For more than three decades, a brand and a directory you can count on...

SELECT REGISTRY, Distinguished Inns [...] guide to exceptional travel and lodging [...] that special place that will make your ne[...]

Whether you're traveling for business or [...] your family, this guidebook will help you to locate extraordinary places to stay throughout the U.S. and Canada. And, no matter what the season or the type of property that you find most appealing, SELECT REGISTRY likely has something for you.

Most importantly, you can rest assured that our member properties have been selected as among the most comfortable and welcoming—unique lodging alternatives in an increasingly cluttered and impersonal travel marketplace.

In years past, the registry book in the lobby of hotels and inns welcomed guests and provided a connection between innkeepers and travelers. The historical registry "quill"—the original instrument of guest registration—has been incorporated into our Association's graphic identity, and the predicates of hospitality, comfort, and authenticity establish our members as "the best of the best"—select properties that will exceed your highest expectations when it comes to lodging.

Look for the plaque with the quill on it when you visit our members' inns, and you'll know that you are "traveling the SELECT REGISTRY way..."

se·lect (si-lekt') *v.* **-lect·ed**, **-lecting**, **-lects**. —*tr.* To choose from among several; pick out, —*intr.* To make a choice or selection. —*adj.* Also **se·lect·ed** (-lek'tid). **1.** Singled out in preference; chosen. **2.** Of special value or quality; preferred. —*n.* One that is select. [Lat. *seligere*, select-: se-, apart+legere, to choose.] —**se·lect'ness** *n.*

...*different styles, different places. All Select*...

The Eastman Inn, New Hampshire

Pearson's Pond Luxury Inn, Alaska

Elizabeth Pointe Lodge, Florida

Los Poblanos Inn, New Mexico

Montford Inn, Oklahoma

Geneva On The Lake, New York

Manoir Hovey, Quebec

Stafford's Bay View Inn, Michigan

Weasku Inn, Oregon

In the late 1960s, one man had an interesting idea. A travel writer named Norman Simpson drove throughout North America in a paneled station wagon, identifying unique places that offered what he called, "good honest lodging, good honest food, and good honest feeling." Hailed as "the Father of Country Inn Travel," Simpson—through his pioneering book, *Country Inns and Back Roads*—introduced an entirely new type of lodging experience to the traveling public. Today, the Association of independent innkeepers started by Norman Simpson includes more than 400 of the "finest country inns, luxury B&Bs, and unique small hotels" from California to Nova Scotia.

We hope that you enjoy this complimentary copy of our directory—which is a gift from your hosts. Use it in good health as you travel; we look forward to welcoming you along the way!

The Innkeepers of Select Registry

Our Quality Assurance Program

Perhaps the most important distinction that sets a SELECT REGISTRY member apart from other inns or B&Bs is our Quality Assurance Program.

SELECT REGISTRY carries out a quality assurance inspection for each of its more than 400 member properties. This program involves independent inspectors—not employees of SELECT REGISTRY—with years of experience in the hospitality industry. The inspectors arrive unidentified, spend the night, and evaluate the inn on a detailed point system, which translates into a pass/fail grade for the inn. Hospitality, the physical plant, and cuisine of the property are all evaluated. Inns applying for membership are inspected, as are existing members on a periodic schedule. Not all properties have what it takes to pass the inspections, and this process provides an assurance to the traveling public that a SELECT REGISTRY inn is in a class of its own. **No other online directory or organization of innkeepers has a comparable inspection program.**

As one inspection report observed, "I could see that all of your guests were being treated like the inspector."

"Among all the different ratings existing today, the most coveted innkeeping award should be an eager referral from a satisfied guest to a friend planning a trip." – Norman Simpson

For the convenience of our guests, an index of the properties by state and province is provided at the front of the book. At the back of the book, you'll find an alpha-listing of all member properties.

Each SELECT REGISTRY member property is represented with its own page of information in this guidebook. The page includes one or two pictures, a brief description of the experience a guest can expect at that property, and contact information. The innkeepers/owners are listed, and the property is identified by a general style/type descriptor (e.g., "Elegant In-Town Breakfast Inn" or "Rustic Country Inn"). ❶

The Rooms/Rates section gives the number of rooms and pricing structure for the property. ❷ Cuisine describes the food and beverage specialties for which our members are famous, including whether the property serves only breakfast or is full service. ❸ The Directions section gives you an easy to follow "road map" to reach the property. ❺ Nearest Airport(s) tells you where you might fly in. ❹

Some of our members wish to indicate certain awards, ratings or memberships (e.g., DiRoNA or PAII—the Professional Association of Innkeepers International), and guests will find the appropriate symbols in the sidebar. ❻ Ratings from organizations such as AAA, Mobil or Canada Select are at the bottom of the inn's description, along with the date when the property became a member of SELECT REGISTRY. ⓬

The guidebook is organized in alphabetical order, by state and province (our Canadian members have a separate section, which begins on page 443). A map of the state or province at the beginning of each section shows the location of each property, relative to major cities and highways. For larger map images, go to the SELECT REGISTRY web site, www. SelectRegistry.com.

Generally speaking, properties are grouped within each state or province by travel area. All Camden, Maine properties, for example, are listed together.

SelectRegistry.com

For many years, while we were known as the Independent Innkeepers' Association, our logo was a lit lantern, symbolizing "the Shining Light in Hospitality." Members who have been in the Association for many years and since before the brand changed to SELECT REGISTRY are identified with the IIA lantern logo. **7**

Many of our inns feature "business friendly amenities," including such things as corporate rates, Internet access, meeting areas, flexible check-in times, and more. If an inn meets at least 12 of 14 criteria we've identified as catering to the business traveler, they will have a briefcase icon at the top of their page. **8**

At the bottom of each page, there is an Amenities and Policies grid—a brief indication of the services each SELECT REGISTRY member property offers its guests. Briefly stated, the icons stand for: **9**

☺ 12+	Suitable for Children	●—●	Exercise Facilities
Ⓝ	Not Suitable for Children	✖	Spa Services
Ⓢ	Non-smoking Inn	📠	Reservations by Travel Agents
♿	Handicap accessible guestrooms	@	Internet Access
💳	Credit cards accepted	🐈	Pets Welcome
Ⓨ	Corporate/Business Rates	≋	Pool
📂	Conference Facilities	🔥	Fireplaces
♥	Wedding Facilities	◎	Whirlpool Tubs
Ⓢ	Eco-tourism*	✳	Air-conditioning
☕	Collectible mug, i.e., Cloth & Clay		

🍽	🍴	🍽	🍷
Breakfast	Lunch	Dinner	Wine/Cocktails

Each of our inns has a slightly different mix of food and beverage services. Although these are often described in more detail in the Cuisine section for each inn, we want to give our guests a quick snapshot of what each inn offers in-house. The icons near the top of each page tell you whether the inn serves breakfast, lunch, and/or dinner, and whether or not wine or cocktails are available. **11**   In many cases, at the very bottom of each page, you'll find a guest quote or some recognition garnered by the property. This tells you something, in particular, for which the property is known. **10**

*For more information on eco-tourism and eco-tourism friendly properties, go online at www.selectregistry.com/ecotourism.

www.SelectRegistry.com
www.innbook.com

If you see something you like in the SELECT REGISTRY guidebook, and also look for travel information on the Internet, we encourage you to visit our central Association web site or the home web sites of our individual members. On the SELECT REGISTRY site, you'll find thousands of pages of information all in one place, including recipes, descriptions and photos of individual rooms, area attractions and other details that complement the information contained in this book. The SELECT REGISTRY web site includes: user-friendly "Find an Inn" search functions, trip planner itineraries, and innovations such as email postcards utilizing the extensive photo archives we have for our inns. In most cases, you'll also be able to check availability and request a reservation online from our members. And, of course, if you want even more in-depth information on a particular member property, there is a hot-link to the home web page for the inn or B&B of interest to you, as well as links to regional and local portals featuring SELECT REGISTRY members.

On our central web site, you'll also find a place to register for our monthly guest e-newsletters, which include featured inns, recipes, stories, and specials. Sign up today, and keep in touch with SELECT REGISTRY on a regular basis!

Be our guest!...

SELECT F R
DISTINGUISHED INNS

Vol. 22, Issue 1 • June 2006

"By far, the most attractive, complete directory of top quality inns, B&Bs, and small hotels and resorts on the Internet! Loads of information."

Gift Certificates

The gift of an overnight stay or a weekend at an exceptional inn or B&B can be one of the most thoughtful and appreciated gifts you can give your parents, children, or dear friends. Employers are discovering that a gift certificate for a "getaway" is an excellent way of rewarding their employees, while at the same time giving them some much needed rest. A few ideas:

- Weddings
- Anniversaries
- Holiday & Birthday gifts
- Employee rewards/incentives
- Retirement

Our gift certificates are valid at any of our more than 400 member properties. We process orders daily, packaging certificates with our complimentary Association guidebook and your personal message. Certificates may be ordered online or by phone, and expedited shipping is available at an additonal cost. The next time you think about gift-giving, think about our Gift Certificate Program—the perfect gift for that special person.

The Golden Quill Club: SELECT REGISTRY'S guest loyalty program

Because we value our many return guests, for the past several years SELECT REGISTRY has administered a modest frequent traveler reward—The Golden Quill Club Loyalty Program.

In the back of this book, you'll find a detachable post card that serves as a passport *and* a voucher, all rolled into one. Completed cards entitle guests to a value-added reward from our member properties and may qualify you for ongoing SELECT REGISTRY contests and promotions. Rules and instructions are printed on the card and posted online.

Start collecting Loyalty Rewards today while staying at SELECT REGISTRY inns. We think you'll find that some experiences are worth repeating!

"Select Registry Gift Certificates — a unique gift for brides and grooms."
-Good Morning America

Alaska
(pg. 17)

Nunavut

British
Columbia
(pg. 452)

Alberta
(pg. 445)

Saskatchewan

Manitoba

Washington
(pg. 421)

Montana

North Dakota

Minn.
(pg. 193)

Oregon
(pg. 300)

Idaho

South Dakota

Iowa

Wyoming

California
North
(pg. 31)

Nevada

Utah
(pg. 375)

Colorado
(pg. 68)

Nebraska

California
South
(pg. 32)

Kansas
(pg. 117)

Arizona
(pg. 19)

New Mexico
(pg. 240)

Oklahoma
(pg. 297)

*Pacific
Ocean*

Texas
(pg. 367)

Kauai

Niihau

Oahu

Molokai

Lanai

Maui

Kahoolawe

Hawaii

Hawaii

Mexico

*Gulf of
Mexico*

SelectRegistry.com

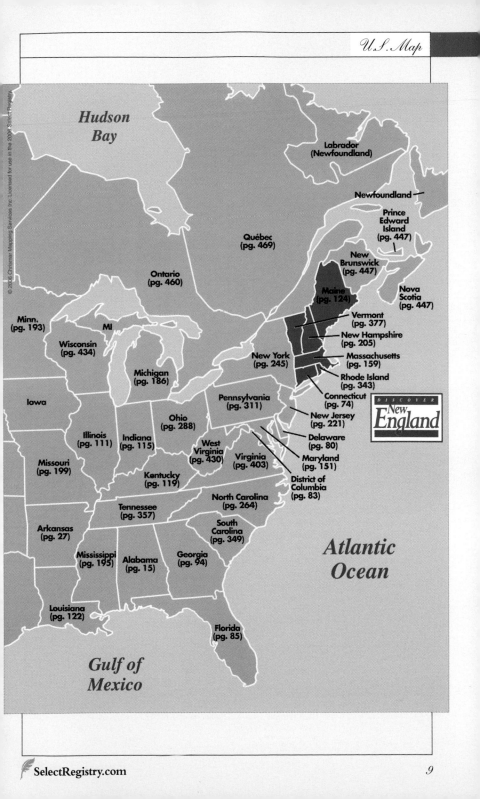

Hudson Bay

Labrador (Newfoundland)

Newfoundland

Prince Edward Island (pg. 447)

Québec (pg. 469)

New Brunswick (pg. 447)

Nova Scotia (pg. 447)

Ontario (pg. 460)

Maine (pg. 124)

Vermont (pg. 377)

Minn. (pg. 193)

MI

New Hampshire (pg. 205)

Wisconsin (pg. 434)

Michigan (pg. 186)

New York (pg. 245)

Massachusetts (pg. 159)

Rhode Island (pg. 343)

Connecticut (pg. 74)

Iowa

Pennsylvania (pg. 311)

New Jersey (pg. 221)

DISCOVER
New England

Illinois (pg. 111)

Indiana (pg. 115)

Ohio (pg. 288)

West Virginia (pg. 430)

Virginia (pg. 403)

Delaware (pg. 80)

Maryland (pg. 151)

Missouri (pg. 199)

Kentucky (pg. 119)

District of Columbia (pg. 83)

Arkansas (pg. 27)

Tennessee (pg. 357)

North Carolina (pg. 264)

South Carolina (pg. 349)

Atlantic Ocean

Mississippi (pg. 195)

Alabama (pg. 15)

Georgia (pg. 94)

Louisiana (pg. 122)

Florida (pg. 85)

Gulf of Mexico

SelectRegistry.com

9

Alabama

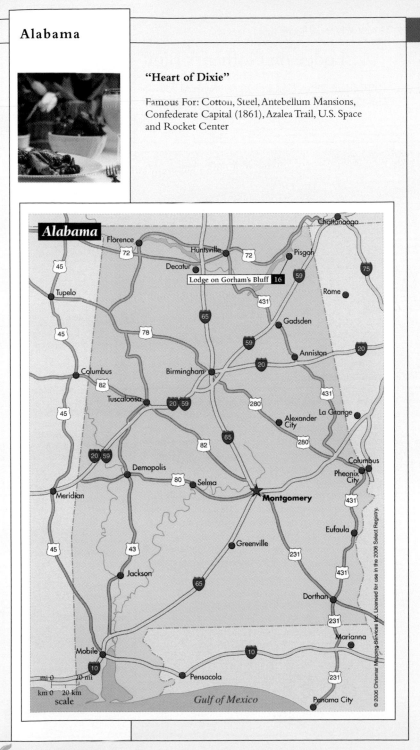

"Heart of Dixie"

Famous For: Cotton, Steel, Antebellum Mansions, Confederate Capital (1861), Azalea Trail, U.S. Space and Rocket Center

Alabama

Chattanooga

Florence
72

Huntsville
72

Pisgah

Decatur
59

Lodge on Gorham's Bluff 16

45

Rome

Tupelo
431

45

78
65

Gadsden

59

Columbus
82

Anniston
20

Birmingham
20

431

Tuscaloosa
20 59
280

La Grange

Alexander City
280

65
82

Columbus

Pheonix City

20, 59

Demopolis
80
Selma

Meridian

★ Montgomery
431

45

43

Greenville
231

Eufaula

Jackson
65

431

Dorthan
231

Mobile
10
Marianna

10

mi 0   20 mi
km 0   20 km
scale

Pensacola

231

Panama City

Gulf of Mexico

© 2006 Christmas Mapping Services Inc. Licensed for use in the 2006 Select Registry.

Lodge on Gorham's Bluff

www.srinns.com/gorhamsbluff
101 Gorham Drive, Gorham's Bluff, Pisgah, AL 35765
256-451-VIEW • 256-451-8439 • Fax 256-451-7403
reservations@gorhamsbluff.com

Proprietors
McGriff Family

Traditional Country
Retreat/Lodge

The Lodge on Gorham's Bluff is perched high on the bluffs overlooking the Tennessee River Valley. Although the atmosphere is one of mannered Southern charm, the daily routine is low-key and casual dress is encouraged. Furnished in an elegant, traditional country style the Lodge and Cottage suites are appointed with antiques, CD/DVD players, in-room snacks, luxurious his/her bathrobes, fine Egyptian cotton linens, feather mattresses, down pillows and remote-controlled fireplaces. Generously sized windows and multiple sets of French doors and private balconies bring the mountain-high views indoors. Amenities include hiking trails, biking, fishing, bird watching, pool, fitness center and seasonal events. *Southern Living* Magazine rated Gorham's Bluff as the most romantic destination in Alabama for the April 2005 issue.

Rooms/Rates
Six Suites $185/$225 per evening, double occupancy. Breakfast is included. Tax and service charge is additional
Number of Rooms: 6

Cuisine
A regionally inspired 4-course gourmet meal, prepared w/only the freshest locally grown ingredients, is served in the candlelit dining room each evening. Fresh flowers, fine linens & flawless service enhance the romantic experience. Gourmet picnic lunches available. Reservations required for dinner & lunch. Additional charges apply.

Nearest Airport(s)
Chattanooga, TN

Directions
Directions available on website and from the innkeeper

Member Since 2003

12+

"Gorham's Bluff smoothes the wrinkles of my soul."
"Beautiful room, glorious food, marvelous view!"

Alaska

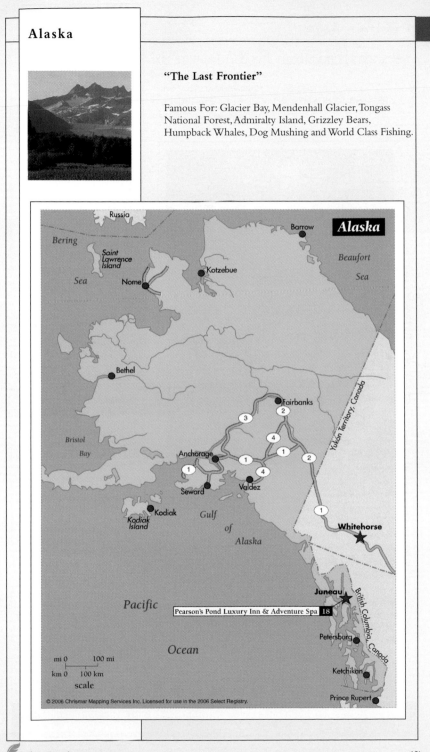

"The Last Frontier"

Famous For: Glacier Bay, Mendenhall Glacier, Tongass National Forest, Admiralty Island, Grizzley Bears, Humpback Whales, Dog Mushing and World Class Fishing.

Alaska

Russia

Barrow

Bering

Saint Lawrence Island

Beaufort Sea

Sea

Nome

Kotzebue

Bethel

Fairbanks 2

3

4

Bristol Bay

Anchorage

1

1

2

1

4

1

Yukon Territory, Canada

Seward

Valdez

Kodiak Island

Kodiak

Gulf

of

Alaska

1

Whitehorse

Juneau

Pearson's Pond Luxury Inn & Adventure Spa 18

British Columbia, Canada

Pacific

Petersburg

Ocean

mi 0   100 mi

km 0   100 km

scale

Ketchikan

Prince Rupert

© 2006 Chrismar Mapping Services Inc. Licensed for use in the 2006 Select Registry.

Pearson's Pond Luxury Inn & Adventure Spa

www.srinns.com/pearsonspond
4541 Sawa Circle, Juneau, AK 99801
888-658-6328 • 907-789-3772 • Fax 907-790-1965
book@pearsonspond.com

Innkeepers/Owners
Diane & Steve Pearson

Contemporary
Waterside Retreat

The opportunity to visit Alaska with our newest Select Registry property! Relax with a book or visit with guests around the fireplace. Listen to the serenity of the water fountain as you view original artwork. Soak in hot tubs-one by the pond, one overlooking the famous Mendenhall Glacier. Stay fit in the gym, take a yoga class or enjoy an aromatherapy massage. Watch wild ducks playing on the pond, eagles soaring & an occasional bear eating wild blueberries. Borrow a bike or hike to the river, ocean, glacier or mountains. Roast marshmallows or sip wine by the campfire, even in the midnight sun. Your knowledgable Alaskan hosts help you plan & customize an Alaska Adventure or Glacier Wedding Package, including whale watching, kayaking, dog mushing or hiking on the glacier, bear viewing, rainforest zip line, native culture, sightseeing, world-class fishing, Glacier Bay and more.

AAA ◆◆◆   *Member Since 2005*

Rooms/Rates
5 Efficiencies, 2 demi-suites w/private bath, fireplace, canopy bed, Wi-Fi, DVD, phone, kitchenette, some w/whirlpool. $129/$429. Breakfast, snacks, afternoon tea, evening reception & unlimited Wi-Fi/laptop. Open year-round.
Number of Rooms: 7

Cuisine
Flexible self-serve extended continental 24/7. Fresh baked breads, healthy choices plus eggs, cheese, meat. Enjoy breakfast in bed or alfresco on your deck, dock, or gazebo overlooking the glacier or waterfall.

Nearest Airport(s)
Juneau International

Directions
Close to key attractions & historic downtown. www.pearsonspond.

"The view of the Mendenhall Glacier from my hot tub will be imprinted on my mind forever. "...an exceptional haven near the Alaskan wilderness."

Arizona

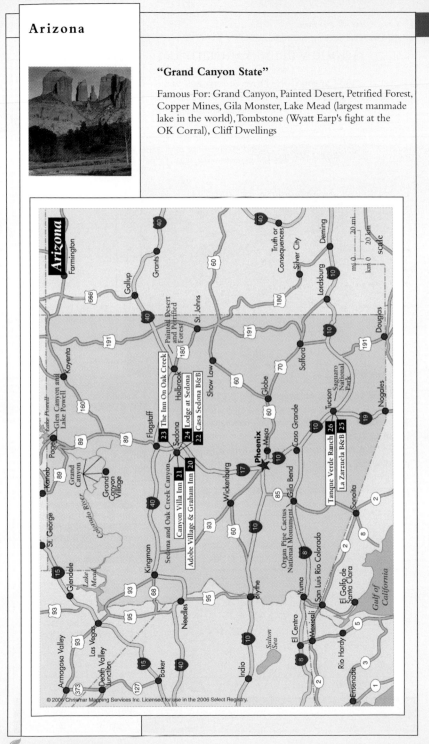

"Grand Canyon State"

Famous For: Grand Canyon, Painted Desert, Petrified Forest, Copper Mines, Gila Monster, Lake Mead (largest manmade lake in the world), Tombstone (Wyatt Earp's fight at the OK Corral), Cliff Dwellings

Arizona

Farmington

Gallup

Grants

Truth or Consequences

Silver City

Deming

Lordsburg

Douglas

mi 0 _____ 20 mi.
km 0 _____ 20 km
scale

St. Johns

Painted Desert and Petrified Forest

23 The Inn On Oak Creek

Holbrook

24 Lodge at Sedona

22 Casa Sedona B&B

Show Low

Globe

Safford

Saguaro National Park

Tucson

26 Tanque Verde Ranch

25 La Zarzuela B&B

Nogales

Kayenta

Glen Canyon and Lake Powell

Lake Powell

Page

Flagstaff

Sedona

Sedona and Oak Creek Canyon

21 Canyon Villa Inn

20 Adobe Village & Graham Inn

Phoenix

Mesa

Casa Grande

Sonoita

Kanab

Grand Canyon

Grand Canyon Village

Wickenburg

Gila Bend

Organ Pipe Cactus National Monument

San Luis Rio Colorado

El Golfo de Santa Clara

Gulf of California

St. George

Colorado River

Kingman

Blythe

Yuma

San Luis Rio Colorado

Mexicali

Rio Hardy

Ensenada

Glendale

Lake Mead

Needles

El Centro

Las Vegas

Salton Sea

Indio

Baker

Amargosa Valley

Death Valley Junction

© 2006 Chrismar Mapping Services Inc. Licensed for use in the 2006 Select Registry.

Adobe Village Graham Inn

www.srinns.com/adobevillage
150 Canyon Circle Drive, Sedona, AZ 86351
800-228-1425 • 928-284-1425 • Fax 928-284-0767
info@sedonasfinest.com

Innkeepers/Owners
Stuart & Ilene Berman

Elegant Southwestern
Village Breakfast Inn

This world renowned Inn has received the AAA Four Diamond Award of Excellence for the past 9 years. Acclaimed for its stunning red rock views and located within walking distance of dining, shopping, art galleries, hiking and biking trails, and in view of Bell Rock, the most photographed monument in Sedona. All guests receive gourmet breakfast, hot afternoon hors d'oeuvres, and evening pastries, complimentary use of Internet Center, mountain bikes and hiking packs, swimming pool and in-ground jetted spa. Received 5 star award "Best Bed & Breakfast Inn in North America."

Rooms/Rates
7 Rooms in main inn $169/$599. 4 Luxury Casitas $389/$469. Spacious and distinctive theme rooms with fireplaces, Jetted tubs, TV/VCRs, CDs.
Number of Rooms: 11

Cuisine
Full, gourmet breakfast. Afternoon hors d'oeuvres, evening pastries. Casitas have bread makers allowing guests to come in to the aroma of fresh-baked bread each day. Guests are welcome to bring their own spirits.

Nearest Airport(s)
Phoenix Sky Harbor Intl.

Directions
From Hwy 179, turn W onto Bell Rock Blvd. Drive two blocks passing the first Canyon Circle Drive. You will see us on the R, on the corner of Bell Rock Blvd. and Canyon Circle Drive. You're home.

AAA ◆◆◆◆   *Member Since 2000*

"...from the red rocks to the stained glass window in our casita,
every detail is perfect."

Canyon Villa Bed & Breakfast Inn

Innkeepers/Owners
Les & Peg Belch

Elegant Village Inn

www.srinns.com/canyonvilla
40 Canyon Circle Drive, Sedona, AZ 86351
800-453-1166 • 928-284-1226 • Fax 928-284-2114
canvilla@sedona.net

Rooms/Rates
11 Rooms. Red Rock View Rooms $229/$324. Limited-View room $199. Discounts available for AAA, AARP, and Slow-Season.
Number of Rooms: 11

Cuisine
Three course served breakfast, afternoon refreshments, and appetizers included. Coffee, tea, and original light deserts are available throughout the entire evening in the dining area. Guests welcome to bring their own spirits.

Nearest Airport(s)
Phoenix PHX

Directions
From I-17, use Exit 298 and go N on SR 179 for 8 mi. L on Bell Rock Blvd. After 1 block turn R on Canyon Circle Dr. The Inn is on the R. Please call for directions if arriving from SR 89-A.

A past recipient of the elite "Best U.S. Bed and Breakfast" award from Harper's *Hideaway Report*, this B&B Inn was custom designed to provide guests with spectacular bedside views of the Red Rocks of Sedona. Themed intimate guest rooms open through arched French doors onto private balconies or lush garden patios. Guestrooms include cable TV, phone, radio, CD player, and some have gas-log fireplaces. Ceramic baths include jetted tubs and luxurious lounge robes. Guests relax daily in the warm Arizona sun by the on-premises pool, hike desert trails from the premises, and stargaze cool evenings by fireside.

Recommended by Frommers, Conde-Nast Johansens and Exxon-Mobil travel guides. One of only six Arizona B&Bs listed in Zagat Survey's 2006 "Top U.S. Hotels, Resorts, & Spas." Awarded AAA Four Diamond Award of Excellence for past 14 years.

AAA ◆◆◆◆   *Member Since 1995*   Mobil ★★★

12+

"One night is too short to stay in a place as wonderful as this.
The views are spectacular."

SelectRegistry.com

21

Casa Sedona Inn

www.srinns.com/casasedona
55 Hozoni Drive, Sedona, AZ 86336
800-525-3756 • 928-282-2938 • Fax 928-282-2259
casa@sedona.net

Innkeepers/Owners
Paul & Connie Schwartz

Elegant Adobe Style In Town B&B Inn

Beautifully landscaped acre at the base of Sedona's highest Red Rock peak, Thunder Mountain. Casa Sedona is an adobe style inn designed by a protégé of Frank Lloyd Wright featuring sun terraces with awe-inspiring 180-degree views, a large garden patio, and fountains. Recipient of the AAA 4-Diamond Award of Excellence for 9 years. Enjoy the tranquil ambiance of the inn, beautifully landscaped grounds, evening appetizers, a hot tub for stargazing, and bountiful breakfasts served in the garden, or fireside. Casa Sedona is a mere three miles from the town's center making it the perfect quiet respite from the city, yet only minutes from fine restaurants and shops. Luxury, elegance, privacy, and exceptional cuisine have guests returning time and time again. Featured by The Travel Channel on its "Best of the Best" series.

Rooms/Rates
$189/$299. Each room is unique: choose Contemporary Southwest to Cowboy to Lace! Amenities include gas fireplaces, king or queen beds, private baths, snuggly robes, whirlpool tubs, TV/VCR's, CD players, wireless Internet, balcony, or porch.
Number of Rooms: 16

Cuisine
Two course breakfast. Late afternoon hor d'ouevres, beverages and homemade cookies. Guests are welcome to bring their own alcoholic beverages.

Nearest Airport(s)
Phoenix Sky Harbor

Directions
From Hwy. 89A, turn N onto Tortilla Dr. then L at the first stop sign (Southwest Drive). Take an immediate R onto Hozoni Drive.

AAA ◆◆◆◆   *Member Since 2004*   Mobil ★★★

12+

The Inn on Oak Creek

Owner/ Manager
Jim Matykiewicz

Contemporary Waterside
Breakfast Inn

www.srinns.com/innonoakcreek
556 Hwy. 179, Sedona, AZ 86336
800-499-7896 • 928-282-7896 • Fax 928-282-0696
theinn@sedona.net

Rooms/Rates
11 Rooms, $200/$295 DBL; 1 Suite, $350. All rooms feature private marble baths, whirlpool tubs, gas fireplaces, TV/VCR/ HBO, Cable, data ports, luxurious bathrobes, hairdryers, phones. Creekside rooms have decks w/dramatic views.
Number of Rooms: 11

Cuisine
Full gourmet breakfast, afternoon beverages, cookies & hors d'oeuvres included in price. Guests are welcome to bring their own adult beverages. All served creekside during warm weather.

Nearest Airport(s)
Flagstaff (30 min.), Phoenix (2.5 hrs.)

Directions
In Sedona proper on Hwy. 179 just 0.4 mile S of the intersection of Hwy 179 & Hwy 89A.

Initially built in 1972 as an art gallery, then totally refurbished and transformed in 1995, the Inn perches on a bluff overlooking Oak Creek, one of Arizona's premier year-round spring-fed streams. Within easy walking distance are Sedona's best art galleries, boutique shops, several fine restaurants and Tlaquepaque shopping village. Yet, almost as close, are National Forest trails that will take you to the heart of red rock country. So, while guests are constantly surprised that an Inn so centrally located in Sedona can offer such privacy and relaxation, the luxurious AAA Four Diamond accommodations, professional staff, and culinary delights (Five Star Food!) are what really please them.

AAA ◆◆◆◆   *Member Since 2001*   Mobil ★★★

12+ 🚭 ♿ 💳   ♥ ✂ 🖼 @   🖼 ◎ ✳ 🕹

"This is the way all B&Bs ought to be. You've thought of everything. Thank you! Thank you!"

The Lodge at Sedona

www.srinns.com/lodgeatsedona
125 Kallof Place, Sedona, AZ 86336
800-619-4467 • 928-204-1942 • Fax 928-204-2128
Info@LODGEatSEDONA.com

Proprietors
Ronald & Shelley Wachal

Elegant Village
Breakfast Inn

paii

"Romance and intrigue, comfort & luxury, beauty and character, escape & adventure - the Lodge at Sedona has it all" AZ News. Elegant Mission/Arts & Craft estate set on three acres of grand seclusion in the very heart of Sedona. Awarded Top 10 Inns in US by Forbes.com, Best B & Bs by *Phoenix* Magazine. Recommended by Small Elegant Hotels, Historic Lodging Directory, *Bon Appetit*, Fodors.com, and Frommer's. Spectacular Red Rock views, sculpture gardens, fitness center priviledges and pools adjacent, fountains and a magical labyrinth. Artful King suites with fireplaces, jet tubs, robes, large decks, stereo TV, CD, DVD. Complete concierge service and full gourmet breakfast served daily. "The Lodge at Sedona is one of the most romantic Inns in Arizona." - AZ Foothills Magazine.

Member Since 2003   Mobil ★★★

Rooms/Rates
14 Rooms & King Suites: $160/$325 B&B; Kings w/ fireplaces, jet tubs, view decks, stereo TV/DVD. Hot Tubs available.
Number of Rooms: 14

Cuisine
Professionally prepared & served gourmet breakfast w/ Sedona Gold coffee & Lodge Granola w/ yogurt. Sunset appetizers, spring water & snacks daily. Complimentary wine setups. Guest beverages welcome!

Nearest Airport(s)
Phoenix (PHX)

Directions
In W. Sedona at 125 Kallof Place, S off Hwy 89A, 2 mi. W of Hwy 179, a block W of Mountain Shadows Dr, or a block E of Coffee Pot Dr. in the very Heart of Sedona. Refer to map on website.

11+ ⊘ ♿ 🛏 🛎 📁 ♥ ↦ ✕ 🎐 @ 🐕 ≋ 🎦 ◎ ✱ ☕

"The Lodge at Sedona - A Luxury Bed & Breakfast Inn,is a grand setting for small Meetings and Retreats"

Innkeepers/Owners
Cliff Aberham, Lew Harper & Pauline Spurgiesz

Southwestern Villa
Bed & Breakfast

La Zarzuela, A Bed and Breakfast Inn
www.srinns.com/lazarzuela
455 No. Camino de Oeste, Tucson, AZ 85745
888-848-8225 • 520-884-4824 • Fax 520-903-2617
stay@zarzuela-az.com

Rooms/Rates
5 Rooms. $250/$325. All accommodations with private facilities, TV,VCR,DVD,CD Player, Coffee Maker, Hairdryer, and Refrigerator.
Number of Rooms: 5

Cuisine
Fresh coffee is ready at 7:00am, and breakfast is served from 8:00am-8:30am. Breakfast is a gourmet, full course meal including: baked breads, fruit, fresh homepade pastries and a hot baked dish. Teas from Harrods of London, England.

Nearest Airport(s)
Tucson International Airport

Directions
Located in the mountains off Gates Pass only 10 min. from downtown Tucson's historical Presidio District & Convention Center. Refer to website for map

Imagine that you have a very well-to-do friend, with very good taste, who owns a large, private villa in the Tucson Mountains (think carefree). This friend, being a very good friend, offers you the use of the villa and its staff, who have been instructed to do anything your heart desires: arrange flights, limos, massages, dinner, whatever - anything to make you blissfully happy. That's La Zarzuela, "the operetta," in a nutshell. The Frank Lloyd Wright-inspired architecture resonates Southwestern culture, with scored concrete floors and walls painted in vibrant hues. With five lovely casitas, La Zarzuela is small enough to provide you the personal level of service we are committed to, yet large enough for the vacationer to meet new people, if you wish. Our new Sonoran Desert Terrace is perfect for small group functions and for the enjoyment of our guests.

Member Since 2004

"Exemplary, there simply are no superlatives big enough for the music, the beauty, the food and hospitality. A profoundly wonderful experience."

Tanque Verde Ranch

www.srinns.com/tanqueverde
14301 East Speedway, Tucson, AZ 85748
800-234-3833 • 520-296-6275 • Fax 520-721-9426
dude@tvgr.com

Innkeepers/Owners
Robert and Rita Cote

Traditional Southwestern
Country Ranch

Founded on a Spanish land grant in 1868 in the spectacular Sonoran Desert, Tanque Verde Ranch has evolved into one of the Southwest's most complete vacation destinations. A 4-star quality resort, it maintains the cowboy traditions and spirit unique to this western cattle ranch. Sonoran-style with adobe walls, high saguaro rib ceilings, beehive fireplaces and mesquite corrals, the Ranch setting provides expansive desert and mountain views. The facilities are just as remarkable, with 140 horses, tennis courts, indoor/outdoor pools, saunas, spa, guided hiking, mountain biking, nature programs, children's program, outdoor BBQs, breakfast rides and more, in a casual relaxed atmosphere!

Rooms/Rates
Nightly rates include room accommodations, three meals a day & all of the wonderful ranch activities! The Ranch offers 51 charming rooms and 23 spacious suites, is open year round and has three rate seasons. Rates vary by room type & number of people.
Number of Rooms: 74

Cuisine
In addition to the activities, three delicious meals are included in the rate! Meals are served daily from 8:00-9:00am, 12:00-1:30pm and 6:30-8:00pm. 4-star quality, fully licensed.

Nearest Airport(s)
Tucson International

Directions
From Tucson, east on Speedway Blvd. to the dead-end, in the Rincon Mountain foothills.

Member Since 1970

Voted one of The Top Ten Family Resorts in North America
by The Travel Channel, March 2003!

26

Arkansas

"The Land of Opportunity"

Famous For: Natural Hot Springs, The Ozarks, Waterfalls, Diamonds, Oil, Aluminum.

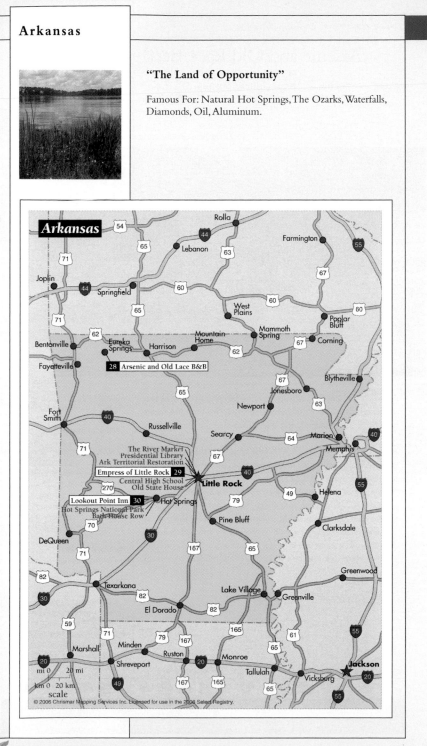

Arkansas

Map locations include:

- 28 Arsenic and Old Lace B&B
- The River Market
- Presidential Library
- Ark Territorial Restoration
- Empress of Little Rock 29
- Central High School
- Old State House
- Lookout Point Inn 30
- Hot Springs National Park
- Bath House Row

Cities and towns: Rolla, Lebanon, Farmington, Joplin, Springfield, West Plains, Poplar Bluff, Bentonville, Eureka Springs, Harrison, Mountain Home, Mammoth Spring, Corning, Fayetteville, Blytheville, Jonesboro, Newport, Fort Smith, Russellville, Searcy, Marion, Memphis, Little Rock, Helena, Hot Springs, Pine Bluff, Clarksdale, DeQueen, Greenwood, Texarkana, Lake Village, Greenville, El Dorado, Marshall, Minden, Ruston, Monroe, Shreveport, Tallulah, Vicksburg, Jackson

scale: mi 0 — 20 mi / km 0 — 20 km

© 2006 Chrismar Mapping Services Inc. Licensed for use in the 2006 Select Registry.

Arsenic and Old Lace B&B

www.srinns.com/arsenicoldlacebb
60 Hillside Avenue, Eureka Springs, AR 72632
866-350-5454 • 479-253-5454 • Fax 479-253-2246
arsenicoldlacebb@aol.com

Innkeepers/Owners
Beverly and Doug Breitling

Intimate Village Bed and Breakfast

Arsenic and Old Lace is located on a heavily wooded hillside in the Historic District of Eureka Springs. The beautiful Ozark Mountains surround this step back to a quieter, more relaxed time. From our Morning Room's balcony or windows, guests enjoy the mixed white squirrels, birds, chipmunks and sometimes even deer, although it is only a short walk to the shops and historic homes and buildiings. The mood is relaxed luxury, and your hosts strive to make each guest feel as if they are at home. The relaxed feel continues to your room, where you will find comfortable furnishings, jetted tubs, lurury showers, televisions, VCRs, CD players and Wifi. Enjoy the video library to watch a movie, curl-up with a good book or your loved one. Relax, unwind. You've stepped back in time without leaving modern necessities.

Rooms/Rates
$139/$259. Rates vary seasonally & midweek.
Number of Rooms: 5

Cuisine
Enjoy custom blended coffee, tea or hot chocolate; our full gourmet breakfast starts with a delicious fruit course, breakfast breads or scones, & a unique main course. Enjoy homemade snacks all day & a well stocked refrigerator.

Nearest Airport(s)
NW Arkansas Regional (XNA)

Directions
Exit airport turn L on Hwy 264 to I-540. R on to I-540 S to US 412 exit. L on US 412 through Springdale AR then 18 mi. E on 412 to AR 45. L on AR 45 to AR 12. R on AR 12 to AR 23. L on 23 to Eureka Springs. Lost? Call 1-800-243-5223.

AAA ◆◆◆   *Member Since 2006*   Mobil ★★★

12+

SelectRegistry.com

Innkeepers/Owners
**Robert Blair and
Sharon Welch-Blair**

Small Luxury Hotel
and Breakfast Inn

The Empress of Little Rock
www.srinns.com/TheEmpress
2120 Louisiana Street, Little Rock, AR 72206
877-374-7966 • 501-374-7966 • Fax 501-375-4537
Email: hostess@theempress.com

Rooms/Rates
8 Rooms, 3 Spa Suites, 3 Mini-Suites, $135/$285 Featherbeds/Cable/DSL/Jacuzzi/Fireplaces
Number of Rooms: 8

Cuisine
Gourmet 2-course breakfast by candlelight served 'Before the Queen' w/formal Victorian pomp & circumstance—silver, china, & a bow-tied 'butler.' Plethora of excellent restaurants available. Complimentary wine and liqueur.

Nearest Airport(s)
Little Rock

Directions
From I-30, take I-630 W. Exit Main St. L on Main to 22nd St. R on 22nd-1 block. From Airport: I-440 W to I-30 E to I-630. Follow above directions. I-430: I-430 to I-630. Take Center St. exit thru light to Main to 22nd St.

Visit the most Victorian of Bed & Breakfasts, the Award-Winning EMPRESS OF LITTLE ROCK SMALL LUXURY HOTEL, for an adventure far from the cares of today! Named Best of the Best by the *Arkansas Democrat Gazette* consecutively since 1998. Winner of the Great American Home Award; the coveted Arkansas Henry Award for Heritage. Named one of the Top 25 Inns in the South by the *National Geographic Traveler*, referred to by Delta *Sky Miles Magazine* as the "Grand Dame of the Ozarks." Watch for us on HGTV: "If Walls Could Talk"; "Porches" and "Homes Across America." Experience a sample taste of the "forgotten experience." The Empress of Little Rock!!

AAA ◆◆◆   *Member Since 2001*   Mobil ★★★★

6+

"In over 80 countries on 6 continents, The Empress is the very best B&B we have ever visited."

Lookout Point Lakeside Inn

www.srinns.com/lookoutpoint
104 Lookout Circle, Hot Springs, AR 71913
866-525-6155 • 501-525-6155 • Fax 501-525-5850
innkeeper@lookoutpointinn.com

Innkeepers/Owners
Kristie and Ray Rosset

Arts & Crafts, built
2002 Waterside

paii

A true sanctuary for body, mind and soul--Lookout Point is a slice of paradise. This newly constructed Arts & Crafts inn is located on the soothing waters of beautiful Lake Hamilton in the low lying Ouachita Mountains. Experience an exceptional inn, with a fine attention to detail as its hallmark. Understated luxury invites relaxation, romance, and rejuvenation. The magnificent gardens with waterfalls and meditation labyrinth are perfect for small, intimate weddings.

Canoe the bay, watch the birds, nap in the hammock, or soak in the nearby historic Hot Springs bathhouses. The well-stocked library and video collection, puzzles, and board games enhance the experience of simplifying life. Come relax, feast, and play!
www.lookoutpointinn.com

Member Since 2005

Rooms/Rates
$150/$325. Corporate weekday rates available. All rooms overlook the gardens/waterfalls and Lake Hamilton.
Number of Rooms: 10

Cuisine
Fresh and hearty breakfast included, plus afternoon snack with wine and tea. Complimentary snack bar with coffee/tea available. Famous Hot Springs bottled mineral water in every room.

Nearest Airport(s)
Little Rock, 60 m.

Directions
From East: I-30 to US 70 (exit 111) to exit 6 (bypass to Mt. Ida). Go to AR Hwy 7. S on 7 3.5 mi. L on Lookout Pt to stop sign; R on Lookout Circle. From West: I-30 to AR Hwy 7 (exit 78). N 24.5 mi. R on Central Terr. to hill top.

"A beautiful blend of water, architecture, comfort and style, Lookout Point embraces the very best of its natural surroundings." *Southern Living* 2005

"The Golden State"

Famous For: Spanish Missions, Gold Rush, Golden Gate Bridge, Wine Country, Citrus, Giant Sequoia Redwoods, Hollywood, Disneyland, Lake Tahoe, Sierra Nevada, Yosemite National Park, Big Sur, Earthquakes, and Death Valley

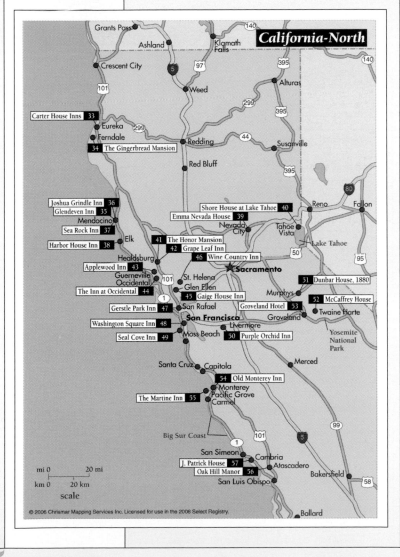

California-North

Grants Pass
Ashland
Klamath Falls
140
Crescent City
97
395
140
Weed
Alturas
101
299
395
Carter House Inns 33
Eureka
299
Redding
44
Susanville
Ferndale
34 The Gingerbread Mansion
Red Bluff
395
Joshua Grindle Inn 36
Glendeven Inn 35
Mendocino
Shore House at Lake Tahoe 40
Emma Nevada House 39
Reno
Fallon
80
Sea Rock Inn 37
Nevada City
Tahoe Vista
Harbor House Inn 38
Elk
41 The Honor Mansion
Lake Tahoe
42 Grape Leaf Inn
Healdsburg
46 Wine Country Inn
50
95
Applewood Inn 43
Guerneville
Occidental
101
St. Helena
★ Sacramento
The Inn at Occidental 44
Glen Ellen
51 Dunbar House, 1880
45 Gaige House Inn
Murphys
52 McCaffrey House
Gerstle Park Inn 47
San Rafael
Groveland Hotel 53
Twaine Harte
Washington Square Inn 48
San Francisco
Groveland
Seal Cove Inn 49
Moss Beach
50 Purple Orchid Inn
Livermore
Yosemite National Park
Santa Cruz
Capitola
Merced
54 Old Monterey Inn
Monterey
The Martine Inn 55
Pacific Grove
Carmel
99
Big Sur Coast
1
101
San Simeon
5
J. Patrick House 57
Cambria
Atascadero
Oak Hill Manor 56
Bakersfield
San Luis Obispo
58
mi 0   20 mi
km 0   20 km
scale
Ballard

© 2006 Chrismar Mapping Services Inc. Licensed for use in the 2006 Select Registry.

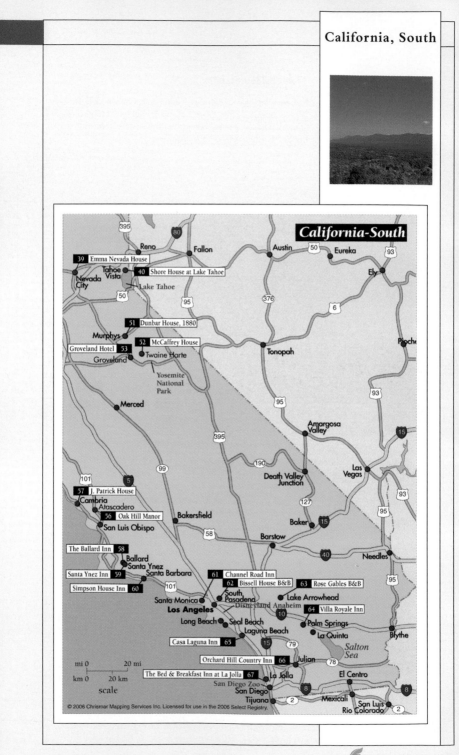

California-South

39 Emma Nevada House
Reno
Fallon
Austin
50
Eureka
93
Tahoe Vista
40 Shore House at Lake Tahoe
Nevada City
Lake Tahoe
Ely
50
95
376
6
51 Dunbar House, 1880
Murphys
52 McCaffrey House
Groveland Hotel 53
Twaine Harte
Tonopah
Groveland
Yosemite National Park
93
Merced
Amargosa Valley
15
395
190
Las Vegas
99
127
57 J. Patrick House
Death Valley Junction
Cambria
Atascadero
93
56 Oak Hill Manor
Bakersfield
San Luis Obispo
Baker
15
95
58
Barstow
The Ballard Inn 58
Ballard
40
Needles
Santa Ynez
Santa Ynez Inn 59
Santa Barbara
61 Channel Road Inn
95
Simpson House Inn 60
62 Bissell House B&B
63 Rose Gables B&B
101
South Pasadena
Lake Arrowhead
Santa Monica
Disneyland Anaheim
64 Villa Royale Inn
Los Angeles
10
Long Beach
Seal Beach
Palm Springs
Casa Laguna Inn 65
Laguna Beach
La Quinta
Blythe
15
79
Salton Sea
Orchard Hill Country Inn 66
Julian
The Bed & Breakfast Inn at La Jolla 67
La Jolla
78
San Diego Zoo
El Centro
mi 0   20 mi
San Diego
8
km 0   20 km
Tijuana
Mexicali
San Luis
scale
2
Rio Colorado
2

© 2006 Chrismar Mapping Services Inc. Licensed for use in the 2006 Select Registry.

SelectRegistry.com

Innkeepers/Owners
Mark and Christi Carter

Elegant Victorian In
Town Inn

Carter House Inns

www.srinns.com/carterhouse
301 L Street, Eureka, CA 95501
707-444-8062 • 707-445-1390 • Fax 707-444-8067
reserve@carterhouse.com

Wine Spectator
GRAND
AWARD

Rooms/Rates
9 Rooms, $155/$350 B&B, 2
Suites, $275/$595 B&B. Open
year-round.
Number of Rooms: 11

Cuisine
Full service award-winning restaurant open nightly, full breakfast.
Full bar, wine shop—3,880 wine
selections. With a recent 95-point
rating from James Laube, Carter
Cellars wine is quickly becoming
a cult classic.

Nearest Airport(s)
Eureka-Arcata Airport is 16 miles
north of Eureka.

Directions
From Highway 101 heading
South turn right on L Street. From
Highway 101 heading North turn
left on L Street. The Inn is located
on the corner of 3rd & L Street.

Northern California's premier inn is an enclave of 3 magnificent Victorians perched alongside Humboldt Bay in Old Town
Eureka. The luxurious accommodations at Carter House Inns
and the sumptuous dining at its Restaurant 301 (considered
among Northern California's best restaurants) set an indulgent
tone for a marvelous visit to the giant redwood forests, rugged
Pacific beaches and the other wonders of Northern California's
Redwood Coast. Our AAA Four Diamond rated accommodations and service are unparalleled; our award-winning cuisine is
prepared w/local organic products and fresh herbs, greens, and
vegetables harvested daily from the Inn's extensive gardens. The
Inn also produces its own wine under the label Carter Cellars,
specializing in limited production cabs & merlots from some
of the finest vineyards in Napa. Check out our incredible food
and wine lover's packages, featuring romantic dining and accommodations in the heart of the Redwood Empire! We offer
Humboldt County's finest accommodations, an outstanding full-
service restaurant, an online wine shop, a wine club, and information about our wonderful region here at the heart of California's
Redwood Country.

AAA ◆◆◆◆   *Member Since 2003*

"I'll never forget my stays at the Carter House Inns. "Lora Finnegan, *Sunset*
Magazine

Gingerbread Mansion Inn
www.srinns.com/gingerbreadmansion
400 Berding Street, P.O. Box 1380, Ferndale, CA 95536
800-952-4136 • 707-786-4000 • Fax 707-786-4381
innkeeper@gingerbread-mansion.com

Innkeepers/Owners
Vince & Sue Arriaga
Robert & Juli
McInroy

Elegant Victorian Village
Breakfast Inn

Exquisitely turreted and gabled, the Gingerbread Mansion Inn is truly a visual masterpiece. Located in the Victorian village of Ferndale, the Inn is surrounded by lush English gardens. Featuring two of the West Coast's most luxurious suites—the 'Empire Suite' and 'Veneto.' Garden views, and old-fashioned tubs and fireplaces for fireside bubble baths are featured. Amenities include a morning tray service, full gourmet breakfast, afternoon tea, turn-down service with bedside chocolates, bathrobes. Near the Giant redwood parks and ocean beaches.

Rooms/Rates
11 rooms and suites, $150/$400. All private baths; many luxurious with clawfoot tubs and fireplaces as big as bedrooms. Office hours 7:00 a.m. to 7:00 p.m. Open year-round.
Number of Rooms: 11

Cuisine
Full gourmet breakfast with hot entree, side dish, and many other items. Afternoon tea service. Complimentary port served in four premium suites. Wine and champagne available.

Nearest Airport(s)
Arcata Airport

Directions
101 4-1/2 hours N of S.F. Ferndale exit, 5 miles to town, L at Bank, 1 block to Inn. From Oregon, 20 minutes S of Eureka. Ferndale exit.

AAA ◆◆◆◆   *Member Since 1988*   Mobil ★★★

6+

Conde Nast Johansen's 2001 "North America Inn of Year"

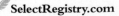

Proprietors
**Sharon Williams &
Higgins**

Elegant Country Breakfast
Inn

Glendeven Inn

www.srinns.com/glendeven
8205 North Highway One, Little River, CA 95456
800-822-4536 • 707-937-0083 • Fax 707-937-6108
innkeeper@glendeven.com

Rooms/Rates
6 rooms, 4 suites in the inn:
$145/$300 B&B; K & Q beds;
2 people per room. Ocean view
luxury cottage: $320/$410 (up to 4
people, including children) EP Open
year-round.
Number of Rooms: 10

Cuisine
Delicious homemade, hot country
breakfasts are brought to your room to
begin the day. Informal early evening
gatherings in the Farmhouse living
room with wine & hors d'oeuvres.
Coffee, teas and homemade cookies
always available in the living room.

Nearest Airport(s)
Sacramento, Oakland and San
Francisco

Directions
From San Francisco: Hwy 101 N
to Hwy 128 W to Hwy 1 N; then
8.2 miles.

Unwind at a tranquil, 1867 country estate on a headland meadow
above Little River, minutes south of historic Mendocino Village.

Glendeven Inn blends the best of the Mendocino coast: gracious
accommodations of a first-class inn, ocean views and a contemporary art gallery.

The heart of Glendeven is a beautifully restored New England-
style farmhouse surrounded by ever-flowering gardens.

Guest quarters provide undisturbed luxury, combining tasteful
antiques, comfortable furniture, featherbeds and fine art.

All accommodations feature well lighted reading areas, and most
include wood burning fireplaces, private decks and stirring views
of the ocean.

AAA ◆◆◆   *Member Since 2002*

"Dreamy ... I give it '5 Pillows' ... no wonder Glendeven rhymes with Heaven!"

Joshua Grindle Inn

www.srinns.com/joshuagrindle
P.O. Box 647, 44800 Little Lake Road, Mendocino, CA 95460
800-474-6353 • 707-937-4143
stay@joshgrin.com

Proprietors
Charles & Cindy Reinhart

Traditional Victorian Village Bed & Breakfast Inn

Experience Mendocino at its best. Our welcoming home sits atop a two-acre knoll overlooking the village and ocean. Park and forget about your car, as galleries, shops, restaurants and hiking trails are just a short stroll away. Tastefully decorated, comfortable, and exceptionally clean rooms await you. Charles and Cindy and our friendly staff will attend to your every need, and serve a full gourmet breakfast. Enjoy chatting with fellow guests over evening refreshments in our parlor, or escape to a private, quiet nook in our gardens. Relax on our front veranda and watch the whales spout in the distance. Recommended by prestigious Andrew Harper's *Hideaway Report*.

Rooms/Rates
10 Rooms Main House, Cottage, Water Tower, $160/$259 B&B. Ocean view luxury Grindle Guest House (2 bdrm) $250/$400 (EP).
Number of Rooms: 10

Cuisine
Full gourmet breakfast specializing in fresh local ingredients. The highly regarded Cafe Beaujolais is just a two-block stroll from the Inn. Wineshop on premises with selection of premium Mendocino wines. Complimentary wine in room & Cream Sherry in Parlor.

Nearest Airport(s)
Little River Airport, San Francisco Int'l, Oakland Int'l

Directions
From San Francisco, take Hwy. 101 N to Hwy. 128 West to Hwy. 1 N. From Hwy. 1 turn west onto Little Lake Road. First driveway on your right.

AAA ◆◆◆◆   *Member Since 1996*   Mobil ★★★

"The hospitality, food, service, & property are among the best we have experienced."

 SelectRegistry.com

Sea Rock Inn

Innkeepers/Owners
Andy and Susie Plocher

Contemporary Country
Seaside Inn

www.srinns.com/searockinn
11101 Lansing Street, PO Box 906, Mendocino, CA
95460
800-906-0926 • 707-937-0926 • Fax 707-676-9008
innkeeper@searock.com

Rooms/Rates
6 Cottages, 4 Jr.Suites, 4 Suites.
$179/$395.
Number of Rooms: 14

Cuisine
Guests enjoy an attractive breakfast buffet with daily changing quiche, hard boiled eggs, yogurt, fresh pastries, juices, fruit and more. Upon check in to the room, guests may relax with a complimentry split of fine local wine.

Nearest Airport(s)
SFO or Oakland, 3 1/2 hrs

Directions
From SF area take Hwy 101 north to Hwy 128 West (scenic) at Cloverdale-Turn right onto Hwy 1 at ocean & go north (scenic) 10 mi to Mendocino. Turn left on Little Lake Rd & make a right on Lansing - inn is 1/3 mi ahead on right.

One of the few inns in Mendocino with ocean views from every hillside accommodation, The Sea Rock Inn beckons with crashing surf and inviting firelit rooms. From your suite or cottage you will experience the true beauty of the Mendocino Coast with spectacular panoramic views of the ocean and dramatic rocky cliffs of the Mendocino Headlands State Park. The setting is perfect for a memorable getaway. Hand hewn wood treatments accent luxuriously comfortable coastal contemporary design and appointments of virtually every amenity imaginable. Stroll through colorful gardens, curl up by the fire or relax on your deck and watch the sunset from your private oceanview cottage or suite. Hiking trails abound nearby, as does ocean and river kayaking, canoeing and many other outdoor actvities. Gourmet dining is a short walk or minute's drive away, and the charming village of Mendocino is a National Historic Register community laden with special shops and attractions. Great rooms, stunning views and nice people...The Sea Rock Inn.

AAA ◆◆◆   *Member Since 2005*

12+ 🚭 💳   ✂ 🛎 @   🧺 ◎ ⑤

Harbor House Inn by the Sea

www.srinns.com/harborhouseinn
P.O. Box 369, 5600 S. Highway, Elk, CA 95432
800-720-7474 • 707-877-3203 • Fax 707-877-3452
innkeeper@theharborhouseinn.com

Innkeeper/Owner
Edmund Jin & Eva Lu
General Manager
Jennifer Monnier

Elegant Country Inn

Built in 1916, the Harbor House is at the throne of the Redwood Empire, standing vigil on a cliff overlooking Greenwood Cove with its spectacular rock formations and powerful surf. Pathways meander through magnificent seaside gardens and lead to the private beach below. The drama continues throughout the Inn's ten guest rooms, its stately sitting room, and breathtaking ocean-view dining room. Refurbished with luxury in mind, the Inn features antique and classic appointments throughout. Creative California cuisine, fresh daily. *Wine Spectator* 'Award of Excellence.' Prix-fixe four-course dinner included. Distinctive lodging, fine dining and timeless luxury; only three hours from San Francisco.

Rooms/Rates
10 Rooms (6 in Main House, 4 Cottages) $300/$475 MAP. Open year-round.
Number of Rooms: 10

Cuisine
Dramatic ocean-view dining. Full breakfast and highly rated 4-course gourmet dinner included in rates. Extensive wine cellar featuring local and international selections.

Nearest Airport(s)
Santa Rosa, San Francisco, Oakland

Directions
From San Fancisco take 101 N, in Cloverdale take Hwy. 128 W to Hwy. 1, S 5 miles to Elk.

Member Since 1975

16+

"This inn has it all: views, elegant rooms, and meals that alone make the trip worthwhile."

SelectRegistry.com

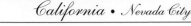

Innkeepers/Owners
Andrew & Susan Howard

Elegant Victorian B&B

Emma Nevada House
www.srinns.com/emmanevadahouse
528 East Broad Street, Nevada City, CA 95959
800-916-3662 • 530-265-4415
mail@emmanevadahouse.com

Rooms/Rates
$179/$229
Number of Rooms: 6

Cuisine
Guests enjoy a sit down three course breakfast that many guests say is worth the trip by itself. Menus are seasonal, with variations on fluffy soufflés and fruit or berry stuffed French toast as frequent choices.

Nearest Airport(s)
Sacramento, Reno, San Francisco & Oakland

Directions
From Sacramento Take Interstate 80 north to Auburn, then Highway 49 north to the Broad Street exit in Nevada City. Go left on Broad Street and up the hill. We are on the right.

Experience the charm of the California Gold Country from a setting of warmth and elegance, in a truly historic place. Our welcoming home sits in a quiet enclave of unique and beautiful Victorians, just on the edge of an authentic gold rush town in the Sierra Foothills. Park and forget your car, as the historic allure of Nevada City is just a short stroll away. Beyond the fascinating shops, galleries and history, there are also trails alongside boiling river rapids, and sixteen unique and interesting wineries to visit. All this is capped by a proliferation of exceptional restaurants that will delight even the most cosmopolitan of travelers. It is not uncommon to hear favorable comparisons to the most notable restaurants of San Francisco and the Napa Valley.

At the Emma Nevada House, you will find comfortable rooms characterized by their fine linens, exceptional cleanliness and thoughtful touches. Wrap around porches, beautiful gardens, and a babbling brook invite guests to linger and unwind in this graceful retreat.

AAA ◆◆◆   *Member Since 2006*

8+

"What a wonderful place for a romantic getaway!"

Shore House at Lake Tahoe

www.srinns.com/tahoe

7170 North Lake Blvd., P.O. Box 499, Tahoe Vista, CA 96148

800-207-5160 • 530-546-7270 • Fax 530-546-7130

innkeeper@shorehouselaketahoe.com

Innkeepers/Owners
Barb & Marty Cohen

Mountain Waterside
Breakfast Inn & Spa

The Shore House is the ultimate romantic getaway on the shore of spectacular Lake Tahoe. Surrounding decks offer fabulous views of the pristine lake and mountains. Relax in the large outdoor lakefront hot tub. Enjoy fine lakefront restaurants, art galleries, and casinos close by. This winter wonderland offers downhill and x-c skiing at 29 resorts, ice skating, snowmobiling, sleigh rides. Summer activities include spectacular hiking, biking, golf, rafting, parasailing, and lunch cruises on the Shore House 36' cabin cruiser, *Lady of the Lake*. Rent kayaks right from the Shore House. Intimate lakefront weddings are our specialty. Enjoy romantic couples' massage packages in the spa overlooking the Lake and Mountains.

Rooms/Rates
All King or Queen Rooms, $190/$290. Each room has a gas log fireplace, custom-built log furnishings, down comforter, featherbed and TV. All private baths, most with whirlpool tubs.
Number of Rooms: 9

Cuisine
Award-winning gourmet breakfasts, wine and appetizers served daily in lakefront dining room or in lakeside gardens. Walk to extraordinary lakefront restaurants.

Nearest Airport(s)
Reno International

Directions
Take Hwy 80E from San Francisco or 80W from Reno. Take Exit 188B onto Hwy 267 towards Kings Beach & North Lake Tahoe. Turn R on Hwy 28 (N Lake Blvd.). Go 3/4 mile to the Shore House at 7170 N Lake Blvd.

Member Since 2000

"The views, the hospitality, the breakfasts, who could ask for more?"

Owners
Steve & Cathi Fowler

Luxury Resort Inn

The Honor Mansion

www.srinns.com/honormansion
14891 Grove Street, Healdsburg, CA 95448
800-554-4667 • 707-433-4277 • Fax 707-431-7173
innkeeper@honormansion.com

Rooms/Rates
13 Rooms, $220/$600, 2 guests per rm. K & Q beds, fireplaces, soaking tubs, garden spa tubs, private decks, rm service menu, comp. resort grounds.
Number of Rooms: 13

Cuisine
Full gourmet breakfast multiple seatings, as well as room service menu, complimentary evening wine and appetizers, sherry, cappuccino machine, & bottomless cookie jar.

Nearest Airport(s)
Oakland and San Francisco

Directions
From the South: Take Hwy 101 North to Healdsburg. Take the Dry Creek exit to the R for 1 block, turn R on Grove St. We are the first white picket fence on the R. From the North: Take Hwy 101 South to the Dry Creek exit; go L.

A Resort Inn...let us pamper you! Built in 1883, this luxuriously comfortable Resort awaits your arrival. Imagine "World-class" amenities and service with hometown hospitality. Spa Services, Pool, Tennis, PGA Putting Green, Bocce, Competition Croquet lawn, Decks, Fountains and Walking Gardens, situated on more than three acres of landscaped grounds, yet a pleasant walk to the downtown square which is replete with terrific shops, bakeries and restaurants. The perfect "special" occasion get-away. Romantic and private. Located in Healdsburg at the confluence of the world-renowned wine growing appellations of Dry Creek, Alexander and Russian River Valleys, with over 100 wineries. Come enjoy our passion for this incredible area and discover some of our boutique wineries, as well as those that have been here for over 100 years. Our fully trained concierge staff is at your service. Plan day trips, picnics, get that special "private" wine tour in some of the world's best wineries right in our back yard. You will never want to leave!

AAA ◆◆◆◆   *Member Since 1998*

16+

"Far more than 'First Class'-it's more like 'World Class.'" "Consistent Perfection."
"Simply Outstanding." "Fabulous!" "Better than Perfection."

Grape Leaf Inn

www.srinns.com/grapeleafinn
www.grapeleafinn.com, 539 Johnson Street, Healdsburg,
CA 95448
866-433-8140 • 707-433-8140 • Fax 707-433-3140
info@grapeleafinn.com

Innkeepers/Owners
**Richard & Kae
Rosenberg**

Luxury Wine
Country Inn

Surrounded by century-old evergreens and lush award-winning gardens, this luxury wine country Inn is tucked away on a quiet historic street, a short walk from fine shops and restaurants. A ten minute drive takes you to more than 104 world-class wineries and the most picturesque countryside imaginable. This highly acclaimed B&B combines the gracious hospitality of a country inn with meticulous service, fine cuisine and 12 luxurious accommodations. Stylish, contemporary decor paired with timeless antiques meld to create the best of California Wine Country style. The relaxing ambience, attentive staff, and its unmistakable romance have made this B&B one of the most sought after small luxury inns in the Wine Country. The 12 rooms, most with king beds, have TV, DVD, CD, Internet wireless service, plush, down bedding and fine pressed linens. Many rooms have fireplaces and phones. Most baths offer two-person spa tubs, and one has a two-person steam shower and Japanese soaking tub. All have Frette linens and Aveda bath amenities.

Rooms/Rates
12 Rooms. $200/$350.
Number of Rooms: 12

Cuisine
Breakfast is an exquisite culinary experience, not just another morning meal. From your 1st cup of freshly ground coffee, to the four-course gourmet breakfast, created from the freshest local produce and herbs grown in our gardens,--all are prepared with imaginative flair by the owners/chefs to create a delicious start to your day. Join us nightly in our "Speakeasy" wine cellar, hidden behind a bookcase, for award-winning local wines and cheeses.

Nearest Airport(s)
SFO and OAK

Directions
See our website for directions from anywhere.

Member Since 2004

12+

"The Wine Country's beautiful Grape Leaf Inn combines the luxury and amenities of a chic boutique hotel with the romantic charm of a B&B."

Innkeepers/Owners
James Caron & Darryl Notter

Premier Historic Country Inn

🍽️ 🍽️

Applewood Inn
www.srinns.com/applewood
13555 Hwy 116, Guerneville, CA 95446
800-555-8509 • Fax 707-869-9170
stay@applewoodinn.com

Wine Spectator
AWARD OF EXCELLENCE

Rooms/Rates
$185/$345
Number of Rooms: 19

Cuisine
Zagat rated, 4 1/2 ★ restaurant @ Applewood offers Mediterranean inspired wine country fare paired w/ an award winning Sonoma County wine list. The inn's romantic dining room features 2 fireplaces & lovely views over a garden courtyard & towering redwoods. Advanced reservations suggested.

Nearest Airport(s)
San Francisco

Directions
Hwy. 101 N from San Francisco to the River Road exit past Santa Rosa. W on River Road 15 mi. to traffic signal @ Guerneville. Turn L at signal, cross Russian River & proceed 1/2 mi. to the inn.

A gently sloping valley guarded by towering Redwoods in the heart of Sonoma's Russian River Valley is home to Applewood Inn and its acclaimed restaurant. Splashing fountains and whimsical statues add texture to the terraced courtyard and gardens that separate the tiled roofed and stuccoed villas of this gracious Mediterranean complex. The old-world atmosphere of a "Gentleman's Farm" is evoked in lovingly maintained orchards and kitchen gardens that supply the restaurant through the Summer and early Fall. Gourmet picnic baskets provided by Applewood's kitchen help make a day of exploring the wine country and dramatic Sonoma Coast all the more enjoyable while Day Spa services add a touch of indulgent pampering. Located within a short drive of wineries, the Sonoma coast and Armstrong State Redwood Reserve.

Member Since 2004

"We have stayed at 3 other B&B's in the wine country and keep comparing them to Applewood. We just need to stick with the one we love best."

Inn at Occidental of Sonoma Wine Country

www.srinns.com/innatoccidental
3657 Church Street, P.O. Box 857, Occidental, CA 95465-0857
800-522-6324 • 707-874-1047 • Fax 707-874-1078
innkeeper@innatoccidental.com

Innkeepers/Owners
Jerry & Tina Wolsborn

Elegant Village
Breakfast Inn

According to *The Wine Spectator*, "One of the Top Five Wine Country Destinations." The antiques, original art and decor provide charm, warmth and elegance exceeded only by the hospitality you experience. "Tops our List as the Most Romantic Place to Stay" is what *Bride and Groom* said of the featherbeds, down comforters, spa tubs for two, fireplaces and private decks. The gourmet breakfast and evening wine and cheese reception add to a memorable experience. Excellent boutique wineries, nearby Armstrong Redwoods State Reserve, Russian River, the dramatic coast and scenic drives along country backroads make for a great destination. Hiking, biking, horseback riding and golfing nearby. All reasons why *AAA VIA* says of The Inn "The Best Bed and Breakfast in the West." An *Andrew Harper* Recommendation.

Rooms/Rates
3 Suites, 13 Rooms: Fireplaces, Spa Tubs, Decks $199/$339. 2 BR Home $629.
Number of Rooms: 18

Cuisine
Full gourmet breakfast. Local wines, cheeses and hors d'oeuvres nightly. Nightly sweets. Concierge service. Wonderful dining nearby. Special Functions: Wedding, Corporate Retreat, Wine Seminar/Dinner.

Nearest Airport(s)
San Fran. (SFO) or Oakland (OAK)

Directions
From San Francisco (101-N) exit at Rohnert Park/Sebastopol. Take 116-W for 7.4 mi to Sebastopol. Turn left onto Bodega Hwy for 6.4 mi, turn Right onto Bohemian Hwy thru town of Freestone for 3.7 mi to Occidental. At 4-way stop, turn right to Inn's parking.

AAA ◆◆◆◆   *Member Since 1995*   Mobil ★★★

12+ 🚭 ♿ 💳 🛈 📂 ♥   ✂ 🖐 @ 🐾   🔌 ◎ ❀   ☕

"Simply everything you want at a Country Inn" – *Recommended Country Inns.*
"Great to be back!! Just as beautiful as the last time."

Innkeepers
Ken Burnet and Greg Nemrow
Proprietor
Sue Burnet

Elegant Village
Breakfast Inn

Gaige House Inn
www.srinns.com/gaigehouse
13540 Arnold Drive, Glen Ellen/Sonoma, CA 95442-9305
800-935-0237 • 707-935-0237 • Fax 707-935-6411
gaige@sprynet.com

Rooms/Rates
23 Rooms & Suites. $175/$595 & $15 p/p breakfast charge. Most with fireplace, Jacuzzi, decks, TV, DVD, tel., wi-fi, DSL, AC. 2 off-site cottages.
Number of Rooms: 23

Cuisine
Professional chef gourmet breakfasts served w/Peet's Coffee & freshly squeezed juice. Evening wine service w/light appetizers. Complimentary beverages, cookies, snacks. Walk to 4 excellent restaurants.

Nearest Airport(s)
SFO, OAK, SMF, STS

Directions
Fr. San Fran: Rt 101N to Rt 37/460A exit. Follow Rt 37 to RT 121 exit. Follow Rt 121N to Rt 116. Take R exit onto Arnold Drive/Glen Ellen. Proceed N through town of Glen Ellen.

In June, 2000, The Gaige House Inn was named the #1 B&B in America by *Travel + Leisure* magazine. Similarly, the Arts and Entertainment (A&E) channel honored the inn as one of the 'top 10 most romantic getaways in the world.' Only one hour from San Francisco, the inn is in the heart of Napa/Sonoma Wine country. Gently influenced Asian decor helps create a sophisticated, yet comfortable environment. Breakfasts are 'outrageously good,' according to *Random House's Guide to The Wine Country*. Relax by the pool, or walk to nearby restaurants. In-room/outdoor spa treatments! Noting all of this, *Frommer's* calls The Gaige House the 'Best B & B in Wine Country.'

Member Since 1998   Mobil ★★★

The Wine Country Inn

www.srinns.com/winecountryinn
1152 Lodi Lane, St. Helena, CA 94574
888-465-4608 • 707-963-7077 • Fax 707-963-9018
romance@winecountryinn.com

Innkeeper
Jim Smith

Traditional Country Inn

For thirty years, three generations of Ned and Marge Smith's family have been welcoming guests to their little slice of Heaven. The Inn is a tranquil and hidden oasis in the heart of America's center for fine wine and eclectic dining. The antique-filled rooms, lush gardens, sun-drenched pool and star-canopied hot tub make it hard for guests to leave, but for those that do, the Smiths and their staff are eager to use their local knowledge to arrange truly memorable days of sampling the finest the area has to offer. At the end of the day guests gather with the innkeepers to compare experiences over more great wine and tables laden with home-made appetizers.

Rooms/Rates
20 Rooms 4 Suites 5 luxury cottages. Rates are $185/$550 Off-season and $210/$595 Harvest Season. All rates include a full buffet breakfast and wine social in the afternoon; off-season mid-week discounts are available. Open year-round.
Number of Rooms: 29

Cuisine
Fresh fruit, juices, home-made granola and nut-breads compliment an innovative egg dish as well as fun bagel bar. Family-recipe appitizers with great local wines in afternoon.

Nearest Airport(s)
Sacramento

Directions
From San Francisco take I-80 (E) to Hwy. 37 follow signs to Napa (Hwy. 29N) 18 miles N to St. Helena. 2 miles N to Lodi Lane R on Lodi 1/3 mile.

Member Since 1978

"This stay was simply outstanding. The facilities are wonderful and the staff has been great!!"

SelectRegistry.com

Gerstle Park Inn

Owners
Jim & Judy Dowling

Elegant Village
Bed & Breakfast Inn

www.srinns.com/gerstlepark
34 Grove St., San Rafael, CA 94901
800-726-7611 • 415-721-7611 • Fax 415-721-7600
innkeeper@gerstleparkinn.com

Rooms/Rates
12 Rooms, 4 with Jacuzzi tubs;
Cottages and Carriage House Suites
with kitchens $1/9/$245. Open
year-round. Meeting facilities up to
20 people conference style.
Number of Rooms: 12

Cuisine
Accommodations include full hot
breakfast to order during a 2-hour
period. Self service Wine hour in
the evening and 24 hour kitchen
privileges which include cookies,
snacks, fruit, sodas, juice, tea
and coffee.

Nearest Airport(s)
SFO-San Francisco, & OAK-
Oakland A.P., 45 min.

Directions
Hwy-101, Exit Central San Rafael,
West on 4th St, L.on D St., R.on
San Rafael Ave, L.on Grove St. 34
Grove St.

Located 20 minutes north of San Francisco and 30 minutes south of the wine country, the Inn was once the site of a English-style estate built in 1895. Situated on 2 1/2 acres in a quiet and historic neighborhood, giant cedar, oak and redwood trees lend ample shade to terraced gardens and green lawns. In the evening, relax on the veranda during wine hour, play croquet, or pick fruit from the orchard. Also, hike in the woods that border the estate. In the morning, enjoy a full hot breakfast to order at your leisure on the veranda or in the breakfast room. Spacious guest rooms are plush in comfort and color, with fine fabrics, antiques, parlor areas and private decks or patios with beautiful views. Gerstle Park Inn is perfectly located for exploring all of the San Francisco Bay Area. There is nothing like this in Marin County!

AAA ◆◆◆   *Member Since 1998*   Mobil ★★★

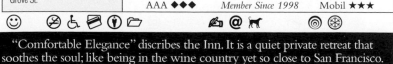

"Comfortable Elegance" describes the Inn. It is a quiet private retreat that soothes the soul; like being in the wine country yet so close to San Francisco.

Washington Square Inn
www.srinns.com/washingtonsquare
1661 Stockton Street, San Francisco, CA 94133
800-388-0220 • 415-981-4220 • Fax 415-397-7242
info@wsisf.com

Proprietors
Maria & Daniel Levin

Traditional Urban Inn

🍽 🍷

Ideally situated in the very heart of San Francisco's legendary North Beach neighborhood, the Washington Square Inn welcomes its guests with the charm and comfort of a small European hotel. Whether traveling for business or recreation, you will find amenities offered at the Inn including free wireless Internet access, complimentary breakfast, afternoon tea, evening hors d'oeuvres & wine, & full office services in the lobby. Rooms feature European antiques, cable TV, soft robes & private baths. Some rooms have sitting areas in bay windows; others offer a cozy atmosphere with private fireplaces. Located in the vibrant neighborhood of North Beach, our historic hotel boasts beautiful views of Coit Tower, Russian Hill, Washington Square Park & the Cathedral of Saint Peter & Paul. The Inn is one of the best San Francisco hotel deals available, offering exemplary lodging & service. As our guest, you'll have a great location from which to explore one of the most beautiful and exciting cities in the world! It's just a short cable car ride or comfortable walk to some of the most famous San Francisco landmarks: Fisherman's Wharf, Pier 39, Coit Tower, China Town, Union Square, Lombard Street, Telegraph Hill (home of the famous wild parrots) and many others.

Member Since 2006   Mobil ★★★

Rooms/Rates
$149/$289. Antiques, telephone, cable TV, soft robes & private baths. Some rooms w/fireplaces overlooking inner courtyard.
Number of Rooms: 15

Cuisine
Nearby high concentration of very good ethnic restaurants.

Nearest Airport(s)
San Francisco,Oakland,San Jose

Directions
From SFO: Take ramp onto US 101 N toward San Francisco & follow US 101 for 8.4 mi. Follow I-280 exit toward Port of SF for 3.2 mi. L on ramp at King St. .9 mi. L on to 3rd Street for approx. .9 mi. 3rd Street becomes Kearny St for the next .7 mi. Bear L onto Columbus Ave for .3 mi. Bear R onto Stockton St for about .1 mi. & Inn will be on the R.

12+   ♿ 💳   @   🧺   🍵

Trip Advisor traveler rating: 5 of 5 stars. "Intimate and elegant. Excellent."

Seal Cove Inn

www.srinns.com/sealcove
221 Cypress Ave., Moss Beach, CA 94038
800-995-9987 • 650-728-4114 • Fax 650-728-4116
Innkeeper@Sealcoveinn.com

Innkeepers/Owners
**Karen Brown Herbert &
Richard Craig Herbert**

Traditional Village
Breakfast Inn

Rooms/Rates
2 Suites, 8 Guestrooms,
$215/$325. All have fireplaces
and TV with VCR. Open year-round
except a few days at Christmas.
Number of Rooms: 10

Cuisine
A full breakfast is served in the
dining room or a freshly baked
continental is offered in the
guest rooms. Complimentary
wake-up coffee outside your door
in the morning and wine & hors
d'oeuvres in the evening.

Nearest Airport(s)
San Francisco Airport is 30
minutes from the Inn.

Directions
From Hwy. 101 or 280 take Hwy. 92
W to Half Moon Bay. Travel N from
Half Moon Bay 6 miles on Hwy.
1, turn W on Cypress Ave towards
the ocean.

Spectacularly set amongst wildflowers and bordered by towering cypress trees, Seal Cove Inn looks out to the ocean over acres of county park. Owned by travel writer Karen Brown and her husband, Rick, the inn is an oasis where you can enjoy secluded beaches, explore tidepools, watch frolicking seals, and follow the tree-lined path tracing the windswept ocean bluffs. Each bedroom is its own private haven with a cozy fireplace and doors opening onto a private deck or patio with views to the distant ocean. Country antiques, lovely watercolors, rich fabrics and grandfather clocks all create a perfect romantic ambiance. Nearby the Inn are the world famous Maverick Surfing Waves, Elephant Seals of Ano Nuevo, majestic coastal Redwood Trees and shopping in the hamlet of Half Moon Bay. The attractions of San Francisco are a mere 30 minutes away. Guests enjoy day trips to Napa/Sonoma and Carmel/Monterey which are 1 1/2 to 2 hours distant.

AAA ◆◆◆◆   *Member Since 1998*

"Seal Cove is truly a special place as are you and your staff. We felt so welcome."

Purple Orchid Inn, Resort & Spa

www.srinns.com/purpleorchid
4549 Cross Road, Livermore, CA 94550
800-353-4549 • 925-606-8855 • Fax 925-606-8880
info@purpleorchid.com

General Manager
Heidi Farah
General Manager
Angela Rauch
Elegant Country
Resort

This distinctive South Livermore Valley Inn offers soaring eagles, singing meadowlarks and the rush of the waterfall - all minutes from the freeway, but miles away in your mind. Our concierge will assist you with reservations for dinner, meeting/conference space or wedding receptions. Located in America's oldest award winning wine country, this elegant estate surrounds your senses with flowers and acres of vineyards and olive orchards. The tranquility will massage your mind with relaxing images of your luxury suite, private jacuzzi tubs in all guest rooms, a leisurely full breakfast, 18 holes of championship golf, a soak in the poolside hot tub, followed by the spa treatment of your choice. Don't forget to enjoy the hors d'oeuvre wine reception and our Estate Grown olive oil tasting nightly! Perfect for corporate getaways.

Rooms/Rates
4 Rooms $150/$195; 4 Suites/
Retreats $225/$260; 2 Patio
Suites, $360/$380. FP/TV/VCR/
Voicemail, concierge service until
8:00pm, Q/K beds,views from all
rooms, Always open.
Number of Rooms: 10

Cuisine
Homemade pastries,fresh fruit,full
gourmet breakfasts, Special
summer themed dinners; Local
dining.

Nearest Airport(s)
Oakland Intl: I880 S to I238 E,
becomes I580 E, see directions
below.

Directions
From SF Intl:Take Hwy 101 S ~5
mi to Hwy 92E to I880 N ~5 mi to
I580 E ~25 mi to exit S Vasco Rd
until it ends at Tesla Rd. Turn L on
Tesla Rd ~2 mi. Turn L on Cross

Member Since 2000

14+

"Better than a cruise and no sea sickness! We felt like a prince and princess."

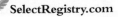

Innkeepers/Owners
**Arline and Richard
Taborek**
General Manager
Anita Miller

Traditional Village Breakfast
Inn

Dunbar House, 1880
www.srinns.com/dunbar
271 Jones Street, Murphys, CA 95247
800-692-6006 • 209-728-2897 • Fax 209-728-1451
innkeep@dunbarhouse.com

Rooms/Rates
3 Rooms, $190/$240; 2 Suites, $250/$260. TV,DVD,data ports, phone,refrigerators, fireplaces,spa baths, down comforters, Q or K beds, AC.
Number of Rooms: 5

Cuisine
Appetizer plate & bottle of wine await in each guest's room. Candlelit breakfast endowed w/edible flowers served in dining room by the fire, in the rose garden, or in the privacy of the guest's room.

Nearest Airport(s)
Sacramento Airport

Directions
From San Francisco: 580 E to Tracy to 205 E to 99 N to Stockton, exit on Hwy. 4 E (Farmington exit), to Angels Camp. 49 S to Hwy. 4 E again. 9 miles to Murphys. L at Main St. L at Jones St.

Arrive at the Inn and begin a visit with history. Located two hours east of San Francisco, between Lake Tahoe and Yosemite, in the Sierra foothills. Murphys remains much the same as it was during the Great Gold Rush. The village is just steps across the bridge over Murphys Creek, and offers fine dining, galleries, wineries, seasonal events, and live theatre. Water fountains and birdhouses abound in the lovingly tended historic rose garden, surrounded by a white picket fence with many private sitting areas. A suite may offer such indulgences as an English towel warmer, balcony in the trees, fine linen, stereo system, champagne and a whirlpool bath for two.

AAA ◆◆◆◆   *Member Since 2001*

12+

"Comfortable & elegant with fabulous food in a gracious setting.
We'll be back soon!"

McCaffrey House

www.srinns.com/mccaffreyhouse
23251 Highway 108, P.O. Box 67, Twain Harte, CA 95383
888–586–0757 • 209–586–0757 • Fax 209–586–3689
innkeeper@mccaffreyhouse.com

Innkeepers/Owners
Michael & Stephanie McCaffrey

Grand Mountain
Home B&B

Pure elegance...in a wilderness setting. This AAA Four Diamond Inn is a delightfully warm and charming three-story country home nestled in the quiet forest hollow of the High Sierras – near Yosemite National Park. Guestrooms are artfully decorated and feature handmade Amish quilts, fire stoves, private bath, TV/VCR, CD players plus exquisite views. McCaffrey House was designed and built by your hosts, Michael and Stephanie McCaffrey. They had one essential theme in mind – warmth and comfort. General gathering areas are spacious and tastefully decorated, with a large collection of furniture and art acquired by Michael and Stephanie during their travels. All appointments have such a welcoming touch that they extend an invitation to come often and stay a while. Enjoy the warmth of friendship along with views of the pristine forest, diverse birds and wildlife, rays of sunshine or snowflakes in flight.

Rooms/Rates
$140/$200
Number of Rooms: 8

Cuisine
Awaken to the aroma of fresh brewed coffee - imported from Costa Rica. Relax in the beautifully decorated dining room for a full country breakfast, prepared by Stephanie McCaffrey, a master of the culinary arts.

Nearest Airport(s)
Sacramento Airport

Directions
McCaffrey House is located 11 miles east of Sonora and one-half mile above the East Twain Harte exit on Highway 108. 3 hour drive from San Francisco; 2 from Sacramento; 3 from Monterey.

AAA ◆◆◆◆   *Member Since 2004*   Mobil ★★★

☺ ⊘ 💳 ⓘ 📂 ♥   ✗ 🖐 @ 🐕   🀫

"McCaffrey House - set off the main road, among trees that reached halfway to heaven ... you could leave the windows open and hear the trees whisper. It's a great place!" Al Martinez, columnist - *Los Angeles Times*

 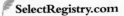

Groveland Hotel

Innkeepers/Owners
Peggy and Grover Mosley

Victorian Country Inn

🍽️ 🍽️ 🍽️ 🍷

www.srinns.com/grovelandhotel
18767 Main Street, P.O. Box 289, Groveland, CA 95321
800-273-3314 • 209-962-4000 • Fax 209-962-6674
guestservices@groveland.com

Wine Spectator AWARD OF EXCELLENCE

Rooms/Rates
Decadent Suites: $225. Truly Decadent Suites: $265/$275. Really Nice Rooms: $135. Extremely Nice Rooms: $145/$155. Luxury Rooms: $165/$175. Rates are for 2 guests. Additional guests: $25. Pets Welcome - $10/pet per night includes treats & use of bowls.
Number of Rooms: 17

Cuisine
Guest Breakfast Buffet, Lunch for Groups and Full Service Dining, open to the public. Full Service Saloon and Wine List.

Nearest Airport(s)
Approximately 2.5 hours from Sacramento (SAC), San Francisco (SFO) or E45.

Directions
E of San Francisco, and S of Sacramento, on Highway 120.

Drive to Yosemite 24/7 - take a picnic and great bottle of wine from our restaurant. We have it all – Tuolumne Whitewater Rafting, a US Top 10 River, over 100 species of wildflowers, hiking, golf, tennis, stables, swim at Rainbow Pool or discover God's Bath on the Clavey River. Four seasons - Spring, with songbirds, incredible flowers and North America's tallest waterfall. Summer's roses, hydrangeas, lavender and balmy evenings to herald Fall's brilliant color and crispness in the air. Winter temps suggest hot cider, cozy fireplaces, toboggans, snowshoes and skis. Lots of wildlife - deer, squirrel, possum, skunk, raccoon, fox, coyote, cougar, and an occasional bear. Feathered species offer a wide variety of birds, and an occasional eagle. *Country Inns* Magazine named it one of the US Top 10 Inns, and *Sunset* Magazine called it 'One of the West's Best Inns.' Romantic parlour dining with fireplace, music, fresh flowers and candlelight. Upscale linens surround your warm, snuggly bed. We provide the ambience – you create the memories! A perfect venue for weddings, receptions, family reunions, company parties, etc. Our Conference Room for 15 people, has a 1900 Belgian conference table. Full service business amenities and free wireless access.

AAA ◆◆◆   *Member Since 2005*   Mobil ★★★

☺ 🚭♿💳🎯📁❤ ✂🔑@🐕 🧺◎

Old Monterey Inn

www.srinns.com/monterey
500 Martin Street, Monterey, CA 93940
800-350-2344 • 831-375-8284 • Fax 831-375-6730
omi@oldmontereyinn.com

Innkeeper/Owner
Patricia Valletta

Elegant In Town Inn

🍽️

'The level of service and accommodations here would rival most any inn or hotel we've visited,' says *The San Franciso Chronicle*. Set amidst an acre of spectacular gardens on a quiet, oak studded Monterey hillside, the Old Monterey Inn exudes romance and warmth. The 1929 half-timbered English Tudor Inn's rooms all overlook the uniquely beautiful gardens. Inside, guests find the attention to detail, which is the hallmark of the Inn--memorably fluffy featherbeds and 24-hour access to mineral waters, juices, tea and coffee. A full gourmet breakfast is served bedside or in our Heritage dining room, or, weather permitting, in our gardens. The owners imbue every element with the extra touches that help the Inn achieve near perfection. Recommended by prestigious Harper's *Hideaway Report* and Conde Nast Gold List.

Rooms/Rates
Cottage, 3 Suites & 6 Rooms w/sitting areas - fireplaces, spa tubs, pvt. baths, feather beds, DSL, TV/VCR, TEL. $270/$450. Open year-round.
Number of Rooms: 9

Cuisine
Evening wine and hors d'oeuvres. Extaordinary restaurants nearby. Port and fresh fruit...

Nearest Airport(s)
Monterey Airport - 10 min.
San Jose Airport - 1 hr. 15 mins.
SFO - 2 hrs. 30 mins.

Directions
SOUTH on Hwy 1: exit Soledad-Munras Ave, cross Munras Ave, R on Pacific. Go about 1 mile, L on Martin St. NORTH on Hwy 1: exit Munras Ave, L to Soledad, R on Pacific, L on Martin. Continue on Martin St 1 long block, Inn is on the R.

AAA ◆◆◆◆   *Member Since 1993*   Mobil ★★★★

14+ 🚭 💳 ❤️ ✗ 📷 @ 📺 ◎ ☕

"Old Monterey Inn: elegance, comfort & room decors that read like poetry" - *Discovery Magazine* "Voted one of California's Top 10 Inns" - ILoveInns.com

Innkeeper/Owner
Don Martine
General Manager
Don Martine

Elegant
Waterside Breakfast Inn

Martine Inn
www.srinns.com/martine
255 Oceanview Boulevard, Pacific Grove, CA 93950
800-852-5588 • 831-373-3388 • Fax 831-373-3896
don@martineinn.com

Rooms/Rates
24 Rooms, 4 Suites. $139/$399.
Number of Rooms: 28

Cuisine
Morning brings a full breakfast on a background of silver, crystal and lace, while evening presents wine and hot hors d'oeuvres. Group lunches and dinners prearranged from 20 to 50, Victorian dinners up to 12 courses.

Nearest Airport(s)
Monterey - 5 miles
San Jose - 70 miles
San Francisco - 90 miles

Directions
Hwy 1 to Pebble Beach Pacific Grove exit. Turn on to Hwy 68 toward Pacific Grove. Stay in R lane on Forest Ave. at the water turn R on Ocean View Blvd turn R at 255 Ocean View Blvd.

Just blocks from Monterey's bustling Cannery Row lies a 24-room Victorian villa that *Bon Appetit* considers "one of the 8 best B&Bs in historic homes" and *Conde Nast Traveler* calls a "spectacular place for a romantic getaway." Welcome to the Martine Inn, built in the 1890s as a lavish private residence just 90 minutes south of San Francisco. Today it's a meticulously renovated resort steps from the water's edge, where every fixture and furnishing is an authentic Victorian-era antique, and every room, many with fireplaces, claw foot tubs and/or ocean views, has its own name and unique decor. Two sitting rooms afford priceless views of the bay, and other inn extras include a library, piano, game room replete with a 1917 nickelodeon, spa and Don Martine's collection of vintage MG autos. Miles of coastal hiking and biking are accessible literally at the inn's front door. All attractions of California's magnificent Monterey Peninsula are nearby, including the Monterey Bay Aquarium, Monarch butterflies.

AAA ◆◆◆   *Member Since 1992*   Mobil ★★★

☺   🚭 ♿ 💳 🛎 📁 ♥   ✂ 🎨 @   🗑 ◎

"One of the 10 Most Romantic Inns in the U.S." - *Vacations* Magazine "It's the kind of place where starry eyed young lovers dream of getting married." - *San Francisco* Magazine

Oak Hill Manor

www.srinns.com/oakhillmanor
12345 Hampton Court, Atascadero, CA 93422
866-625-6267 • 805-462-9317 • Fax 805-462-0331
macare@oakhillmanorbandb.com

Innkeepers/Owners
Risë and Maurice
Macaré

Elegant European
B&B

Oak Hill Manor Bed and Breakfast estate sits graciously on an oak studded hill with a sunset view of the Santa Lucia Mountains and our newly planted Zinfandel vineyard. Eight elegant suites, each styled after a different European country decor, await you. Fireplaces, whirlpool tubs and private decks enhance the ambiance of many suites. Enjoy a quiet conversation in the parlor; play a game of pool or darts in the pub; read a book in the library; enjoy a beautiful sunset; relax on your balcony; share a bottle of champagne; or pamper yourself with a massage. We offer the opportunity to escape from your busy life, relax and unwind, renew your spirit, and enjoy all the charm and beauty the Central Coast has to offer. Relax in our Lincoln Town Car stretch limo as you visit the Paso Robles Wine Country or the Edna Valley Wine Trail. Hike or bike the many trails available in San Luis Obispo County; tour Hearst Castle; shop for antiques or just enjoy the ambiance and hospitality of our European styled B&B. Rediscover your Joie de Vivre!

Rooms/Rates
$180/$280
Number of Rooms: 8

Cuisine
Enjoy full breakfast choices including Eggs Benedict, Orange French Toast, Swiss Quiche, Greek Omelette or Zucchini Pancakes.

Nearest Airport(s)
San Luis Obispo County Airport, 30 minutes

Directions
Oak Hill Manor is located halfway between San Francisco & Los Angeles. Take Hwy 101 to Santa Barbara Rd exit. Turn E on Santa Barbara Rd and drive approx. 1/2 mi. passing the Nazarene Church on the L and 2 stop signs. Turn R at our sign onto Hampton Court. Oak Hill Manor is the large Tudor estate on the hill.

Member Since 2005

2+

"You have thought of every detail for comfort and pleasure ... truly a treasure that we will always remember!" "...the best B&B we have ever stayed at..."

Innkeepers/Owners
**Ann O'Connor and
John Arnott**

Log Home & Carriage
House Breakfast Inn

J. Patrick House Bed & Breakfast Inn
www.srinns.com/jpatrickhouse
2990 Burton Drive, Cambria, CA 93428
800-341-5258 • 805-927-3812 • Fax 805-927-6759
jph@jpatrickhouse.com

Rooms/Rates
$165/$215
Number of Rooms: 8

Cuisine
Enjoy a full gourmet breakfast in our Garden room. Fresh fruit, homemade granola, fresh plump raisins and delicious yogurt for starters. Main entrees such as, Vegetable strata, Blintzes with Raspberry Sauce, Chili Corn Soufflé and Stuffed French Toast with pure Maple syrup to name a few, change daily.

Nearest Airport(s)
San Luis Obispo Airport

Directions
Midway between Los Angeles & San Francisco on the Central Coast of CA. 6 mi. from Hearst Castle.

Country Elegance in Accommodations: Cambria's original – and still the finest – Bed and Breakfast Inn, nestled in the tall Monterey pines above Cambria's charming east village. As you enter the front door of this enchanting log home, the warmth of its embrace will welcome you. The aroma of freshly baked cookies, homemade granola, breads and muffins will transport you to a magical place. The main log home has one guest suite. Stroll through the passion vine covered arbor to the charming carriage house with seven additional "exquisitely appointed" guest rooms. Indulge in wine and hor d'oeuvres in the evening and "killer" chocolate chip cookies and cold milk before bedtime. Each morning a delicious full breakfast is served in the light-filled Garden Room. Enjoy exemplary guest services.

AAA ◆◆◆   *Member Since 2003*   Mobil ★★★

14+ Ⓢ 🖃 ♥ ✕ 🏠

The Ballard Inn

www.srinns.com/ballardinn
2436 Baseline Avenue, Ballard, CA 93463
800-638-2466 • 805-688-7770 • Fax 805-688-9560
innkeeper@ballardinn.com

Innkeepers/Owners
Budi & Chris Kazali
General Manager
Christine Forsyth

Elegant Country Inn

Voted one of America's Top Ten Most Romantic Inns, our comfortably elegant 4 diamond Country Inn is nestled among vineyards and orchards in the charming township of Ballard. Each of the 15 rooms posesses its own special charm and character reflecting local history. Many of our rooms have fireplaces, creating an especially romantic retreat. Borrow our bicycles and take one of our picnic lunches for an adventurous tour of the Santa Barbara wine country. A tasting of local wines, hors d'oeuvres and a full breakfast are included in your stay. The acclaimed Ballard Inn Restaurant features French-Asian cuisine in an intimate dining room complete with a magnificent marble fire place. It is open to the public Wednesday-Sunday.

Rooms/Rates
15 Rooms, $215/$305. Closed Christmas Eve & Christmas Day.
Number of Rooms: 15

Cuisine
French-Asian cuisine.

Nearest Airport(s)
Santa Barbara

Directions
From Hwy. 101, take Solvang exit, follow Route 246 E through Solvang to Alamo Pintado; turn L. Drive 3 miles to Baseline Ave. turn R. The Inn is on your R.

AAA ◆◆◆◆   *Member Since 1993*

12+ 🚭 ♿ 🛏 🛎   ✍ @   🧺

The West's Best Small Inns/*Sunset Magazine*
Top 10 Most Romantic Inn/American Historic Inns

Innkeeper/Owner
Douglas Ziegler
General Manager/Inn-keeper
Rick Segovia
Victorian Breakfast Inn

Santa Ynez Inn
www.srinns.com/santaynezinn
3627 Sagunto St., Santa Ynez, CA 93460
800-643-5774 • 805-688-5588 • Fax 805-686-4294
info@santaynezinn.com

Rooms/Rates
$285/$475
Number of Rooms: 14

Cuisine
Full Gourmet breakfast, Evening Wine & Hors d'oeuvres and Evening Desserts.

Nearest Airport(s)
Santa Barbara Airport

Directions
From the North: Take 101 South to Highway 246. Take 246 East (left) to the town of Santa Ynez and turn left on Edison and right on Sagunto. From the South: Take 101 North to Highway 154. Take 154 over the San Marcos Pass to Highway 246 and make a L onto 246. R on Edison and R on Sagunto.

Our Wine Country Getaway awaits in 14 individually decorated rooms and junior suites. Accommodations feature unique antiques, queen or king-sized beds with Frette linens, remote-controlled gas fireplaces and whirlpool tubs in deluxe marble baths. Most rooms offer a private balcony or patio to savor the beauty and serenity of the Santa Ynez Valley. Take advantage of all that Santa Barbara County has to offer, from wine tasting and antique shopping, to Glider rides and Jeep tours. There's something for everyone in Santa Ynez. After a day of Southern California sightseeing adventures, you may wish to unwind in the heated outdoor whirlpool, lounge on the sundeck, or take a leisurely stroll through the gardens of the Inn. Whatever your needs—whether you wish to arrange for wine tasting tours, shopping, dining, glider rides, bicycle rentals or transportation—our concierge service is eager to assist you.

AAA ◆◆◆◆ *Member Since 2004*

"What a delight to find one such a quality country Inn with such charm. We will return!"

Simpson House Inn

www.srinns.com/simpsonhouse
121 East Arrellaga Street, Santa Barbara, CA 93101
800-676-1280 • 805-963-7067 • Fax 805-564-4811
reservations@simpsonhouseinn.com

Owners
Glyn & Linda Davies
Managing Partner
Nick Davaz

Elegant Victorian Bed
& Breakfast Inn

This elegantly restored 1874 Historic Landmark Victorian Estate is the only Five Diamond Bed & Breakfast Inn in North America. It's comprised of six tastefully apppointed rooms in the original estate home, four private cottages and 4 spacious rooms in our historic carriage house. The Inn is secluded within an acre of beautifully landscaped English gardens, yet just a five-minute walk from the historic downtown, restaurants, shopping, theater and a pleasant walk to the beach. All rooms feature antiques, fine art and Oriental rugs. Fireplaces and whirlpool tubs are available. We serve a delicious full gourmet breakfast, to your room, in the gardens or our dining room. Afternoon dessert tea and lavish evening Mediterranean hors d'oeuvres and wine tasting are not to be missed. Additional complimentary amenities include full access to the Athletic Club a short distance from the Inn, bicycles and English croquet. Our Concierge can arrange spa treatments in your guest room, wine country tours, whale watching or a host of other activies.

AAA ◆◆◆◆◆ *Member Since 1993*

Rooms/Rates
6 Main House and 1 Garden Room $235/$475. Historic Carriage House Rooms $585/$615. Garden Cottages $595/$615. Open year-round. Mid-week and seasonal rates on availability.
Number of Rooms: 15

Cuisine
Complimentary full vegetarian breakfast, afternoon dessert tea and Mediterranean hors d'oeuvres buffet with local wine tasting each evening.

Nearest Airport(s)
Santa Barbara

Directions
From San Francisco - Mission St. exit, L. Anacapa St., R. Arrellaga St., L; From Los Angeles - Garden St. exit, R. Gutierrez St., L. Santa Barbara St., R. Arrellaga St., L.

"The staff and Inn completely exceeded our expectations. We had a beautiful stay!"

SelectRegistry.com

Owner
Susan Zolla
Innkeeper
Christine Marwell

Traditional In Town
Breakfast Inn

Channel Road Inn
www.srinns.com/channelroad
219 W. Channel Road, Santa Monica, CA 90402
310-459-1920 • Fax 310-454-9920
info@channelroadinn.com

Rooms/Rates
$225/$395
Number of Rooms: 14

Cuisine
Delicious hot breakfasts served buffet style or brought to your room or patio when you desire. Informal early evening gatherings w/wine & hors d'oeuvres. Tea, lemonade & cookies.

Nearest Airport(s)
Los Angeles International (LAX)

Directions
From #405 Freeway N or S, take the 10 Freeway W to Pacific Coast Hwy N. (becomes the coast highway going N when it meets the ocean). Continue N 1.8 mi. to stoplight for W. Channel Road & Chautauqua; both streets come off the coast highway. Make very hard R onto W. Channel & proceed 1 block to 219 W. Channel Rd.; the Inn is the big blue house on the L.

A surprise by the beach in the eclectic Los Angeles neighborhood of Rustic Canyon, the Channel Road Inn provides the comfortable elegance of a restored 1915 Santa Monica home and the timeless pleasure of a seashore retreat. Guests enter through the original polished oak doors. The living room is furnished in period antiques and arranged to highlight the Batchelder tiles surrounding the fireplace. The Inn's guest rooms and suites feature blue water or garden views, some with fireplaces or whirlpool tubs, others with sunny decks. All offer fine white linens and upscale amenities. Some of the city's best dining, shopping, and entertainment venues are within minutes of the Inn.

AAA ◆◆◆   *Member Since 2002*   Mobil ★★★

"Please bottle whatever you do so I can remember the Channel Road Inn always."

Bissell House Bed & Breakfast

www.srinns.com/bissellhouse
201 Orange Grove Avenue, South Pasadena, CA 91030
800-441-3530 • 626-441-3535 • Fax 626-441-3671
info@bissellhouse.com

Innkeeper
Juli Hoyman

Elegant Victorian
Breakfast Inn

paii

Restful, elegant and romantic, this 1887 classic Victorian estate will exceed your expectations for charm. The Bissell House offers intimate accomodations for travelers seeking comfort and relaxation amidst the culture and heritage of Old Pasadena. Also nearby are the world-famed Huntington Library and Gardens, Caltech, JPL, Norton Simon Museum and numerous historic locations. Located in the historic Orange Grove Mansion District, the Bissell House is a perfect location for attending annual home and garden tours or the New Year's Rose Bowl Parade. An upscale neighborhood with tree-lined streets of Pasadena cloisters the inn amongst an old-world setting. Delightful breakfasts are served in the dining room where Albert Einstein was once hosted! Le Cordon Bleu trained chefs serve on weekends. Additional complimentary services include: concierge, high speed Internet/wireless access, use of pool/gardens, afternoon tea, desserts, snacks and beverages, and spa services arranged with advance notice. The inn is minutes from downtown Los Angeles. Voted one of the Top Romantic Inns!

Rooms/Rates
5 Rooms and 1 Suite w/jacuzzi, antiques, featherbeds, robes, claw-footed tubs or showers, DSL, and TV/VCR/DVD available select rooms. $150/$350 all inclusive rates.
Number of Rooms: 6

Cuisine
Full gourmet breakfast served by candlelight on Haviland Limoges china with crystal and Victorian silver. Special diets accommodated. Afternoon tea, beverages/snacks. Organic coffees/teas.

Nearest Airport(s)
Los Angeles International-30 min.
Burbank-15 min.

Directions
1.25 miles south of Colorado St., Pasadena on Orange Grove Blvd. Corner of Columbia/Orange Grove Ave. Take 110 or 134 or 210 Fwys at Orange Grove exits.

AAA ◆◆◆   *Member Since 2006*

10+

"Perfect in every detail...I'm spoiled for any place else!"

Rose Gables Bed & Breakfast

Innkeepers/Owners
Laurie and Ray Naud

Victorian Bed and
Breakfast

www.srinns.com/rosegablesbb
29024 Mammoth Drive, P.O. Box 3080
Lake Arrowhead, CA 92352
866-201-4090 • 909-336-9892
rosegables@charter.net

Rooms/Rates
$139/$219
Number of Rooms: 5

Cuisine
Full gourmet breakfast served in dining room at 9 am. Homemade pastries, fresh fruit & an assortment of teas & coffee. You won't go away hungry!

Nearest Airport(s)
Ontario International

Directions
From I-10 take 215 N. Take Hwy 30 E & exit Waterman Ave. N on Waterman Ave.; it becomes Hwy 18 as you head up the mountain. Stay on the 18 until the Lake Arrowhead turn off. Follow it to the bottom of the hill & turn R onto Hwy 173. Go past Cedar Glen, the marina & the hospital. Turn R on Yosemite, R on Yellowstone, R on Banff, and R on Mammoth

Featured in "Best Places in Southern California", Rose Gables is A Victorian style B&B filled with antiques and is the premier B&B in Lake Arrowhead. Elegant, yet comfortable, perfect for that romantic getaway or weekend away. Curl up by your fireplace in your fluffy cotton robes. Enjoy the breathtaking views. Stretch out on your king size bed. Grab a video from our large collection and watch a movie in your room. Peruse our library and find that perfect book to enjoy while lounging on the deck or check out our huge game selection. Sample some of Laurie's homemade treats along with a hot cup of tea. Located just minutes from shopping & restaurants, yet secluded & peaceful. A block from the National Forest where hiking trails await. Our gourmet breakfasts offer an ever-changing menu including such tempting delights as Eggs Florentine, frittatas, soufflés, & more.

AAA ◆◆◆ *Member Since 2006*

"Having been to many Bed and Breakfasts, nothing compares to Rose Gables. The views, the room, and the breakfasts were amazing!"

Villa Royale Inn

www.srinns.com/villaroyale
1620 S. Indian Trail, Palm Springs, CA 92264
800-245-2314 • 760-327-2314 • Fax 760-322-3794
info@villaroyale.com

Innkeepers/Owners
Bambi and David Arnold

Tuscan-style Estate

Framed by breathtaking mountain views, the Villa Royale's intimate three acres echo an ancient Tuscan estate. Wander through tranquil courtyards overflowing with fragrant citrus, jasmine and lavender, gently cascading fountains, two heated pools and a large jacuzzi.

AAA's Westways magazine calls the Villa Royale's AAA Four Diamond Europa Restaurant "a charming hideaway where you'll feel as if you have been transported to an intimate castle in Europe." Europa's bar, with its pool and mountain views, prides itself on its extensive offerings awarded by *Wine Spectator* Magazine. Luxurious full-service amenities, including full complimentary breakfast and fine dining, a daily newspaper, in-room spa services, and an attentive and caring staff make the Villa Royale Inn your ultimate Palm Springs romantic getaway.

Rooms/Rates
Seasonal rates. Hideaway Guestrooms $100/$250. Royale Guestrooms $150/$275. The Villas, 1 Bedroom $200/$400; 2 Bedroom $250/$450. Deposit taken at time of booking w/10 day cancellation policy.
Number of Rooms: 30

Cuisine
Superb cuisine served fireside or by trickling fountains. Small private dinning room for up to 12 ideal for a special occasion or intimate wedding celebration.

Nearest Airport(s)
5 min. from downtown Palm Springs & the airport.

Directions
Driving time subject to traffic & weather. From LA area: approx. 2 hrs. From San Diego: approx. 2 hrs.15 min.

AAA ◆◆◆◆   *Member Since 2006*

"Picturesque...a fountain and beautiful garden entrance, mature trees, meandering brick pathways, stunning mountain views. A very special place to stay."

Innkeepers/Proprietors
Paul Blank & Francois Leclair

Boutique Ocean-view Hotel & Spa

Casa Laguna Inn & Spa
www.srinns.com/casalaguna
2510 South Coast Highway, Laguna Beach, CA 92651
800-233-0449 • 949-494-2996 • Fax 949-494-5009
innkeeper@casalaguna.com

paii

Rooms/Rates
15 Rooms, 5 suites & a Cottage: $150/$600. All rooms are air-conditioned & feature a 9-layer, deluxe bed, CD & DVD players. Some w/ private patios, jetted tubs and/or fireplaces.
Number of Rooms: 22

Cuisine
Full gourmet breakfast & afternoon wine & hors d'oeuvres included. Area fine dining.

Nearest Airport(s)
Orange County - John Wayne, SNA

Directions
From I-5 N: Exit CA-1/Camino Las Ramblas to Beach Cities. Keep L at the fork; merge to CA-1/PCH for 6.7 mi. From I-5 S or I-405 S: Exit CA-133 S to Laguna Beach for 9 mi., then L onto CA-1/PCH for 1.75 mi.

Voted "Best B&B in Orange County" for nine consecutive years by the OC Register. Terraced on a hillside amid tropic gardens and flower-splashed patios, the historic Casa Laguna Inn & Spa exudes an ambiance of bygone days when Laguna Beach was developing its reputation as an artists' colony and hideaway for Hollywood film stars. The mission style inn set below towering palms framing views of the blue Pacific invites you to slow your pace to that of another, less hurried era. The magnificent Palm Court and the ocean-view pool deck will enchant you with fountains and rare Catalina tiles. Two lovely beaches are a few minutes walk from the hotel. Victoria Beach offers a long stretch of white sand while Moss Point offers tide pools and coves. One and a half miles south of Main Beach, the inn is a short distance from the boutiques, pottery shops, and galleries for which Laguna Beach is famous. A Casa Laguna Spa treatment is an excellent way to enhance your stay at Casa Laguna. Guests are pampered, rejuvenated and renewed.

AAA ◆◆◆   *Member Since 2004*

"The perfect getaway! A charming and relaxing retreat. Marvelous setting with wonderful staff."

Orchard Hill Country Inn

www.srinns.com/orchardhill
2502 Washington St., P.O. Box 2410, Julian, CA 92036
800-716-7242 • 760-765-1700 • Fax 760-765-0290
information@orchardhill.com

Innkeepers/Owners
Pat and Darrell Straube

Elegant Contemporary
Country Inn

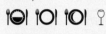

Rooms/Rates
Lodge Rooms $225 and $240.
Cottage Rooms $305 and one
Deluxe $425.
Number of Rooms: 22

Cuisine
Full breakfast and afternoon hors
d'oeuvres included. Dinner is
served on selected nights and picnic lunches are available. Excellent
selection of beer and wine.

Nearest Airport(s)
San Diego International

Directions
60 mi. NE of SD. IS 15 north to
Scripps Poway Pkwy, turn right
(East). Approx. 12 mi, left on Hwy 67
(North). Hwy 67 becomes Hwy 78 in
Ramona and continues straight into
Julian through Santa Ysabel (22 mi.)
In Julian, at the four way stop sign,
continue straight. Orchard Hill Coun-
try Inn is up one block on the left.

Orchard Hill Country Inn is reminiscent of America's great national park lodges. This award-winning premiere inn is nestled
in the heart of Julian's historic district. Orchard Hill Country Inn
features hilltop vistas, a water feature, colorful gardens, and hiking trails leading to abandoned gold mines. Julian has wonderful
opportunities for birding, star gazing, hiking, and nearby desert
wildflower preserves. Our cottage rooms all have our porches or
decks and fireplaces. Some also have whirlpool bathtubs. Our
lodge rooms are cozy and beautifully decorated. All rooms have
private bathrooms, televisions, VCR's and CD players. Our comfortable rooms and warm hospitality will delight you. Orchard
Hill provides relaxation, memorable dining, and romance.

AAA ◆◆◆◆ *Member Since 1998*

Top 9 western lodges – *Sunset* Magazine
"Perfection is now more than a word."

Innkeeper
Gayle Wildowsky

Historic Village Breakfast
Inn

The Bed & Breakfast Inn at La Jolla

www.srinns.com/innatlajolla

7753 Draper Avenue, La Jolla, CA 92037

800-582-2466 • 858-456-2066 • Fax 858-456-1510

BedBreakfast@innlajolla.com

Rooms/Rates
14 Rooms $179/$359; 1 Suite $399. Deluxe, elegant cottage-style rooms w/fresh flowers & fruit. Open year round.
Number of Rooms: 15

Cuisine
Full candlelit breakfast. Gourmet entrees served with fresh fruit, muffins, scones, homemade granola topped with honey and vanilla-laced yogurt, rich coffee and exotic teas.

Nearest Airport(s)
San Diego International

Directions
From the S: I-5 N; exit La Jolla Parkway to Torrey Pines Rd. W, R on Prospect Pl to Draper Ave., L on Draper. From the N: I-5 S; exit La Jolla Village Dr. W, L on Torrey Pines Rd., R on Prospect Pl to Draper, L on Draper.

This elegant historical inn is drenched in sunlight, draped in brilliant bouganvillia and kissed by mild ocean breezes. Located in one of the most beautiful seaside villages in the world, it is only steps to the best beaches and snorkeling in California, as well as the finest shops, restaurants, art galleries, and museums. The inn is central to the main attractions of San Diego, such as the Stephen Birch Aquarium, Sea World, Old Town, Wild Animal Park, and Mexico. After a fun-filled day, return to the peaceful respite of the inn, where, lulled by the melodious garden fountain and surrounded by lush greenery, you will have time to reflect and relax and savor the good life. Each of the thirteen guest rooms and two suites are unique in their personality and decor, embellished with fine antiques and accessories, creating a personalized space you can call your "home away from home." You may like it so much that you may never want to leave. Fine sherry and fresh flowers are in each of the guest rooms to relax the body and delight the senses. Come be our guest and experience all the best that San Diego, and particularly La Jolla, have to offer. "So close yet so far from all!"

Member Since 2002

12+

"Delighted we switched from the Hilton!"

Colorado

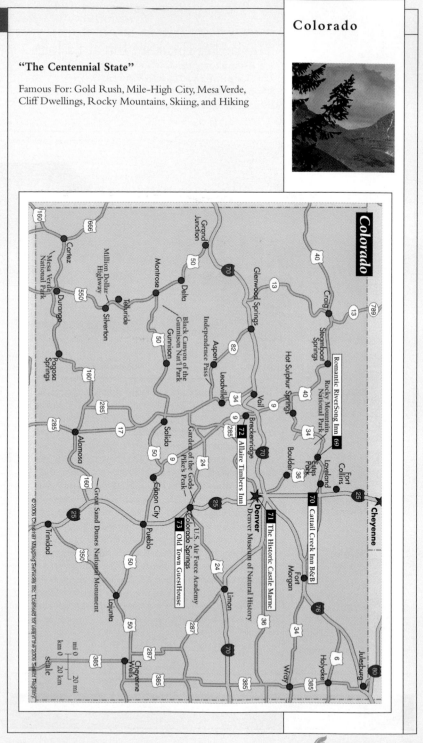

"The Centennial State"

Famous For: Gold Rush, Mile-High City, Mesa Verde, Cliff Dwellings, Rocky Mountains, Skiing, and Hiking

Colorado

- Romantic RiverSong Inn **69**
- Allaire Timbers Inn **72**
- The Historic Castle Marne **71**
- Cattail Creek Inn B&B **70**
- Old Town GuestHouse **73**

Denver Museum of Natural History

Mesa Verde National Park
Rocky Mountain National Park
Black Canyon of the Gunnison Nat'l Park
Gunnison Nat'l Park
Garden of the Gods / Pike's Peak
U.S. Air Force Academy
Great Sand Dunes National Monument
Independence Pass
Million Dollar Highway

Cheyenne

© 2005 Christman Mapping Services Inc. Licensed for use in the 2006 Select Registry

scale
mi 0   20 mi
km 0   20 km

Romantic RiverSong Inn

Innkeepers/Owners
Sue & Gary Mansfield

Traditional Mountain
Retreat/Lodge

🍽️ 🍽️

www.srinns.com/romanticriversong
P.O. Box 1910, 1766 Lower Broadview Rd
Estes Park, CO 80517
970-586-4666 • Fax 970-577-1336
romanticriversong@earthlink.net

Rooms/Rates
4 Rooms, $150/$175 B&B; 5 Cottage
Suites, $225/$295 B&B. Tubs for 2;
and marvelous packages online.
Number of Rooms: 10

Cuisine
Evening dining is reserved for the
first four couples that sign up for
a marvelous five-course dinner by
fireside. The tables are set with fine
china and bone handle silver service
on white lace linens, while softly in
the background the sounds of jazz
classics soothe your soul.

Nearest Airport(s)
Denver International, 1 hour & 45
minutes

Directions
Hwy 36 through Midtown of Estes,
Hwy 36 to Mary's Lk Rd; L at Mary's
Lk Rd; Go 1 bk Cross bridge. Turn
R immediately; take country road
to the end.

Once every three days a couple chooses Romantic RiverSong
Inn as their hideaway in the Colorado Rockies to elope. The inn
is secluded on 27 wooded acres with towering Blue Spruces and
Ponderosa pines, quiet ponds, hiking trails and tree swings. With
only ten guest rooms, the inn has achieved a marvelous balance
with its luxurious rooms (radiant heated floors, jetted tubs for two
by a crackling fire) and nature. These lovely rooms are merely
background to the mountain melodies of songbirds and a rushing
mountain stream. After a great hike in Rocky Mountain National
Park come home to a relaxing "streamside massage." Then, later
that evening enjoy our own chef prepared candlelight dinner by
fireside. It's the warm hospitality that makes the memories of Romantic RiverSong linger long after you've gone from this little bit
of heaven in the Colorado mountains.

Member Since 1987   Mobil ★★★

12+ 🚭 ♿ 💳   ♥   ✂️ 🐾 @ 🐕   🛏️ ◎   ☕

"...the most romantic place my wife and I have stayed. The breakfast is delicious...
phenomenal service & hospitality. Still the best dinner in Estes Park!"

Cattail Creek Inn B&B

www.srinns.com/cattailcreek
2665 Abarr Drive, Loveland, CO 80538
800-572-2466 • 970-667-7600 • Fax 970-667-8968
info@cattailcreekinn.com

Innkeepers/Owners
Sue and Harold Buchman

Contemporary In Town Breakfast Inn

Rooms/Rates
8 Rooms $115/$210. The inn's eight guest rooms have distinctive individual features and are situated for optimal privacy. Open year-round.
Number of Rooms: 8

Cuisine
Full gourmet breakfast, snacks. B&B liquor license.

Nearest Airport(s)
Denver International Airport (most major carriers)

Directions
I-25 to exit 257B to US Hwy. 34 (W). Go (W) on US 34 for 6 miles to Taft. Turn R (N) on Taft and go 3/4 mile to 28th. Turn L on 28th and go one block to Abarr Drive. Turn L on Abarr Drive. Follow Abarr Dr (S) to the inn.

You will sense the feeling of casual elegance and warmth the minute you enter the grand foyer of this luxurious inn. From the finely crafted cherry woodwork, the golden-glazed hand-plastered walls to the fine art and the world-class bronze sculpture, this unique inn is truely an artistic experience! Located on the seventh tee box of the Cattail Golf Course, guests have peaceful views of Lake Loveland and majestic views of the Rocky Mountains. The Inn is across the lagoon from Columbine Art Gallery and is within walking distance to Benson Sculpture Park.

Member Since 2000   Mobil ★★★

14+

"Nothing Short of Heaven!! We've never been so relaxed nor felt so comfortable."

Innkeepers/Owners
**The Peiker Family
Diane, Jim, Melissa, and
Louie**

Elegant Victorian In
Town Breakfast Inn

The Historic Castle Marne Inn

www.srinns.com/castlemarne

1572 Race Street, Denver, CO 80206

800-92-MARNE • 303-331-0621 • Fax 303-331-0623

info@castlemarne.com

Rooms/Rates
9 Rooms, $105/$260
2 Suites with Jacuzzi tubs.
3 Rooms with private hot tubs.
Number of Rooms: 9

Cuisine
Full gourmet breakfast
Elegant Private 6 course Dinners
Afternoon Tea and Luncheons

Nearest Airport(s)
Denver International

Directions
From DIA, Pena Blvd. To I-70 W to
Quebec. L to 17th Ave. R to York St.
L to 16th Ave. R 4 blocks to Race St.
From mountains, I-70 E, R onto 6th
Ave.Frwy (US 6) E to Josephine St. L
to 16th Ave. L to Race St. From Colo
Spgs, I-25 N exit R onto University
Blvd N, R on 16th Ave. to Race St.
From Cheyenne, I-25 S, exit R on Park
Ave. R on Broadway, L on 17th Ave. R
on Race St. one block to 16th Ave.

Denver's grandest historic mansion, listed on the National & Local Historic Registers. Built in 1889, features handhewn lavastone exterior, handrubbed woods, balconies, four-story tower and stained glass Peacock Window. It all blends beautifully with period antiques and family heirlooms to create a charming Victorian atmosphere. Relax in the English garden beside the bubbling fountain. Full gourmet breakfast served in the original Dining Room. Complimentary Afternoon Tea served in the Parlour. Whirlpool spas and private outdoor hot tubs. Lunch & Private candlelight dinners by reservation. In Denver's Wyman Historic District. Near Museum of Nature and Science, Zoo, Botanic Gardens. Five minutes from Downtown and Cherry Creek Shopping area. Walking distance to many restaurants. Wedding and Honeymoon packages available. Small weddings and elopements a specialty. The AIA says, "Castle Marne is one of Denver's great architectural legacies." Free Parking. WIFI. Business meeting space.

AAA ◆◆◆   *Member Since 1991*   Mobil ★★★

Winner of 2004 Condé Nast Johansens Top 3 Inns on the North American continent. "... they pay impeccable attention to details that excite the senses."

Allaire Timbers Inn

www.srinns.com/allairetimbers
9511 Hwy. 9, South Main Street, P.O. Box 4653
Breckenridge, CO 80424
800-624-4904 Outside CO • 970-453-7530 • Fax 970-453-8699
info@allairetimbers.com

Innkeepers/Owners
Sue Carlson and Kendra Hall

Contemporary Mountain
Breakfast Inn

This contemporary log B&B is the perfect Rocky Mountain Hideaway. Located on a tree filled bluff at the south end of historic Main Street, the Allaire Timbers offers 10 guest rooms, each with private bath and deck. Two elegant suites offer a special touch of romance with private hot tub and fireplace. Relax by a crackling fire in the log and beam Great Room. Enjoy the serenity of the tiled sunroom. Retreat to the reading loft, or unwind in the outdoor hot tub with spectacular mountain views. Just steps from downtown Victorian Breckenridge with its many and varied restaurants and shops. Access to the ski area and Breckenridge Riverwalk arts/music amphitheatre via the Free Ride town bus system. Featured in Arrington's Inn Traveler and CNN's Travel Guide.

Rooms/Rates
8 Lodge Rooms, 2 Suites
$145/$400.
Number of Rooms: 10

Cuisine
Hearty breakfast of homemade breads and sweets, fresh juices and fruits, the Inn's special recipe granola and changing menu of hot entrees. Evenings enjoy fresh baked cookies and seasonal herbal iced tea or hot citrus cider.

Nearest Airport(s)
Denver International

Directions
From Denver, I-70 West to exit 203. Hwy. 9 South to Breckenridge, through town past the traffic light at Boreas Pass Road (gas station on right). Take next Right, bear right into private parking lot.

Member Since 1995   Mobil ★★★

13+

"Hospitality, comfort and culinary magic." *Washington Post*

Innkeepers/Owners
Shirley and Don Wick

Elegant In Town
Breakfast Inn

Old Town Guest House
www.srinns.com/oldtownguesthouse
115 South 26th Street, Colorado Springs, CO 80904
888-375-4210 • 719-632-9194 • Fax 719-632-9026
Luxury@OldTown-GuestHouse.com

Rooms/Rates
$99/$235, Corporate rates available, Private hot tubs, steam showers, fireplaces, balconies, TV/VCR/DVD, phones, wireless Internet, A/C, International video-conferencing in private conference room. Attractions: Pikes Peak, Garden of the Gods,and more.
Number of Rooms: 8

Cuisine
Full 3 course sit-down breakfast. Evening wine/beer and hors d'oeuvres.

Nearest Airport(s)
Colorado Springs

Directions
From I-25, exit 141 going West to 26th St. North on 26th, proceed 2 1/2 blocks, turn right into B&B's private parking lot.

The three-story brick guesthouse, built as a B&B, is in perfect harmony with the 1859 period of the surrounding historic Old Town. The urban Inn offers upscale amenities for discerning adult leisure and business travelers. The foyer elevator allows the entire Inn to be accessible. The soundproof, uniquely decorated guestrooms have private porches overlooking Pikes Peak. Relax on the umbrella-covered patio for afternoon wine and hors d'oeuvres. The innkeepers are Pikes Peak area concierges. The elegance and hospitality of the Guest House was awarded AAA's Four Diamond Award for Excellence. Distinctive Inn of Colorado.

AAA ♦♦♦♦   *Member Since 2001*

12+

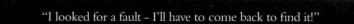

"I looked for a fault – I'll have to come back to find it!"

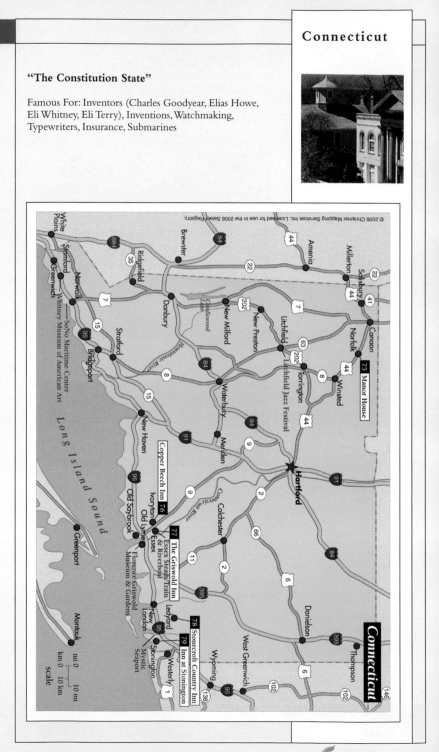

Connecticut

"The Constitution State"

Famous For: Inventors (Charles Goodyear, Elias Howe, Eli Whitney, Eli Terry), Inventions, Watchmaking, Typewriters, Insurance, Submarines

© 2006 Chrismar Mapping Services Inc. Licensed for use in the 2006 Select Registry.

75 Manor House

Copper Beech Inn 76

77 The Griswold Inn

Essex Steam Train & Riverboat

Florence Griswold Museum & Gardens

78 Stonecroft Country Inn

79 Inn at Stonington

SoNo Maritime Center

Whitney Museum of American Art

Litchfield Jazz Festival

Connecticut

scale
mi 0   10 mi
km 0   10 km

Innkeeper/Owner
L. Keith Mullins
Innkeeper/Manager
Lisa T. Auclair

Village Breakfast Inn

Manor House

www.manorhouse-norfolk.com
69 Maple Avenue, Norfolk, CT 06058
Toll Free 866-542-5690 • Fax 860-542-5690
innkeeper@manorhouse-norfolk.com

Rooms/Rates
8 Rooms, 1 Suite, $110/$235. Four rooms offer wood or gas fireplaces, 3 with whirlpools, and two with private balconies.
Number of Rooms: 9

Cuisine
Full country breakfast. Complimentary coffee, hot or iced tea, and hot chocolate available all day, glassware and refrigerator also available.

Nearest Airport(s)
Bradley International

Directions
NYC: I-84 E to exit for Rte. 8 N in Waterbury. At terminus of highway in Winsted take Rte. 44W R to Norfolk. Boston: I-84 W to exit for Rte. 4 Farmington to Rte. 179 to Rte. 44W to Norfolk.

Surround yourself by Victorian Elegance in this 1898 Tudor Estate described by *Gourmet* as "Quite Grand," and designated "Connecticut's Most Romantic Hideaway" by the *Discerning Traveler*. Featured in *National Geographic Traveler*, *Good Housekeeping*'s "Best Weekend Getaways," and listed as one of the top 25 Inns by American Historic Inns. All rooms offer views of the spacious grounds and perrenial gardens, are furnished with period antiques, and luxurious down comforters. Savour a full breakfast in the elegant dining room, relax by the baronial fireplace in the living room, or read a book in the library, all adorned with Tiffany windows and architectual detail. The Manor House is located at the foot of the Berkshires, and travelers can enjoy an array of outdoor activities, shopping, summer theatre, and music festivals.

Member Since 2000

12+

"Connecticut's Most Romantic Hideaway"
The Discerning Traveler

The Copper Beech Inn

www.srinns.com/copperbeech
46 Main Street, Ivoryton, Essex, CT 06442
888-809-2056 • 860-767-0330 • Fax 860-767-7840
info@CopperBeechInn.com

Proprietors
Ian S. Phillips
Barbara C. Phillips
Elegant Country
Hotel

Wine Spectator
AWARD
OF
EXCELLENCE

Selected as *"The Best Country Inn"* in Connecticut by the readers of *Connecticut Magazine*, for the past two years, the Copper Beech Inn is minutes from the Connecticut River and Long Island Sound, and is just a 2-hour drive from either New York or Boston. Lovingly restored over the past three years, the period antiques, Oriental rugs, and richly textured fabrics bring comfort and classic European sophistication to this grand estate. Elegant guest rooms & suites with oversize beds feature Italian marble bathrooms and air-jet thermo-masseur tubs. The highly acclaimed AAA Four Diamond restaurant was named the *"Best Overall"* in the state by the readers of *Connecticut Magazine* in 2005. It features extraordinary food and a *Wine Spectator* award-winning wine list with over 400 selections. Andrew Harper's *Hideaway Report* selected the inn as one of the *"The Best in New England"* and, *The New York Times* said in a recent review "The Copper Beech Inn is a lovely example of what Americans look for in a three or four-star country inn ... the wine list is pretty spectacular ... the dining experience always marvelous." "Worth the 2-hour drive from New York & Boston alone." *Boston Magazine*.

Rooms/Rates
13 Rooms including 2 suites
$150/$395 Full Breakfast. Open
Year-Round. All w/private baths.
Number of Rooms: 13

Cuisine
French with a contemporary flair.
Select from an extraordinary menu
and 400 selection award-winning
wine list. "Crystal sparkles, silver
shines, Oriental rugs glow on polished floors, antiques & masses
of fresh flowers set the scence
for the flawlessly elegant dining"
Connecticut Magazine.

Nearest Airport(s)
Hartford 45 mins., Boston 2
hours, New York 2 hours

Directions
I-95 to Exit 69 to Route 9. Exit 3.
Left off ramp. 1.5 mi on Left.

AAA ◆◆◆◆   *Member Since 2003*   Mobil ★★★★

12+

"Everything was perfect, from the warm hospitatity to the gorgeous flowers to the delicious food to the charming service."

Innkeeper/Owner
Douglas Paul
General Manager
Alan A. Barone

Traditional Village Inn

The Griswold Inn

www.srinns.com/griswold
36 Main Street, Essex, CT 06426
860-767-1776 • Fax 860-767-0481
griswoldinn@snet.net

Rooms/Rates
Seasonal Rates. 14 Guest Rooms,
$100/$220 B&B; 16 Suites
$160/$370 B&B. Open year-round.
Number of Rooms: 30

Cuisine
Complimentary continental breakfast
for inn guests. Lunch, dinner, Sunday
Hunt Breakfast. Authentic American
Cuisine featuring fresh seafood, aged
beef selections and New England
favorites. Inspired "small" plates
served in Wine Bar. Full service,
award-winning Tap Room.

Nearest Airport(s)
Hartford's Bradley Airport - 1 hr.
Boston, JFK

Directions
I-91 S to exit 22 S (left-hand exit).
Rte. 9 S to exit 3 Essex. I-95 (N&S) to
exit 69 to Rte. 9 N to exit 3 Essex. Two
hours from New York and Boston.

This 1776 landmark is located on Main Street in the "storybook" village of Essex, selected as the Best Small Town in America. The Connecticut River Valley, in which Essex is situated, has been designated one of the world's "Last Great Places" by the Nature Conservancy. Mere steps from the Connecticut River, the Inn's connection with the sea is apparent throughout. Filled with brass bells and binnacles, the 'Gris' also houses a renowned maritime art collection. Savor the atmosphere and acclaimed cuisine in its historic dining rooms. Relax in the Inn's stunning Wine Bar featuring a small plate menu concept and an extensive selection of wines by the glass. Step into the award-winning Tap Room where lively music rings out nightly: sea chanteys, banjo, Dixieland, swing and more. Riverboat cruises, shopping, antiquing, hiking, museums and historic homes are just outside the door, while Mystic Seaport and Aquarium, Goodspeed Theatre, outlets, Foxwoods and Mohegan Sun casinos and entertainment complexes are within easy reach.

Member Since 1974

"The hospitable 'Gris' retains a place of honor as an American treasure."

Stonecroft Country Inn

www.srinns.com/stonecroft
515 Pumpkin Hill Road, Ledyard, CT 06339
800-772-0774 • 860-572-0771 • Fax 860-572-9161
stonecroftinn@comcast.com

Owners
Joan R. Egy
Elegant Country
Inn

Relax in quiet country elegance on an 1807 sea captain's six-acre estate, only ten minutes from Mystic Seaport, Foxwoods and Mohegan Sun casinos. Ancient stone walls and lush green lawns surround the Inn, consisting of The Main House, a sunny Georgian colonial, and The Grange, our recently converted 19th century barn. Romantic guestooms feature French, English and American country decor, with fireplaces, whirlpools and heated towel bars, television and internet access. Pamper yourself with an on-site massage, and savor an exquisite dinner fireside in our elegant granite-walled restaurant or the candlelit garden terrace. Open year-round.

Rooms/Rates
4 Rooms Main House: AC, 3 with fireplace; 4 Deluxe Rooms Grange: AC, gas fireplace, TV, 2-person whirlpool; 2 Suites Grange: AC, gas fireplace, TV, bidet, 2-person whirlpool, walk-in shower. All rooms $150/$300.
Number of Rooms: 10

Cuisine
Breakfast included. Dinner in Grange Dining Room or on terrace, contemporary American cuisine, Zagat food rating 28. Full service bar & extensive wine list. Classical guitarist on Sat. night.

Nearest Airport(s)
TF Green (Providence)

Directions
I-95 N: Exit 89, L off ramp, straight 3.75 mi. I-95 S: Exit 89, R off ramp, straight 3.5 mi.

Member Since 2002

"wonderful blend of luxury and simplicity" "cared for, pampered" "kudos to the Chef!" "married 10 years and coming here for 9" "I want to live here"

SelectRegistry.com

Innkeeper/Owner
William Griffin
General Managers
Susan Irvine Anne Starzec
Historic Village Breakfast Inn

Inn at Stonington
www.srinns.com/innatstonington
60 Water Street, Stonington, CT 06378
860-535-2000 • Fax 860-535-8193
www.innatstonington.com

Rooms/Rates
18 Rooms. Seasonal rates
$135/$435. Open Year Round.
Number of Rooms: 18

Cuisine
Continental breakfast served.
Fresh baked breakfast breads,
asst muffins, bagels,croissants,
fresh fruit.

Nearest Airport(s)
T.F. Green, Prov. RI

Directions
North on I-95 Exit 91 turn right at
the bottom of ramp. Proceed 1/2
mile and turn left on North Main
St. Proceed to stoplight & cross
US Rt. 1. At 1st stop turn left. At
next stop, take a right onto Water
St. Proceed over bridge, bear left
and travel approx. 6/10 ths of a
mile to 60 Water St. South on
I-95, turn left at bottom of ramp.
Use same dir. as above.

Named by *Travel + Leisure* as Inn of the Month, this newly constructed 18 room inn is located in the heart of Stonington Borough, one of the last untouched and 'historic' villages in New England. Relax in the privacy of your room, snuggled in front of your fireplace or take a luxurious bath in the soaking Jacuzzi tub. Public rooms include a top floor sitting room overlooking the Harbor, intimate bar with adjoining breakfast room, a cozy living room, and a well equipped gym. During the day stop by one of the local wineries, visit downtown Mystic, or simply take a stroll down Water Street and enjoy the specialty shops and some of the finest antiques in the area. Each evening join us for complimentary wine and cheese before walking to dinner at one of four fabulous restaurants in the village. Area attractions: small beach within walking distance, Mystic Seaport, Mystic Aquarium, Mohegan Sun and Foxwood Casinos, Watch Hill beaches. Come see what *CT Magazine* and *Coastal Living* consider one of New England's most romantic Inns.

Member Since 2005

14+

"There's surely more than one kind of romance in this world, but Stonington Village – and The Inn at Stonington – seem to have most of them covered."

"The First State"

Famous For: Historic Brandywine Valley—Museums
and Gardens, Du Pont Family Mansions, Beaches,
Fishing, Wildlife, Farmland, Bird-watching, Nascar
races, and No-sales-tax shopping.

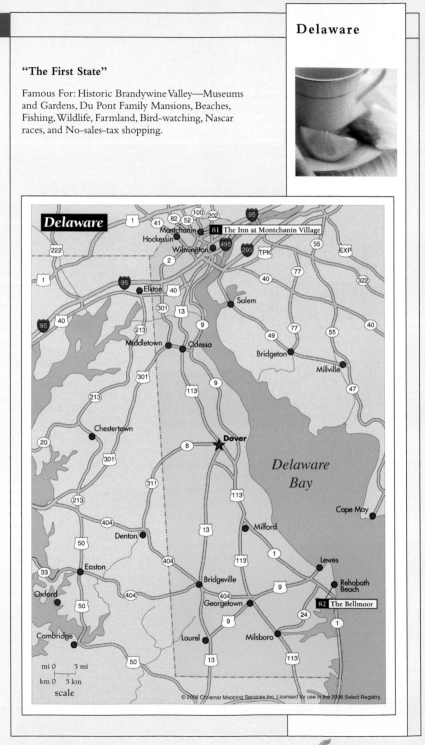

Delaware

81   The Inn at Montchanin Village

Montchanin
Hockessin
Wilmington
Elkton
Salem
Middletown   Odessa
Bridgeton
Millville
Chestertown
Dover
Delaware Bay
Cape May
Denton
Milford
Easton
Lewes
Oxford
Bridgeville
Rehoboth Beach
Georgetown
82   The Bellmoor
Cambridge
Laurel
Milsboro

mi 0   5 mi
km 0   5 km
scale

© 2006 Chrismar Mapping Services Inc. Licensed for use in the 2006 Select Registry.

Innkeeper/Owner
Dan and Missy Lickle
General Manager
Jacques Amblard
Elegant Village Inn

The Inn at Montchanin Village

www.srinns.com/montchanin
Rte 100 & Kirk Road, P.O. Box 130, Montchanin, DE 19710
800-269-2473 • 302-888-2133 • Fax 302-888-0389
inn@montchanin.com

Wine Spectator AWARD OF EXCELLENCE

Listed on the National Historic Register, The Inn at Montchanin Village was once a part of the Winterthur Estate and was named for Alexandria de Montchanin, grandmother of the founder of the Du Pont Gunpowder Company. One of the few remaining villages of its kind, the settlement was home to laborers who worked at the nearby Du Pont powder mills. In eleven carefully restored buildings dating from 1799 to 1910, there are 28 richly furnished guest rooms and suites appointed with period and reproduction furniture. The Inn's renowned Krazy Kat's Restaurant, once the village blacksmith shop, is known as much for its creative cuisine as its whimsical décor.

Rooms/Rates
28 elegant rooms & suites. $169/$375. Marble baths, nightly turndown, *New York Times* daily paper & imported linens.
Number of Rooms: 28

Cuisine
Krazy Kat's Restaurant is part of the Inn. Eclectic continental cuisine, specializing in local ingredients. Private dining rooms available for groups of 10-40.

Nearest Airport(s)
Philadelphia International

Directions
From I-95 N or S: Exit 7 (Delaware Ave.). Follow Rte. 52 N (Pennsylvania Ave.) for 2.2 miles. Turn R onto Rte. 100 N, continue through 2 traffic lights. At the 3rd light, make a R, then a quick L into the parking lot. (Registration in barn).

Member Since 2002 Mobil ★★★

"...from the gardens, to the elegant rooms, to the antiques and imported linens–no detail has been missed."

The Bellmoor

www.srinns.com/bellmoor
6 Christian Street, Rehoboth Beach, DE 19971
800-425-2355 • 302-227-5800 • Fax 302-227-0323
info@thebellmoor.com

Proprietors
Moore Family
General Manager
Chad Moore
Elegant In-Town
Breakfast Inn

Quiet moments in the garden...sunrise on the beach...the crackle of the fire in the Jefferson Library...a leisurely walk to unique boutique shopping and fine dining restaurants...a favorite book in the Sunroom. Our newly expanded Day Spa offers over 30 services to restore and rejuvenate body and spirit. Whether you choose a sea-weed wrap, hot stone pedicure or a soothing springtime facial, you can leave the world behind and experience refined relaxation and well-being. Additional complimentary services: concierge, bellman, high speed Internet access, wireless access on first floor and in garden, guest computer room, two pools, hot tub, fitness room. Enjoy complete relaxation in our beautifully appointed accommodations of unsurpassed comfort combining the warm, residential feel of a B&B with the efficient, professional service of a small European hotel.

Rooms/Rates
55 rooms, $105/$395 B&B. 23 suites, $150/$550 B&B; suites include marble bath, fireplace, whirlpool, wet bar. Adult concierge floor available. Rates change seasonally. Packages available, see website or call.
Number of Rooms: 78

Cuisine
Full country breakfast in Garden Room or in garden. Afternoon refreshments. 24 hour coffee service. Many fine dining options within walking distance. Entire property non-smoking.

Nearest Airport(s)
Philadelphia

Directions
Downtown Rehoboth Beach, residential setting 2 blocks from the ocean. See website or call for detailed directions.

Member Since 2004

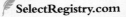

"...like visiting the seaside manor of a longtime friend."

"The Nation's Capital"

Famous For: The White House, the Capitol, Arlington
Cemetery, Cherry Festival, the Smithsonian,
Washington Monument

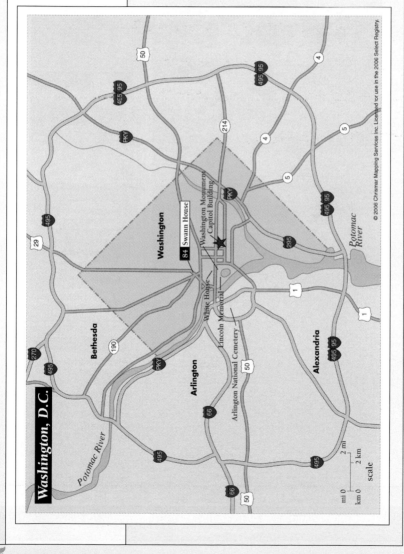

Swann House

www.srinns.com/swannhouse

1808 New Hampshire Ave. N.W., Washington, DC 20009

202-265-4414 • Fax 202-265-6755

stay@swannhouse.com

Innkeepers/Owners
Mary & Richard Ross
General Manager
Rick Verkler

Historic In Town
Breakfast Inn

Rooms/Rates
8 Rooms $165/$365; 4 Suites $195/$365. Each room is unique; all private baths, 5 with fireplace,2 Whirlpool. Open year-round
Number of Rooms: 12

Cuisine
Deluxe continental breakfast daily w/gourmet entree on weekends, afternoon refreshments, evening sherry, dozens of fine restaurants within walking distance.

Nearest Airport(s)
Reagan National (DCA)

Directions
Centrally located, just 12 blocks N of the White House. From Dupont Circle, take New Hampshire Ave. N. Swann House is on the W side, just N of S St., on the corner of Swann.

Elegantly situated in the Dupont Circle Historic District, Swann House shines among its neighboring embassies and stately Victorian homes. Nearby you will find dozens of colorful shops, restaurants, and galleries. We invite you to sip sherry by the fire and savor the ambiance of our 1883 Richardson Romanesque gem. Our sitting rooms, verandas and pool, all graciously appointed for your comfort, beckon you to unwind. Cozy fireplaces, flower-filled balconies and whirlpool bathtubs enhance several of our unique guestrooms, and all offer luxurious down featherbeds, cable TV and telephones with voice mail and data port. An elegant venue for private parties, weddings, receptions, meetings and retreats. Named 'Best B&B in Washington' by *Frommer's* every year since 1999. Voted "Top 10 Most Romantic Inn" in the country *–American Historic Inns* and "Top 10 Urban Inn" *–Forbes*

Member Since 2002

12+

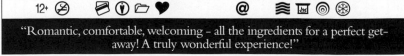

"Romantic, comfortable, welcoming - all the ingredients for a perfect getaway! A truly wonderful experience!"

Florida

"The Sunshine State"

Famous For: Disney World, Busch Gardens, St. Augustine (the oldest city in U.S., founded 50 years before Plymouth), Florida Keys, Everglades, Space Shuttles, Beaches, Alligators, Oranges, Grapefruit, Wildlife

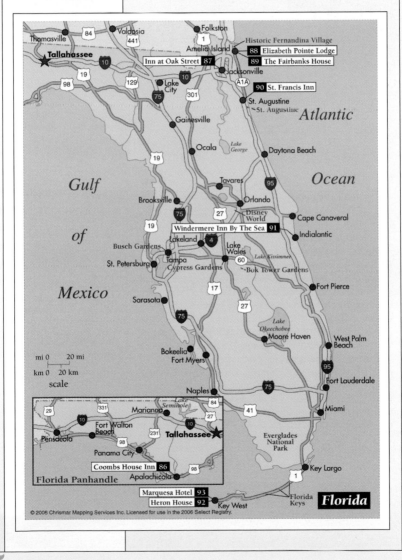

Thomasville
Valdosia
Folkston
84
441
1
Historic Fernandina Village
Amelia Island
88 Elizabeth Pointe Lodge
Tallahassee
10
Inn at Oak Street 87
89 The Fairbanks House
19
Jacksonville
98
129
10
A1A
Lake City
301
90 St. Francis Inn
75
St. Augustine
St. Augustine
Atlantic
Gainesville
Ocala
Lake George
Daytona Beach
19
Ocean
Tavares
95
Gulf
Brooksville
Orlando
75
27
Disney World
Cape Canaveral
of
19
Windermere Inn By The Sea 91
Indialantic
Lakeland
4
Busch Gardens
Lake Wales
Tampa
60
Lake Kissimmee
Mexico
St. Petersburg
Cypress Gardens
Bok Tower Gardens
Sarasota
17
Fort Pierce
75
27
Lake Okeechobee
mi 0   20 mi
Bokeelia
Moore Haven
West Palm Beach
km 0   20 km
Fort Myers
scale
95
Naples
75
Fort Lauderdale
Lake Seminole
84
41
Miami
29
331
Marianna
10
27
Fort Walton Beach
10
Tallahassee
Everglades National Park
Pensacola
98
231
Panama City
Coombs House Inn 86
98
Key Largo
Apalachicola
1
Florida Panhandle
Florida Keys
Marquesa Hotel 93
Florida
Heron House 92
Key West

© 2006 Chrismar Mapping Services Inc. Licensed for use in the 2006 Select Registry.

Coombs House Inn

www.srinns.com/coombshouse
80 Sixth Street, Apalachicola, FL 32320
888-244-8320 • 850-653-9199 • Fax 850-653-2785
info@coombshouseinn.com

Owners
Lynn and Bill Spohrer
Romantic Victorian
Bed and Breakfast

The 1905 Coombs House Inn, located in Apalachicola on Florida's northern Gulf Coast, occupies two elegant Victorian mansions in the historic district of this quaint seaside fishing village, adjacent to St. George Island with its white pristine beaches. Each distinctively decorated room features antique furniture and artwork, has its own full bath, cable TV, telephone and wireless access. Our 3 luxury suites have romantic whirlpool tubs. Guests enjoy complimentary gourmet breakfasts and weekend wine receptions. Check out a complimentary bicycle for a tour of the ante bellum homes. Beach chairs and umbrellas are available for you as well. Camellia Hall, a spacious meeting room enhanced by gardens and a classic gazebo, provides the ideal setting for weddings, and club or business meetings. *Travel + Leisure* Magazine recognized us as one of the "30 Great US Inns." Discover this enchanting town, established in 1831 and rich with maritime history. Relax on the veranda, enjoy a walk to charming restaurants, taste our delicious oysters, visit our museums and theatre, or go fishing or kayaking on the famous Apalachiocola River of the "Forgotten Coast."

AAA ◆◆◆   *Member Since 2006*

Rooms/Rates
16 guestrooms $89/$169. 3 suites $149/$225. Meeting hall seats 50.
Number of Rooms: 19

Cuisine
Baked Strata (like quiche), with eggs, cheese, potatoes, & a daily variety of additional ingredients, like ham, bacon, tomatoes, & mushrooms. We also have a buffet of fresh fruit, many selections of fresh muffins (such as blueberry, sunrise, orange & cranberry), cereals, yogurt, juices, milk, coffee, Starbucks coffee, decaf & imported teas.

Nearest Airport(s)
Tallahassee & Panama City

Directions
Scenic US98 into town. 3 short blocks SW of flashing traffic light, corner of US-98 & 6th St.

"The Inn is peaceful, embracing - a romantic retreat."

　 SelectRegistry.com

Proprietors
Tina Musico & Robert Eagle

Historic Urban Inn

The Inn at Oak Street

www.srinns.com/innatoakstreet
2114 Oak Street, Jacksonville, FL 32204
904-379-5525 • Fax 904-379-5525
innatoakstreet@yahoo.com

Rooms/Rates
$120/$180. Open year-round. Feature flat screen TV with DVD, wine refrigerator, plush robes. 3 rooms with spa tubs and balconies, 1 room with fireplace.
Number of Rooms: 6

Cuisine
Full gourmet breakfast included. Complimentary wine hour and 24 hour coffee bar. We offer a variety of Special Packages which include menu selections for dining at the Inn. Excellent dining within walking distance and a short drive.

Nearest Airport(s)
Jacksonville International Airport

Directions
15 minutes from airport, two miles from downtown Jacksonville. Easily accessible from I-95 North and South, and I-10.

Bordering downtown Jacksonville, the Inn is located in the Riverside National Register Historic District, one of the most diverse collections of historic residential architecture in Florida. The Inn provides luxurious accommodations and superb amenities in the heart of this beautiful neighborhood, just steps from the St. Johns River. Built in 1902, and meticulously renovated by the owners, the Inn offers a vibrant and stylish interior in an urban historic environment. Spacious guestrooms, elegantly furnished, provide modern comforts including flat screen TV with DVD/CD player and wine refrigerator. Business travelers enjoy wireless Internet while lounging on the wraparound porch, while leisure guests relax with a massage in our tranquil spa room. Indulge in our complimentary wine hour, full gourmet breakfast and 24-hour coffee bar. Experience local boutiques, outstanding eateries and art museums, or enhance your stay with a variety of our special packages. Our personal service, fine details and amenities make your visit a memorable one.

Member Since 2005

12+

"A Jewel in Jacksonville...rooms combine comfort with couture."
Travel + Leisure

Elizabeth Pointe Lodge
www.srinns.com/elizabethpointe
98 South Fletcher Avenue, Amelia Island, FL 32034
888-757-1910 • 904-277-4851 • Fax 904-277-6500
info@elizabethpointelodge.com

Innkeepers/Owners
David and Susan Caples

Traditional Waterside
Inn

Rated "One of the 12 best waterfront inns" in America, the Pointe sits overlooking the Atlantic Ocean. Focusing on individualized attention, the inn is Nantucket "shingle style" with an oversized soaking tub in each bath, fresh flowers, morning newspaper, full seaside breakfast and a staff that wants to exceed your expectations. Light food, dessert, and room service available 24 hours. Only a short bike ride to the historic seaport of Fernandina. Horseback riding, tennis, golf and sailing nearby.

Rooms/Rates
24 Rooms, $175/$350 B&B;
1 Cottage, $350 B&B. Open year-round.
Number of Rooms: 25

Cuisine
A complete and tended buffet breakfast in the Sunrise Room or outside on the deck overlooking the ocean. A light fare menu available 24 hours. Complimentary social hour each evening at 6 p.m. Wine and beer available. Our culinary staff welcomes special dietary requests.

Nearest Airport(s)
Jacksonville International Approximately 35 minutes away.

Directions
From I-95 take exit 373 and follow Route A1A to Amelia Island. Our address on A1A is 98 S. Fletcher Avenue, on ocean side.

AAA ◆◆◆   *Member Since 1998*

"The ideal place for a waterside escape." *Country Inns* Magazine

 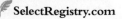

The Fairbanks House

Innkeepers/Owners
Bill & Theresa Hamilton

Elegant Victorian In
Town Breakfast Inn

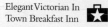

www.fairbankshouse.com
227 South 7th Street, Amelia Island, FL 32034
888-891-9880 • 904-277-0500 • Fax 904-277-3103
email@fairbankshouse.com

Rooms/Rates
6 Rooms, 3 Cottages, 3 Suites,
$180/$395 B&B. Open year-round.
Number of Rooms: 12

Cuisine
Sumptuous gourmet breakfast
served in our formal dining room,
or on piazzas and patios amid our
hidden gardens by the pool. Lively
daily social hour with beverages,
hot and cold hors d'oeuvres. Three
minute walk to casual cafes, taverns
and fine-dining restaurants.

Nearest Airport(s)
Jacksonville, FL

Directions
Use exit 373 from I-95 and follow
the signs for Fernandina Beach
along Highway A1A, 200 East. After
bridge go 3.3 miles to Cedar. L onto
Cedar and R onto 7th. 25 minutes
from JAX, FL airport, 15 minutes
from I-95.

Featured in *The Best Romantic Escapes in Florida* and built in 1885, Fairbanks House is an 8000 sq. ft. Italianate villa rising above a quiet Victorian village on Amelia Island. Surrounded by soaring magnolias and live oaks with dripping Spanish moss, the mansion, cottages and pool rest on a strikingly landscaped acre where guests enjoy a serene 100% smoke-free stay. Rooms are elegantly furnished with period antiques and romantic reproductions. Numerous upscale amenities are designed for a carefree getaway, honeymoon or vacation. King beds, Jacuzzis, bikes, beach gear, Romance Packages, and full concierge service are but a few examples of our attention to detail. Close to secluded beaches and 1100 acre park. Ask for details on seasonal specials and Girls Just Wanna Have Fun Getaways.

Member Since 1998

12+

"Your packages are so creative – they make trip-planning simple.
Love your social hours!"

St. Francis Inn
www.srinns.com/stfrancisinn
279 St. George Street, St. Augustine, FL 32084
800-824-6062 • 904-824-6068 • Fax 904-810-5525
info@stfrancisinn.com

Innkeepers/Owners
Joe and Margaret Finnegan

Historic In Town
Bed & Breakfast Inn

Come visit the past! Antique filled rooms and suites, private balconies with rocking chairs, rooms with fireplaces, kitchenettes, and Jacuzzis. Walk to everything from the Inn's Old City location. This historic Inn overflows with hospitality, set in a lush courtyard on brick paved streets with horse drawn buggys. A historic treasure, but modern comforts abound! Great value, with many guest amenities: swimming pool, gourmet Southern breakfasts, bikes, social hour, evening sweets, "day at the beach," VCR, wi-fi, courtesy local transportation, health club privileges, private parking, free and discounted attractions tickets, coffee and inn-baked cookies, sherry and flowers in your room. Add in-room massages, gift baskets, in-room breakfasts, picnic baskets, flowers, champagne and other "extras." Tropical setting provides endless outdoor activity, plus sightseeing, historic landmarks, cultural events and celebrations. Many packages available to enhance your stay with added value and savings, themed for romance, history, beaching, golf, midweek savings.

Rooms/Rates
12 Rooms $129/$259; 4 Suites $149/$249; 2-BR Cottage $249/$319. Many great amenities included. Special packages and extras.
Number of Rooms: 17

Cuisine
Homemade breakfast entrees and more, enjoyed in our dining room, your room, balcony or courtyard! Appetizers & beverages at social hour; evening sweets; homemade cookies. Mimosas, Bloody Marys at weekend breakfast.

Nearest Airport(s)
St. Johns County (SGJ); Jacksonville Internat'l (JAX)

Directions
I-95 to exit 318 St. Augustine SR16, to US 1, south to King St, go L. 2/3 mi to St. George St, turn R. Inn is 3 blocks on L, park on R.

AAA ◆◆◆   *Member Since 2002*

"It's wonderful to be able to choose your room or suite, each so unique, with all of them pictured and described in great detail on www.stfrancisinn.com!"

Windemere Inn By The Sea

Innkeeper
Elizabeth G. Fisher

Luxury Oceanfront
B&B

www.srinns.com/windemereinn
815 S. Miramar Avenue (A1A), Indialantic, FL 32903
800-224-6853 • 321-728-9334 • Fax 321-728-2741
stay@windemereinn.com

Rooms/Rates
7 Guest Rooms. $140/$250. 2 two bedroom suites $300 and $400. AAA and pre-registered corporate discounts offered. Open year round.
Number of Rooms: 9

Cuisine
Start each morning with the sunrise over the Atlantic, and a full gourmet breakfast. A fruit course is followed by alternating sweet and savory dishes. Home made pasteries and desserts served at "tea time" daily. We are able to cater to most dietary needs upon request.

Nearest Airport(s)
Melbourne Int'l 15 minutes, Orlando Int'l 1 hour

Directions
I-95, exit #180 (Hwy. 192) E to A1A, R/S 1/4 mi. on L/ocean side.

Imagine ... a luxury, oceanfront bed and breakfast, only an hour east of Orlando. Guest rooms and suites are furnished with antiques and fine linens, most with ocean views, some with balconies, porches, whirlpool tubs or TVs. Start each morning with a full, gourmet breakfast, enjoy pastries and sherry at "tea time." Windemere is the ideal spot for your corporate retreat, small wedding, honeymoon or special getaway, for watching a rocket launch form Kennedy Space Center, or witnessing sea turtles nest and hatch. The grounds have several gardens, including herbs for cooking. The central point is a lily pond alive with marine plants and animals. Sit on our Beachside Pergola and watch dolphins and surfers play in the waves, or the moon rise. We have private beach access, and provide beach gear. Windemere is 45 minutes south of Kennedy Space Center, an hour east of Orlando and 10 minutes from Historic Downtown Melbourne with shopping, arts and entertainment and casual and fine dining.

To view our rooms please visit www.windemereinn.com.

AAA ◆◆◆   *Member Since 2005*

18+   🚭   💳 🛈   ♥   @   ◎

"Our stay far exceeded our expectations. You made our 12th Anniversary very special. We will be back before our 13th."

Heron House

www.srinns.com/heronhouse
512 Simonton Street, Key West, FL 33040
888-265-2395 • 305-294-9227 • Fax 305-294-5692
heronkyw@aol.com

Proprietors
Roy and Christina Howard
General Manager
Jeffrey Brannin
Historic In Town Inn

The Heron House is located on Simonton Street in the Historic District of Old Town Key West, only one block from the main street known as Duval. The Heron House is a 23-room small romantic Inn, comprised of three historical conch-style homes. An elegantly tiled swimming pool is nestled between two of the homes. Luxuriously landscaped, Heron House features an orchid nursery, as well as exotic tropical plants. Centrally located, the Heron House provides easy access to numerous restaurants and beaches. Winner of *American Bed & Breakfast Association* 4-Crown award.

Rooms/Rates
23 Rooms, $129/$369; 3 poolside, 3 Premium Poolside, 4 Garden, 7 Deluxe Garden, 4 Garden Terrace Junior, and 2 Honeymoon Junior Suites. Newly renovated, designer furnished, AC, phones, color cable TV.
Number of Rooms: 23

Cuisine
Poolside expanded continental breakfast; wine and cheese served nightly before sunset.

Nearest Airport(s)
Key West International Airport

Directions
Take Truman Ave (US 1) S. Head W on Simonton St. The Heron House is on the S side, between Southard and Fleming.

AAA ◆◆◆◆   *Member Since 2002*

16+

"Unique...rich and luxurious; an orchid lover's paradise!"

Innkeeper/Owner
Carol Wightman
Owners
**Richard Manley and
Erik DeBoer**

Elegant
In Town Hotel

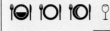 ♀

The Marquesa Hotel
www.srinns.com/marquesahotel
600 Fleming St., Key West, FL 33040
800-869-4631 Reservations Only • 305-292-1919
Fax 305-294-2121
info@marquesa.com

Rooms/Rates
14 Rooms, $175/$320; 13 Suites, $270/$430. Open year-round.
Number of Rooms: 27

Cuisine
Poolside or room service dining for breakfast; fine dining in Cafe Marquesa with an inventive and delicious menu. Excellent wine list.

Nearest Airport(s)
Key West International Airport 3 miles

Directions
US 1, R on N Roosevelt Blvd, becomes Truman Ave. Continue to Simonton, turn R, go 5 blks to Fleming. Turn R. Hotel on R.

In the heart of Key West's Historic District, the Marquesa Hotel and Cafe is a landmark 120-year-old home, restored to four-diamond status. Floor-to-ceiling windows, large bouquets of flowers, two shimmering pools and lush gardens are Marquesa trademarks. Rooms and suites are luxurious with private marble baths, bathrobes, and fine furnishings. Located one block from Duval Street for shops, galleries, restaurants and night life. *The Miami Herald* rated it as one of Florida's top 10 Inns, and *Zagat's* rated it 17th in the U.S.A. Named an "Orvis-Endorsed Lodge" for fishing expeditions.

AAA ◆◆◆◆   *Member Since 1991*

12+ ⊗ ♿ 🖻   ☜   ≋

"Bravo! Beautifully appointed, gorgeous setting, accomodating and knowledgeable staff."

"The Peach State"

Famous For: Stone Mountain, Okefenokee Swamp,
Live Oak Trees, Islands, Beaches, Peaches, Historic Savannah

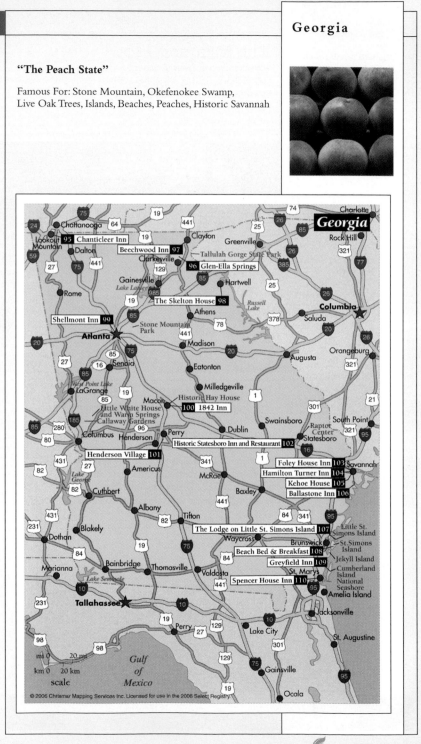

Chanticleer Inn

www.srinns.com/chanticleer
1300 Mockingbird Lane, Lookout Mountain, GA 30750
866-777-7999 • 706-820-2002 • Fax 706-820-7976
info@stayatchanticleer.com

Innkeepers
Kirby & Judy Wahl

Historic Mountain Top
Breakfast Inn

Rooms/Rates
$110/$295 per night includes full breakfast. King, queen, or 2 queen beds. Rates based on room size and amenities such as whirlpool tub. Suites available.
Number of Rooms: 17

Cuisine
Breakfast is freshly prepared each day. We recommend local restaurants for lunch and dinner. We also host weddings, conferences, & meetings, see www.meetat-grandview.com.

Nearest Airport(s)
Chattanooga

Directions
From Chattanooga take Broad Street S to Lookout Mountain & follow the signs to Rock City. From I-24 take the Lookout Mtn. exit and follow the signs to Rock City.

THIS HISTORIC INN combines the ambiance of yesteryear with the comfort and amenities of today. Built in 1927, Chanticleer Inn offers 17 luxurious guest rooms each decorated with antiques and classic fabrics. Nestled among gardens and stone walkways, the cottage rooms have modern conveniences and some extras such as private patio, fireplace, or Jacuzzi. Perfect for romance, relaxation, sightseeing, business, or weddings, the Chanticleer Inn caters to each guest with gracious hospitality. Located high atop Lookout Mountain near all Chattanooga attractions, Chanticleer Inn is convenient yet tranquil. Guests enjoy our National Parks, waterfalls, golf, shops, spas, and many nearby restaurants.

Member Since 2003

12+ ⊘ ⅙ 🗋 ⓟ 🗁 ♥   ✂ 🗲 @   ≋ 🗔 ◎ ✺

"You are such wonderful hosts! This was so relaxing. We cannot wait to return. Thank you."

Glen-Ella Springs

www.srinns.com/glen-ella
1789 Bear Gap Rd, Clarkesville, GA 30523
888-455-8886 • 706-754-7295 • Fax 706-754-1560
info@glenella.com

Innkeepers/Owners
Barrie & Bobby Aycock
Rustic Mountain
Inn

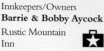

Wander down the gravel road at the southernmost tip of the Blue Ridge Mountains and discover the peaceful setting of Glen-Ella Springs Country Inn. Listen to the birds sing while you rock on the porch. Stroll around the extensive perennial and herb gardens, and eighteen acres of meadow bordered by Panther Creek. Relax by the massive stone fireplace in our century-old inn, a rare example of the traditional small hotels that once dotted the North Georgia Mountains. Relish the comfort of the inn's tasteful décor. Savor the outstanding food, from bountiful country buffet breakfasts to elegant dinners. The constantly changing menu in our award-winning restaurant, named one of Georgia's Top Ten Dining Destinations in 2004 and 2005, guarantees a memorable dining experience in an atmosphere of casual elegance. Spend leisurely days fishing world class trout streams, hiking numerous scenic trails, boating on nearby rivers and lakes, or exploring charming historic villages filled with fine art and crafts by local artisans.

Rooms/Rates
16 Rooms, $140/$265 B&B.
Open year-round.
Number of Rooms: 16

Cuisine
Bountiful country breakfasts. Dinner by reservation from a constantly changing menu of up-scale southern-American cuisine prepared by our professional staff, guaranteeing a memorable dining experience. Guests must bring their own wine and spirits.

Nearest Airport(s)
Greenville, SC or Atlanta, GA

Directions
At the edge of the Blue Ridge Mtns, 90 miles north of Atlanta. 3 miles off 4-lane US 441 between Clarkesville & Clayton; Go west on T. Smith Rd. at mile marker 18, then N. on Historic Old 441. Take the first left on Orchard Rd., then follow the signs.

Member Since 1990

12+

"Delicious food, beautiful scenery, fine hospitality." "God smiles on Glen-Ella."

SelectRegistry.com

Innkeepers/Owners
Gayle and David Darugh

Elegant Rustic Mountain Inn

Beechwood Inn

www.srinns.com/beechwoodinn
P.O. Box 429, 220 Beechwood Dr, Clayton, GA 30525
866-782-2485 • 706-782-5485 • Fax 706-782-7644
david-gayle@beechwoodinn.ws

Rooms/Rates
2 rooms, 4 suites $159/$179 B&B. Private baths. Open year-round. Complimentary afternoon appetizers and wine.
Number of Rooms: 6

Cuisine
Beechwood Bountiful Breakfast daily. 5 course Prix Fixe dinners w/ wine on most Saturdays, advance reservations. Extensive wine list. Visit our website for information on gourmet wine events, winetastings & special weekend packages.

Nearest Airport(s)
Atlanta, GA. and Asheville, NC each 90 minutes.

Directions
In Clayton, Georgia, at intersection of Hwys 441 & 76, turn E on 76. Go 1/10 mi., turn L on Beechwood Dr. Follow inn signs.

Georgia's premier wine country inn provides rustic elegance in a romantic setting overlooking the historic town of Clayton. The Inn was voted "Number One Inn in North America for a Weekend Escape - 2005." Filled with antiques and primitives, yet warm and inviting, Beechwood Inn is altogether homey and comfortable. Food and wine enthusiasts will want to experience wine weekend packages and culinary events, when celebrated winemakers and chefs from around the world collaborate to expand guests' epicurean horizons. Nearby mountains, trails and rivers offer activities and experiences for a lifetime of memories. Explore mountain villages, raft the Chattooga River, hike to a waterfall or drive along bucolic country lanes. History buffs will want to visit the Foxfire Museum. Close to three mountain golf courses. Everyone will enjoy relaxing in our 100 year old gardens with a good book and a glass of wine. Romantic guest rooms have fine linens, robes, private porches or balconies, fireplaces, wonderful views, and cozy privacy.

Member Since 2005

12+

"Innkeepers Dave & Gayle Darugh will make you so glad you visited. We consider a trip to the Beechwood Inn one of life's finest pampering experiences."

The Skelton House
www.srinns.com/skeltonhouse
97 Benson Street, Hartwell, GA 30643-1991
877-556-3790 • 706-376-7969 • Fax 706-856-3139
t.skeltonhouse@comcast.net

Innkeepers/Owners
Ruth and John Skelton
Historic Village
Breakfast Inn

The Skelton House is an 1896 National Register Victorian Inn, located in the historic downtown area of the small town of Hartwell. The charm, grace and hospitality of the original Skelton family and their grand home has been retained by today's generation of Skeltons as their home, restored in 1997, enjoys its new life as The Skelton House. Wrap yourself in luxury while enjoying the beauty of the Victorian period joined with the comfort and elegance today's discerning guests expect. Enjoy the beautiful Victorian parlor, the sunny morning room, the cozy receiving room, the spacious dining room, or one of the many porches and balconies. Two beautiful acres of landscaped gardens are also available for outdoor events. Located only 13 miles South of I-85 in the NE corner of GA. Less than 2 hours from the metro Atlanta area or 1 hour from the local Greenville/Spartanburg airport. The perfect getaway for vacationers and business travelers alike. Come experience what many believe to be the ultimate in Southern Hospitality.

Rooms/Rates
7 Guestrooms, $100/$135.
Antiques, cable TV/HBO, private phones, wireless internet, room thermostats, queen beds, luxury linens, private baths/hairdryers.
Number of Rooms: 7

Cuisine
Creative full service hot breakfasts made fresh daily with the best seasonal and local ingredients. Nearby casual dining with a lunch & dinner menu of southern regional cuisine and full service bar (Tues-Sun).

Nearest Airport(s)
Greenville, SC (GSP) 65 miles.

Directions
I-85 to GA exit 177. 13 miles S on GA Hwy. 77 to Hartwell. Turn R at 5th traffic light onto Carter St. Look for us on the immediate L. past the Presbyterian Church.

AAA ◆◆◆   *Member Since 2001*

☺ ⊘ ♿ 🛏 🕐 📂 ♥   ✍ @   ◎ ❋ ☕

"From the rose & herb gardens into this gracious family home--my soul was renewed. It must be a calling to make this house so warm and wonderful."

Shellmont Inn

Innkeepers/Owners
Ed and Debbie McCord

Traditional Victorian
In Town Breakfast Inn

www.srinns.com/shellmontinn
821 Piedmont Ave. N.E., Atlanta, GA 30308
404-872-9290 • Fax 404-872-5379
innkeeper@shellmont.com

Rooms/Rates
Standard Rooms $145/$200;
Whirlpool Suites $185/$235;
Carriage House $215/$325.
Open year-round.
Number of Rooms: 5

Cuisine
Full gourmet breakfast,
complimentary beverages, fresh
fruit basket, evening chocolates,
evening turn-down service. Fully
licensed and inspected. Atlanta's
smallest Historic Hotel.

Nearest Airport(s)
Hartsfield-Jackson Int'l - 8 miles

Directions
From airport, I-75/85 N, exit 248-C
(International Blvd), turn L at 2nd
traffic light (Ellis St), turn R at next
traffic light (Piedmont Ave). Go N 1
1/4 mile. Located at the intersection
of Piedmont Ave and 6th. Street
on the R.

The Shellmont Inn is an impeccably restored 1891 National
Register mansion in Midtown Atlanta's theatre, restaurant and
cultural district. The Inn is a treasure chest of stained, leaded and
beveled glass, intricately-carved woodwork and hand-painted
stenciling. Guest rooms are furnished with antiques, oriental
rugs and period wall treatments. Wicker-laden verandas overlook
manicured lawns and gardens—including a Victorian fishpond.
The experience is unforgettable. National Register of Historic
Places Property. City of Atlanta Landmark Building. Recipient of
Mayor's Award for Excellence for Historic Preservation.

AAA ◆◆◆   *Member Since 1994*   Mobil ★★★

"A jewel in the heart of Atlanta. Southern hospitality at its finest. Exquisite!"

1842 Inn

www.srinns.com/1842inn
353 College Street, Macon, GA 31201
800-336-1842 • 478-741-1842 • Fax 478-741-1842
management@1842inn.com

Innkeeper
Nazario Filipponi

Elegant In Town
Breakfast Inn

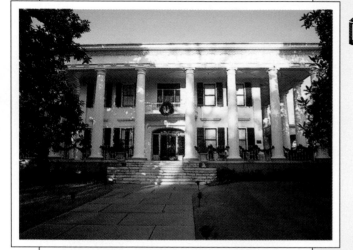

The 1842 Inn boasts 19 luxurious rooms and public areas tastefully designed with fine English antiques, tapestries and paintings. A quaint garden courtyard and garden pool greet guests for cocktails or breakfast. Nightly turndowns, shoeshines and fresh flowers enhance many other gracious grand hotel amenities. Rooms available with whirlpool tubs and fireplaces. High level of service. Valet parking on request. Considered 'One of America's Top 100 Inns in the 20th Century' by the International Restaurant and Hospitality Rating Bureau.

Rooms/Rates
19 Guest Rooms, $139/$230 B&B. (Rates subject to change without notice.) Open year-round.
Number of Rooms: 19

Cuisine
Full breakfast and hors d'oeuvres included. Dinner in nearby private club. Full service bar.

Nearest Airport(s)
Macon, Atlanta

Directions
Exit 164 on I-75 turn L fm N; R fm S go to College St; turn Left; Inn is 2 blocks on left.

AAA ◆◆◆◆   *Member Since 1994*

12+

Zagat top 50 US Inns and Resorts.

General Manager
Heather Bradham
Traditional Victorian
Country Resort

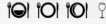

Henderson Village
www.srinns.com/hendersonvillage
125 South Langston Circle, Perry, GA 31069
888-615-9722 • 478-988-8696 • Fax 478-988-9009
info@hendersonvillage.com

Rooms/Rates
24 Rooms/Suites $175/$350. Cottages are elegantly rustic; houses are subtly refined. Office hours are 7 a.m. to 10 p.m. EDT.
Number of Rooms: 24

Cuisine
Excellent a la carte breakfast, lunch and dinner menu, hot country breakfast, homemade pastries, fruit; room service available. Full bar and extensive wine list.

Nearest Airport(s)
Atlanta International

Directions
I-75 to Exit 127; Hwy. 26 W 1 mile. Henderson Village is at the crossroads of GA Hwy. 26 and US Hwy. 41. 40 miles south of Macon, 10 miles south of Perry.

Authentic Southern Hospitality awaits, with twelve historic homes beautifully restored and relocated to create a most charming country resort with thousands of acres to relax, unwind and recuperate in traditional southern style. Delight in our gourmet restaurant voted 'The absolute best dining experience in Georgia,' by *Georgia Trend* Magazine. Unwind as you ride horses alongside the cotton fields and through our pecan orchards. Test your skills shooting sporting clays or spend a lazy day in the sun fishing for bass. Rejuvenate your spirit with massage and an afternoon by the pool. Henderson Village is a rare find. Top Ten Most Romantic Inn for 2003.

AAA ◆◆◆◆　　*Member Since 2002*

"This is my kind of country living! Great food, great service, great place. Thank you."

Historic Statesboro Inn and Restaurant

www.statesboroinn.com
106 S. Main Street, Statesboro, GA 30458
800-846-9466 • 912-489-8628 • Fax 912-489-4785
frontdesk@statesboroinn.com

Innkeepers/Owners
Tony Garges
Deman Dubose

Traditional
In Town Inn

A 1905 historic Victorian oasis where porches, rockers, and gardens adorned with small tranquil ponds are blended with gratious Southern hospitality. Our style is eclectic yet comfortable, with furnishings from three generations and a small pub adds a European feel. Our service is attentive, just right for that relaxing get away. Our spacious banquet room fronted with a Southern style brick veranda makes the Inn a natural setting for that special occasion or executive retreat. While you are at the Inn, visit the Georgia Southern Botanical Garden, or see birds of prey at the Raptor Center. Attend a show or tour exhibits at the Averitt Arts Center. History and antiques are also a treat. Small pets under 20lbs. are welcome.

Rooms/Rates
15 Rooms, 1 two-room Suite,
$85/$130 B&B. Open year-round.
Number of Rooms: 16

Cuisine
Homemade treats await your arrival, and a hearty country breakfast is complimentary for guests. Enjoy our Sunday buffet of traditional southern cooking. Catering available. Please call for special holiday meals and Sunday brunch schedules.

Nearest Airport(s)
Savannah International Airport

Directions
From Savannah: I-16 W to Exit 127 (Rt. 67) to Statesboro to 301N (Main St.); From Atlanta, I-75S to Macon I-16E to exit 116, (301N) to Statesboro. (Do NOT take 301 bypass).

Member Since 1998

"The Statesboro Inn is wonderful: Thank you for making our trip great...highly recommended."

Innkeepers/Owners
Beryl W. and Donald G. Zerwer

Elegant Historic
Breakfast Inn

Foley House Inn
www.foleyinn.com
14 West Hull Street, Chippewa Square, Savannah, GA 31401
800-647-3708 • 912-232-6622 • Fax 912-231-1218
info@foleyinn.com

Rooms/Rates
$230/$355. Closed Christmas Day.
Number of Rooms: 18

Cuisine
Complimentary gourmet breakfast, afternoon tea with sweets,and hors d'oeuvres with complimentary wine in the evening...all prepared by our critically-acclaimed chef. Treats w/ turndown service. Premium wines & champagnes for sale by the bottle or glass at any time. Short walk to fine restaurants.

Nearest Airport(s)
Savannah/Hilton Head Int'l

Directions
From I-95 to I-16 to end at Montgomery St. Right at 2nd light onto Oglethorpe St., R onto Bull St., R onto Hull St. 1st red brick building on R. Beautiful Chippewa Square is our front yard.

An upscale AAA 4-diamond Southern B&B with a European appeal. Common areas & guest rooms decorated with British period decor and stunning architecture. Gas fireplaces in most rooms; canopied and four-poster beds. Some rooms with oversized Jacuzzi baths and private balconies. Enjoy a complimentary gourmet breakfast, afternoon tea with sweets, and hors d'oeuvres with wine in the evening...all prepared by our critically-acclaimed chef. Our concierge will make dinner and tour reservations. Amazingly short walk to restaurants, theatres, antique stores, art galleries, etc. from this perfectly central location. Some rooms have private balconies overlooking historic Chippewa square, the site where "Forrest Gump" was filmed eating chocolates and waiting for the bus. Our park-like setting leads to Bull Street and one of the most historic walks in America. All the luxor of the 1800s without sacrificing modern conveniences. Wireless internet connections and spa services are available complete with a fitness room.

AAA ♦♦♦♦　　*Member Since 1998*　　Mobil ★★★

"One of the top ten romantic inns in all of North America!"
- *Vacation* Magazine

Hamilton Turner

www.hamilton-turnerinn.com
330 Abercorn Street, Savannah, GA 31401
888-448-8849 • 912-233-1833 • Fax 912-233-0291
info@hamilton-turnerinn.com

Innkeepers/Owners
Jim and Gay Dunlop
Elegant In Town
Historic Mansion

"Historically, the talk of the town," the photogenic Hamilton-Turner Inn is the quintessential Savannah society mansion. With stylish comforts and chic Southern hospitality reminiscent of the Savannah 400 era, the inspiring Mid-Victorian, Second Empire architecture woos travelers to the "elegant and historic" manor on the park (circa 1873). The culture-rich walking vacation begins from the low key, high style of relaxation at the inn with a lazy stroll (or brisk walk) from the prestigious garden park of Lafayette Square -- one of the hallmark convivial spaces of the world-famous planned city. Unpretentious luxuries include imaginative cultural tours; romantic honeymoon or getaways, business travel-with-leisure retreat; full house group reservations; and last minute macro vacation packages. Leisure in the slowed Southern pace. Featured in *Esquire, Conde' Nast Traveler,* and *Country Discoveries.*

Rooms/Rates
13 bedrooms, 4 suites from $175 per night, double occupancy. King, double queen, queen, & double twin beds. Carriage house offers 3 clustered rooms. ADA & small pet friendly lodging.
Number of Rooms: 17

Cuisine
Complimentary cuisine features the signature " full southern mansion breakfast" ... afternoon wine and hors d'oeuvres, bedtime brandy or port and a sweet surprise; plus special diet menus.

Nearest Airport(s)
Savannah-Hilton Head, 8 mi.

Directions
I-16 East to Savannah. Exit on Montgomery St. R on Liberty St. R on Abercorn St. to Lafayette Square. The Cathedral is on the square.

AAA ◆◆◆◆   *Member Since 2003*

12+

"Stay at the Hamilton Turner and enjoy the magical views of Lafayette Square." - *Southern Living.* "...a step back to a more gracious era."

Owner
Kessler Collection
Innkeeper
Sarah Hartman

Historic In Town Breakfast Inn

Kehoe House
www.srinns.com/kehoehouse
123 Habersham Street, Savannah, GA 31401
800–820–1020 • 912-232-1020 • Fax 912-231-0208
info@kehoehouse.com

Rooms/Rates
Low Season $249/$379, High Season $299/$429. Special Packages, Wedding/Meeting Space. All-white Q or K-size bedding w/contrasting colors, armoire, wireless high-speed Internet access, CD player, color TV & private bath with unique accoutrements.
Number of Rooms: 13

Cuisine
Gourmet made-to-order breakfast, afternoon tea service, and evening hors d'oeuvres with wine. Coffee and tea available 24 hours.

Nearest Airport(s)
Savannah Airport

Directions
I-95 to I-16 to end at Montgomery. Right on Liberty, left on Habersham to Columbia Square.

The Inn, built in 1892 in the Renaissance Revival style, is one of Savannah's most distinctive landmarks and a perfect venue for a luxury Bed & Breakfast Inn. It enjoys a prime location on Columbia Square in the Historic District. Antiques, oriental carpets, and intriguing art accent the gracious and inviting décor. Generous guestrooms are distinctively decorated from romantic to stately. Verandahs and private balconies are favorite outdoor retreats. For your convenience the Inn offers complimentary private parking and elevator service to all floors. You'll be welcomed at the Inn by an attentive staff dedicated to serving you in the true tradition of Southern hospitality. The recent renovation and refurbishment enhanced the interior and guestrooms, which now reflect a sense of Southern hospitality, history and romance with gilded mirrors, opulent fabrics and antique chandeliers.

Member Since 2003

12+

"We have never had such a lovely time. The house is beautiful and the staff is fantastic!"

Ballastone Inn

www.srinns.com/ballastoneinn
14 East Oglethorpe Avenue, Savannah, GA 31401
800-822-4553 • 912-236-1484 • Fax 912-236-4626
inn@ballastone.com

Innkeepers/Owners
Jennifer and Jim Salandi

Historic In Town
Luxury Hotel

The four-story Italianate Ballastone Inn, built in 1838 and located in the heart of Savannah's historic district, offers 16 exquisite rooms and suites, each with fireplace. "Table for Two Privacy" (SM), a handsome Victorian bar, 24/7 concierge services, off-street parking and private elevator distinguish the Ballastone Inn, a nine-year AAA Four Diamond property. Details including softly-scented Egyptian 400 thread count linens, French down blankets, fresh flowers, Gilchrist and Soames English Spa Collection amenities and distinctive antiques are why the Ballastone Inn has been voted "Most Romantic Inn" by Savannah Magazine and in 2006 "Most Romantic" by Coastal Living Magazine. Rates include a full Southern breakfast; formal afternoon tea served on a sterling silver tea service, fine china, hors d'oeuvres and premium boutique wines during evening cocktail hour. A National Register historic site, The Ballastone is a 2005 Andrew Harper's Hideaway Grand Award Winner and is recommended by Condé Nast Johansens, Fodor's, and Frommer's.

Rooms/Rates
$215/$395 Double occupancy. Courtyard, deluxe, and superior rooms, plus luxury suites which overlook the lush garden.
Number of Rooms: 16

Cuisine
An elegant, personally prepared "table for two," made-to-order breakfast, afternoon high tea enjoyed with fragrant antique linens, pre-dinner hors d'oeuvres, and private bar with premium liquors and boutique wines. Smoking is permitted out-of-doors.

Nearest Airport(s)
Savannah-Hilton Head International

Directions
East on I-16 to Savannah. Exit on Montgomery St. R on Oglethorpe Avenue to Drayton Street. U-turn L around the median to the Inn.

AAA ◆◆◆◆ *Member Since 2005*

16+

"If there was a hall of fame for bed and breakfasts, Ballastone would be at the top." -- North Carolina guests. "A splendid oasis!" -- England guests.

General Manager
Joel Meyer

Private Island Getaway

The Lodge on Little St. Simons Island

www.srinns.com/lodgeonlittlestsimons
P.O. Box 21078, Little St. Simons Island, GA 31522-0578
888-733-5774 • 912-638-7472 • Fax 912-634-1811
Lodge@LittleStSimonsIsland.com

Rooms/Rates
Open year-round. Children of all ages welcome May - Sept, children over 8 years Oct - Apr. All inclusive rates 11 Rooms $450/$675; 2 Suites $1100/$1200; Full House $1650/$2500; Exclusive Full Island $7700/$8000 - See website for SPECIALS!
Number of Rooms: 15

Cuisine
Delicious regional cuisine served family-style. 3 meals daily. Snacks, personal picnics, oyster roasts, crab boils, cocktail cruises and beach picnics.

Nearest Airport(s)
Brunswick, GA (BQK), Savannah, GA (SAV), Jacksonville, FL (JAX)

Directions
Accessible only by boat with departures twice daily from St. Simons Island.

Nature prevails on this pristine Georgia island where 10,000 acres are shared with no more than 30 overnight guests at a time. Accessible only by boat, Little St. Simons Island unfolds its secrets to those eager to discover a bounty of natural wonders. Seven miles of shell-strewn beaches meet acres of legendary moss-draped live oaks, glistening tidal creeks, and shimmering salt marshes to provide an unparalleled setting for a host of activities and total relaxation. Guests enjoy interpretive tours, birding, canoeing, kayaking, fishing, bicycling and horseback riding. Creature comforts include gracious accommodations, delicious regional cuisine and Southern hospitality.

Member Since 1993

"Great getaway, perfect balance of seclusion and comfort, relaxation and activity."

Beach Bed & Breakfast

www.srinns.com/beachbb
907 Beachview Drive, St. Simon's Island, GA 31522
912-634-2800 • 912-638-5042 • Fax 912-634-4656
reservations@beachbedandbreakfast.com

Innkeeper/Owner
Joe McDonough

Waterside Resort
B&B

Rooms/Rates
7 Suites, $240/$500. Southern breakfast served at your oceanfront table each morning along with Capt Joe's internationally famous fresh fruit bowl.
Number of Rooms: 7

Cuisine
Delightful full breakfast served on an oceanfront deck.

Nearest Airport(s)
Brunswick

Directions
Take exit 38 (I-95) towards US17 Brunswick. Take US17 S and turn L onto St. Simons Causeway (Torres Causeway). Coming off the last bridge, take R at traffic light. Go to yield sign and turn L onto King's Way. Go straight thru 2 traffic lights, then .4 mi. Turn R onto 5th Street around the 90 degree curve. 2nd unit on the L.

The Beach Bed & Breakfast is a beautiful 13,000 square feet oceanfront Spanish-Mediterranean villa. Its seven suites are furnished with exquisite décor and detail. Guests can take advantage of ocean-front decks for a hot served breakfast, pool, Jacuzzi and home theatre, and the property is perfectly located within walking distance of ten of the island's best restaurants. In-Suite Complimentary beverages and snacks are an added bonus, along with complimentary bicycles and local airport pickup. Site-seeing tours, golf, tennis, boating, fishing and dinner boat tours are available through the B&B. A full-service staff awaits your arrival. 10 top Romantic Inns.

Member Since 2003

12+

"The St. Simon's Suite would make the most discerning mermaid come in from the sea and stay ashore!" "Absolutely the Best."

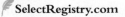

Innkeepers/Owners
The Ferguson Family

Traditional
Waterside Retreat/Lodge

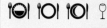

Greyfield Inn
www.srinns.com/greyfieldinn
Post Office Box 900, Fernandina Beach, Fl 32035
Cumberland Island, GA 32035
888-243-9238 • 904-261-6408 • Fax 904-321-0666
seashore@greyfieldinn.com

Rooms/Rates
16 Rooms, $395/$575 AP.
Open year-round.
Number of Rooms: 16

Cuisine
Hearty southern breakfast,
delightful picnic lunch, gourmet
dinner. Full bar; wine, beer,
liquor, cocktail hour with hors
d'oeuvres.

Nearest Airport(s)
Jacksonville, Florida

Directions
I-95 to Highway A1A (Exit 373)
to Amelia Island. 14.8 miles to
Centre St. Turn left and go to
waterfront. Meet at Dock 3 at the
"Lucy R. Ferguson/Greyfield"
sign. Call for parking instructions.

This turn-of-the-century Carnegie mansion is on Georgia's largest and southernmost coastal island. Miles of trails traverse the island's unique ecosystems along with a beautiful, undeveloped white sand beach for shelling, swimming, sunning and birding. Exceptional food, lovely, original furnishings, and a peaceful, relaxing environment provide guests with a step back into another era. Overnight rate includes an island outing with our naturalist, bicycles and kayaks for exploring the island, round-trip boat passage on our private ferry, and meals.

Member Since 1982

5+

"We took away memories that will last a lifetime...we felt right at home."

Spencer House Inn

www.spencerhouseinn.com
200 Osborne Street, St. Marys, GA 31558
877-819-1872 • 912-882-1872 • Fax 912-882-9427
info@spencerhouseinn.com

Innkeepers/Owners
Mary and Mike Neff

Historic Village
B&B Inn

Spencer House Inn, built in 1872, is located in the heart of the St. Marys Historic District within walking distance to restaurants, shops, museums and the ferry to Cumberland Island National Seashore. We can make your ferry reservation and pack a picnic lunch for you as you head off for your adventure on a beautiful, undeveloped and pristine barrier island - the beach was voted "one of the best wild beaches" by *National Geographic Traveler* magazine - and we're on the Colonial Coast Birding Trail. You'll enjoy relaxing in the cypress rockers on the Inn's verandahs. For your convenience, the Inn has an elevator. Walk to the waterfront park, fishing pier, boat ramp and marsh walk. Take a leisurely stroll around our historic village, or rent a bicycle or golf cart. There are golf courses nearby and also an outfitters shop for a kayak trip. Okefenokee Wildlife Refuge is 45 minutes away. The beaches of Jekyll, St. Simons and Amelia Islands are a short drive. We are nine miles east of I-95 by the St. Marys River on the Georgia/Florida border.

Rooms/Rates
$115/$200. Rates subject to change. All private baths. Elevator & outside ramp. Open year-round.
Number of Rooms: 14

Cuisine
Full buffet breakfast. Picnic lunches available. Walk to restaurants for lunch and dinner. Guest refrigerator. Afternoon iced tea, coffee and homemade treats.

Nearest Airport(s)
Jacksonville, FL

Directions
On Georgia/Florida border. From I-95 take Georgia Exit 3, turn L at stop light and travel 9 miles E on Highway 40 which becomes Osborne Street. The Inn is on the L at the corner of Osborne & Bryant Streets. Ample parking & lobby entrance are on Bryant St.

AAA ◆◆◆ *Member Since 2003*

"Your hospitality is outstanding, we're already looking forward to our next stay."
"Your personal service is an asset & distinguishes you from the rest."

Illinois

"The Prairie State"

Famous For: Hogs, Pigs, Cattle, Electronics, Chemicals, Manufacturing, Ancient Burial Mounds, Lake Michigan, Chicago "Windy City", Sears Tower, Wrigley Building

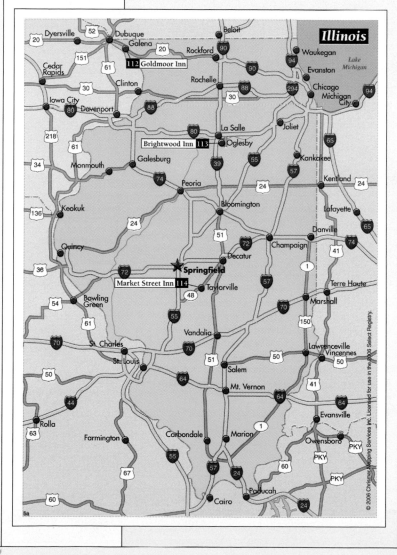

Illinois

112 Goldmoor Inn

Brightwood Inn **113**

Market Street Inn **114**

© 2006 Chrismar Mapping Services Inc. Licensed for use in the 2006 Select Registry.

Goldmoor Inn

www.srinns.com/goldmoor
9001 Sand Hill Road, Galena, IL 61036
800-255-3925 • 815-777-3925 • Fax 815-777-3993
goldmoor@galenalink.com

Innkeepers/Owners
Patricia and James Goldthorpe

Elegant Country Inn

Contemporary luxury country Inn atop a bluff overlooking the Mississippi River, 6 miles south of historic Galena. The Goldmoor features the perfect setting for small weddings, romantic getaways, anniversaries, and honeymoons. Our grand deluxe suites and cottages, and log cabins feature fireplaces and whirlpools, some even overlooking the Mississippi. We pamper you with first-class amenities such as full gourmet breakfast with free room service, European terry robes, the finest linens, heated towel bars in each bath, VCR/DVD stereo systems with Bose surround sound and complimentary video and DVD library, TVs with digital satellite systems and multi-line phones with modem hook-ups and free long distance. Complimentary mountain bikes. Top rated Inn in Illinois from 1993 to present by ABBA. Evening gourmet dining overlooking the Mississippi River with extensive wine cellar.

Rooms/Rates
13 Suites $215/$345, 3 Cottages $275/$345, 2 Cabins $255/$295.
Number of Rooms: 18

Cuisine
Full gourmet breakfast served 8:30-10:00 overlooking Mississippi River, or your choice of great room dining or free room service. Homebaked cookies in your room. Evening 6-course gourmet dinner w/ extensive wine cellar. Custom catering for groups or wedding receptions.

Nearest Airport(s)
Dubuque, IA, 25 minute drive; Chicago, 2.45 hours.

Directions
6 miles S of Galena on Blackjack Rd to Sand Hill Rd: follow signs on Blackjack Rd. Turn R on Sand Hill, 1/4 mi. on the L.

Member Since 2001

"This was the perfect spot. We loved it! We'll be back next year."
(Ask us for more.)

Innkeepers/Owners
Jo and John Ryan

Traditional Country
Inn

Brightwood Inn

www.srinns.com/brightwood
2407 N. IL Rt. 178, Oglesby, IL 61348
888-667-0600 • 815-667-4600 • Fax 815-667-4727
brtwood@starved-rock-inn.com

Rooms/Rates
7 Rooms, $115/$210; 1 Suite, $225/$255. Each of the eight rooms features its own unique personality and style. All rooms have gas fireplace, private bath and TV/DVD. Open year-round.
Number of Rooms: 8

Cuisine
Full breakfast. Elegant dining 3-course meal on weekends. Simple suppers available Sun-Thur. Reservation required. Beer, wine & liquor. Lunch totes available.

Nearest Airport(s)
Midway Airport/Chicago

Directions
From I-80 take exit 81, go S on IL Rte 178 for 6 mi. Inn will be on R side. From I-39 take Tonica exit. Go E 2nd stop sign turn L on IL Rte 178. Follow for 3 mi., Inn on L side.

Newly constructed in 1996 and nestled on 14 acres of meadow within the confines of Matthiessen State Park, the Brightwood Inn was designed to resemble a vintage farmhouse complete with a veranda and rocking chairs. The Inn will provide you with a romantic, peaceful and luxurious stay amid the beauty of nature. All rooms have TV & DVD and phones with modem hookup. Six rooms have large Jacuzzi tubs and three have private balconies. Starved Rock State Park and the I&M Canal are located just two miles north. Intimate dining room with seasonally adjusted menu features herbs fresh-picked from our garden. The entire inn is smoke-free and pets are not allowed.

AAA ◆◆◆   *Member Since 2000*   Mobil ★★★

12+ 🚭 ♿ 📷 🌐 📁 ♥   @   🔥 ◎ ❄   ☕

"Where do we start? AMAZING! The food, atmosphere, ...a perfect romantic getaway."

Market Street Inn
www.srinns.com/marketstreet
220 E. Market Street, Taylorville, IL 62568
800-500-1466 • 217-824-7220 • Fax 217-824-7229
jhauser@chipsnet.com

Innkeepers/Owners
Myrna & Joseph Hauser
Historic In Town
Breakfast Inn

paii

Rich in architectural detail, this romantic 1892 Queen Anne Victorian jewel boasts six original fireplaces and mantels, ornate woodwork, fretwork over pocket doors and beveled glass windows. Sit by the parlor fireplace and feast your eyes upon the antiques, semi-antiques and Oriental rugs to appreciate the blend of history, luxury, charm and hospitality. In the main inn, the grand oak staircase beckons one to unwind in one of the 8 guest rooms--each with delightfully different decor. Our CARRIAGE HOUSE has two rooms: a King Grand Deluxe with two fireplaces, a wet bar, a double whirlpool and separate shower & HANDICAP SUITE. Modern amenities include central air, private baths--most with double whirlpool tubs/showers, fireplaces, cable TV, in-room phones and wireless DSL. At day's end stroll through the perennial gardens to view over 200 hostas & relax in the gazebo of the Victorian wrap-around porch. Lincoln Library and sites are 30 minutes away. Lincoln Prairie Bike Trail is six blocks away. Golfing & skydiving in area.

Rooms/Rates
10 Rooms, $125/$275. 2 King Jr. Suites w/dbl whirlpools, most w/fireplaces
Number of Rooms: 10

Cuisine
Full hearty candlelight breakfast served daily. Complimentary wine served each evening and hors d'oeuvres on weekends. Complimentary: coffee, tea, soda & bottled water. Fine dining 2 blocks away.

Nearest Airport(s)
Springfield Airport

Directions
3.5 hrs. from Chicago. I-55 to Springfield: Rt. 29 S to Taylorville; R on Walnut, L on Market. From Decatur: Rt. 48 W to Taylorville, L on Walnut, L on Market. 90 minutes from St Louis: I-55 north, exit 63 onto Rt. 48 go 25 miles, exit L at 1 mile sign for Taylorville; R on Market.

AAA ◆◆◆   *Member Since 2002*

☺   🚭♿📖ⓘ📂❤   ✍@   🧺◎   ☕

"Peaceful! I lost all sense of time while soaking in the hot tub just talking for 2 1/2 hours."

Indiana

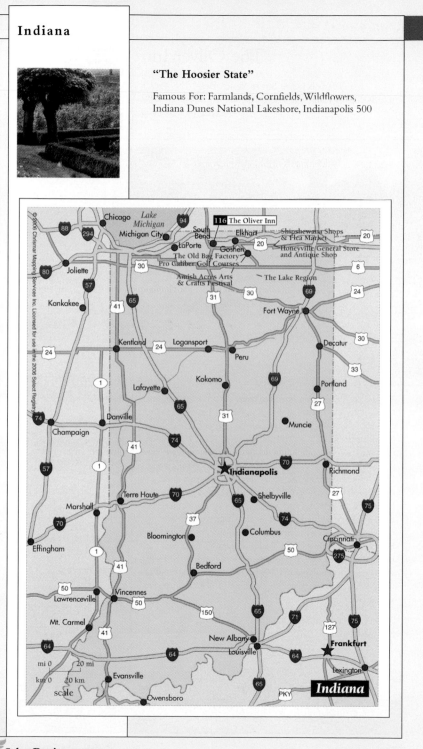

"The Hoosier State"

Famous For: Farmlands, Cornfields, Wildflowers,
Indiana Dunes National Lakeshore, Indianapolis 500

The Oliver Inn

www.srinns.com/oliverinn
630 W. Washington Street, South Bend, IN 46601
888-697-4466 • 574-232-4545 • Fax 574-288-9788
oliver@michiana.org

Innkeepers/Owners
Tom and Alice Erlandson

Victorian In Town Breakfast Inn

The Oliver Inn Bed & Breakfast offers a 'turn-of-the-century' feeling with all of today's important amenities. Experience Victorian elegance in this historic mansion surrounded by a lush acre of manicured gardens, gazebo and lawn swings. Nine beautiful rooms in main house, private baths, double whirlpools, A/C, fireplaces, CD players, sound machines, hairdryers, luxurious robes. Enjoy candlelight breakfast by the fire to live piano music and complimentary snacks, gourmet coffees and soft drinks from the Butler's Pantry. For dinner, stroll next door to Tippecanoe Place Restaurant in the Studebaker Mansion. Come discover why The Oliver Inn was voted the Michiana area's 'Best Bed & Breakfast'. Experience the ultimate in relaxation, luxury and serenity in our Carriage House Suite. Two bedrooms, two baths, jetted marble shower, double whirlpool tub, living room with fireplace and entertainment center, screened in porch and full kitchen stocked with goodies.

Member Since 2000

Rooms/Rates
9 Rooms $130/$195, 2 two-bedroom suites, King/Queen beds, A/C, telephone, hairdryers, cable TV. Some with fireplace, balcony, or whirlpool tub.
Number of Rooms: 9

Cuisine
Full candlelight breakfast with live piano music. Complimentary drinks and snacks from Butler's Pantry. Dine at Tippecanoe Place Restaurant in the Studebaker Mansion right next door.

Nearest Airport(s)
South Bend (SBN)

Directions
From the North: Indiana Toll Road (I-80/90), exit 77, S at light on 31/933, 2 miles to R on Washington St. From the South: N on Hwy 31 into downtown South Bend, L on Washington.

"We haven't been this relaxed in a long time; warm and gracious hospitality; lovely décor."

Kansas

"The Sunflower State"

Famous For: "Home on the Range," Wild West, Dodge City, Buffalo, Agriculture, Aircraft Manufacturing, Sunflowers, Grain, Great Plains

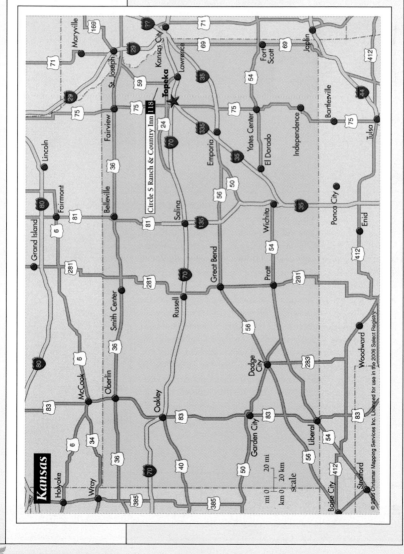

Circle S Ranch & Country Inn

www.srinns.com/circlesranch
3325 Circle S Lane, Lawrence, KS 66044
800-625-2839 • 785-843-4124 • Fax 785-843-4474
circlesinn@aol.com

Innkeepers/Owners
Mary and Jack Cronemeyer

Rustic Country Inn

Nestled amid 1,200 acres of gently rolling hills fifty minutes west of Kansas City, is a place where visitors can experience a rare vestige of the once vast tallgrass prairie. The Circle S Ranch, owned and operated by Mary's family since the 1860s, offers a romantic retreat where couples' favorite pastime is connecting with one another and nature. Each of the elegantly rustic country inn's uniquely-themed guestrooms feature gracious comforts, luxurious amenities, air conditioned with sweeping views of the prairie landscape where buffalo still roam. Conference and Wedding facilities are available in our Party Barn, Conference Room, or Great Room. Open Year round. You can reserve a room at a moment's notice, and online reservations are accepted. Voted best Inn in the U.S. by bedandbreakfast.com, and one of the 'Top 15 B&B/Inns' for business travelers by *Arrington's Bed and Breakfast Journal*. Best in the Midwest 2003. We also recieved an award for Best for Honeymoon/Anniversary in Arrington's *Inn Traveler* 2005 Book of Lists.

Rooms/Rates
8 rooms, $155-$175/$225. 4 Suites, $190/$275. Unique decor; rooms available w/whirlpool tubs & fireplaces. All rooms have robes, phones & sitting areas.
Number of Rooms: 12

Cuisine
Hearty country style breakfast, with soft drinks, bottled water, guest refrigerator, and ice. Dining schedule varies seasonally, with many items coming from our kitchen garden. Fine wines, beer and liquors available.

Nearest Airport(s)
Kansas City International Airport

Directions
From Kansas City: I-70 W toward Topeka. Exit at E. Lawrence exit 204. R on 59 Hwy. NW for 3 mi. R on CR-1045 N for 5.5 mi. R on 35th St. E for 2 mi.

AAA ◆◆◆   *Member Since 2002*

"There is something magical...with its serene surroundings. You can't help relaxing..."

Kentucky

"The Bluegrass State"

Famous For: Horses, Kentucky Derby, Tobacco Farms, Fine Bourbon, Lakes, Hardwood Forests, Daniel Boone Bluegrass music, "My Old Kentucky Home"

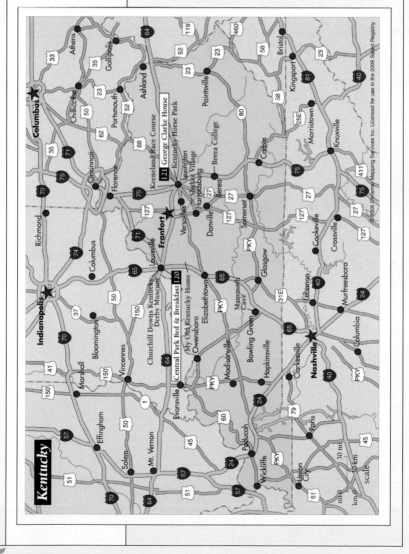

Central Park Bed & Breakfast

www.srinns.com/centralparkbb

1353 South Fourth Street, Old Louisville Historic District,
Louisville, KY 40208

877-922-1505 • 502-638-1505 • Fax 502-638-1525

centralpar@win.net

Proprietors
Robert & Eva Wessels
General Managers
Merle Meyer & Linda Rexroat

Historic District
Bed & Breakfast

paii

Central Park Bed & Breakfast is the perfect destination for accommodations outside the ordinary. The casual, yet stately ambiance, delicious breakfasts and attentive hosts make for a memorable stay. All rooms have luxurious linens, fireplaces, a comfortable sitting area, work desk with phone and high speed Internet connections, and private ensuite bathrooms, some with 2-person whirlpool tubs. Central Park Bed & Breakfast is an architectural delight of comfortable elegance. This fine three story Victorian is located in the heart of "Old Louisville Historic District," America's largest collection of Victorian homes. The marvelous 1884 craftsmanship is present throughout including splendid reverse painted glass ceiling of the front porch, hand carved oak woodwork and fireplace mantels, beautiful stained glass windows, German tile floors, and intricately hammered brass hardware.

AAA ◆◆◆   *Member Since 2006*

Rooms/Rates
Queens $110/$135; Kings/suites $135/$175; Carriage House (kid & pet friendly) $135/$150. Corp. rates for single bus. travelers @$95 w/automatic check-in upgrade.
Number of Rooms: 7

Cuisine
Creative 3-course breakfasts served fireside or on the garden patio or rear veranda. Fresh roasted coffee, teas, juices, & fresh baked pastries. Afternoon beverages, snacks & evening desserts. Fine & casual dining less than 2 blocks from inn.

Nearest Airport(s)
Louisville International, 10-min.

Directions
I-65 to ex 135 (W. St. Catherine), L on 3rd St to 3rd lt, R on Magnolia, R 3/4 block on 4th.

"A Statement in Casual Elegance"

Proprietress
Kathryn L. Bux

Historic
Urban Bed & Breakfast

paii

George Clarke House
www.srinns.com/georgeclarke
136 Woodland Ave., Lexington, KY 40502
866-436-1890 • 859-254-2500
jeeves@georgeclarkehouse.com

Rooms/Rates
All guest rooms have fireplaces, en suite private baths (some with whirlpool tubs), and queen or king beds. High Season: $189/$299 Low Season: $149/$229. Resident cats greet you upon arrival
Number of Rooms: 4

Cuisine
Breakfasts are sumptuous affairs. Delicacies such as crême brûlée French toast, waffles with Grand Marnier strawberries, or Crab Cakes Benedict are served fireside on delicate china with gleaming silver and sparkling crystal. Our private blend gourmet coffee completes your dining experience.

Nearest Airport(s)
Bluegrass Airport - 5mi from GCH

Directions
Located in historic, residential downtown neighborhood.

The year was 1890. It still is. . .here.

Priceless antiques, hand-tied Persian rugs, historic wall-coverings and draperies tantalize the senses as you cross the threshold of this National Historic Register home. Experience the luxury and pampering that entice our guests to return time and again. Each guest room offers sanctuary from the stressors of modern life. Opulent king or queen rooms feature gas fireplaces, elegantly appointed beds, and breathtaking, en suite private baths. Selections range from a queen room w/antique, carved walnut bed and English maid's tub in the bath to an exquisite 2-room suite featuring a carved-mahogany king bed w/private parlor and 2-person Ultra Therapeutic whirlpool in the bath. See our website for complete details. Distinctive amenities include, high-thread count, cotton linens, Egyptian cotton towels, Penhaligon's bath products, and gourmet chocolates. For those who can't leave the 21st Century, each room has private phone, TV, complimentary high-speed wireless Internet.

Prepare to be enchanted!

Member Since 2005

12+ 🚭 💳 ① ↔ ✂ 📠 @ 🧺 ◎ ✳ ☕

"Everything was just PURRRRRFECT." "...like a home away from home."
"Absolutely Enchanting." "All done to perfection. Thank you for your excellence."

Louisiana

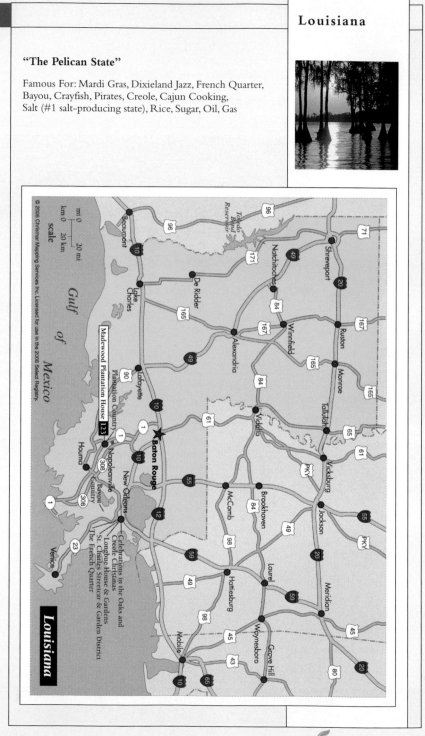

"The Pelican State"

Famous For: Mardi Gras, Dixieland Jazz, French Quarter, Bayou, Crayfish, Pirates, Creole, Cajun Cooking, Salt (#1 salt-producing state), Rice, Sugar, Oil, Gas

Gulf of Mexico

Madewood Plantation House 123
Plantation Country

Celebrations in the Oaks and Creole Christmas
Longhue House & Gardens
St. Charles Streetcar & Garden District
The French Quarter

Louisiana

© 2006 Chrismar Mapping Services Inc. Licensed for use in the 2006 Select Registry.

mi 0   20 mi
km 0   20 km
scale

Toledo Bend Reservoir

Beaumont
Lake Charles
De Ridder
Natchitoches
Shreveport
Winnfield
Alexandria
Ruston
Monroe
Tallulah
Vicksburg
Vidalia
Lafayette
Baton Rouge
Houma
Napoleonville
Bayou Country
New Orleans
Venice
McComb
Brookhaven
Jackson
Hattiesburg
Laurel
Meridian
Waynesboro
Grove Hill
Mobile

SelectRegistry.com

Owners
Keith and Millie Marshall
Manager
Christine Gaudet

Traditional Southern
Country Inn

Madewood Plantation House

www.srinns.com/madewoodplantation
4250 Highway 308, Napoleonville, LA 70390
800-375-7151 • 985-369-7151 • Fax 985-369-9848
madewoodpl@aol.com

Rooms/Rates
6 Rooms; 2 Suites, $259/$289 double occupancy. Seasonal package rates MAP (Dinner, Breakfast). Open year-round, except Thanksgiving, Christmas and New Year's Eves and Days. **Number of Rooms:** 8

Cuisine
Wine and cheese hour. Candlelit Southern/Cajun dinner served with other guests in plantation dining room. Full service liquor. Full plantation breakfast.

Nearest Airport(s)
Ryan Airport - Baton Rouge

Directions
I-10 W. from New Orleans to exit 182, Cross Sunshine Bridge and follow LA Hwy 70 to Spur 70, then L on LA Hwy 308, 2.2 miles past Napoleonville.

Madewood Plantation House offers elegant accommodations in a homelike atmosphere. The National Historic Landmark is lovingly maintained by its longtime staff, who provide the relaxed atmosphere for which Madewood is noted. Guests enjoy antique-filled rooms and canopied beds along with a house party ambiance that includes a wine and cheese hour prior to a family-style candlelit dinner prepared by Madewood's cooks. Selected one of the top 12 Inns by *Country Inns* magazine, featured in *National Geographic Traveler* and named by *NGT* in 1999 as one of the top 54 inns in US, *Travel Holiday* magazine and *Time* magazine. French spoken.

Member Since 1993

12+

The "Queen of the Bayou"

"The Pine Tree State"

Famous For: Lobsters, Lighthouses, Rocky Coastlines, Potatoes, Pines, Ports, Paper

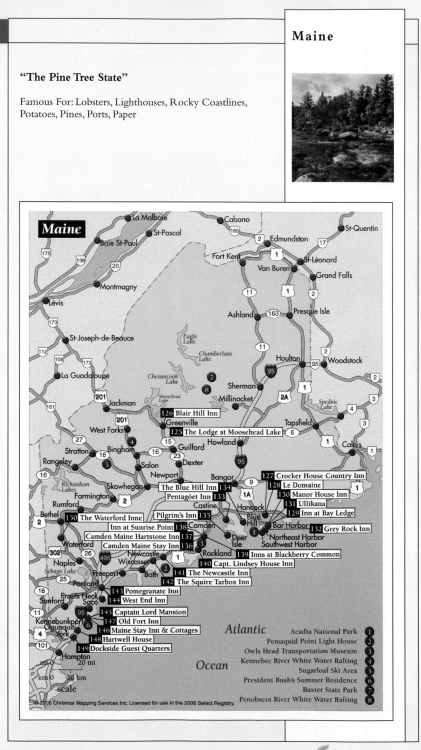

Maine

La Malbaie · Cabano · St-Quentin
St-Pascal · Edmundston · St-Léonard
Baie St-Paul · Fort Kent · Van Buren · Grand Falls
Montmagny · Ashland · 163 · Presque Isle
Lévis · Houlton · Woodstock
St-Joseph-de-Beauce · Eagle Lake · Chamberlain Lake
La Guadalupe · Chesuncook Lake · Sherman · Spednic Lake · Calais
Jackman · Millinocket · Topsfield
126 Blair Hill Inn
Greenville · Howland
125 The Lodge at Moosehead Lake
West Forks · Guilford · Dexter
Stratton · Salon · Newport · Bangor
Rangeley · Skowhegan
127 Crocker House Country Inn
128 Le Domaine
Farmington · **The Blue Hill Inn 134**
Rumford · **Pentagöet Inn 133** · Castine · **130** Manor House Inn
Bethel · **131** Ullikana
150 The Waterford Inne · **Pilgrim's Inn 135** · **129** Inn at Bay Ledge
Waterford · **Inn at Sunrise Point 138** · Camden · Bar Harbor · **132** Grey Rock Inn
Camden Maine Hartstone Inn 137 · Northeast Harbor
Naples · **Camden Maine Stay Inn 136** · Rockland · **139** Inns at Blackberry Common
Freeport · **140** Capt. Lindsey House Inn
Portland · **141** The Newcastle Inn
142 The Squire Tarbox Inn
Prouts Neck · **143** Pomegranate Inn
Saco · **144** West End Inn
Kennebunkport · **145** Captain Lord Mansion
Ogunquit · **147** Old Fort Inn
York · **146** Maine Stay Inn & Cottages
148 Hartwell House
Hampton · **149** Dockside Guest Quarters

Atlantic

Ocean

Acadia National Park ❶
Pemaquid Point Light House ❷
Owls Head Transportation Museum ❸
Kennebec River White Water Rafting ❹
Sugarloaf Ski Area ❺
President Bush's Summer Residence ❻
Baxter State Park ❼
Penobscot River White Water Rafting ❽

mi. 0   20 mi
km 0   20 km
scale

© 2006 Chrismar Mapping Services Inc. Licensed for use in the 2006 Select Registry.

Owners
Sonda and Bruce Hamilton

Traditional Country Retreat/Lodge

Lodge at Moosehead Lake
www.srinns.com/mooseheadlake
368 Lily Bay Road, P. O. Box 1167, Greenville, ME 04441
800-825-6977 • 207-695-4400 • Fax 207-695-2281
innkeeper@lodgeatmooseheadlake.com

Rooms/Rates
5 elegantly appointed Lodge Rooms, 3 exquisite Carrige House Suites, $205/$475. All have luxurious spa baths and magnifient lake and mountain views. Some w/ private decks.
Number of Rooms: 8

Cuisine
Gourmet Breakfast served en suite, on the verandah or in the dining room. Fine dining offered Friday - Monday in season. Enjoy the candlelit dining room with sweeping views of Moosehead Lake. Full bar and impressive wine cellar. 24 hour guest pantry.

Nearest Airport(s)
Bangor

Directions
95N to Newport, 7N to Dexter, 23N to Guilford, 15N to Greenville. 1.5 hrs drive from Bangor, 2.5 from Portland, 4.5 from Boston.

In the small town of Greenville, on a forty- mile lake, in the northern reaches of Maine the Lodge at Moosehead Lake can be found. Perched gracefully atop a rise overlooking the broad waters of Moosehead Lake with direct access to it's shores, this award winning Inn with spectacular lake views, sensational sunsets, peaceful atmosphere, warm hospitality and pampered service is the ideal retreat. This exquisite and stately Colonial, built in 1917 abounds with elegance, sophistication and comfort. Revel in the ever-changing vista across Moosehead Lake that is both stunning by day and magical by moonlight. This ultra private Lodge is filled with unique imports, rich custom designer fabrics and one-of-a kind furnishings. Meticulous in every conceivable detail, this luxury Inn is a timeless masterpiece that captures the very essence of Maine. 2005 Grand Award winner in the Andrew Harper's Hideaway report listing the Worlds top 24 captivating hideaway hotels and resort. Inland Maine's only AAA 4 diamond.

AAA ◆◆◆◆   *Member Since 1995*

12+

"You have done the State of Maine a great service by creating this experience. We depart relaxed, pampered, and impressed. Anxious to return this summer."

Blair Hill Inn at Moosehead Lake

www.srinns.com/blairhillinn
351 Lily Bay Road, Greenville, ME 04441
207-695-0224 • Fax 207-695-4324
info@blairhill.com

Innkeepers/Owners
Dan and Ruth
McLaughlin

Historic Country Estate

It's hard to imagine that such a beautiful place exists. Rising up from the hillside atop massive stone walls, the 1891 mansion will take your breath away. As the centerpiece of 15 acres of gardens, woodland trails, ponds & flower fields, Blair Hill Inn is renowned for its soaring views of Moosehead Lake and the mountain wilderness beyond. With a perfect balance of warmth and elegance, the inn is stripped of packaged pretense and brimming with genuine beauty. The relaxed atmosphere, together with service that speaks thoughtfully to your needs, will set you instantly at ease. Hilltop breezes, jazz, and brilliant lake views create that special vacation evening. This 9,000 square foot estate has grand and architecturally exquisite spaces with the air of a country-house hotel. The decor reflects pedigree but is unpretentious. It is a rare, refreshing find. Beautiful guest rooms, gorgeous baths, breathtaking views, abundant flowers, award-winning dining and summer evening concerts await you. Sitting on the broad porch as the sun sets across the lake, you'll realize that this is the hidden gem you've been looking for.

Member Since 2005

Rooms/Rates
8 Beautiful Guest Rooms
$275/$450
Number of Rooms: 8

Cuisine
A Top Ten restaurant of Maine, dinner is served weekends from mid-June to mid-Oct. Wood-grilled meats & seafood, fresh produce from the inn's gardens and greenhouse. Instead of eating dinner, you're experiencing an event. Breakfast, served each morning, lives up to the sumptuousness of its surroundings.

Nearest Airport(s)
Bangor International

Directions
95N to Newport; 7N to Dexter; 23N to Guilford; 15N to Greenville. 1.5 hours from Bangor, 2.5 from Portland, 4.5 from Boston.

10+

"Your love and skill have worked together to create a masterpiece. Thank you for your pursuit of perfection. This is heaven on earth."

Innkeepers/Owners
Richard and Elizabeth Malaby

Traditional Country Inn

🍽️　🍽️ 🍷

🏮

Crocker House Country Inn

www.srinns.com/crocker
967 Point Road, Hancock Point, ME 04640
877-715-6017 • 207-422-6806 • Fax 207-422-3105
info@crockerhouse.com

Rooms/Rates
$110/$160 in-season, $85/$120 off-season B&B. Late April until New Year's Day. MAP available-off season.
Number of Rooms: 11

Cuisine
Breakfast and dinner. Wine list and full bar. Classic continental cuisine with a downeast flair. Extensive use made of organic and indigenous products.

Nearest Airport(s)
Bar Harbor - 17 miles
Bangor - 42 miles

Directions
If you are travelling N on Rt. 1 proceed to Ellsworth. If you are travelling N on US 95 proceed to US 395 in Bangor. Follow US 395 to the end. Take Rt 1A 23 miles to Ellsworth. From Ellsworth go 8 miles N on U.S. Rt. 1, turn R on Point Road. Continue 5 miles to Inn on R.

The Crocker House Country Inn is tucked away on the peninsula of Hancock Point. Its quiet, out of the way location, fine cuisine and individually appointed guest rooms, all combine to make the Crocker House a refreshing and memorable destination. The restaurant, open to the public, continues to draw guests from distant places for its extraordinary cuisine and live piano on Friday and Saturday nights. A three-minute walk to Frenchman Bay and public moorings. An ideal location for wedding receptions, family reunions and small business retreats. Pet friendly. Wireless.

Member Since 1987

☺　🚭　💳🏦📁❤　✍️　🐕

"Don't really have the right words to thank you for our stay. Your staff is incredible!"

Le Domaine

www.srinns.com/ledomaine
P O 519, Hancock, ME 04640
800-554-8498 • 207-422-3395
info@ledomaine.com

Owner
F.E. Dixon
General Manager
Beth Clark

Elegant Village Inn

Rooms/Rates
3 Rooms, 2 Suites $200/$285.
June 9 to October 18.
Number of Rooms: 5

Cuisine
Renowned French restaurant named 'One of the Best Restaurants in the World for Wine' by *Wine Spectator*. French provencal cooking using the finest Maine seafood, local produce & meats.

Nearest Airport(s)
Bar Harbor/Trenton 20 minutes.
Bangor 40 minutes

Directions
Located on U.S. Rte 1, in Hancock, ME. Just 10 min. E of Ellsworth, 45 min. from Bangor. From I-95 in Bangor, take I-395, follow signs to Ellsworth. From Bar Harbor Airport or Cat Ferry from Nova Scotia, take Rte. 3 N to Ellsworth, then U.S. Rte.1 E.

The colorful, sun-soaked atmosphere of Provence surrounds you when you step into Le Domaine. The scent of lavender and fresh flowers, French furnishings, cheerful prints, antiques and art create a truly unique atmosphere. There are many delights to savor... breakfast overlooking the garden, the elegant dining room, selecting from the delicious dinner offerings, studying our award-winning list of French wines, the waft of wonderful aromas, delectable desserts. However you choose to spend your days - at a concert, hiking in Acadia National Park or shopping for treasures in this lively area of Coastal Maine - Le Domaine makes any visit truly memorable.

Member Since 2002

12+

"Le Domaine was a unique experience that transported me back to my days in Provence. Now it is a happily anticipated destination when visiting Maine."

Inn at Bay Ledge

Innkeepers/Owners
Jack and Jeani Ochtera

Elegant Rustic Waterside
Breakfast Inn

www.srinns.com/bayledge
150 Sand Point Road, Bar Harbor, ME 04609
207-288-4204 • Fax 207-288-5573
bayledge@downeast.net

Rooms/Rates
8 rooms, $110/$375 low season; high season $160/$475. 4 cottages $125/$375 low season; high season $175/$475. All rooms are king or queen with private baths. Inn rooms have bay view. Cottages enjoy a pine view. Summer Cottage has bay view.
Number of Rooms: 12

Cuisine
Full gourmet breakfast served in the sunroom overlooking the bay. Afternoon tea & refreshments on the porch.

Nearest Airport(s)
Bar Harbor 15 minutes, Bangor 1 hour, Portland 3 hours

Directions
From the head of the island follow Rt. 3 for 5 mi. L onto Sand Point Rd. The inn is on the L overlooking the bay.

Amidst the towering pines, The Inn at Bay Ledge literally clings to the cliffs of Mt. Dessert Island, which is locally and aptly referred to as "The Eden of New England." The veranda, appointed with comfy wicker, overlooks the spectacular coastline and is extremely inviting. Guests may enjoy a swim in our pool, relax in a hammock or take a stroll along our private beach. The elegant bedrooms compliment the style of the inn which was built in the 1900s and possesses an upscale country ambiance. Beautifully decorated with antiques, all rooms are unique with views of Frenchmen Bay. King and queen beds are covered with designer linens, down quilts and feather beds. Our new Summer Cottage sits just 25 feet from the cliff's edge!

AAA ◆◆◆   *Member Since 2002*   Mobil ★★★

"We don't want to leave-Can't wait to return. This is one of the prettiest places on earth!"

Manor House Inn

www.srinns.com/manorhouseinn
106 West Street, Bar Harbor, ME 04609
800-437-0088 • 207-288-3759 • Fax 207-288-2974
manor@me.acadia.net

Innkeepers/Owners
Stacey and Ken Smith

Traditional Village
Breakfast Inn

Built in 1887 as a 22-room mansion, Manor House Inn has been authentically restored to its original splendor and is now on the National Register of Historic Places. The moment you step into the front entry a romantic Victorian past becomes the present. Enjoy comfort, convenience, and privacy while staying within easy walking distance of Bar Harbor's fine shops, restaurants and ocean activities. Each morning wake up to a delicious home-baked breakfast such as baked stuffed blueberry French toast. Then spend your day exploring Acadia National Park.

Rooms/Rates
18 Rooms/Suites $140/$237.
Off-season $77/$200.
Open Mid April - Late October.
Number of Rooms: 18

Cuisine
Full breakfast and afternoon tea.

Nearest Airport(s)
Hancock County Airport;
Trenton, Maine, 20 miles

Directions
As you approach Bar Harbor on Route 3, turn Left onto West Street. Manor House Inn will be 3 blocks down, on the right.

AAA ◆◆◆   *Member Since 1998*   Mobil ★★★

12+

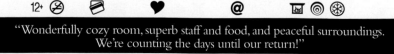

"Wonderfully cozy room, superb staff and food, and peaceful surroundings.
We're counting the days until our return!"

Ullikana & A Yellow House

Innkeepers/Owners
Helene Harton and
Roy Kasindorf

Traditional In Town
Breakfast Inn

🍽️   🍷

www.srinns.com/ullikana
15 The Field, Bar Harbor, ME 04609
207-288-9552 • Fax 207-288-3682

Rooms/Rates
16 Rooms, high season:
$150/$285; low season:
$100/$225. All our rooms have
king or queen beds. All have
private baths. Some have porches
overlooking harbor. Some rooms
have fireplaces.
Number of Rooms: 16

Cuisine
We serve a full breakfast on our
patio, looking out on the water.
Also we have afternoon refreshments on the patio.

Nearest Airport(s)
Bangor and Bar Harbor

Directions
Rte 3 to Bar Harbor. L onto
Cottage St. R onto Main St. L
after Bar Harbor Trust Company
building. Take gravel road towards
water.

Ullikana, a secluded, romantic haven, overlooking the harbor, and
our sister Inn, A Yellow House, only steps away, are two of the few
remaining cottages from the 1800s in Bar Harbor. Only a minute
walk from the center of town, our quiet location offers a haven of
hospitality. Watch the lobster boats in the harbor from the garden
or the patio, where sumptuous breakfasts are served. Relax in the
casual elegance of these historic Inns, where art is an important
part of our decor. We invite you to share the history and hospitality of Ullikana and A Yellow House with us.

Member Since 2000

⊘   ⊘   💳   🗳️

"When in Bar Harbor, I always stay at Ullikana!" (Roy's Mom)

Grey Rock Inn
www.srinns.com/greyrock
Harbourside Road, Northeast Harbor, ME 04662
207-276-9360 • Fax 207-276-9894

Innkeepers/Owners
Janet, Karl & Adam Millett

Elegant Country Breakfast Inn

This beautifully situated mansion on seven acres overlooks the harbor lighthouse and outer islands off Mt. Desert. Built in 1910 as a private residence, Grey Rock has been a gathering place, hosting many of the famous families that built their homes in NE Harbor. With warmth and charm, Grey Rock offers elegant rooms that are pleasingly decorated. To assure your pleasure and relaxation, fireplaces are featured throughout the public rooms and in many of the bedrooms. Grey Rock is a seven-minute walk to the picturesque village of NE Harbor with its quaint old-fashioned shops and to our marina, a popular yachting basin. Elegant, Cottage style, country inn with breakfast.

Rooms/Rates
7 Rooms, 1 Suite, May to June 20, $110/$275. July thru October, $165/$375.
Number of Rooms: 8

Cuisine
Breakfast only; 110 restaurants on this island. We make reservations for you. Guests are welcome to bring their own spirits. We supply ice and glassware. Afternoon Tea.

Nearest Airport(s)
Bangor International

Directions
Follow RT 198 on Mount Desert Island. We are the first property bordering the National Park as you approach the Village.

Member Since 1998

12+

"Maine Coast Living at its Best!"

SelectRegistry.com

Innkeepers/Owners
Jack Burke & Julie Van de Graaf

Historic Waterside Inn

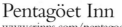

Pentagöet Inn
www.srinns.com/pentagoet
P.O. Box 4, Castine, ME 04421
800-845-1701 • 207-326-8616
stay@pentagoet.com

Rooms/Rates
16 Rooms, all private baths, mostly kings, 95/245. Open May-October.
Number of Rooms: 16

Cuisine
Full country breakfast and afternoon refreshments. Dinner served nightly featuring lobster and local shellfish, native fish and game, New England specialities and fine desserts. There is a well stocked wine cellar and a full bar.

Nearest Airport(s)
Bangor International Airport

Directions
From I-95 to Augusta, Rte 3 to Belfast, Rte 1 N to Bucksport, Rte 175/166 to Castine, left on Main Street

"Overlooking Penobscot Bay, this picturesque little town is one of the most authentic New England fishing villages you will ever encounter," noted *National Geographic* in May of 2000. The Pentagoet, a whimsical Queen Anne Victorian, is one of Maine's original "summer hotels" built for the 1890s steamship trade. The inn has been lovingly restored, and you will feel at home with the charming mix of antiques and collectibles. Just being here in this vintage seaside village is often all our guests desire. Day trips to Camden, Stonington, Acadia and Bar Harbor are all just an hour away. We can plan itineraries for kayaking, sailing, hiking, antiques, art galleries, and light houses and will tell you about the best lobster roll in the area. We invite you to dinner; it's casual by candlelight, with Ella and Louie in the background. Enjoy our exceptional home cooking that honors the classic in its soulful simplicity and bows to the seasons. Have a nightcap in our cozy, old world bar, the inn's "utterly fascinating Passports Pub," according to *Andrew Harper's Hideaway Report* in August of 2004.

AAA ◆◆◆   *Member Since 2005*

"Be sure to try the 'exceptional bouillabaisse...'"
Discerning Traveler 2004:"Most Romantic Hideaway"

The Blue Hill Inn

www.srinns.com/bluehill
40 Union Street, P.O. Box 403, Blue Hill, ME 04614
800-826-7415 • 207-374-2844 • Fax 207-374-2829
mary@bluehillinn.com

Innkeepers/Owners
Mary & Don Hartley
Traditional Village Breakfast
Inn

The coastal village of Blue Hill wraps around the head of Blue Hill Bay and is centrally located for exploring Acadia National Park, Deer Isle, Castine, and Blue Hill Peninsula. The beauty of the area's rugged coastlines, blueberry barrens, pine trees, crystal blue waters, lobster buoys, lighthouses, and small villages is complemented by fine arts, crafts, and food. Evening skies are brilliant with stars. The Inn is situated in the historic district and is a short walk to the harbor, Kneisel Chamber Music Hall, Blue Hill Mountain, art and antique galleries. The circa 1830 clapboarded hostelry retains many original features and the fireplaces, gleaming 19th Century floors, and antique furnishings contribute to an intimate atmosphere. After a day of hiking, kayaking, bird-watching, gallery hopping, or reading in the garden, guests return for a perfect pot of tea or espresso. Hors d'oeuvres are served before dinner; down comforters and turn-down service await after dinner. Guest rooms are air conditioned for those warmer days.

Rooms/Rates
11 Rooms, $138/$195 B&B; Cape House luxury suite, $225/$285 B&B. Fpls, AC. Inn opened mid-May to Oct 31. Cape House available as self-catering Nov-May - $165. 7% tax.
Number of Rooms: 12

Cuisine
Multi-course breakfasts with several entrees, afternoon refreshments, evening hors d'oeuvres. Locally grown organic produce and Maine seafood featured. Fine wines & liquors. Fine & casual dining within walking distance.

Nearest Airport(s)
Bangor-1 hr.; Portland-3 hrs.

Directions
From S, ME 95N to 295N to Augusta exit 113, 3E to 15S to Blue Hill. In BH, right at High St. From N, 95S to Bangor. Exit 395W to 15S.

Member Since 1994

12+

"Stay here if you enjoy antiques, warm hospitality, and classic New England Inns." Maine Handbook.

Innkeeper/Owner
**Tony Lawless &
Tina Oddleifson**

Historic Waterside Country Inn

Pilgrim's Inn
www.pilgrimsinn.com
P.O. Box 69, 20 Main Street, Deer Isle, ME 04627
888-778-7505 • 207-348-6615 • Fax 207-348-6615
innkeeper@pilgrimsinn.com

Rooms/Rates
12 Rooms and 3 cottages; $99/$269, B&B. Most rooms have views of the mill pond or Northwest Harbor. All rooms have private baths. Open May through October.
Number of Rooms: 15

Cuisine
Full Country Breakfast; Afternoon refreshments; and Dinner at the Whale's Rib Tavern featuring American Heritage cuisine in an historic setting.

Nearest Airport(s)
Bangor International Airport

Directions
I-95 to Augusta, Rte 3 to Belfast, Route 1 N, in Bucksport take Rte 15 S. Go 25 miles, over Deer Isle bridge, go 5 miles to Village, Right onto Main St, Inn on left 200 yds.

Overlooking Northwest Harbor and a picturesque millpond, this 1793 colonial is surrounded by the unspoiled beauty of remote Deer Isle in Penobscot Bay. Glowing hearths, colonial colors, pumpkin pine floors, antique furnishings, combined with warm hospitality and flavorful meals in the cozy Whale's Rib Tavern have pleased many contented guests. Easy access to Haystack Mountain School of Crafts, the busy fishing village of Stonington, Isle au Haut, views of lighthouses and numerous galleries. Day-trips to pleasant coastal villages and Acadia National Park make it an ideal location for an extended stay. A kayaking, sailing and hiking paradise. On the National Register of Historic Places. An Editors' Choice in the 2006 *Yankee Magazine Travel Guide to New England*; chosen as of one of the Country's Best B&Bs by Forbes. com; and designated as an Environmental Leader by the State of Maine. In addition to 12 rooms in the inn, three cottages on the property are perfect for families with children and pets.

Member Since 1980   Mobil ★★★

10+

"The Inn is splendid and everything was absolutely out of this world, from our room to the meals. A wonderful seaside getaway."

Camden Maine Stay

www.srinns.com/camdenmainestay
22 High St., Camden, ME 04843
207-236-9636 • Fax 207-236-0621
innkeeper@camdenmainestay.com

Innkeepers/Owners
Bob and Juanita Topper

Historic Village
Breakfast Inn

Relaxed, warm, romantic, and very friendly the Maine Stay is located in the historic district of one of America's most beautiful seaside villages. A short walk down tree-lined streets brings you to the harbor park, shops and restaurants. Built in 1802, the striking main house, attached carriage house, and four-story barn are outstanding examples of early American architecture and old New England taste and charm. Spacious common areas with an eclectic collection of furnishings and artwork, exquisite guestrooms, and a big country kitchen enchant and delight. A perfect getaway for any season. Chosen by *Frontgate* as one of *America's Finest Homes*. In the words of *Vacations Magazine*, "Down east hospitality at its very best." *Frommer's* comments, "Camden's premier Bed and Breakfast," and *Fodor's* agrees, "Camden's best B&B."

Rooms/Rates
8 Rooms, all with private baths, $125/$250. Spacious and tastefully decorated common areas with wood burning fireplaces. Open year-round.
Number of Rooms: 8

Cuisine
Full breakfast, which may be taken at our antique harvest table in the dining room or at a table for two on our sun porch overlooking our beautifully landscaped one-acre garden. Tea is served in the afternoon and nearby restaurants offer fine dining and casual harbor settings...lobster at its best.

Nearest Airport(s)
Rockland (RKD); Bangor (BGR); Portland (PWM)

Directions
US Rte 1 (High Street) 3 blocks N of the village.

Member Since 1995

12+

"I've stayed in 40 B&B's (inc. Europe) and the Maine Stay is, by far, the best. Perfect, absolutely perfect...." J. Kast

Owners
Mary Jo Brink and
Michael Salmon

Elegant Village Inn

Camden Maine Hartstone Inn
www.srinns.com/camdenhartstone
41 Elm Street, Camden, ME 04843
800-788-4823 • 207-236-4259 • Fax 207-236-9575
info@hartstoneinn.com

Rooms/Rates
6 rooms, 6 suites, $100/$250 B&B. Gourmet Getaway packages and Cooking Class weekends available. Open year-round. Tour our rooms & check availability at hartstoneinn.com.
Number of Rooms: 12

Cuisine
Memorable full breakfast, afternoon cookies and tea, and a five-course gourmet dinner by reservation. Dinner is served Wed.-Sun, July-Oct. (Thurs.-Sun, Nov.-June). Fine wine selection from our cellar list.

Nearest Airport(s)
Bangor or Portland

Directions
US Rt. 1 into Camden, the Inn is on your left as you enter the village from the South.

An enchanting hideaway in the heart of Camden village that *Fodor's* considers "An elegant and sophisticated retreat and culinary destination," this Mansard style Victorian built in 1835 offers a unique experience in pampered luxury. "From Quimper faince and luscious linens in the guest rooms to the world-class cuisine in the dining room and the collection of 400 live orchids in the common areas, Mary Jo and Michael Salmon get absolutely everything right," says the *Maine Explorers Guide*. Each air conditioned guestroom combines carefully chosen furnishings and original artwork to create a mood of lavish comfort and romance. Luxurious amenities include: soft robes, memorably fluffy featherbeds, fine linens, gas fireplaces, Jacuzzi tubs, CD players, TV and WiFi. Reward yourself and your taste buds with our sumptuous multi-course breakfast presented on the sunny dining room porch. In the late afternoon indulge in our wine and cheese pairings and sneak away for some solitude to our beautiful English style gardens or to the privacy of your guestroom. Elegant china, fine crystal and internationally award winning cuisine make dinner a truly memorable experience. Gourmet getaway packages, chef for the day and cooking class weekends are available.

Member Since 2002

12+

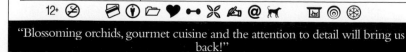

"Blossoming orchids, gourmet cuisine and the attention to detail will bring us back!"

Inn at Sunrise Point

www.srinns.com/sunrisepoint
PO Box 1344, Camden, ME 04843
207-236-7716 • Fax 207-236-0820
info@sunrisepoint.com

Proprietors/Hosts
Stephen T. & Deanna Tallon
Innkeepers
Joerg & Patty Ross
Elegant Waterside
Breakfast Inn

🍽️   🍷

A pampering seaside haven, this Andrew Harper Best Hideaways-recommended bed and breakfast inn offers spectacular ocean views and all the luxuries you can expect from a AAA Four-Diamond property. Set within a secluded four-and-a half-acre oceanfront hideaway and just minutes from picturesque Camden. Sleep soundly in the wonderful sea air, comforted by the gentle murmur of waves outside your window. Awaken to the breathtaking sight of the sunrise across Penobscot Bay before enjoying a complimentary gourmet breakfast in the inn's bright conservatory or ocean room. Later, browse in the cherry-paneled library with a glass of fine wine and select a good book. Stay in an elegantly furnished room in the main house, a wonderfully restored 1920s shingle-style Maine summer "cottage," or in one of the beautifully furnished cottages or suite at the water's edge. Perhaps a romantic loft above all of the cottages and high in the trees will let you dream with the birds. A luxurious, romantic and elegant retreat for discerning travelers.

Rooms/Rates
3 rooms $240/$350. 4 cottages $290/$510. Suite $270/$365. Loft $310/$420. Open Mid-April to Mid-November. All accommodations with partial to full ocean views and all with private decks.
Number of Rooms: 9

Cuisine
Gourmet Breakfast

Nearest Airport(s)
Portland - 80 minutes

Directions
From S I-95 N to Portland. Joins Rte 295 N to Coastal Exit 31 (formely exit 24) at Topsham. Make right from the off-ramp and continue until signs directing you to Rte 1 N to Bath. Follow Rte 1 N through Camden and inn is 4 miles N on right hand side down to water's edge.

AAA ◆◆◆◆   *Member Since 2005*   Mobil ★★★

12+ 🚭 ♿ 💳   ❤   ✂️ ✈️ @   🔲 ◎   🅢 ☕

"Heaven on Earth! We were lulled to sleep by the sound of waves on Penobscot Bay. Wake up to a gourmet delight each morning. Sheer Luxury! Wonderful!"

Innkeepers/Owners
Jim and Cyndi Ostrowski

Traditional Village Bed & Breakfast

Inns at Blackberry Common

www.srinns.com/blackberrycommon
82-84 Elm Street, Camden, ME 04843
800-388-6000 • 207-236-6060 • Fax 207-236-9032
innkeepers@blackberryinn.com

Rooms/Rates
$99/$249. Open all year. Fireplaces, whirlpools, luxury linens. Seasonal lighthouse & special dining packages.
Number of Rooms: 18

Cuisine
A multi-course gourmet breakfast, brimming with local Maine specialties and our own fresh garden herbs & berries served in our candlelit dining room or on the garden patio. Complimentary afternoon refreshments.

Nearest Airport(s)
Portland Bangor

Directions
I-95 N to Rte 295 N at Exit 44 at Portland. Exit 28 to Brunswick & Rte 1 N. Take Rte 90 W toward Camden. L on Rte 1 N again. Inns are on R entering Camden from S.

Just three blocks to the picturesque schooner filled harbor, our Inns are a quiet romantic oasis surrounded by over an acre of Maine gardens.

Three gracious parlors of the 1849 Victorian boasting original tin ceilings and plaster moldings welcome guests to enjoy afternoon refreshments or a quiet read before the fire. Our extensive gardens, complete with a blackberry patch, are a quiet retreat after a day of sailing, hiking or kayaking.

Choose an elegant guestroom in Maine's only authentic "Painted Lady" Victorian Inn. Select a Carriage House cottage room tucked amid the gardens. Or stay in a stately guestroom in our Federal Colonial Inn celebrating 200 years! Cozy gas fireplaces and baths with soaking clawfoot or whirlpool tub for extra pampering. Create a special memory! Lighthouses are our specialty!

Member Since 2006

"Top notch...Best of the rest." "Casual elegance, lovely gardens & breakfast is ambrosia for the gods!" "Hospitality spoken here."

Captain Lindsey House Inn

www.srinns.com/captainlindsey
5 Lindsey Street, Rockland, ME 04841
800-523-2145 • 207-596-7950 • Fax 207-596-2758
lindsey@midcoast.com

Innkeepers
Pam & Drew Schultz

Elegant In Town
Inn

The Captain Lindsey House is an elegantly restored sea captain's home located in the heart of Rockland's Waterfront District. This historic inn offers old world charm with all modern amenities and features private baths in each guest room. Our location affords a great place from which to walk to the many fine restaurants, galleries and unique boutiques along Main street. Antiques and artifacts from around the world grace our spacious guest rooms, cozy parlor and library. Linger by the fire or relax outside on our garden terrace. Guests are welcome to gourmet breakfast each morning, afternoon refreshments & homemade cakes, cookies and pies. Close by you'll enjoy the Farnsworth Art Museum, fine galleries and a taste of "Down East" coastal life. Friendly, genuine hosts await you.

Rooms/Rates
$105/$150 off season (Oct 15th to June 15th), $160/$230 in season. Business rates available year-round. Many packages available. Open year-round.
Number of Rooms: 9

Cuisine
Lunch and dinner in the Waterworks Restaurant. Pub favorites, local fare and seafood. Microbrewed beers, wines and spirits.

Nearest Airport(s)
Portland Jetport, Portland, ME
Bangor International

Directions
From Boston: Rte. I- 95 N to Rte. I-295N to Rte. I-95N to exit 28 (Coastal Rte. 1) into Rockland, Main St. to L. Summer St (by Ferry terminal), L on Union, 1st L to Lindsey.

AAA ◆◆◆   *Member Since 1998*

12+ 🚭 ♿ 🧳 🛎 ♥ 🖋 @ 🖼 ❄

"Great hosts, you made us feel like old friends. The service, beds and breakfast were first class and your inn is beautiful!"

Innkeepers/Owners
Peter and Laura Barclay

Traditional Village
Country Inn

The Newcastle Inn

www.srinns.com/newcastleinn
60 River Road, Newcastle, ME 04553
800-832-8669 • 207-563-5685 • Fax 207-563-6877
innkeep@newcastleinn.com

Rooms/Rates
15 Rooms including 4 Suites.
2006 rates: $155/$295 in season
$125/$225 off season.
Number of Rooms: 19

Cuisine
Multi-course breakfast served
from 8-9:00 a.m. Exceptional
6-course candlelight dining by
reservation (weekends only in
winter season). Full bar and
extensive wine list.

Nearest Airport(s)
Portland

Directions
Take I-95 North to exit 44, I-295
North. Take Exit 31 and turn right
onto Rte 196 heading south. After
2.5 miles, take Route 1 North
toward Bath. 7 miles past Wiscasset bridge, turn right on River Rd.
Inn is 1/2 mile on the right.

A romantic Country Inn located in Maine's Mid-Coast, famous for its beaches, lighthouses and rocky shore. The Inn's living rooms, sunporch and deck are a quiet, peaceful, and relaxing place from which to enjoy the wonders of Coastal Maine. Overlooking the harbor, the Inn's gardens abound in lupines and other perennials. Many of the inn's guest rooms feature canopy or four-poster beds, fireplaces, water views, Jacuzzis, or soaking tubs and all are air-conditioned. The inn was awarded the prestigious Waverly/Country Inns Magazine Room of the Year Award for its decorating. Renowned for its dinner service, the Inn's restaurant, Lupines, is open to the public and offers New England style French cuisine with an emphasis on local, seasonal ingredients. Enjoy your specially prepared dinner in the Inn's dining rooms featuring water views, a wood-burning fireplace and a mural of the Damariscotta River and the village beyond. Lupines was referred to as "on a cloud near culinary heaven" by the Maine Sunday Telegram.

AAA ◆◆◆   *Member Since 1990*

12+

"Exactly what we dreamed about a Maine Country Inn;
comfort, hospitality, and superb food!"

The Squire Tarbox Inn

www.srinns.com/squiretarbox
1181 Main Road, Westport Island, Wiscasset, ME 04578
800-818-0626 • 207-882-7693 • Fax 207-882-7107
squiretarbox@prexar.com

Innkeepers/Owners
Roni and Mario De Pietro

Traditional Country Inn

Once upon a time, there was a Country Inn conspicuous from all others. After a restoration for your comfort, this colonial farm created an alternate luxury, amidst the splendor of nature. Set within fields, stone walls, and woods, and with kindness to all creatures great and small, pristine barns are filled with gentle animals. The Inn offers you peace and tranquility, away from tourist crowds, but convenient to coastal adventures. Relax on our screened in deck while watching the wild life. Dine leisurely in our 1763 dining room with meals created by our Swiss/owner chef, using all local and home grown organic vegetables. Sleep with the luxury of down duvets and pillows. On the National Register of Historic Places.

Rooms/Rates
$99/$190 double occupancy.
Open April 1 thru' Dec. 31.
Number of Rooms: 11

Cuisine
A full hot breakfast is served. Fresh goat cheese at the cocktail hour, and chocolate chip cookies all day. A la carte dinner menu is prepared by Mario Swiss/owner chef. Enjoy dining on the deck or in the dining room. We have a full liquor license.

Nearest Airport(s)
Portland Jetport

Directions
I-295 to exit 28/Brunswick; Rt. 1 N through Brunswick & Bath; from Bath bridge continue 7 miles on Rt. 1; turn R on Rt. 144 & take it 8.5 miles, it twists & turns but is well marked; you can't miss us - The Rambling Colonial Farmhouse on R.

Member Since 1974

12+

"Fantastic food. Very friendly caring innkeepers.
Beautiful quiet location. Excellent place."

Innkeeper/Owner
Isabel Smiles
General Manager
Chris Monahan

Elegant In Town
Breakfast Inn

Pomegranate Inn
www.srinns.com/pome
49 Neal St., Portland, ME 04102
800–356–0408 • 207-772-1006 • Fax 207-773-4426

Rooms/Rates
8 Rooms, 1 Suite, 1 Garden Room, $95/$165 off season. $175/$285 in season. Open year-round.
Number of Rooms: 10

Cuisine
Full, served breakfast included in price. Complimentary wine and tea upon arrival.

Nearest Airport(s)
Portland International Jetport

Directions
Fr. South: I-95N. ex. 44 to I-295N ex. 4 ex. 5 to 22E. R Bramhall St. immediate L Vaughan St. 4th L Carroll St. Inn at intersection Neal and Carroll St. From North: ex. 6A onto Rte.77 (State St.). R on Pine L on Neal.

Portland's beautiful Western Promenade District, an historic residential neighborhood, is the location of this special city inn. It is a small sophisticated hotel which offers a quiet haven from the tensions of travel. The bustle of downtown is forgotten when you step through the Pomegranate's doors. Antiques and modern art abound in the eclectic atmosphere as featured in the *New York Times, Boston Globe* and *Travel + Leisure* Magazine. For real seclusion, the carriage house offers a first floor guest room with its own private terrace(seasonal). The main house also has a lovely urban garden. A lot of elegance with a touch of panache.

Member Since 1995

12+ 🚭 ♿ 💳   ✒ @   🏨   ❀

"There's a very special place to stay in Portland, Maine...the Pomegrante, a place with a sense of peace and privilege."

West End Inn

www.srinns.com/westend
146 Pine St., Portland, ME 04102
800-338-1377 • 207-772-1377
innkeeper@westendbb.com

Innkeepers/Owners
Dan & Michele Brown
Manager
Pam Bouchard-Nee

Elegant Victorian In Town
Bed and Breakfast

Located in the Western Promenade Historic District, this Georgian style brick townhouse is one of a collection of Victorian-era homes, all reflecting a wealth of architectural detail. The comfort and elegance of the West End Inn creates an oasis within the city and is located in one of the best preserved Victorian neighborhoods in the country. A quiet location and six comfortable guest rooms invite an exceptional night's sleep. The sumptuous breakfast is served in the beautiful dining room with its twelve-foot decorative ceilings and afternoon tea is served in the adjoining library. The residential location provides convenience to the downtown, Arts District and Museums, Public Market, Old Port, Ferry, Civic Center, and Financial District, while offering a refuge and an opportunity for quieter contemplation and a walk on the Promenade. Enjoy city life the Maine way!

Rooms/Rates
6 Rooms Queen/King/Twin beds $139/$199, quiet season $89/$139. All with cable TV and wireless internet.
Number of Rooms: 6

Cuisine
Sumptuous full breakfast, afternoon tea, many exceptional restaurants within short walk.

Nearest Airport(s)
Portland International (PWM)

Directions
From South:I-95 exit 44 onto I-295. Exit 6A, Forest Ave South, before first light bear R onto Rte 77, State St, continue up hill cross Congress St (Longfellow statue on your left), immediate R onto Pine St, several blocks corner Neal St and Pine. From North: I-295 to Exit 6A then same directions as above.

AAA ◆◆◆   *Member Since 2004*

10+

"It is great to find another B&B that is doing things right!"

Innkeepers/Owners
Bev Davis and Rick Litchfield

Elegant
Village Breakfast Inn

Captain Lord Mansion

www.srinns.com/captainlord
6 Pleasant Street, P.O. Box 800, Kennebunkport, ME 04046-0800
800-522-3141 • 207-967-3141 • Fax 207-967-3172
innkeeper@captainlord.com

Rooms/Rates
15 Rooms, $149/$449 B&B;
1 Suite $299/$499 B&B.
Open year-round.
Number of Rooms: 16

Cuisine
Full 3-course breakfast. Afternoon Tea and refreshments. Guests are welcome to bring their own spirits.

Nearest Airport(s)
Portland, ME

Directions
ME Tpke (I-95) to Exit #25. L onto Rte. 35S, go 1.7 mi. to light, cross over Rte.1, bearing R, continue on Rte. 35S/9A for 3.5 miles. At light, turn L onto Rte. 9 E, In Dock Square, @ monument, turn R onto Ocean Ave. Go .3 mile, turn L on Green St. Mansion on 2nd block on L. Parking behind inn.

Come enjoy an unforgettable experience with us! Your comfort, serenity and relaxation are important to us. Our warm hospitality, personal service, central location and large, beautifully-appointed guest rooms are dedicated to your complete satisfaction. Each guest-room offers such amenities as an oversize four-poster bed, a cozy gas fireplace and a heated marble bath floor. Several baths have multiple body-jet showers; 9 have double jacuzzi-style tubs. Find fresh flowers, freshly-prepared breakfasts, afternoon refreshments and lots of personal attention. The Inn is situated at the head of a sloping green, overlooking the Kennebunk River. Our picturesque, quiet, yet convenient, location affords you a terrific place from which to walk to explore the shops, restaurants and galleries in this historic village.

AAA ◆◆◆◆   *Member Since 1975*   Mobil ★★★

"An experience of hospitality at its finest!"

Maine Stay Inn & Cottages

www.mainestayinn.com

34 Maine Street, P.O. Box 500A, Kennebunkport, ME 04046

800-950-2117 • 207-967-2117 • Fax 207-967-8757

innkeeper@mainestayinn.com

Innkeepers/Owners
George and Janice Yankowski

Traditional Village Breakfast Inn

Step back in time to a place where exceptional warmth and hospitality will make your visit to the Southern Maine coast a most memorable experience. Listed on the National Register of Historic Places, the Maine Stay Inn and Cottages at the Melville Walker House offers a charming and comfortable ambiance within the quaint seaside village of Kennebunkport. Choose the Victorian romance of a 19th century Inn Room, or the private intimacy of an English Country Cottage Suite. Relax around a cozy fire or enjoy a double whirlpool Jacuzzi tub. Perfectly located in the quiet residential Historic District, you are just a short stroll along tree-lined streets to the fine shops, galleries and restaurants of Kennebunkport's Dock Square. Sandy beaches and quiet coves provide the tranquility that will soothe your soul.

Rooms/Rates
4 Inn Rooms, $109/$229; 2 Inn Suites, $179/$289; 11 Cottage Rooms/Suites, $109/$289. Open year-round.
Number of Rooms: 17

Cuisine
Awaken to a full New England breakfast served in our dining room or, in summer, on the porch. Guests staying in our charming cottage suites may opt to have their breakfast delivered in a delightful wicker basket! Join us for Afternoon Tea on the sunny porch, or in cooler weather, around a cozy fire.

Nearest Airport(s)
Portland

Directions
ME Tpke., Exit 25 (formerly Exit 3). L on Rte. 35, 6 mi. to Rte. 9. Turn L on Rte. 9, Go over bridge, thru village to stop sign. Turn R on Maine St. Go 3 blks.

AAA ◆◆◆   *Member Since 1996*   Mobil ★★★

"One of the most relaxing and enjoyable places we have ever stayed."
"We cannot wait to return!"

Innkeepers/Owners
Sheila & David Aldrich
Innkeepers/General
Managers
Shana & Tom Hennessey

Elegant Waterside
Breakfast Inn

Old Fort Inn

www.srinns.com/oldfortinn
P.O. Box M, 8 Old Fort Avenue, KennebunkPort, ME 04046
800-828-3678 • 207-967-5353 • Fax 207-967-4547
info@oldfortinn.com

Rooms/Rates
16 Rooms, $175/$395 B&B.
Open April to mid-December.
Number of Rooms: 16

Cuisine
Buffet breakfast, fresh fruit, cereals, homemade breads croissants, quiche, waffles, and other hot entrees. Afternoon treats. Guests are welcome to bring their own alcoholic beverages, or special orders may be made.

Nearest Airport(s)
Portland-30 miles

Directions
I-95/Maine Turnpike to Exit 25(Kennebunk exit), turn L on Rte. 35 for 5 1/2 mi. L at light on Rte. 9 for 3/10 mi. R on Ocean Ave. for 9/10 mi. to Kings Hwy@Colony Hotel. Turn L. Follow road to "T" intersection go R up hill to Old Fort Avenue-3/10 mi. Inn on L.

One of Maine's exceptional Country Inns. Tucked away on 15 acres of immaculately maintained grounds and woodlands; the Inn has been described as "sophisticated, elegant, complete tranquility two minutes from the activities of downtown Kennebunkport"★. Just 1 block from the ocean, The Old Fort Inn offers the visiting guest a quiet atmosphere. The antique appointed guest rooms, rich in nostalgic ambience, are located in a turn-of-the-century carriage house of red brick and ocal stone. Done with a meticulous eye for detail, guest rooms are tastefully decorated with wonderful wall coverings and elegent fabrics, with either four-poster or canopy beds and down comforters. Some rooms have fireplaces and Jacuzzis. Amenities include A/C, phones, cable TV, enclosed honor bars, heated tile floors in all baths, a scrumptious buffet breakfast, afternoon treats, heated pool, tennis court and Antique Shop. The Inn is just 1-1/4 miles from the village and 5 minutes from two 18-hole golf courses. ★S. Schatzki–guest

Member Since 1976

"To recommend your Inn to our friends requires only one word, IMPECCABLE."

Hartwell House Inn & Conference Center

www.srinns.com/hartwell

312 Shore Rd., P.O. Box 1950, Ogunquit, ME 03907
800-235-8883 • 207-646-7210 • Fax 207-646-6032
innkeeper@hartwellhouseinn.com

Owners
James & Trisha Hartwell
Innkeepers
Paul & Gail Koehler
Elegant Village Breakfast Inn

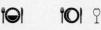

The romantic Hartwell House Inn, a 16-room inn and conference center, is located in the quaint town of Ogunquit, southern Maine. Open year-round and within easy reach of Boston (1-1/2 hours) and New York City (5 hours), the inn and conference center are steps from the beach, shopping and diverse four-season activities. The Marginal Way, a cliff walk bordering Ogunquit's rugged coastline, is steps from the Inn. Guests can park at the Inn and walk to the sweet village of Ogunquit or Perkins Cove for boating, fishing, boutiques and waterfront lobster dining. The Inn's intimate 36-seat restaurant, S.W. Swan Bistro, is across the street. "Antique Alley," Kittery and Freeport outlet shopping are an easy drive. The dedicated conference center offers private conference rooms accommodating groups from 12 to 75. Outstanding views, state-of-the-art equipment and a customized catering menu create an atmosphere conducive to productive thinking. The Inn offers a romantic site for off-season small weddings and celebrations.

Member Since 1981

Rooms/Rates
16 A/C guest rooms, suites and apartments, some with deck, kitchenette and/or sitting room with sofa bed, $120/$270. Open year-round. Weekly rates available.
Number of Rooms: 16

Cuisine
Complimentary full gourmet breakfast, afternoon tea with sweets and pastries. The inn's 36-seat restaurant serves French-inspired American Bistro cuisine.

Nearest Airport(s)
Portland International Jetport is 25 miles away.

Directions
From I-95N: exit 7 to Rte 1 N. 6.5 miles to R on Bourne Lane. R on Shore Rd. 1/4 mile to Inn on R. From I-95S: exit 19, L on Rte 109 E. R on Rte 1 S to Ogunquit. L on Shore Rd, .6 miles to Inn on R.

"Warm, relaxing, beautiful. We can't wait to come back!"
www.hartwellhouseinn.com

SelectRegistry.com

Dockside Guest Quarters

www.srinns.com/dockside
22 Harris Island Rd., York, ME 03909
800-270-1977 • 207-363-2868 • Fax 207-363-1977
info@docksidegq.com

Innkeepers/Owners
The Lusty Family

Traditional Waterside Inn

Rooms/Rates
19 rooms $96/$215, 6 suites
$193/$265. Off & Mid Season.
Packages available year-round. EP
Number of Rooms: 25

Cuisine
Dining on porch, overlooking
York Harbor, a favorite of locals
and visitors. Specialties: roast
duckling, bouillabaisse, lobster
dublin lawyer, grilled salmon
maison. Lunch & Dinner are
served in the restaurant. Breakfast
is available in the Maine House.

Nearest Airport(s)
Manchester, NH 1hr

Directions
From I-95 exit at York, ME (exit #7).
Go S on Rt 1. First traffic light, turn
L on Rte 1A. Follow 1A through
York Village and turn R on Rte 103.
Take the 1st L immediately after
bridge, follow signs.

The Dockside captures the essence of Maine with its natural
beauty, gracious hospitality, and abundant sights, recreation and
activities. Uniquely situated on a private peninsula overlooking
York Harbor and the Atlantic Ocean, each room has a panoramic
water view. Accommodations are in the Maine House, a classic
'New England cottage,' furnished with antiques and marine art,
and multi-unit buildings at the water's edge. Warmth and charm
are found throughout. The Dockside Restaurant boasts a water
view from every table. A creative menu specializes in fresh Maine
seafood.

AAA ◆◆◆   *Member Since 1975*   Mobil ★★★

"The location, serenity and warm hospitality makes this one of our favorites."

The Waterford Inne

www.srinns.com/water

Box 149, 258 Chadbourne Road, Waterford, ME 04088

207-583-4037 • Fax 207-583-4037

inne@gwi.net

Innkeeper/Owner
Barbara Vanderzanden

Traditional Country Inn

A 19th century farmhouse on a country lane midst 25 acres of fields and woods, distinctively different, a true country inn offering uniquely decorated guest rooms, a charming blend of two centuries – the warmth of early furnishings combined with contemporary comforts. An air of quiet simple elegance pervades the common rooms rich with antiques and art, pewter and primitives. An intimate library with an eclectic collection to appeal to all tastes--travel, nature, history... Step outside to explore the pleasures of country simplicity, to listen to the quiet or the songbirds, to smell the freshness of a summer morning or perhaps the winter fragrance of a woodburning fire. Wander through the gardens which provide a colorful array of flowers and a bounty of fresh fare for your dining table. Return inne-side to pamper your palate with country chic cuisine. The road to the Waterford Inne is traveled by hikers and cyclists, antiquers and skiers, discriminating travelers who delight in the charm and personal attention of a country inn.

Rooms/Rates
$100/$200 B&B; Open year-round.
Number of Rooms: 8

Cuisine
Breakfast included. Fine dinners available with advance reservation. Guests are welcome to bring their own spirits.

Nearest Airport(s)
Portland, ME

Directions
From ME Tpke: take Exit 63 to Rt. 26 N for 28 mi. into Norway, then Rt. 118 W for 9 mi. to Rt. 37. Turn L, go 1/2 mi. to Chadbourne Rd. Take R and go 1/2 mile up hill. From Conway NH: Rt. 16 to Rt. 302 E to Fryeburg, ME. Rt. 5 out of Fryeburg to Rt. 35 S, continue to left fork onto Rt. 118 E. for approx. 5 miles to Rt. 37. Turn R, go 1/2 mi. to Chadbourne Rd. Turn R and go 1/2 mile up hill.

Member Since 1979   Mobil ★★★

"The Waterford Inne was one of our inspirations to move to this area! Atmosphere: friendly! We were amazed by the care given to dinners--exquisite!"

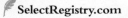

SelectRegistry.com

Maryland

"The Old Line State"

Famous For: Maryland Crabs, Chesapeake Bay, Ocean City, Atlantic Coast, River Valleys, Rolling Hills, Forests, Appalachian Mountains, Fort McHenry, Tobacco

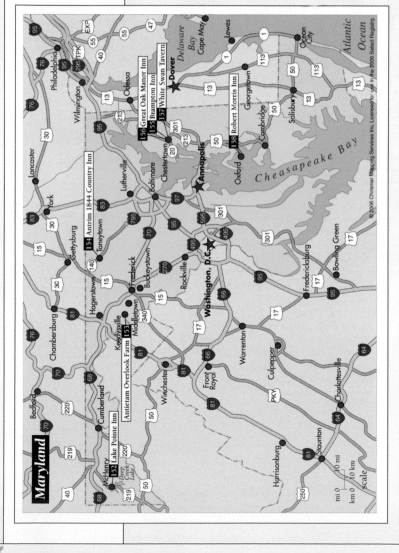

Lake Pointe Inn

www.srinns.com/lakepointe
174 Lake Pointe Drive, Deep Creek Lake, MD 21541
800-523-LAKE • 301-387-0111 • Fax 301-387-0190
relax@deepcreekinns.com

Innkeeper
Caroline McNiece

Traditional Waterside
Breakfast Inn

The Lake Pointe Inn decorated in the Arts & Crafts style, embraces you with an exceptionally warm welcome when you enter the chestnut paneled Great Room with it's Mission Style furnishings. Nestled in the Lake Pointe Community, in Western Maryland, the Inn is perched just 13 feet from water's edge. The wraparound porch invites you to relax in a rocking chair, read or watch the waterfowl frolic. It is easy to enjoy Garrett County's 4 season activities while staying at the Inn. Golf, skiing and snowboarding await you at the Wisp Resort, adjacent to the Lake Pointe Community. Tour the area using our complimentary canoes, kayaks and bicycles or hike in the 5 nearby State Parks. The outdoor fireplace, herb garden and hammock provide a perfect haven for private conversation or stargazing. Frank Lloyd Wright's Fallingwater and Kentuck Knob are nearby. Lake Pointe Inn is a perfect getaway in any season for any reason!

Rooms/Rates
8 Rooms $158/$259; 2 Suites $219/$269; Some amenities include: Fireplaces, Spa Tubs, Steam Shower, Sauna, CAC, TV/DVD, Bose CD player/alarm (MP3 aux.), Wireless internet, Private Telephone. Massage available. Closed Dec. 24, 25.
Number of Rooms: 10

Cuisine
Full breakfast & light hors d'oeuvres included in daily rate; dinners served to Inn guests on 3-day holiday weekends. Meeting space available 8-20 persons.

Nearest Airport(s)
Pittsburgh International

Directions
From I-68 in Western MD, take Rte 219 S for 12.5 mi.; R onto Sang Run Rd; 2 blocks, L onto Marsh Hill Rd., go 1/4 mile; L onto Lake Pointe Dr just past Wisp Resort.

Member Since 2000

16+

"This is the most relaxing place I have ever been... simply put, EXCEPTIONAL!"

SelectRegistry.com

Innkeepers/Owners
**Mark Svrcek and
Rudy Novak**

Traditional Mountain
Country Manor

Antietam Overlook Farm
www.srinns.com/antietam
4812 Porterstown Rd., Keedysville, MD 21756
800–878–4241 • 301–432–4200 • Fax 301–432–5230
Reservations@antietamoverlook.com

Rooms/Rates
6 Suites, $165/$325 B&B. Open year-round. Attractions: Antietam National Battlefield, Harpers Ferry, antiquing, Charlestown horse track, hiking, biking and relaxing. Complimentary beverages, wine & liqueurs.
Number of Rooms: 6

Cuisine
Unforgettable, three course country breakfast included. Fine dining nearby.

Nearest Airport(s)
Hagerstown airport is about 25 minutes away. Washington Dulles Airport about 1hr. away

Directions
Located in the Western Maryland Mountains about one hour from Baltimore and Washington, D.C. Call or check on-line for availability and booking. Directions sent with booking confirmation.

Our 95-acre mountaintop country manor inn overlooking Antietam National Battlefield has extraordinary views of four states. You will marvel at the hand-hewn timber framing and rough-sawn craftsmanship. Cozy fireplaces, fabulous furnishings and fine crystal create a warm, comfortable atmosphere. In the winter months, guests are invited to spend time in front of the grand fireplace where interesting conversation adds to the warmth. The views are spectacular year round, but in the spring and summer our large "Overlook" porch is wonderful. Spacious suites include fireplaces, sumptuous queen beds, stress relieving bubble baths, and private screened porches. While our seclusion and tranquility are unparalleled, many guests also enjoy visiting the Civil War battlefields at Gettysburg and Bull Run.

Member Since 1992

"Unbelievable food and quiet seclusion...ah!"
Visit us on-line at www.AntietamOverlook.com

Antrim 1844 Country Inn

www.srinns.com/antrim
30 Trevanion Road, Taneytown, MD 21787
800-858-1844 • 410-756-6812 • Fax 410-756-2744
info@antrim1844.com

Proprietors
Dorothy and Richard Mollett
General Manager
John Vonnes
Elegant Country Inn

One of the most prestigious inns in the country, Antrim 1844 is near Baltimore and Washington, DC, and just 12 miles from historic Gettysburg. Set on 24 acres of rolling Maryland countryside, Antrim's mansion, dependencies and other outbuildings have been restored to their antebellum grandeur. Each guestroom or suite is individually appointed with feather beds and antique furnishings. Fireplaces, Jacuzzis, decks, high speed internet and luxurious baths abound. Expect exquisite dining and incredible wines in an old-world setting. Enjoy outdoor swimming, tennis and croquet amid Antrim's elaborate formal gardens. Golf, historic tour and special getaway packages are also available.

Rooms/Rates
29 Guest Rooms and Suites, $160/$375. Open year-round. Activities: Gettysburg, Baltimore & Washington attractions, golfing, antiquing, hiking, biking, swimming, tennis.
Number of Rooms: 29

Cuisine
Afternoon tea. Evening hors d'ouevres. Elegant 6-course prix fixe dinner $65. Morning wake up tray at your door, plus full country breakfast. Full bar and 1200-selection wine list.

Nearest Airport(s)
BWI

Directions
From Wash DC: I-495 to I-270W; 15N to 140E to Taneytown through light; 1 block & bear R on Trevanion Rd. From Balt/BWI: I-695N to I-795W to 140W to Taneytown; L on Trevanion Rd.

Member Since 1993

"Perfection in every way," "magnificent," "opulent," "superb." *Zagat* Survey

 SelectRegistry.com

Innkeepers/Owners
Danielle and Michael Hanscom
Innkeeper
Rita Scardino

Elegant Country Breakfast Inn

Brampton Inn

www.srinns.com/brampton

25227 Chestertown Road, Chestertown, MD 21620

866-305-1860 • 410-778-1860 • Fax None

innkeeper@bramptoninn.com

Rooms/Rates
8 rooms, $175/$295; 2 Cottage Suites, $255/$295. Spacious rooms, simple elegance, wood-burning fireplaces, whirlpools. Open year-round.
Number of Rooms: 10

Cuisine
Full gourmet breakfast with individual table service. Afternoon Tea.

Nearest Airport(s)
Baltimore (BWI)and Philadelphia (PHL)

Directions
0.9 miles outside of Chestertown on Route 20 West.

The Brampton Bed and Breakfast Inn is Maryland's Eastern Shore romantic oasis, located on 20 wooded acres, just one mile outside the charming town of Chestertown, Maryland. Brampton B&B Inn brilliantly blends the grand elegance of a historical estate with the comfort and modern amenities today's stressed-out travelers crave.

Ignite or rekindle romance in one of our spacious and well-appointed guest rooms, offering wood-burning fireplaces, whirlpool tubs and glorious views. Enjoy a full country breakfast, lovingly prepared and graciously served at individual tables in Brampton Inn's beautiful dining room. Attention to detail, personal service, and friendly innkeepers will make your visit a relaxed and memorable one.

Chestertown, Maryland with the state's second highest concentration of eighteenth century homes, is a colonial village with abundant activities, and serves as a perfect base for exploring all that Maryland's Eastern Shore has to offer. "Meticulously restored, in a pastoral setting..." *The New York Times.*

Member Since 2001

12+

"The Brampton Inn is the perfect setting to relax, rejuvenate and to remember the important things in life"

Great Oak Manor

www.srinns.com/greatoak
10568 Cliff Road, Chestertown, MD 21620
800-504-3098 • 410-778-5943 • Fax 410-810-2517
innkeeper@greatoak.com

Innkeepers/Owners
Cassandra & John Fedas

Elegant Waterside
Manor House

F. Scott Fitzgerald wrote of blue lawns and country houses such is Great Oak Manor. From the estate's walled garden bordered by 65-year old boxwoods and its circular drive on the estate side, to its magnificent view of the Chesapeake Bay and private beach on the water side, this country estate provides the appropriate setting for a relaxing getaway and a weekend of romance. Our guest and public rooms are spacious and beautifully furnished. Built at a time when grandeur was more important than cost, guests are swept away by the majesty of the house. This is a true Manor House with fine details, beautiful furnishings, Orientals, and an 850 volume library to browse. We offer complimentary 9-hole golf, tennis, a swimming pool, and a private beach. The Manor will meet your every need, with 1200 feet of waterfront on the Chesapeake Bay, and the most beautiful sunsets on the Eastern Shore of Maryland. Our newest addition, the "Conservatory," which overlooks the Bay, is popular for small business retreats or family reunions.

Rooms/Rates
9 rooms, $140/$275, 3 suites, $190/$275. Elegant spacious rooms, fireplaces, gracious public rooms. Massage Therapy available.
Number of Rooms: 12

Cuisine
Complete & Scrumptous Breakfast. Individual Egg dishes or French Toast daily, "Manor" baked muffins, & fresh fruits year round. Afternoon refreshments, snacks, & complimentary coffee, tea, water, & soda. Evening Port & Sherry.

Nearest Airport(s)
BWI,PHL

Directions
8.5 mi. from High St. Chestertown Rt. 514 N. past pastoral fields until you reach the Chesapeake Bay.

Member Since 2003

"Gracious, lovely ambiance. Thank you for your peaceful refuge that catered to all of our senses."

 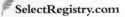

Innkeepers/General
Managers
**Mary Susan Maisel,
Wayne McGuire**

Elegant In Town Breakfast
Inn

White Swan Tavern

www.srinns.com/whiteswan
231 High Street, Chestertown, MD 21620
410-778-2300 • Fax 410-778-4543
info@whiteswantavern.com

Rooms/Rates
4 Rooms, $140/$180; 2 Suites,
$210 & $240. Open All Year
Number of Rooms: 6

Cuisine
Complimentary Continental
breakfast, afternoon tea, fruit
basket. Fine restaurants and cafes
within walking distance.

Nearest Airport(s)
Baltimore, Philadelphia,
Washington

Directions
Rte. 213 to Chestertown. W on
Cross St. L on High St. White
Swan on R. Ring doorbell. Off
street parking in rear off Cannon
Street.

The White Swan has been a familiar landmark in Chestertown
since pre-revolutionary days. Close to the great Eastern cities,
yet quietly nestled in the history of Maryland's eastern shore,
the Inn is for those who treasure serene streets, birdsong mornings, impeccable service and the grace of New World tradition.
All rooms are elegantly appointed with antiques, reproductions
and artwork within a museum quality restoration. Guests enjoy
working fireplaces in our common rooms, a lovely garden terrace
and meadow, central heat, air conditioning, and off street parking.
Experience the historic feeling of this special place.

Here, our forefathers and their families gathered to share ideas and
to draft a way of life that continues today in the spirit of timeless values. Take a refreshing scenic walk to the Chester River
waterfront two easy blocks away, shop for collectables or quality
gifts, browse the many galeries and studios of master craftsmen
and artists, dine is a variety of settings around town. Relax and
restore yourselves.

Member Since 2001

12+ 🚭 ♿ 💳 🛈 📁 ❤️   🖐 @   📺   ❄️

"A picturesque, delightful, comfortable and tastefully decorated place. We'll be
back!" "A lovely Inn, warm & welcoming." "Remarkable place, love it."

Robert Morris Inn

www.srinns.com/BestCrabCakesOvernight
314 N. Morris St., P.O. Box 70, Oxford, MD 21654
888-823-4012 • 410-226-5111 • Fax 410-226-5744
robertmorrisinn@webtv.net

Innkeeper/Active Owners
Jay Gibson, Wendy & Ken Gibson

Traditional Colonial
Waterside Inn

Come to our country romantic (1710) inn and step back in time. Explore the Chesapeake Bay and all the unique things the Eastern Shore of Maryland has to offer. We are indeed the "Land of Pleasant Living." Guests staying overnight can choose between accommodations at our historic Main Inn or Sandaway Lodge where many rooms have porches overlooking the river and beach. We tell guests they have two choices for activities. One, you can take the scenic car ferry across the river for a short-cut to St. Michaels (6 mile drive) and then explore the nearby towns of Tilghman and Easton. We call this "doing the loop." Second choice is to find yourself a lounge or adirondack chair at the Sandaway property to linger away the day watching workboats, sailboats, yachts and wildlife go by. After seeing a fabulous sunset, just walk up Lovers Lane to the inn for a relaxing dinner. James Michener, author of "Chesapeake" used to frequent our inn and wrote the outline for his book in the tavern. He rated our crab cakes the best of any restaurant on the Eastern Shore. We now ship crab cakes nationwide! To order call 1-866-MICHENER (642-4363). For more information visit www.BestCrabCakes.com or www.SurfandTurf.com - Better Than Lobster TM.

Member Since 1970

Rooms/Rates
$110/$290 EP. Historical & Waterfront. Mid-week reduced.
Number of Rooms: 34

Cuisine
March Weekends, Season Apr-Nov Breakfast & Lunch Daily, Dinner Thur-Mon (Breakfast not included in rate). Dining room w/historic murals, rustic tap room, colonial tavern. Full-service bar. Specialty drinks, beer & wine.

Nearest Airport(s)
BWI & National - 1.5 hours.
Dulles - 2 hrs. 15 min.

Directions
Hwy 301 to Rte 50 E. Turn R on Rte 322 for 3.4 mi, turn R on Rte 333 for 9.6 mi. 1 hr from Annapolis, 1 1/2 hrs from DC, 1 3/4 hrs from Baltimore, 2 1/2 hrs from Philadelphia. Speed limit in Oxford 25 mph and is strictly enforced.

"Best crab cakes, a place to fall in love again, ask for the surf and turf, great river views, romantic...a walk back into a more relaxed time."

Massachusetts

"The Bay State"

Famous For: Pilgrims, Thanksgiving, Salem Witch Trials, Boston Tea Party, Birth of the American Revolution, Minutemen, Freedom Trail, Swan Boats, Cape Cod, Education, Arts, Technology, and Medicine.

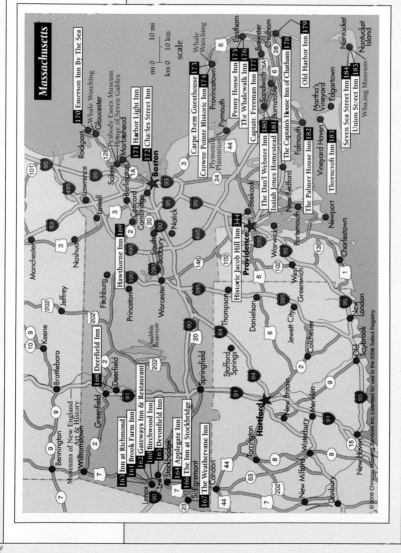

Birchwood Inn

www.srinns.com/birchwood
7 Hubbard Street, P.O. Box 2020, Lenox, MA 01240
800-524-1646 • 413-637-2600 • Fax 413-637-4604
innkeeper@birchwood-inn.com

Innkeeper/Owner
Ellen Gutman Chenaux

Historic Village
Breakfast Inn

paii

Experience comfortable country elegance at Birchwood Inn. The oldest home in Lenox has been welcoming friends since 1767. Its tranquil hilltop setting is a short walk from the village's celebrated restaurants, shops and galleries, while year-round culture -- including Tanglewood, the summer home of the Boston Symphony -- and recreation are a stone's throw away. The Colonial Revival mansion's antiques, collectibles, quilts, canopy beds, and nine fireplaces create the idyllic ambience for a romantic getaway. Renown for sumptuous breakfasts and afternoon tea, the inn offers blossoms in stone-fenced gardens in spring, Berkshire breezes and fireflies on the gracious porch in summer, vibrant foliage on the doorstep in autumn, and the welcoming warmth of firesides in winter.

Rooms/Rates
$125/$295. Rates change seasonally. Distinctly & comfortably decorated guestrooms, 6 w/ fireplaces & TV, antiques, private bath, air-conditioning, hairdryer, outgoing telephone, free wireless Internet access. Open year-round.
Number of Rooms: 11

Cuisine
Fireside "best breakfast in New England," featuring seasonal fruit dish, homemade breads, & hot entrée served at individual tables. Afternoon tea w/homemade pastries.

Nearest Airport(s)
Albany and Hartford airports

Directions
Mass Pike (I-90), Exit 2, Rte. 20W for 4 mi., L at 1st light (183/7A), bear R at monument, up the hill, R on Hubbard.

Member Since 2003

12+

"Wonderfully romantic! Thank you for memories we will cherish forever."

Brook Farm Inn

Innkeepers/Owners
Linda and Phil Halpern

Elegant Victorian Village
Breakfast Inn

www.brookfarm.com
15 Hawthorne Street, Lenox, MA 01240
800-285-7638 • 413-637-3013 • Fax 413-637-4751
innkeeper@brookfarm.com

Rooms/Rates
$120/$395 B&B. Furnished w/antiques, canopy beds. 9 w/fireplaces, some w/whirlpool tubs, all with A/C, hairdryers, phones. Heated outdoor pool. Open year-round. WIFI access.
Number of Rooms: 15

Cuisine
Full breakfast and afternoon tea with homemade scones. Well-stocked guest pantry with refrigerators, ice, instant hot water, tea, coffee, hot chocolate, and homemade cookies.

Nearest Airport(s)
Albany, NY and Hartford, CT

Directions
Mass. Tpke. (I-90), exit 2, R on Rte. 20W 5 miles, to L on Rte. 183, 1 mile to Town Hall, sharp L on Old Stockbridge Rd., 2/10 mi then R on Hawthorne St.

There is poetry here. Nestled in a wooded glen, Brook Farm, a Victorian inn surrounded by award-winning gardens, is just a short walk to historic Lenox village. Built in 1882, and furnished with antiques, the inn features a library filled with poetry, history and literature, where the sounds of classical music can be heard. Brook Farm is close to Tanglewood and all Berkshire cultural attractions. Your friendly hosts offer gracious hospitality and assistance in planning a memorable Berkshires vacation. The sumptuous buffet breakfasts are unsurpassed. Seasonal activities include downhill and xc-skiing, hiking, antiquing and museum tours. Special winter packages are offered. Attractions: Tanglewood, Berkshire Theatre Festival, Rockwell Museum, Shakespeare & Co., Hancock Shaker Village, Clark Art Institute.

AAA ◆◆◆   *Member Since 2001*   Mobil ★★★

"There is poetry here" is indeed a most fitting expression of what the Inn and the innkeepers are all about...beauty and romance...warmth and hospitality.

Gateways Inn

www.srinns.com/gatewaysinn
51 Walker Street, Lenox, MA 01240
888-492-9466 • 413-637-2532 • Fax 413-637-1432
gateways@berkshire.net

Innkeepers/Owners
Fabrizio and Rosemary Chiariello

Elegant In Town Inn

🍴 🍴 🍴 ♉

Wine Spectator
AWARD OF EXCELLENCE

Gateways Inn, a turn-of-the-century neoclassical mansion built for Harley Procter, offers European hospitality in an elegant setting—a relaxing atmosphere, in the center of town. The beauty of Stanford White's staircase and Tiffany-style rose windows enhance the building. The inn features charming rooms, each uniquely decorated with antiques, many with fireplaces and modern amenities including centralized air-conditioning, TV, phones with dataport and voice mail. The aroma of fresh-brewed coffee and warm croissants fills the air each morning, as guests awake to breakfast and to another day of being pampered by the owners and staff. Our award-winning Bar offers the largest selection of Single Malt and Grappas in the country and is also famous for special cocktails. After theater, light meals are served until midnight. By request, we can organize balloon trips, massages, personal guided hiking, biking and fly fishing excursions. (One week minimum advance notice needed).

Member Since 2001

Rooms/Rates
11 Rooms, $100/$190; 1 Suite, $230/$350. Antiques, 4-poster canopy & sleigh beds. Peak season premium.
Number of Rooms: 12

Cuisine
Full breakfast and elegant, yet casual, dining Tues-Sun. After-theatre desserts & light meals available. Open to the general public. Extensive selection of American & Italian wines & a fully-stocked bar.

Nearest Airport(s)
Albany, NY

Directions
Boston: I-90 W to Lee, exit 2. R on Rte. 20 W.—stay on until intersect Rte. 183 S. L onto Rte.183 S (Walker St.). 1 mi. on R. New York: Taconic Pkwy. to I-90E, exit 2 Lee (as above).

☺ 🚭 💳🛈📁❤ ✍@ 🧺 ◎

"Charming, a little bit of Europe right here. A memorable weekend. We got engaged!"

Carl M. Dunham, Jr.
Innkeeper/Owner

Historic Country
Inn

The Inn at Richmond

www.srinns.com/innatrichmond

802 State Road (Route 41), Richmond, MA 01254

888-968-4748 • 413-698-2566 • Fax 413 698-2100

innkeepers@innatrichmond.com

Rooms/Rates

9 Rooms, Suites, Cottages. $180/$380. Weekly rates, special packages. A/C, Cable TV & VCR/CD, wireless internet access; phones; some fireplaces, whirlpools, kitchens, decks. Open year-round
Number of Rooms: 9

Cuisine

The innkeeper/staff prepares a sumptuous country continental plus breakfast featuring locally grown foods and innovative seasonal specialties. Complimentary beverages and sweets are offered.

Nearest Airport(s)

Albany and Hartford

Directions

NYC-Taconic Pkwy Rte 295 Exit, right to Rte 41, left 1 mile to inn. Boston-I90 Exit 1, N 7 mi. on Rte 102/41 to inn.

This Inn is nestled in the countryside just west of Tanglewood and Lenox on 27 exquisite acres with gardens, meadows, and woodland paths and is the home of the prestigious Berkshire Equestrian Center. The 1770s Main House and surrounding structures have been restored preserving the 18th and 19th Century architectural details. Modern amenities have been discreetly introduced for comfort and luxury. All accomodations are individually decorated with antiques, heirlooms and fine reproductions. Children are welcomed in the cottages. The innkeeper offers many unique special touches to ensure a memorable visit. Guests delight in gathering in the evenings to enjoy cocktails and conversation. Further indulgences might include a massage or a horseback riding lesson, requested in advance. Amidst the perennial gardens, the Inn is a perfect setting for retreats, conferences or weddings.

AAA ◆◆◆   *Member Since 2006*

"Charming, hospitable, beautifully decorated, and delicious breakfasts. With the Berkshire Equestrian Center, the inn offers a unique experience."

Applegate Inn

www.srinns.com/applegate
279 West Park Street, Lee, MA 01238
800-691-9012 • 413-243-4451 • Fax 413-243-9832
lenandgloria@applegateinn.com

Owners/Innkeepers
Gloria and Len Friedman

Elegant Country Breakfast Inn

paii

Once inside the iron gate, the circular drive, lined with lilac bushes reveals this elegant 1920s white-pillared Georgian mansion. It is situated on a 6 acre country estate across the road from a golf and tennis club one-half mile from the historic town of Lee and about 3 miles from Stockbridge. The inn's spacious public rooms are furnished with antiques and antique reproductions. The 11 guest accommodations are uniquely decorated and luxuriously appointed. From the screened porch look beyond the heated swimming pool to the lawns, towering trees and gardens. This is tranquility itself—a relaxing place to rejuvenate while pampered with attentive service, candlelit breakfasts, and wine and cheese served each afternoon. Explore Tanglewood, theater, dance, Norman Rockwell Museum, golf, tennis, hiking, swimming, boating, skiing, antiquing, shopping and other natural and cultural wonders of the Berkshires, or linger at the inn by a roaring fire, rest in a hammock for two under an old apple tree, or stroll the perennial gardens.

Rooms/Rates
Rooms $120/$250; Suites $200/$360; Cottage $200/$340. Central AC, TV, VCR, CD, many with fireplace, jacuzzi, mini-fridge, balcony and patio. One room has a steam shower for two. All have robes, hair dryer, phone, fresh flowers, brandy & chocolate. Gift shop.
Number of Rooms: 11

Cuisine
Multi-course gourmet candlelit breakfast served on china & crystal. Wine & cheese served in the afternoon. Fruit bowl, cookie jar & guest pantry always available.

Nearest Airport(s)
Albany Int'l & Bradley Airports

Directions
I-90 to Exit 2 (Lee); Rte. 20 W to stop sign. Go straight .5 mile on L, across from Greenock Country Club.

AAA ◆◆◆ *Member Since 2002*

12+

"A lovely place for relaxation and gracious hospitality - a perfect 10!"

Innkeepers/Owners
Ronnie & Bruce Singer

Elegant Country Inn

Devonfield Country Inn B & B
www.srinns.com/devonfield
85 Stockbridge Road., Lee, MA 01238
800-664-0880 • 413-243-3298 • Fax 413-243-1360
innkeeper@devonfield.com

Rooms/Rates
6 Rooms; 3 Suites; 1 Guest Cottage.
Mid-week: $140/$210; In Season:
$180/$260. Weekend: $180/$260; In
Season: $225/$325
Number of Rooms: 10

Cuisine
Full gourmet breakfast.

Nearest Airport(s)
Bradley, CT (63 mi); Albany (45)

Directions
From NY: Taconic Pkwy to Hillsdale,
NY; Rte 23 E to Great Barrington, MA;
Rte 7 N to Stockbridge. At stop, R on
Main. L @ fire station, continue on
Rte 7 for .8 mi. R on Lee (becomes
Stockbridge Rd) & go 1.9 mi. Inn on
R. From Mass Pike: Ex 2 off Pike. Af-
ter toll, R to Lee (Rte 20/Housatonic).
Follow into town to stop. (Landmarks:
park on R & Carr Hardware on L)
Straight on W. Park (Stockbridge) for
.9 mi. Inn on L.

Built in 1800, Devonfield is set on a 29 acre pastoral meadow shaded by graceful birch trees, with the rolling tapestry of the Berkshire Hills beyond. The main house is beautifully appointed with period antiques and also includes a guest pantry that is always fully stocked with coffee, tea, hot chocolate, popcorn and fresh baked cookies. A full sized refrigerator is available should you choose to bring any special refreshments. Devonfield's guest accommodations are all spacious, with private baths that include hairdryers and make-up mirrors. Quilts, down comforters, plush sheets, towels and TV/VCRS are in every room. Many have wood-burning fireplaces and some have Jacuzzis and include fine terry robes. All rooms have complimentary cognac, hand-made chocolates and bottled water. You'll start your day with a delicious full country breakfast that proudly features food items that are locally grown and/or prepared. Dine accompanied by classical music and by candlelight (or fireside during the fall and winter months). Picnic baskets are also available. Devonfield has its own exercise room, tennis court and 20' X 40' heated pool and Greenock Golf Club is a "6 iron away."

Member Since 2003 Mobil ★★★★

"From the moment we stepped in to this elegant English country inn, we felt at home. The innkeepers were welcoming and warm."

The Inn at Stockbridge

www.srinns.com/innatstockbridge
RTE 7N, Box 618, Stockbridge, MA 01262
888-466-7865 • 413-298-3337 • Fax 413-298-3406
innkeeper@stockbridgeinn.com

Innkeepers/Owners
Alice & Len Schiller
Manager
Annette Perelli
Elegant
Village Breakfast Inn

Enjoy peaceful charm and elegance in a 1906 Georgian style mansion secluded on 12 acres in Stockbridge, a town described by Norman Rockwell as the best of New England and the best of America. Awaken to the aroma of fresh coffee, stroll the beautiful grounds, take a dip in the heated pool, exercise in the fitness room, relax on the wrap around porch and take time away from the cares of the world. Antiques, collectibles and luxury are very much at home here. Amenities and attention to detail found only in upscale properties for the discriminating traveler await you here. Fireplace and double whirlpool rooms with a private deck are available. Voted by the Discerning Traveler as one of the Most Romantic Inns for 2005. Centrally located to all Berkshire cultural attractions including the Norman Rockwell Museum and Tanglewood.

Rooms/Rates
8 Rooms $140/$275-8 Fireplace and/or Whirlpool Suites $225/$375 Rates vary by room and season.
Number of Rooms: 16

Cuisine
Gourmet candlelit breakfast. Complimentary wine and cheese. Self service butlers pantry with snacks and beverages. Complimentary bottled water.

Nearest Airport(s)
Albany,NY-Hartford,CT

Directions
MA Pike to exit 2, W on Rte 102 to Route 7N 1.2 miles to Inn on Rt. From NYC: Saw Mill Pkwy N to Taconic Pkwy N to Rte 23E to MA to Rte 7N past Stockbridge village 1.2 m N. From NJ: NYS Thruway (RT 87N) to exit 17 to Rt 84E to Taconic State Parkway N. Follow above from NY.

AAA ◆◆◆   *Member Since 1986*   Mobil ★★★

12+

"Wonderful as always. Great hospitality, breakfast and a wonderful time. Loved the poodle. Excellent, elegant, beautiful, comfortable & delicious."

Innkeepers/Owners
Jeffrey and Maxine Lome

Traditional Village Breakfast Inn

The Weathervane Inn

www.srinns.com/weathervaneinn
17 Main Street, Route 23, South Egremont, MA 01258
800-528-9580 • 413-528-9580 • Fax 413 528-1713
innkeeper@weathervaneinn.com

Rooms/Rates
Guestrooms: $115/$200. Suites: $225/$300.
Number of Rooms: 11

Cuisine
Full Country Breakfast each morning and afternoon tea. Dinner available to parties of ten or more by prior arrangement. We have a Liquor License and sell and serve a variety of beverages.

Nearest Airport(s)
Albany, NY - 1 hour
Hartford/Bradley, CT - 90 miles

Directions
From NYC: Taconic Pkwy to Rte. 23 E 13 miles to Inn on R. From Mass Tpke: exit 2 to Rte. 102 to Rte. 7 S to Rte. 23 W to Inn on L.

Nestled in the quaint and historic village of South Egremont, this charming landmark Country Inn has been offering gracious hospitality to visitors to the Berkshires for over 18 years. The Lome family invites you to enjoy all the Berkshires has to offer in the comfort of our ten charming and beautifully-appointed guest rooms. We offer a bountiful country breakfast to start your day and a fireside tea for your relaxation after a full day of activities. The Berkshires offer four seasons of cultural and recreational activities including Tanglewood summer stock, historic homes, hiking, skiing and antiquing. Our newly renovated barn offers Yoga, Chikitsa, and Swadhyaya classes. You can also schedule a private Bodywork or Massage session. Please call for more details. Rekindle your romance and get away from it all at the Weathervane.

AAA ◆◆◆   *Member Since 1984*

Deerfield Inn

www.srinns.com/deerfieldinn
81 Old Main Street, Deerfield, MA 01342-0305
800-926-3865 • 413-774-5587 • Fax 413-775-7221
info@deerfieldinn.com

Innkeepers
Karl & Jane Sabo

Traditional Federal
Village Inn

One of the few original country inns in the northeast, this classic hostelry opened its doors in July 1884, despite a plague of grasshoppers devouring its way across a drought-stricken county. Located along a charming mile-long way known simply as "The Street," the Deerfield Inn is still the centerpiece of Old Deerfield with 11 rooms in the main inn and 12 in the south wing. A National Historic Landmark, this unspoiled 350-year-old village is a perfect destination for those looking for the real New England. Enjoy Deerfield's farms, museums, attractions, country walks, boutique shops, friendly folk, and beautiful scenery. Dinner at the Inn is a well-deserved reward after a busy day of touring, antiquing, and browsing. We look forward to welcoming you here.

Rooms/Rates
$173/$277 DBL. Rates include tea, full country breakfast, waitstaff gratuity, state & local taxes. Rates, availability, reservations, packages, available on our website. AAA discount. Open year-round except Dec. 23-26.
Number of Rooms: 23

Cuisine
Relaxing, friendly restaurant using local, seasonal produce fresh from the field, orchard, and stream. Convivial tavern, good selection of single malts, local beers, and wide-ranging wine list.

Nearest Airport(s)
Bradley Field, CT

Directions
FROM NYC: 3.5 hrs. I-91 N to exit 24. Follow signs to Historic Deerfield. FROM BOSTON 2 hrs. I-90 W to Exit 4 & I-91 N to exit 24.

AAA ◆◆◆   *Member Since 1996*   Mobil ★★★

"Visiting Deerfield is like stepping back in time.
We love the inn, our home away from home."

Innkeepers/Owners
Gregory Burch and Marilyn Mudry

Traditional Village
Breakfast Inn

Hawthorne Inn

www.srinns.com/hawthorn

462 Lexington Road, Concord, MA 01742-3729

978-369-5610 • Fax 978-287-4949

Inn@ConcordMass.com

Rooms/Rates
Seven graciously appointed guestrooms offering Canopy or Four-poster Bed. $105/$305. Recognized by *Forbes* Magazine "10 Best Inns of New England."
Number of Rooms: 7

Cuisine
Breakfast is served each morning, around a convivial common table, on hand-painted Dedham Pottery. Inn guests enjoy a robust selection of fresh-baked breads, breakfast cakes, specialty jams, seasonal fruit offerings and fresh-roasted organic coffee.

Nearest Airport(s)
Logan Airport/Boston

Directions
From Rte 128-95: take exit 30 B (Rte 2A West) for 2.8 miles. Bear Right at fork, go toward Concord for 1.5 miles. Inn is opposite Hawthorne's home.

Just 19 miles from Boston, three rivers wend through a Colonial landscape of Minutemen's fields where lichen-covered walls embrace the homes of Hawthorne, Alcott and Emerson. Under shade of ancient trees you find the Hawthorne Inn an intimate refuge filled with much to share: poetry and literature to entertain and enlighten you, artworks and archaic artifacts that are a wonder to behold, weavings and coverlets to snuggle on a crisp autumn eve and burnished antique furnishings that speak of home and security. Vibrant guestrooms, inspired by a refreshing sense of tradition melded with an artist's whimsy, are highlighted with wonderful colors to rest the soul and warm the heart.

AAA ◆◆◆   *Member Since 1980*   Mobil ★★★

"Everything about our stay was wonderful, with beautiful accommodations and gracious hosts."

Emerson Inn By The Sea

www.srinns.com/emersoninn
One Cathedral Avenue, Rockport, MA 01966
800-964-5550 • 978-546-6321 • Fax 978-546-7043
info@EmersonInnByTheSea.com

Innkeepers/Owners
Bruce and Michele Coates
General Manager
Jennifer Messier
Traditional Waterside Inn

Ralph Waldo Emerson called the Inn "Thy proper summer home." Today's guests enjoy the relaxed 19th Century atmosphere from our broad oceanfront veranda, but can savor the 21st Century amenities of a heated outdoor pool, sauna, room phones, air conditioning, television, private baths and spa tubs. Nearby are hiking trails along the oceanfront, tennis, golf, sea kayaking, scuba diving and the always popular whale watches. Halibut Point State Park features the history of the Rockport Quarries and downtown Rockport is famous for shops and art galleries. The historic Emerson is the ideal ocean front location for weddings, retreats and conferences. "Editors Pick," *Yankee Travel Guide to New England*. And as featured in Zagat's *2005 & 2006 Top U.S. Hotels, Resorts, and Spas.*

Rooms/Rates
36 Rooms, $99/$350 B&B; Rooms with ocean views, spa tubs, fireplaces. Two Seaside Cottages, each accommodates 8, available for a weekly rental. Open all year.
Number of Rooms: 38

Cuisine
Award-winning Restaurant. 'Unparalleled ambiance' - *The Boston Globe*. Outdoor oceanfront dining and elegant turn-of-the-century dining room serving breakfast daily; dinner and live music schedules vary by season.

Nearest Airport(s)
Boston Logan International Airport

Directions
Rte. 128 N to traffic light in Gloucester L on Rte.127 to Pigeon Cove. R at our sign on Phillips Ave.

AAA ◆◆◆   *Member Since 1973*   Mobil ★★★

"Lovely view of sunrise, comfortable bed, lots of pillows; it was perfectly wonderful."

Innkeepers/Owners
Peter & Suzanne Conway

Elegant
In Town Inn

Harbor Light Inn
www.srinns.com/harborlight
58 Washington Street, Marblehead, MA 01945
781-631-2186 • Fax 781-631-2216
info@harborlightinn.com

Rooms/Rates
21 Rooms, $145/$345; Suites, $195/$345 B&B. Open year-round.
Number of Rooms: 21

Cuisine
Breakfast buffet. 7 restaurants within 2 blocks of Inn. Wine & liquor within 2 blocks of Inn.

Nearest Airport(s)
Boston Logan International

Directions
From Boston & airport: take Rt. 1A N to Rt. 129 E to Marblehead. Take first R at Hunneman Caldwell Banker Real Estate, onto Washington St. Follow approx 1/3 mile to Inn.

Winner of numerous national awards for excellence, including *Vacation* magazine's "America's Best Romantic Inns." The Inn offers first-class accommodations and amenities found in the finest of lodging facilities. Elegant furnishings grace these two connected Federalist mansions. Formal fireplaced parlors, dining room and bed chambers, double Jacuzzis, sundecks, patio, quiet garden and outdoor heated pool combine to ensure the finest in New England hospitality. Located in the heart of historic Harbor District of fine shops, art galleries and restaurants.

AAA ◆◆◆   *Member Since 1996*   Mobil ★★★

12+

"Impeccable accommodations out done only by the staff and their eagerness to please!"

Charles Street Inn

www.srinns.com/charlesstreet
94 Charles St., Boston, MA 02114
877-772-8900 • 617-314-8900 • Fax 617-371-0009
info@charlesstreetinn.com

Innkeepers/Owners
Sally Deane & Louise Venden

Historic Beacon Hill B&B

A luxury inn located in historic Beacon Hill within blocks of Boston's shopping, touring, and subway stops, the Charles Street Inn offers unique comfort and privacy in nine spacious rooms with elevator access. Each room features a private bath with whirlpool tubs, working marble fireplaces, fresh flowers, BOSE radio/CD player, Cable TV, VCR, DVD, HVAC controls, DSL and Wireless Internet, and Sub-Zero refrigerator. Authentic Victorian-era antiques, king & queen size canopy and sleigh beds, and rich imported linens complete each elegant setting. Relax in front of a fire or enjoy any of the fabulous restaurants that are literally steps from the inn. Recognized among Boston's Best by *Travel + Leisure, Boston Magazine*, and as one of the top 10 romantic inns in the US by America's Historic Inns. Concierge services available.

Rooms/Rates
9 Rooms. $225/$425 depending on room, season, and day of the week. Call for rates (US toll-free 877-772-8900) or visit "Reservations" on our web site.
Number of Rooms: 9

Cuisine
Arrive to sweets, fresh fruit, snacks and refreshments in the lobby and in your room (kitchenette w/dishes, tea kettle, coffee pot and mini-fridge). Then, schedule your in-room breakfast with so many choices we call it "deluxe continental".

Nearest Airport(s)
Boston

Directions
Find Storrow Drive & take Gov't Ctr Exit. Turn S onto Charles Street and go 2 blocks.

Member Since 2004

"A business executive, tired of waiting for elevators in larger chain hotels might find solace here." *Washington Post*

Carpe Diem Guesthouse

Innkeepers/Owners
Rainer Horn, Jürgen Herzog, Hans van Costenoble

Historic Village Breakfast Inn

www.srinns.com/carpediem
12 Johnson Street, Provincetown, MA 02657-2312
800-487-0132 • 508-487-4242 • Fax 508-487-0138
info@carpediemguesthouse.com

Rooms/Rates
14 rooms and suites, $95/$345. Open year round.
Number of Rooms: 14

Cuisine
Jürgen's homemade German-style breakfast is famous. The family-size dining table is the meeting point for all guests who like a good cup of coffee, German bread, cakes, Belgian waffles, quiche, omelets or other specials. Afternoon wine & cheese hour and refreshments.

Nearest Airport(s)
Boston & Providence

Directions
Entering Provincetown on Rt. 6 take the second L at the street light. Go down Conwell Street which ends at Bradford Street. Take a R and Johnson Street is your first L.

Seize the day – make your Provincetown stay extraordinary! The Carpe Diem is an intimate Cape Cod Guesthouse and a romantic hideaway combined with luxurious amenities and personal service. Quietly located in the center of town each room is named after a renowned writer, decorated with European antiques and ambience and offers private bath, queen size bed, down bedding, bathrobes and luxury products. Some feature fireplaces, whirlpool tubs, private entrance and/or private patios. Our garden is a green oasis with a heated spa. Let classical music carry you away along a journey of the heart and imagination. Enjoy our homemade gourmet breakfast and join us for our daily Wine and Cheese hour. The common rooms are a great place to relax, read a good book, meet people or chat with new friends. There is a fireplace, video library, complimentary Sherry and Port, a 24-hour coffee station as well as a guest office for those that need to stay connected to the "real" world. And for those who like the excitement of shopping and nightlife, Commercial Street, the pulsating lifeline of Provincetown, is only steps away. Carpe Diem – a magical place on the edge of the continent!

Member Since 2003

12+

"A perfect paradise, it will stay in our memories forever--a wonderful place to wake up in."

Crowne Pointe Historic Inn & Spa
www.srinns.com/crownepointe
82 Bradford Street, Provincetown, MA 02657
877-276-9631 • 508-487-6767 • Fax 508-487-5554
welcome@crownepointe.com

Innkeepers/Owners
**David M. Sanford,
Thomas J. Walter &
Mom**

Historic Breakfast
Inn & Spa

Wine Spectator

AWARD
OF
EXCELLENCE

A prominent Sea Captain built this historic mansion, which has been fully restored to its 19th Century glory. The inn's stunning Victorian architecture includes two-story wrap around porches complete with turret and harbor views. The *New York Daily News* raves "Five Star Luxury Without the Cost." Revive at our full service on-site Shui Spa featuring many treatments and massage options. Shui Spa offers guests an intimate spa experience. Crowne Pointe is a AAA Four Diamond property located in the center of town. Our signature gourmet hot breakfast and afternoon wine and cheese social are included. Heated in-ground pool, two hot tubs, fireplaces and in-room whirlpools are offered. Spa packages are available. Our restaurant captures our guests with exquisite gourmet cuisine, and our hotel bar is a treasured place to socialize. The finest menu creations from our talented chefs, carefully selected labels from our wine cellar, and excellent service in a charming setting are waiting for you to indulge.

Rooms/Rates
40 Rooms. $110/$465 depending upon season. Min stay req's may apply. Many special packages available, call for details.
Number of Rooms: 40

Cuisine
The freshest regional ingredients arriving daily, our distinctive full hot breakfasts are unsurpassed. The main selections change daily and special dietary needs are accommodated.

Nearest Airport(s)
Provincetown Airport (PVC) or Boston Logan Airport

Directions
Rt 6 E. 63 m. to Provincetown. Turn L at the 2nd Provincetown exit onto Conwell St. Take Conwell St. to the end & make R onto Bradford St. Follow Bradford to 82. Inn sits on a bluff.

AAA ◆◆◆◆   *Member Since 2003*

15+

"Faaaabulous"-Eartha Kitt

Innkeepers/Owners
Margaret & Rebecca Keith

Traditional Village
Breakfast Inn

paii

Penny House Inn
www.srinns.com/penny
4885 County Rd (Route 6), Eastham, MA 02642
800-554-1751 • 508-255-6632 • Fax 508-255-4893
pennyhouse@aol.com

Rooms/Rates
9 guestrooms $179/$350
3 Suites $325/$395
Number of Rooms: 12

Cuisine
Traditional full breakfast with a gourmet flair. Specialties: Eggs Benedict, French Toast Croissants & Pecan Waffles w/fresh fruit. Special dietary needs accommodated (Vegetarian, Diabetic, Gluten-free) advance notice.

Nearest Airport(s)
Boston & Providence

Directions
Cross the Cape Cod Canal, take Route 6 towards Provincetown. Go past exit 12, highway ends at a traffic circle, take 2nd exit (Rt6) through 3 traffic lights, exactly 5 mi. from circle on L (cnr of Bayside Dr & Rt6) across from St.Aubin's Nursery.

A little slice of heaven hides behind a large hedge on the Outer Cape, just minutes away from breathtaking beaches and sand dunes of the Cape Cod National Seashore. Relax, rejuvenate and reconnect at this 1690 restored sea captain's home. Guestrooms at the inn are characterized by their own personal charm. Modern bathrooms, AC, TV/VCR, phone, fireplaces, whirlpool tubs, suites, wireless internet, seasonal heated salt water pool, high thread count sheets, fluffy towels and comfortable beds are among the many modern amenities the inn offers. Several rooms are hidden away, perfect for romantic escapes and honeymoons. For complete pampering our spa offers massage, manicures, wraps & facials. A short walk away is a full service health club with indoor tennis.

AAA ◆◆◆   *Member Since 2003*   Mobil ★★★

8+ 🚭 ♿ 💳   🏋 ✂ 🖨 @ 🌊 📺 ◎ ❋ ☕

SelectRegistry.com

175

The Whalewalk Inn and Spa

www.srinns.com/whalewalkinn
220 Bridge Road, Eastham, Cape Cod, MA 02642
800-440-1281 • 508-255-0617 • Fax 508-240-0017
reservations@whalewalkinn.com

Innkeepers
Elaine and Kevin Conlin

Traditional Village Breakfast
Inn

Abandon every day life. Rekindle your romance and rejuvenate your body and mind. Relax at Cape Cod's most romantic country Inn and Spa. Secluded, but centrally located to all the attractions which make Cape Cod so special. After a gourmet breakfast, walk the "Outer Cape" beaches, listening to the soothing sound of the waves, lapping on Cape Cod Bay or crashing at the National Seashore. At the end of a day on the beach, riding the Rail Trail, kayaking, shopping or museum hopping, restore your inner balance and harmony at The Spa, a very special place with your comfort and exercise regime in mind. Forget the weather; you can pamper your mind and body with a massage or facial package; feel the heat of the dry sauna; or workout in the indoor resistance pool or on the cardiovascular machines. Stay in the luxurious Spa Penthouse or in another of our beautiful accommodations. All rooms are individually decorated, have air-conditioning, TV/VCR, CD players and phones. Come and enjoy our impeccable service and heartfelt hospitality.

AAA ◆◆◆   *Member Since 1993*

Rooms/Rates
$205/$395. Call for off-season rates. Open March to December 31.
Number of Rooms: 16

Cuisine
Full-service gourmet breakfast with fresh home-baked delights and entrees including: Pecan Waffles, Eggs Benedict, Corn Pancakes with Dill Shallot Sauce and Salmon Rosettes, Grand Marnier Oatmeal Pie, Frittata Primavera, and Captain Harding Omelet. Evening hors d'oeuvres are served.

Nearest Airport(s)
Boston, MA; Providence, RI

Directions
Rte. 6 to Orleans Rotary, Rock Harbor Courthouse Exit off Rotary, L on Rock Harbor Road (1/4 mile), R on Bridge Road (1/4 mile). Driving time, Boston or Providence—2 hours.

"We discovered many treasures on the Cape, but none as treasured as The Whalewalk Inn. Another fabulous visit! Thank you for making Cape Cod so memorable."

Innkeepers/Owners
Donna and Peter Amadeo

Elegant Waterside Breakfast Inn

The Captain Freeman Inn

www.srinns.com/captainfreeman
15 Breakwater Road, Brewster, Cape Cod, MA 02631
800-843-4664 • 508-896-7481 • Fax 508-896 5618
stay@captainfreemaninn.com

Rooms/Rates
12 Rooms, 6 w/fireplaces, whirl-pool tubs and TV's, $150/$250 B&B. Open year-round.
Number of Rooms: 12

Cuisine
Full gourmet breakfast, afternoon tea, winter weekend cooking school with wine-tasting and dinner.

Nearest Airport(s)
ProvidenceBoston Logan International

Directions
From route 6 (Mid Cape Highway) take exit 10 (route 124) toward Brewster. At the end of 124 go Right on Route 6A, then Left on Breakwater. Our driveway is the first one on the Left.

Built just a short stroll from beautiful Breakwater Beach, The Captain Freeman Inn is a lovingly restored Victorian sea captain's mansion furnished with canopy beds and period antiques. Luxury accommodations include fireplace, two-person whirlpool, garden and pool views. Breakfast is served poolside on the wraparound porch overlooking lush perennial gardens. In cooler winter weather you will dine fireside in the garden-view dining room. Bicycles are provided to our guests. Venture out to watch hump-back whales at play or bike miles of wooded trails. Return for a glass of wine and a dip in our heated pool. See sunset on Cape Cod Bay. Sail, surf, fish, golf, or rock on our wraparound porch.

Member Since 1998

10+ ⊘ ▭ 🗀 ❤ ✍ @ ≋ ▨ ◉

"A honeymoon made in heaven! We were in awe when we entered our room."

The Captain's House Inn of Chatham

www.captainshouseinn.com
369-377 Old Harbor Rd, Chatham, MA 02633
800-315-0728 • 508-945-0127 • Fax 508-945-0866
info@captainshouseinn.com

Innkeepers/Owners
Jan and Dave McMaster

Elegant Village
Breakfast Inn

Rooms/Rates
12 Rooms, $250/$350; 4 Suites, $250/$450 Summer; $185/$250; $225/$295 Winter. All rooms are air conditioned. Open year-round.
Number of Rooms: 16

Cuisine
Breakfast, poolside lunches, afternoon tea, evening snacks.

Nearest Airport(s)
Providence or Boston

Directions
Rte. 6 (Mid-Cape Hwy) to exit 11(S) Rte. 137 to Rte 28, L approx. 3 miles to rotary. Continue around rotary on Rte. 28 toward Orleans 1/2 mile on L.

Perhaps Cape Cod's finest small Inn, this historic 1839 sea captain's estate on two acres is the perfect choice for a romantic getaway or elegant retreat. Gourmet breakfasts, English afternoon teas, beautifully decorated rooms with king and queen size four-poster beds, fireplaces, seating areas, telephones with data ports, WI-FI capability and TV/VCR's; some with whirlpool tubs. Enjoy uncompromising service from our enthusiastic international staff and enjoy the Inn's many gardens and fountains, heated outdoor pool, fitness centre, and savor the scenic beauty of the historic seafaring village of Chatham with its spectacular views of the ocean.

AAA ◆◆◆◆   *Member Since 1989*   Mobil ★★★

12+ 🚭 ♿ 💳 🛎 📁 ♥ ✂ 📷 @ ≋ 🏋 ◎ ❄

"Fantastic service and accommodation. Can't wait to tell our friends."

Innkeepers/Owners
Judy & Ray Braz

Village Breakfast
Inn

Old Harbor Inn
www.srinns.com/oldharborinn
22 Old Harbor Road, Chatham, MA 02633
800-942-4434 • 508 945-4434 • Fax 508 945-7665
info@chathamoldharborinn.com

Rooms/Rates
$199/$289 in the summer. Rates in the spring and fall shoulder seasons are $169/$249. Winter rates are $139/$199. Minimum stay requirements. Special packages available.
Number of Rooms: 8

Cuisine
Breakfast of homemade specialties. Coffee, tea, soft drinks and snacks anytime.

Nearest Airport(s)
Barnstable County Airport- Approximately 20 miles

Directions
Rte 6 (Mid Cape Hwy) to exit 11 S to Rte 137 go 3 mi. to Rte 28 S approx. 3 mi. to rotary stay on 28 around rotary. We are immediately on R. Please call for directions from Boston, Providence, or New York.

The Inn offers all the amenities that the sophisticated traveler requires, while maintaining an intimate ambiance. Ideally located steps from the major attractions that Chatham offers. Many guests truly enjoy not having to use their cars for several days as they explore the village. Judy, Ray and their knowledgeable staff will offer suggestions for maximizing your leisure activities. Chatham serves as a centralized base for exploring all of Cape Cod and the islands of Nantucket and Martha's Vineyard. Itineraries for day trips to Sandwich or Provincetown or anywhere in between can be arranged based on what activities you enjoy the most. Explore the natural beauty of Cape Cod. Discover the breathtaking vistas of the National Seashore. Be pampered at The Old Harbor Inn. Every day you get our best!

AAA ◆◆◆   *Member Since 2004*   Mobil ★★★

12+

"You have met and exceeded all of our expectations." "Wonderful, restful, stay." "Breakfast to die for!" "Perfection... we will return."

The Dan'l Webster Inn & Spa

www.srinns.com/danlwebsterinn
149 Main St., Sandwich, MA 02563
800-444-3566 • 508-888-3622 • Fax 508-888-5156
info@danlwebsterinn.com

Innkeeper/Owner
Catania Family
General Manager
Gary Cremeans

Traditional Village
Inn & Spa

AWARD OF EXCELLENCE
DiRoNA

This award-winning Inn set in the heart of Historic Sandwich, offers guests the romance of the past with today's conveniences. Canopy and four-poster beds, fireplaces and oversized whirlpool tubs await your arrival. Each guest room and suite has been individually appointed with exquisite period furnishings. The new Spa at The Dan'l Webster offers the ultimate in luxury for Men and Women...from completely organic Body Treatments and relaxing Massages to soothing Facials and more, we will pamper your mind, body and soul! Enjoy a romantic dinner in one of our distinctive dining rooms. Savor delicious award-winning cuisine and creative chef's specials complemented by an acclaimed wine selection, or relax in our casual Tavern at the Inn and enjoy lighter fare and a warm, friendly atmosphere.

All suites are furnished with Keurig coffee makers, purifing e-showers, 300 ct. Pima cotton triple sheeting, selection of high quality pillows, photo-catalytic ionization air purifiers and silky micro fiber robes.

Rooms/Rates
53 Traditional/Deluxe/Superior Rooms, $109/$249; 17 Suites, $179/$379. Open year-round. Closed Christmas.
Number of Rooms: 70

Cuisine
Breakfast, lunch, dinner, & Sunday Brunch. Tavern on premise. Fine & casual dining menus available serving contemporary and traditional American cuisine.

Nearest Airport(s)
Logan Airport (Boston)

Directions
From Boston, MA: Rte. 3 S to Rte. 6 to exit 2 turn L on Rte. 130 approx. 2 miles–R at fork. Inn will be on L.

AAA ◆◆◆   *Member Since 1994*   Mobil ★★★

"The boutique inn is located between heaven, history and the ocean..."

Innkeepers/Owners
Cecily Denson and
Richard Pratt

Elegant Victorian
Village Breakfast Inn

Isaiah Jones Homestead
www.srinns.com/isaiahjones
165 Main Street, Sandwich, MA 02563
800-526-1625 • 508-888-9115 • Fax 508-888-9648
info@isaiahjones.com

paii

Rooms/Rates
7 Rooms, $120/$210, includes
a full, three course breakfast. Air
conditioned. Open year-round.
Number of Rooms: 7

Cuisine
Breakfast is served in our cherry
paneled dining room. Enjoy a full
three-course breakfast of fresh
fruit, juices, hot entrees, home-
baked scones and coffeecakes,
and a 'bottomless' pot of our
special blend of coffee.

Nearest Airport(s)
Logan Airport, Boston, MA;
TF Green, Providence, RI

Directions
Rte. 6 (Mid-Cape Hwy.) Exit 2,
Left at the end of the ramp onto
Rte.130 to the village center. Bear
right at the fork, go 2/10 mile, Inn
is on the Left - 165 Main.

Relax in pampered elegance in this 1849 Italianate Victorian
Inn. The main house has five exquisitely appointed guest rooms,
with private baths, feature queen beds, antique furnishings, oriental carpets, all with fireplaces or glass-front stoves and two with
oversize whirlpool tubs. The unique Carriage House has been
recently renovated to include two spacious junior suites each with
a fireplace and whirlpool bath. Located in the heart of Sandwich
village, you are within easy walking distance of many attractions
of the Cape's oldest town. Unwind by strolling the meandering
garden paths around the goldfish pond, by sitting in comfortable Adirondack chairs that are placed around the well-manicured
yard or by relaxing by the original antique-tiled fireplace in the
gathering room. A full breakfast, served in our cherry-paneled
dining room, sets a warm tone to start your day. Chosen Editors
Choice, *Cape Cod Travel Guide*, Spring, 2005. Selected as "Insider
Pick" for Romantic Getaways by *Destination Insider*.

AAA ◆◆◆   *Member Since 1989*   Mobil ★★★

12+

"All of the little details were wonderful." "Thank you for making our honeymoon
very special." "We will never forget such a special place". "Pure pleasure!"

Palmer House Inn

www.srinns.com/palmerhouse
81 Palmer Avenue, Falmouth, MA 02540
800-472-2632 • 508-548-1230 • Fax 508-540-1878
innkeepers@palmerhouseinn.com

Innkeepers/Owners
Pat and Bill O'Connell
Elegant Village
Breakfast Inn

On a tree-lined street in the heart of the Historic District, The Palmer House Inn is an elegant Victorian home. Stained glass windows, rich woodwork, gleaming hardwood floors and antique furnishings create an overall sense of warmth and harmony. Beautiful beaches, quaint shops, ferry shuttles, and excellent restaurants are only a short stroll away. The innkeepers pamper you with meticulous housekeeping, fresh flowers, extra pillows, fluffy robes, fine linens and good reading lights. The Palmer House Inn is the perfect place to stay, in splendid comfort and gracious care. Local activities include golf, swimming, cycling on the Shining Sea Bike Path, fishing, charter sailing, kayaking, hiking, bird watching and more.

Rooms/Rates
16 Rooms, $109/$259; 1 Cottage Suites, $245/$299. K,Q,DBL beds, AC, cable TV & phones. Some have whirlpools, fireplaces. Open year-round.
Number of Rooms: 17

Cuisine
Full gourmet breakfast served with candlelight and classical music. Afternoon and evening refreshments. Early morning coffee.

Nearest Airport(s)
TF Green (Providence) Logan (Boston)

Directions
After crossing the Bourne Bridge, follow Rte. 28 S for approximately 15 miles. A half-mile past the only traffic light at Jones Road/Ter Heun Drive, Rte. 28 turns left into Falmouth Village. The Inn is on the L just after the turn.

AAA ◆◆◆◆ *Member Since 2001*

12+

"How visually appealing everything is...the decor, the gardens, the porches. We loved it!"

Thorncroft Inn

www.srinns.com/thorncroftinn
460 Main St., P.O. Box 1022, Martha's Vineyard, MA 02568
800-332-1236 • 508-693-3333 • Fax 508-693-5419
innkeeper@thorncroft.com

Proprietors/Innkeepers
Lynn and Karl Buder

Traditional Village Breakfast Inn

Rooms/Rates
14 antique appointed rooms, 10 with working wood burning fireplaces, some with two person whirlpools or private in-room hot tubs. $225/$550 B&B
Number of Rooms: 14

Cuisine
Full country breakfast served in two dining rooms at individual tables for two or an ample continental breakfast in bed; Traditional or healthful entrees. Afternoon tea and pastries.

Nearest Airport(s)
Martha's Vineyard Airport (MVY) 5 miles

Directions
Year-round car & passenger Steamship Authority Ferry at Woods Hole, MA. (508-477-8600) Take left off dock and right at stop sign. Take next right onto Main St. Inn is 1 mile on left.

Thorncroft Inn is situated in three restored buildings on 2 1/2 acres of quiet, treed grounds on the Island of Martha's Vineyard. It is secluded, exclusively couples-oriented and first-class. All rooms have phone, TV/VCR, high-speed internet access, air-conditioning, irons, ironing boards and deluxe bathrobes. Most rooms have working, wood-burning fireplaces and canopied beds. Some have two-person whirlpool bathtubs or private in-room 300-gallon hot tubs. Several offer private exterior entrances or furnished private porches or balconies. Our concierge service is renowned and focuses on the specific needs of each couple. Thorncroft Inn is an ideal setting for honeymoons, anniversaries, elopements, engagements, birthdays or any romantic getaway for couples.

AAA ◆◆◆◆   *Member Since 1994*   Mobil ★★★

"Thorncroft is the kind of place, where we find ourselves falling in love all over again. The perfect place to escape the real world for a time."

Seven Sea Street Inn

www.srinns.com/sevenseastreet
7 Sea Street, Nantucket, MA 02554
800-651-9262 • 508-228-3577 • Fax 508-228-3578
innkeeper@sevenseastreetinn.com

Innkeepers/Owners
Matthew and Mary Parker
Assistant Innkeeper
Emily McDowell

Traditional Village
Breakfast Inn

Enjoy Seven Sea Street Inn, a truly charming Nantucket bed and breakfast Inn, where we pride ourselves on the attentive service and elegant accommodations that will make your stay with us a fond memory. Our Inn is distinguished by its beautiful red oak post and beam style, designed and constructed with an authentic Nantucket ambiance in mind. We are the only Inn on the Island which offers guests both a relaxing Jacuzzi Spa and a stunning view of Nantucket Harbor from our Widow's Walk deck. All of our guest rooms are furnished with luxurious Stearns and Foster queen or king mattresses, the world's finest bedding. Each Main house guest room and suite is furnished with rainshower shower-heads, ACs, high definition TVs, high speed wireless connectivity and a bow box of Nantucket's famous chocolate covered cranberries. Our location, nestled on a quiet tree-lined side street and less than a five-minute walk from Main Street shopping, restaurants, museums and the beach, couldn't be better. Indulge yourself at our lovely Inn this year.

Rooms/Rates
9 Guest Rooms, $99/$269 B&B; 2 Suites, $159/$339 B&B. Seasonal rates.
Number of Rooms: 11

Cuisine
Expanded Buffet Continental Breakfast served daily. Two seatings, 8 a.m. and 9 a.m. Gourmet coffee, tea, soda, bottled water and homemade cookies available anytime.

Nearest Airport(s)
Nantucket Memorial Airport

Directions
Flights available from Boston, NYC, Providence, & Hyannis. Ferry service from Hyannis to Steamboat Wharf in Nantucket. Less than a 5 minute walk from the wharf to the Inn. Take your 1st right onto South Beach Street then your 2nd left onto Sea Street. The Inn is on the left at 7 Sea Street.

AAA ◆◆◆   *Member Since 1996*

5+ ⊘ 💳 ⓣ ✂ 🏠 @ 🔲 ◎ ✳

"We loved every moment of our stay at your beautiful Inn.
Our room was perfect thanks!"

Union Street Inn

Innkeepers/Owners
Deb & Ken Withrow

Elegant Village Breakfast
Inn

www.srinns.com/unionstreetinn
7 Union Street, Nantucket, MA 02554
800-225-5116 • 508-228-9222 • Fax 508-325-0848
unioninn@nantucket.net

Rooms/Rates
12 Rooms. High Season:
$275/$445; Shoulder Seasons:
$160/$350. Closed November
through March.
Number of Rooms: 12

Cuisine
Full Gourmet Breakfast. Afternoon
Treats. Coffee, Tea, Bottled Spring
Water always available.

Nearest Airport(s)
Nantucket Memorial Airport-10
minute taxi ride.

Directions
Flights from Boston, NYC, New
Bedford & Hyannis. High season
from Providence, Washington
D.C. & Philadelphia. Ferry
service from Hyannis-short walk
from ferries.

Nantucket's luxury B&B. "Ken worked in the hotel business,
Deborah in high-end retail display, and guests get the best of both
worlds. This 1770 house, a stone's throw from the bustle of Main
Street, has been respectfully yet lavishly restored. Guests are treated to Frette linens, plump duvets, lush robes and a full gourmet
breakfast served on the tree-shaded garden patio."-Fodors.

Professionally decorated in 2005, the inn is ideally located in the
heart of the historic village just off Main Street's cobblestones and
the harbor. Rooms have air conditioning, cable TV, "fresh" bath
amenities and Wi-Fi high speed Internet access. Several rooms
have wood burning fireplaces. Nantucket's restaurants, shops, galleries, and museums are a short stroll. Walk or bicycle to Nantucket's beautiful beaches.

Member Since 2005

12+ ⊘ ▱ @ ▥ ✺

"In a word, lovely. The Union Street Inn has an excellent central location, and
the rooms were tastefully decorated and kept very clean."

"The Wolverine State"

Famous For: Famous For: Great Lakes (borders on four of the five Great Lakes), Fishing, Swimming, Water Sports, Holland (Tulip Center of America), Cherries, Farmland, Auto Manufacturing

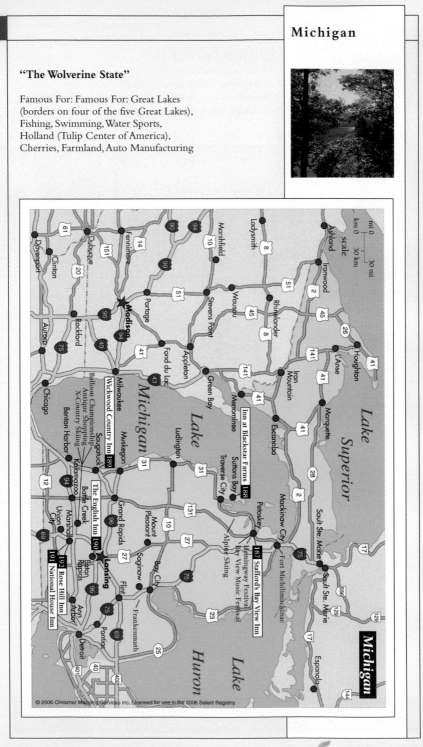

© 2006 Chrismar Mapping Services Inc. licensed for use in the 2006 Select Registry.

SelectRegistry.com

Proprietors
Stafford Smith Family
General Manager
Chad McDonald

Traditional Victorian
Country Inn

Stafford's Bay View Inn

www.srinns.com/staffordsbay

2011 US 31 N, P.O. Box 657, Petoskey, MI 49770

800-258-1886 • 231-347-2771 • Fax 231-347-3413

bayview@staffords.com

Rooms/Rates
31 Rooms, $89/$170; 9 Spa-Fireplace Suites $119/$240; Bridal Suite $119/$260; B&B, Double Occupancy.
Number of Rooms: 40

Cuisine
Breakfast & Dinner: May–Oct. and winter weekends. Lunch: Late May –Oct. Sunday Brunch: June-Oct. & Holidays. Visit www.staffords.com for menus, dining schedules and info on full-service, year-round, innkeeper-owned properties nearby.

Nearest Airport(s)
Pellston (PLN) - 17 miles
Traverse (TVC) - 65 miles

Directions
From Detroit: I-75N to Gaylord exit 282, Rte. 32W to US 131N to Petoskey. From Chicago: I-94 to I-196N to US 131N to Petoskey. From the North: I-75S across Mackinac Bridge to Petoskey Exit, US 31S.

"Bay View Inn" was purchased by Stafford and Janice Smith in 1961. Stafford and his family has owned, operated, and lovingly restored, this grand Victorian Country Inn on the shores of Lake Michigan's Little Traverse Bay. Built as a rooming house in 1886 in the Historic Landmark District of Bay View, this Inn sets the standard in country inn dining and gracious service. Each beautifully appointed guest room features a private bath, and individual climate controls. Visitors to the area enjoy summer Chautauqua programs, championship golfing, our fall color tours, winter ski packages, and sleigh rides around the Bay View cottage grounds. Petoskey's Historic Gaslight Shopping District and marina are located nearby. Our inn is an exquisite place to hold weddings, rehersal dinners, receptions and reunions. Many quiet corners offer a wonderful environment for company meetings and conferences. Landmark Hospitality where yesterday and today come together. Voted 'Michigan's Best Brunch' by *Michigan Living*

AAA ◆◆◆   *Member Since 1972*   Mobil ★★★

"Perfect! The staff-decor-food! The view! Everything at this charming inn is wonderful! Warm caring smiles, yummie cookies, and we love the new color."

Inn at Black Star Farms

www.srinns.com/blackstarfarms
10844 E. Revold Rd., Suttons Bay, MI 49682
877-466-9463 • 231-271-4970 ext. 150 • Fax 231-271-6321
innkeeper@blackstarfarms.com

Proprietor
Don Coe
Inn Manager
Corey Wentworth
Winery Breakfast
Inn

Our year-round Inn is nestled below a hillside of vineyards in the heart of Leelanau Peninsula wine country. Its eight contemporary guestrooms, each with private bath and some with fireplaces and spa tubs, have fine furniture, luxurious linens, and down comforters. Amenities include a bottle of our Red House Wine, cozy robes, and satellite TV/VCR. Massage services and sauna are available. A full gourmet breakfast is prepared for you daily using local seasonal products. You can sample our award-winning wines and spirits at our on site tasting room – also home of the artisanal Leelanau Cheese Co. The farm also features boarding stables and wooded recreational trails that are great in any season. Meetings, reunions and receptions welcomed.

Member Since 2003

Rooms/Rates
May 26-October 28, 2006: $280/$375. October 29-May 24, 2007: $215/$295.
Number of Rooms: 8

Cuisine
Our breakfasts feature fresh fruit and juices, homemade baked goods, a seasonal gourmet entree using local products, and coffee & tea.

Nearest Airport(s)
Cherry Capitol Airport (TVC)

Directions
From Traverse City: Follow M-22 N toward Northport. The Inn will be on your L after approx. 12 mi. L on Revold Rd. and L again into our driveway. From Cherry Capital Airport: Exit the airport and turn R. At Garfield turn R. At Front St. (M-72) turn L. Follow M-72 to M-22 and proceed as above.

12+

"Our Black Star wedding was magical. We've returned to celebrate our anniversary and plan to be back each and every year to be pampered again."

Innkeepers/Owners
**Julee Rosso Miller and
Bill Miller**

Elegant Village Breakfast Inn

Wickwood Inn
www.srinns.com/wickwood
510 Butler Street, Saugatuck, MI 49453-1019
800-385-1174 • 269-857-1465 • Fax 269-857-1552
innkeeper@wickwoodinn.com

Rooms/Rates
7 traditional rooms, 4 suites with sitting areas, fireplaces & private baths. $155/$355 K & Q or twin.
Number of Rooms: 11

Cuisine
She changed the way America eats—*New York Newsday*. Great eclectic food is evident in a warm complimentary Country Breakfast, daylong Serendipity Sips & Sweets, Candlelight Evening hor's d'ouvres & Brandies & Chocolate finalé.

Nearest Airport(s)
Grand Rapids

Directions
Southwestern Michigan, downtown in Village of Saugatauck on Lake Michigan. Two and one-half hours from Chicago and Detroit. Take I-96 to Exit #36 from the S, Exit #41 from the N on to the Blue Star Highway into Village to Butler Street.

Travel + Leisure says, "Wickwood is one of America's most romantic Inns, a jewel with delicious food!!" Foodlovers, romantics and art connoisseurs gather at Silver Palate Cookbook author Julee Rosso's Inn in this charming art village on the shores of Lake Michigan. "She changed the way American eats," New York's Newsday compliments. Everyday terrific "surprises" are served including Chocolate Strawberries, lush Evening Hor's d'ouvres, great Champagne Brunch, Biscotti & Vin Santo. This exquisite getaway has a sophisticated décor, stunning artwork, antiques, gazebos and gardens. Guest rooms are appointed with featherbeds, fireplaces, cozy robes, stereos, books and spa secrets. "The décor is breathtaking—the food perfection," raves Zagat. The villages feature one of the "World's Top Ten Beaches," nature and bike trails, antique shops, 50 art galleries, berry and apple orchards, wineries, 150 shops and boutiques, four golf courses, theater, music and film festivals. The Inn is exquisite all year, especially magical at The Holidays.

Member Since 2002

12+

"Every time we visit, now twelve times and counting, we marvel at all of Wickwood's efforts to make our stay ever more memorable during every season."

The English Inn
www.srinns.com/englishinn
677 S. Michigan Rd., Lansing/Eaton Rapids, MI 48827
517-663-2500 • Fax 517-663-2643

Innkeepers/Owners
Gary and Donna Nelson

English Tudor
Country Inn

Rooms/Rates
10 Rooms, $105/$175 B&B; includes 6 Inn Rooms, Two Cottages include 4 bedrooms w/jacuzzi tubs and fireplaces. Open year-round.
Number of Rooms: 10

Cuisine
Breakfast w/room, Lunch M-F, Dinner 7 days. Continental-French cuisine, daily chef specials. Specialty of House; Chateaubriand for Two, carved tableside. Authentic English pub. Wine, beer, ale, liquor. Banquet Facilities 15-200+.

Nearest Airport(s)
Lansing Capitol City

Directions
From I-96 in Lansing, take M-99 S (exit 101) 8 mi. From I-94, take M-99(N) 22 mi. Ninety miles W of Detroit, 15 miles S of State Capitol (Lansing), and Michigan State Univ.

A former auto baron's residence, this 1927 Tudor mansion will make you feel as though you've been transported to the English countryside. Perched on a hillside overlooking the Grand River, the Inn is part of a 15-acre estate that includes formal gardens and wooded nature trails. The main house has six well-appointed bedrooms named for English towns or the royal family, a cozy pub, library and two cottages include 4 bedrooms w/fireplaces and Jacuzzi tubs, common sitting areas. The Inn's award-winning restaurant includes a wine list bestowed with the Award of Excellence by *Wine Spectator*. A perfect setting for get-aways, executive retreats and family gatherings. In addition, a 200-seat, 10,000 sq.ft. banquet facility sits adjacent to the main house.

AAA ◆◆◆   *Member Since 1991*

12+

"The Inn is a 'magical' place - thanks for the memories!"

Innkeeper/Owner
Barbara Bradley

Rustic Village Breakfast Inn

National House Inn
www.srinns.com/nationalhouse
102 S. Parkview, Marshall, MI 49068
269-781-7374 • Fax 269-781-4510
innkeeper@nationalhouseinn.com

Rooms/Rates
15 Rooms, $105/$115 B&B;
2 Suites, $145.
Number of Rooms: 17

Cuisine
Breakfast, afternoon tea, catered
dinners for receptions.

Nearest Airport(s)
Kalamazoo

Directions
I-94 to exit 110 Rte. 27(S) 2 miles
to Michigan Ave (SW corner
of circle, located in downtown
Marshall).

Nestled in the heart of Historic Marshall, National House Inn
is Michigan's oldest operating Inn. The first brick building in
the county, National House has been restored as a warm, beautifully furnished, hospitable Inn with lovely gardens. Marshall--
nicknamed "The City of Hospitality"--has many citations for its
850 19th Century architectural structures, and is included on the
National Register of Historic Places, where the Inn is also listed.
In 2004, Marshall was chosen as one of 12 distinctive destinations
for the National Trust for Historic Preservation, has a prestigious
National Historic Landmark District designation and is home
to Schuler's Restaurant and the annual fall Historic Home Tour.
Come join us for afternoon tea at a turn of the century pace in a
turn of the century Inn.

Member Since 1978

National House Inn has been featured in *Midwest Living* - April 2004

Rose Hill Inn

www.srinns.com/rosehillinn
1110 Verona Road, Marshall, MI 49068
269-789-1992 • Fax 269-781-4723
rosehillinnkeeper@cablespeed.com

Innkeepers/Owners
Gerald & Carol Lehmann

Historic Bed & Breakfast

paii

The Rose Hill Inn is an elegant 1860 Victorian mansion, once the summer home of William Boyce, flamboyant self-made millionaire and founder of the American Boy Scouts. Twelve-foot ceilings, tall windows, lovely views, fireplaces, and fine antiques combine to create a mood of tranquility and escape from the modern world.

Guest rooms are decorated in luxurious nineteenth century style with vintage art work, period decor, and antique lighting but feature all the contemporary conveniences: A/C, private baths, cable TV, and wireless Internet. A card room and billiard room are also available for your enjoyment.

Situated on three acres of landscaped grounds, Rose Hill offers a private swimming pool, tennis court, porches, patios, gardens, and fountains. Located in historic Marshall, Michigan, within walking distance of fine dining, museums, and shops. The Rose Hill Inn provides the rare opportunity to step back into the Gilded Age and create a unique memory--the perfect choice for your wedding, family reunion, or corporate event.

AAA ◆◆◆   *Member Since 2004*

Rooms/Rates
$99/$260. Other rates may apply for special events/holidays, off-season & business travel. Some discounts available. Some queen beds and/or fireplaces. Guests may use pool or tennis court w/o fees.
Number of Rooms: 6

Cuisine
Full breakfast served fireside on Haviland China includes a hot specialty d'jour, seasonal fruit, juice, yogurt, & home-baked goods. Complimentary snacks, coffee/tea, bottled water & soft drinks always available.

Nearest Airport(s)
Kalamazoo

Directions
I-94: Exit 110, S to Mansion St., W .8 mi. I-69: Exit 36, E to Fountain St., N 2 blks.

"Rose Hill is the standard for B&B's. First cabin all the way." "The Rose Hill Inn reminds one of a Tuscan villa." *New York Times* Travel Section

Minnesota

"The Gopher State"

Famous For: Hi-Tech, Grain, Timber, Corn, Sugar Beets,
Dairy, Rice, Pillsbury Dough Boy, Twin Cities
(St. Paul & Minneapolis), Prairies, Lake Superior, Falls

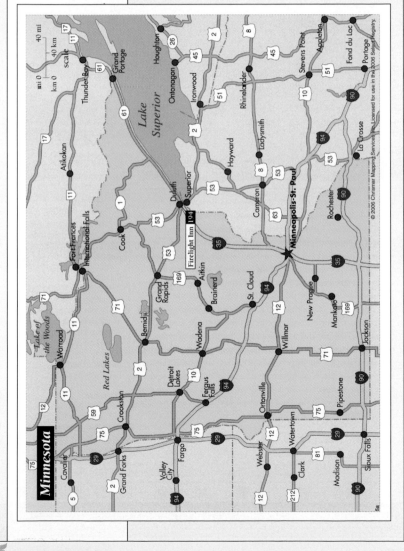

The Firelight Inn on Oregon Creek

www.srinns.com/firelightinn
2211 East Third Street, Duluth, MN 55812
888-724-0273 • 218-724-0272 • Fax 218-724-0304
info@firelightinn.com

Innkeepers/Owners
Jim & Joy Fischer

Elegant In Town Breakfast Inn

paii

Duluth resides on the tip of the largest freshwater lake in the world--Lake Superior. Over 1,100 vessels slip silently into Canal Park and anchor here each year. The Firelight Inn is located in a historic Duluth neighborhood on a secluded street adjoining Oregon Creek and is a perfect setting for your relaxing getaway. In keeping with the history of the mansion which was built in 1910, it has been renovated and furnished in a lasting and timeless traditional style. Comfortable common areas include the Firelight Room pictured above, the formal living room, original butler's pantry and the original glass enclosed front porch overlooking the creek. The Barnum and Brookside Suites with access to an outdoor second floor deck overlooking the creek give beautiful winter views of Lake Superior. In summer, your breakfast may be enjoyed on the deck listening to the babbling creek. The third floor suites offer spectacular Lake Superior views. Hot stone, seaweed wraps, couples teaching massage and relaxation massage therapy available on site.

Rooms/Rates
5 suites with private bath, fireplace, AC, two person Jacuzzi tub, featherbed, TV/VCR/DVD. Open all year. $179/$259
Number of Rooms: 5

Cuisine
Our specialty is delivering your delicious full breakfast in a basket to your suite. Special packages include soup suppers, picnic lunches, gift baskets, wine selection and champagne.

Nearest Airport(s)
Duluth International.

Directions
From I35 North, exit 21st Ave. East. Left and continue up hill to 4th St. Right turn and travel two blocks to 23rd Ave. East. Right turn to Third St. Another right turn and The Firelight Inn is the second property on your right.

Member Since 2003

17+

"Everything says luxury--you've thought of every detail--makes it a little piece of heaven!"

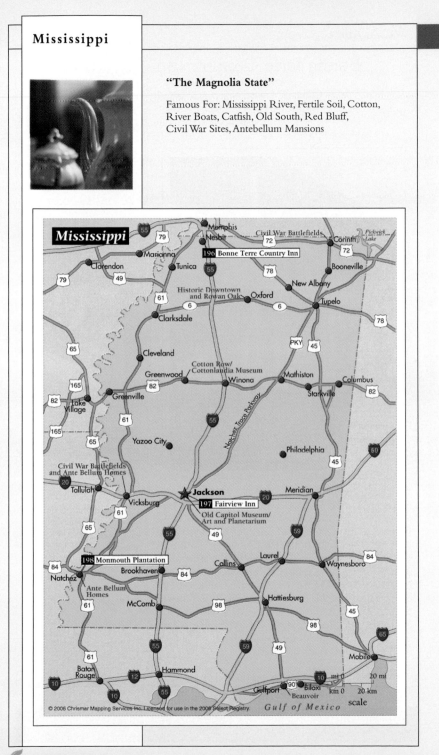

"The Magnolia State"

Famous For: Mississippi River, Fertile Soil, Cotton, River Boats, Catfish, Old South, Red Bluff, Civil War Sites, Antebellum Mansions

Mississippi (map)

- Memphis
- Nesbit
- Civil War Battlefields
- Corinth
- Pickwick Lake
- Marianna
- Tunica
- 196 Bonne Terre Country Inn
- Booneville
- Clarendon
- New Albany
- Historic Downtown and Rowan Oaks
- Oxford
- Tupelo
- Clarksdale
- Cleveland
- PKY
- Greenwood
- Cotton Row/Cottonlandia Museum
- Winona
- Mathiston
- Columbus
- Greenville
- Lake Village
- Starkville
- Yazoo City
- Philadelphia
- Civil War Battlefields and Ante Bellum Homes
- Tallulah
- ★ Jackson
- 197 Fairview Inn
- Meridian
- Vicksburg
- Old Capitol Museum/Art and Planetarium
- 198 Monmouth Plantation
- Brookhaven
- Collins
- Laurel
- Waynesboro
- Natchez
- Ante Bellum Homes
- McComb
- Hattiesburg
- Baton Rouge
- Hammond
- Mobile
- Gulfport
- Biloxi
- Beauvoir
- *Gulf of Mexico*

© 2006 Chrismar Mapping Services Inc. Licensed for use in the 2006 Select Registry.

scale: mi 0 — 20 mi / km 0 — 20 km

Bonne Terre Country Inn

www.srinns.com/bonneterre
4715 Church Rd. West, Nesbit, MS 38651
662-781-5100 • Fax 662-781-5466
info@bonneterre.com

Innkeepers/Owners
Charles and Kimbel Orr

Elegant Country
Inn

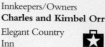

Rooms/Rates
14 Rooms, $165/$250. Special rates are available for corporate groups. All rooms are decorated with fine antique décor and feather beds. Special touches include fireplaces, whirlpool tubs, and balconies.
Number of Rooms: 14

Bonne Terre, French for the "good earth," is a 14–room Country Inn nestled in Nesbit, Mississippi just 15 minutes south of Memphis. Our 23 beautifully wooded acres of Mississippi highlands are within a short drive from anywhere in the Mid-South. In our restaurant, a double sided fireplace is a romantic focal point while the indoor veranda paints a beautiful portrait of the woods and one of our picturesque lakes. Bonne Terre also includes a New England-style Wedding Chapel, a gazebo,and Ashley Hall, our grand Colonial Williamsburg-style reception and banquet hall where countless memorable weddings, receptions and special occasions are held. Bonne Terre is ranked as the premier bed and breakfast property in the Memphis area, consistently rated #1 in readers polls for both dining and lodging.

Cuisine
The Bonne Terre Cafe, the heart of our lovely inn, presents an exquisite fine dining experience for our guests. Our award-winning chefs prepare an array of American Continental cuisine set in an elegant, intimate setting.

Nearest Airport(s)
Memphis International

Directions
Just 15 minutes S of Memphis off I-55. Take Church Rd. exit and go W 4.4 miles to Bonne Terre. 3 hours north of Jackson, Miss.

Member Since 2003

"It's the most beautiful place I've ever seen. A romantic, peaceful retreat beyond compare."

Innkeepers/Owners
Carol and William Simmons

Elegant In Town
Breakfast Inn

Fairview Inn
www.srinns.com/fairview
734 Fairview Street, Jackson, MS 39202
888-948-1908 • 601-948-3429 • Fax 601-948-1203
fairview@fairviewinn.com

Rooms/Rates
3 Rooms, $115 B&B;
15 Suites, $165/$350 B&B.
Open year-round.
Number of Rooms: 18

Cuisine
Full breakfast each morning. Fine Dining Thursday-Saturday 5:30 to 9:00 p.m. Sunday Brunch 11:30 a.m. to 2:00 p.m. Banquet and meeting facilities for groups to 100. Wine and liquor available.

Nearest Airport(s)
Jackson International

Directions
I-55 exit 98A on Woodrow Wilson, L at second traffic light at North State, L one block past second traffic light at Fairview St., Inn is first on L.

Fairview Inn & Restaurant, located in the Belhaven Historic District of Jackson, Mississippi, offers luxury accommodations with all modern amenities such as high speed Internet access and voice mail. Enjoy its well-stocked library, replete with military history and many first editions, its formal garden, flowering magnolia and crepe myrtle trees, and the relaxed ambiance of a two-acre estate on the National Register of Historic Places.

Named a Top Inn of 1994 by *Country Inns* magazine, cited "Southern hospitality at its best" by *Travel + Leisure* in 1998, selected by the National Trust for Historic Preservation for inclusion in the 1998 wall calendar featuring Historic Bed & Breakfast Inns and Small Hotels, named a Top Ten Romantic Inn of 2000 by American Historic Inns, featured in *Southern Living* in 2001, winner of Conde Nast Johansens "Most Outstanding Inn 2003, North America."

AAA ◆◆◆◆   *Member Since 1994*

"This is a place to sustain the body and rest the soul." Jane Goodall

Monmouth Plantation

www.monmouthplantation.com
36 Melrose Avenue, Natchez, MS 39120
800-828-4531 • 601-442-5852 • Fax 601-446-7762
luxury@monmouthplantation.com

Owners
Lani & Ron Riches
Elegant In Town
Inn

Monmouth Plantation, a National Historic Landmark (circa 1818), is a glorious return to the Antebellum South, rated "one of the ten most romantic places in the USA" by *Glamour* magazine and *USA Today*. It waits to enfold you in luxury and service. Walk our beautifully landscaped acres. Thirty rooms and suites in the mansion and the seven other historic buildings hold priceless art and antiques while providing every modern comfort. Mornings begin with a delightful complimentary Southern breakfast. Nights sparkle under candlelight during 5-course dinners. *Conde Nast Traveler* 2005 Gold List.

Rooms/Rates
17 Rooms, $155/$210; 13 Suites, $190/$380. Open year-round.
Number of Rooms: 30

Cuisine
Breakfast and dinner, lunch for private parties only. Wine, liquor, and beer.

Nearest Airport(s)
Jackson, Baton Rouge

Directions
E on State Street, 1 mile from downtown Natchez on the corner of John Quitman Parkway and Melrose Avenue.

AAA ◆◆◆◆   *Member Since 1993*

Selected by *Travel + Leisure* as among the
"500 Greatest Hotels in the World." 2005

Missouri

"The Show-Me State"

Famous For: Center of Continental United States, "Gateway to the West," Livestock, Ozark Plateau, Cottontail Rabbits, Dairy, Corn, Wheat, Cotton, Lead, Zinc, Lime, Cement, Timber, Aircraft, Automobiles, Spacecraft

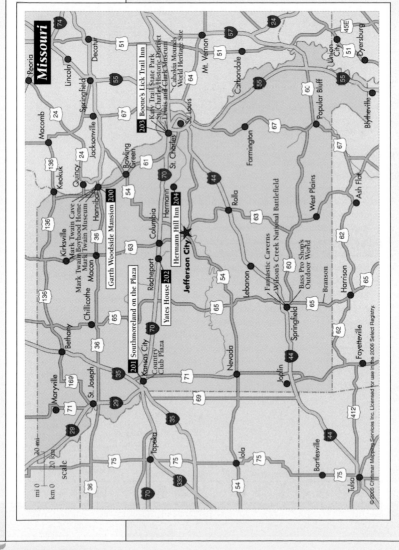

Garth Woodside Mansion

www.garthmansion.com
11069 New London Road, Hannibal, MO 63401
888-427-8409 • 573-221-2789 • Fax 573-221-9941
innkeeper@garthmansion.com

Innkeepers/Owners
Col. (Ret.) John and Julie Rolsen

Traditional Victorian
Country Breakfast Inn

Rated #1 B&B in Missouri. Step back in time in this beautifully restored 1871 Second Empire Victorian mansion, nestled in 39 acres of gardens, rolling meadows, ponds, and woodlands. Relax among original antiques that fill the parlors, library, sitting and dining rooms. Savor the solitude of natural surroundings or enjoy beautiful architecture including the famed 'flying staircase.' Stretch out on the grand porch or hide away on the romantic second floor balcony. Afternoon treats with tea or your favorite beverage are complimentary upon check-in. Stay where Samuel Clemens opted to be a frequent overnight guest. Cottages provide total privacy. We offer the finest wines and a full bar. Dine indoors on site at the Woodside Restaurant or in the garden area al fresco with our fresh Missouri Cuisine.

Rooms/Rates
8 Rooms $139/$225; 3 Cottages $279/$395. Original antiques, hypo-allergenic Queen and King feather beds, central heat/air. 2 rooms offer oversized two-person whirlpool tubs. Open all year.
Number of Rooms: 11

Cuisine
Romantic Dining nestled among the 100+ yr old oak trees. Menu changes nightly, reflecting the daily purchase of the freshest Missouri ingredients available.

Nearest Airport(s)
STL

Directions
From St. Louis: N on SR 61, 75 mi. N of I-70. R on Warren-Barrett, R on New London. Follow signs. From SR 36 or I-72 S on SR 61, L on Warren-Barrett, R on New London. Follow signs.

AAA ◆◆◆   *Member Since 2001*   Mobil ★★★

12+

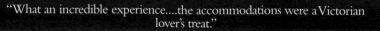

"What an incredible experience....the accommodations were a Victorian lover's treat."

Innkeepers/Owners
**Mark Reichle and
Nancy Miller Reichle**

Traditional Urban
Breakfast Inn

Southmoreland on the Plaza
www.srinns.com/southmoreland
116 East 46th St., Kansas City, MO 64112
816-531-7979 • Fax 816-531-2407
southmoreland@earthlink.net

Rooms/Rates
12 Rooms in Main House,
$135/$200 Summer, $130/$215
Winter, $250 Carriage House (less
$20 SGL.)
Number of Rooms: 13

Cuisine
Gourmet breakfast served daily.
Complimentary afternoon wine &
hors d'oeuvres, with hot beverages and sweets served in the
evening. Courtyard breakfast BBQ
served weekends, Apr-Oct.

Nearest Airport(s)
Kansas City International

Directions
From I-70 or I-29 in downtown KC,
take Broadway (S) to Cleaver II Blvd.
(47th St.), L on Cleaver II Blvd, L on
Main, R on E 46th St. About 1.5 blks
down E 46th on the lefthand side.
From I-35, take Main St. (S) to E 46th.
Make L onto E 46th-down 1.5 blks.

Award-winning Southmoreland's 1913 Colonial Revival styling
brings New England to the heart of Kansas City's historic, arts,
entertainment, and shopping district - The Country Club Plaza.
Business and leisure guests enjoy individually decorated rooms
offering decks, fireplaces or Jacuzzi baths. Business travelers find
respite at Southmoreland with its rare mix of corporate support
services: in-room phones, fax, copier, voice mail, wireless internet
access, 24-hour access and switchboard. Featured on the Food
Channel's "Barbecue with Bobby Flay." Six time winner of Mobil's Four Star Award. Visit us at www.southmoreland.com.

Member Since 1992

12+

"Southmoreland on the Plaza is as restful and alluring a place as I've ever
experienced." - *Southern Living* Magazine.

Yates House Bed & Breakfast

www.srinns.com/yateshouse
305 Second Street, Rocheport, MO 65279
573-698-2129
yateshouse@socket.net

Innkeepers/Owners
Conrad and Dixie Yates

Traditional Village
Breakfast Inn

Change your pace at this beautiful, Historic Rocheport Bed & Breakfast. Everything you'll need for luxurious and relaxing enjoyment is provided or within easy walking distance. Guest rooms are large, beautifully furnished, and well equipped. All have private, attached baths. Two have Bain-Ultra jetted tubs. A fireplace is located in the spacious Suite. Digital cable TV/DVD, complimentary DVD library, and wireless DSL service provided. Twenty four seat dining/meeting room available and catered for small groups. Individual table or inroom breakfast service provided. Famous for seasonal, gourmet breakfast menu. "Dixie can flat cook," observed *Southern Living* magazine. Within a block of Katy Trail State Park. Photogenic trails, bluffs, tunnels, and Missouri River within short walking distance. Vinyards, winery, shops, and restaurants nearby. Voted "Favorite Day Trip" by readers of the *Kansas City Star*. Fortunately located midway between Kansas City and St.Louis and fifteen minutes from University town of Columbia.

Rooms/Rates
5 rooms, $119/$225. 1 suite $239/$269. Corporate rates. Premium quality Queen and King beds. Two jetted tubs. One fireplace. Digital cable/DVD. Wireless DSL. Plentiful outdoor seating in garden areas. Open year-round.
Number of Rooms: 6

Cuisine
Full, seasonally changing, gourmet breakfast menu with individual table or inroom service. Afternoon cookies and beverage.

Nearest Airport(s)
Columbia Regional, 30 min.

Directions
I-70 to Exit 115 (Rocheport) at Missouri River Bridge. 2 miles N on BB. L one block on Columbia St to 305 Second St.

Member Since 2005

12+ ⊘ 💳 ⓘ 📁 ✍ @ 🎱 ◎

"Unpretentious hospitality, superior breakfasts, and lovely accommodations."

Innkeepers/Owners
V'Anne and Paul Mydler, and Venetia McEntire (daughter)

Traditional In Town Breakfast Inn

🍽️

paii

Boone's Lick Trail Inn
www.srinns.com/booneslick
1000 South Main Street, Saint Charles, MO 63301 USA
888-940-0002 • 636-947-7000 • Fax 636-946-2637
innkeeper@booneslick.com

Rooms/Rates
4 Rooms, $120/$175; 1 Attic Loft & 1 Master Bedroom, $145/$205. Cottage Whirlpool Suite $195/$275. All private baths. Open year-round.
Number of Rooms: 7

Cuisine
Traditional full or continental-plus breakfast served in dining room. Breakfast brought to Attic Loft, Master Bedroom & Cottage for extra fee.

Nearest Airport(s)
STL Int'l - 8 miles

Directions
From downtown St. Louis take I-70 Westbound to exit 229 (St. Charles Fifth St.), Go North 3 blocks to Boone's Lick Rd., Rt. 4 blocks to Main St. Inn on SE corner of Main & Boone's Lick Rd. From I-70 Eastbound exit Fifth St. Go N on Fifth to Boone's Lick Rd.

Explore this 1840's Federal-style inn with antiques where Daniel Boone & Lewis and Clark trekked along the wide Missouri River. In the heart of a colonial village with 100 shops, 30 restaurants, museums & Katy Trail State Park at our door. The old river settlement with its brick street, gas lamps & green spaces, is the start of the Boone's Lick Trail (8 mi. to STL airport & 25 minutes to St. Louis' sights). V'Anne's delicate lemon biscuits, freshest fruits, and hot entrees are served amidst Paul's working duck decoy collection; a perfect escape for new inngoers, return guests and corporate seekers of a different style lodging. Cottage whirlpool suite now available.

AAA ◆◆◆   *Member Since 1992*   Mobil ★★★

☺   🚭 ♿ 💳 ⓘ 📂 ♥   ✍ @   ◎ ❀   ☕

"Where you are only a few steps away from history–sleep just 50 yards away from where Lewis and Clark slept."

Hermann Hill Vineyard & Inn
www.srinns.com/hermannhillinn
P.O. Box 555, 711 Wein Street, Hermann, MO 65041
573-486-4455 • Fax 573-486-5373
info@hermannhill.com

Innkeepers/Owners
Peggy and Terry
Hammer

Luxury Country Inn &
Vineyard

Enjoy the ultimate country inn experience. We have eight exquisitely appointed guestrooms and five new cottages with spectacular views from your own balcony or patio, luxurious private baths with Jacuzzi-style tubs for two, and the privacy and freedom to set your own pace. Sited on a bluff, the backdrop for your stay is an ever-changing panorama of Hermann and the Missouri River Valley. Sleep late, have breakfast in bed, walk to a nearby winery, explore a quiet old river town, or simply relax and contemplate the view. Later, as the day wanes, enjoy the late afternoon on your private balcony/patio and revel in the luxury that is Hermann Hill's speciality. The choice is all yours. Visit us at www.hermannhill.com to check availability at both Hermann Hill Inn and Hermann Hill Village. Our guests love the consistent amenities at each property that assures the highest level of customer satisfaction. Cottages will generally accomodate up to two couples, with one built for up to four couples. Check out our website for details.

Rooms/Rates
2006 rates $148/$312, all rooms have king-size oak sleigh bed, fireplace, large whirlpool tub, large separate showers, TV/DVD/VCR
Number of Rooms: 8

Cuisine
A full country breakfast with choice of entree served either to your room, or in kitchen, dining room, or outside deck.

Nearest Airport(s)
70 miles west of St. Louis Lambert Airport

Directions
From Exit 175 of I-70, take Hwy 19 south into Hermann, continue south on Hwy 19 to West 6th St. Turn right on W. 6th St., then left on Washington St. At West 10th St., turn right and go 3 blocks up hill, around sharp right turn and watch for our sign on right.

AAA ◆◆◆   *Member Since 2005*

"Hermann is a B&B town... but a trip to the region would not be complete without a stay at Hermann Hill Vineyard & Inn." *Southern Living* Magazine

"The Granite State"

Famous For: Granite, White Mountains, Lakes, Beaches, Prime Primary (The first state to hold presidential primary elections)

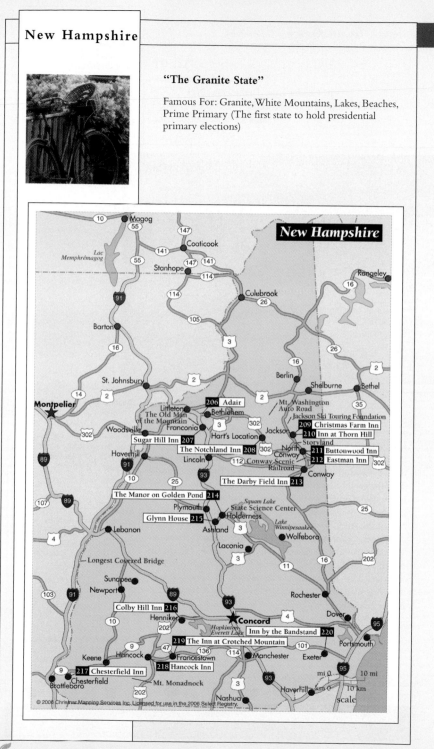

New Hampshire

206 Adair
207 Sugar Hill Inn
208 The Notchland Inn
209 Christmas Farm Inn
210 Inn at Thorn Hill
211 Buttonwood Inn
212 Eastman Inn
213 The Darby Field Inn
214 The Manor on Golden Pond
215 Glynn House
216 Colby Hill Inn
217 Chesterfield Inn
218 Hancock Inn
219 The Inn at Crotched Mountain
220 Inn by the Bandstand

© 2006 Christmas Mapping Services Inc. Licensed for use in the 2006 Select Registry.

Adair

www.srinns.com/adair
80 Guider Lane, Bethlehem, NH 03574
888-444-2600 • 603-444-2600 • Fax 603-444-4823
innkeeper@adairinn.com

Owners
Betsy and Nick Young
Innkeepers
Janet and David Matteucci
Elegant Country Inn

Get away from it all and unwind at this peaceful country home. Enter a woodland oasis via a long drive bordered by rock walls, stately pines, and white birch. This comfortably elegant inn sits atop a knoll, affording magnificent views of the Presidential Range, and surrounded by sweeping lawns, ponds, perennial gardens, and 200 acres of woods. The Olmstead Brothers originally designed the inn's landscaping with its signature iron gates. Adair serves as an intimate, romantic retreat for adults who wish to relax, observe wildlife and/or take advantage of the nearby White Mountains. The inn's relaxing ambiance and casual dress belie uncompromising attention to detail, highly personalized, warm service, and flavorful food. Adair is within a short drive of Franconia Notch, Mt Washington, Mt Lafayette, The Flume, superb hiking, numerous cross-country venues, and 3 major ski areas. Named a "2005 Top 10 Most Romantic Country Inn/Bed & Breakfast" by American Historic Inns. Deliberately small, naturally quiet.

Rooms/Rates
$195/$325 B&B. Comfortable guest rooms w/ private baths, most with fireplaces and mountain views, several w/ 2-person tubs. Two-week closures possible in Apr & Nov.
Number of Rooms: 9

Cuisine
Full breakfast, featuring fresh fruit, steaming popovers, and hot entree. Afternoon tea with scratch-baked sweets. Fine, new American dining at Tim-bir Alley (W-Su) seasonally. Full set-ups in Tap Room. Guests can bring their own spirits.

Nearest Airport(s)
Manchester, NH. Approx. 95 miles

Directions
From I-93 N or S, take exit 40 onto Rt. 302 E; take sharp L at the Adair sign and follow the signs to the inn. From the E, take Rt. 302 W 3+ miles past Bethlehem and make a R at the Adair sign.

AAA ◆◆◆◆   *Member Since 1995*   Mobil ★★★

12+

"Our whole experience here was glorious: the smells, sights, sounds that soothe the soul."

Sugar Hill Inn

Innkeeper/Owner
Steven Allen

Traditional Country Inn

www.srinns.com/sugarhill
Scenic Rte. 117, Sugar Hill, NH 03586
800-548-4748 • 603-823-5621 • Fax 603-823-5639
info@sugarhillinn.com

Rooms/Rates
Classic Rooms $100/$290;
Cottages, $155/$320;
Luxury Rooms, $175/$380.
Open year-round.
Number of Rooms: 15

Cuisine
Full breakfast and afternoon
tea and sweets daily. Dinner
Thursday-Sunday by reservations.
Wine and liquor available. Nice
selection of Port Wine.

Nearest Airport(s)
Manchester Airport - 100 miles.

Directions
From I-93 N : Take exit 38, left
at bottom of ramp to Rte. 18 N.
Travel .5 (1/2) miles L at bridge
Rte 117. The Inn is .5 (1/2) miles
up the hill on R. From I-91 N or
S: take exit 17 onto Rte. 302 E 20
miles on R is Rte. 117. The inn is
8 miles on the left.

"Romance is virtually guaranteed." *Boston Globe* 2003. This 18th
Century classic farmhouse is perched on a hillside on acres of
woodlands, rolling lawns and perennial gardens, enhanced by unparalleled views of the White Mountains. Guestrooms are tastefully appointed, several have fireplaces, whirlpool tubs and private
decks, all are impeccably kept. Enjoy three spacious common
rooms, a large verandah, scrumptious breakfast, afternoon tea,
gourmet dining, selected wine list and casual atmosphere. Steve
is a graduate of the French Culinary Institute. With these amenities, your stay here is sure to be an unforgettable experience. Also,
with abundant outdoor activities, museums, chamber concerts
and theatre, your time here will be rewarding.

Member Since 2001

"Perfect Getaway. A fantastic location-beautiful rooms-a wonderful time. Great Food."

The Notchland Inn

www.srinns.com/notchlandinn
US Route 302, Hart's Location, NH 03812
800-866-6131 • 603-374-6131 • Fax 603-374-6168
innkeepers@notchland.com

Innkeepers/Owners
Les Schoof and Ed Butler

Traditional Tudor
Mountain Country Inn

Get away from it all, relax and rejuvenate at our comfortable granite manor house, completed in 1862, within the White Mountain National Forest. Settle into one of our spacious guest rooms, individually appointed and each with woodburning fireplaces and private baths. Children and pets are welcome in our newly completed river or mountain view cottages, ranging in size from 1 to 2.5 bedrooms and all with whirlpool baths. A wonderful 5-course dinner and full country breakfast are served in a fireplaced dining room overlooking the gardens. Nature's wonders abound at Notchland. We have 8,000 feet of Saco River frontage on our property and two of the area's best swimming holes! Top off an active day, in any season, with a soak in our wooden hot tub, which sits in a gazebo by the pond. Visit with Abby and Crawford, our Bernese Mountain Dogs. Secluded, yet near to all the Mt. Washington Valley has to offer. Notchland...a magical location.

Member Since 1996

Rooms/Rates
8 Deluxe Rooms, 7 Suites, 3 Cottages $199/$395, B&B. Open year-round.
Number of Rooms: 16

Cuisine
5-course distinctive dinners Weds-Sun, hearty country breakfast daily. Fully licensed: wine/spirits/beer. At Notchland, the table is yours for the evening. Dinner is a leisurely affair, taking about 2 hours. $35 per person for in-house guests. $40 Wed, Thur, Sun and $45 Fri, Sat & Holidays for others.

Nearest Airport(s)
Manchester, NH, approx. 125 miles
Burlington, VT, approx. 130 miles

Directions
Take Rt 93N to exit 35, Rt 3N, go 10 miles to Rt 302, turn R, continue 16.5 miles E on 302 to Inn on R.

Chosen one of America's 54 Best Inns by *National Geographic Traveler* magazine.

Proprietors
The Tolley Family
Innkeeper
Tom Spaulding
Traditional Country
Inn & Spa

Christmas Farm Inn
www.srinns.com/christmasfarminn
P.O. Box CC Route 16B, Jackson, NH 03846
800-HI-ELVES • 603-383-4313 • Fax 603-383-6495
info@christmasfarminn.com

Rooms/Rates
42 Units, $227/$342 All rates include full breakfast and candle light dinner for two. Taxes and gratuities are additional. Seasonal packages available. Open year-round. Enjoy our all new SPA, opening in June 2004.
Number of Rooms: 42

Cuisine
Full, cooked-to-order country breakfast, exquisite candlelit dinner, Inn-baked breads and desserts. Mistletoe Pub - full bar available.

Nearest Airport(s)
Portland, ME

Directions
Follow Rte. 16 to Jackson. From Rte. 16 to 16B. Go through covered bridge. 1/2 mi. to school house on R. Keep school house to R and go up hill 1/2 mi. Inn on R.

AN INN FOR ALL SEASONS. Nestled in the majestic White Mountains on ten breathtaking acres, the Christmas Farm Inn offers a taste of the good life. Accommodations include colonial guestrooms in the main inn, private fireplaced cottages and luxury two-room suites with gas fireplaces, Jacuzzi tubs, private balconies and more.... Stroll along our award-winning gardens, swim in the outdoor pool, or soak in the hot tub after a day of cross-country skiing alongside the inn. Enjoy our full service SPA. New American cuisine is featured in the Inn's dining room, complimented by a thoughtful wine list. Conference and intimate wedding settings are available throughout the property.

AAA ◆◆◆   *Member Since 1988*   Mobil ★★★

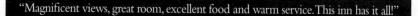

"Magnificent views, great room, excellent food and warm service. This inn has it all!"

Inn at Thorn Hill

www.srinns.com/thornhill

Thorn Hill Road, P.O. Box A, Jackson Village, NH 03846

800-289-8990 • 603-383-4242 • Fax 603-383-8062

stay@innatthornhill.com

Innkeepers/Owners
James & Ibby Cooper

Elegant 19th Century Village Inn

Situated grandly on a knoll overlooking Jackson Village and the Presidential Mountains, the Inn offers 25 uniquely decorated guestrooms, suites, and cottages. The Main Inn features four suites and 12 luxury rooms, all with fireplaces, spa baths, and TV/DVDs, some with steam showers, wet bars, and mountain views. Common areas include a wrap-around porch with views and dining; a lounge with a separate, casual menu; library; and spa level. Spa Facilities include an exercise room, sauna, yoga, manicure/pedicure and three treatment rooms. Activities are available in all seasons at the Inn and throughout the White Mountains. Outdoor pool, year-round outdoor hot tub, cross-country skiing, and tobogganing at the Inn—hiking, golf, tennis, shopping, skiing, and sleigh rides are all nearby. Only AAA Four Diamond Inn and Restaurant in Mt. Washington Valley. *Conde Nast Traveler's* Gold List 2006.

Rooms/Rates
Main Inn: 4 suites, 12 luxury rooms; Carriage House: 6 North Country rooms; 3 Cottages; Open year round. Breakfast, tea & three-course dinner included. $195/$360. Off Season Spa Packages.
Number of Rooms: 25

Cuisine
New England Cuisine with Mediterranean influences & mountain views. Separate lounge menu. Well stocked bar with over thirty single malt scotches & the wine list has over 1300 selections.

Nearest Airport(s)
Portland, ME

Directions
Boston: I-95 to Spaulding Turnpike Rt.16N to Jackson; Portland: Rt.302 to Rt.16N; Montreal, Canada: Can 55 to I-91/I-93, Exit 40-Rt. 302 to Rt.16N to Jackson. Follow signs to Inn.

AAA ◆◆◆◆   *Member Since 1998*   Mobil ★★★

"Nobody does it better and we look forward to being in your home again very soon."

Innkeepers/Owners
Jeffrey and Elizabeth Richards

Traditional Country
Bed and Breakfast

The Buttonwood Inn on Mt. Surprise

www.srinns.com/buttonwood
P.O. Box 1817, Mt. Surprise Rd., North Conway, NH 03860
800-258-2625 • 603-356-2625 • Fax 603-356-3140
innkeeper@buttonwoodinn.com

Rooms/Rates
10 Guestrooms, air-cond, all private baths, $95/$265. Fireplaces common rooms, DVD.
Number of Rooms: 10

Cuisine
Full breakfast; delicious entree changes daily. Served at individual tables, special dietary requests honored.

Nearest Airport(s)
Portland, ME - 65 miles
Manchester, NH - 100 miles

Directions
From SOUTH: I-95 to Rte. 16 N (Spaulding Tpke.) to North Conway. In North Conway Village, at light, turn R on Kearsarge Rd. At 'T,' bear L, Continue approx. 1.2 mi. to stop. Straight across intersection, up Mt. Surprise Rd. 3/10 mi. From NORTH: Rte. 302 S, L to Hurricane Mountain Rd., L to Mt. Surprise Rd., travel 3/10 mi.

Enjoy the peaceful surroundings of this 1820's, ten room Inn, hugging the base of Mount Surprise. At Buttonwood, designated "THE MOST PERFECT STAY," Arrington's Inn Traveler Book of Lists, and "BEST FOR REST AND RELAXATION", guests find romance; retreat; family reunions; intimate wedding celebrations; small business meetings, and our holiday shopping packages are all specialties. Air-conditioned Guest-Chambers feature wide pine floors, stenciling, and antiques. Deluxe rooms offer fireplaces, or fireplace and Jacuzzi-for-two. Common living rooms with wood-burning fireplaces welcome you home to afternoon tea and treats. Relax by the outdoor pool, surrounded by memorable perennial gardens while spying on Ruby-Throated Hummingbirds. Revisit favorite hiking trails and ski-slopes, or discover new ones. Plan adventures to the Cog Railway, or the Flume Gorge. Shopping and fine dining are available a few minutes away in Historic Jackson Village and North Conway. Make plans to visit... we'll blend hospitality and laughter especially for you.

Member Since 1999

12+

"What a treasure! The Buttonwood is perfect privacy, memorable breakfasts, warmth, and special memories to visit again and again."

Eastman Inn

www.srinns.com/eastman

P.O. Box 882, North Conway, NH 03860

800-626-5855 • 603-356-6707 • Fax 603-356-7708

BePampered@eastmaninn.com

Innkeeper/Owner
Lea Greenwood

Traditional Village Bed & Breakfast

Built in 1777 by the Noah Eastman family, the Inn, one of the oldest homes in North Conway, boasts a history rich in tradition in the development of the social and economic growth of the Mt. Washington Valley. The 1930 edition of the New Hampshire Guidebook described the Eastman Inn as "...an all-season house, where hospitality is extended to guests desiring mountain vacations in the quiet comfort of a private home." Seventy-five years later, hospitality remains our priority. Join us for a relaxing, quiet vacation in a home steeped in tradition either for pleasure or on business, and let us treat you to warm, attentive bed and breakfast hospitality in the splendor and style of a bygone era. An eclectic mix of antiquity and modern conveniences makes your journey to an earlier time far more comfortable than our ancestors perhaps imagined. Relax, enjoy gracious Southern hospitality with New England flair, and ... be pampered!

2005 Winner of the "Best Breakfast" category, Best of BedandBreakfast.com Award; Best of BedandBreakfast.com Award 2004 "Best Hospitality" winner; one of the Top Ten Best Overall B&Bs, Best of BedandBreakfast.com Award.

Member Since 2004

Rooms/Rates
$110/$240 w/private baths. Deluxe rooms, fireplaces, whirlpool and antique soaking tubs, cable television, telephone, wraparound porch, lending library.
Number of Rooms: 14

Cuisine
Breakfast is not traditional country inn fare but a gastronomic adventure with the menu changing daily. Dietary restrictions available. Fine dining within minutes.

Nearest Airport(s)
Portland, ME - 60 milesManchester, NH - 100 miles

Directions
1/2 mile S of Schouler Park in the Village of North Conway on Rte 16/302.

15+

"...we felt peaceful and pampered."

Innkeepers/Owners
Marc & Maria Donaldson

Traditional Full Service Country Inn

The Darby Field Inn
www.srinns.com/darbyfield
185 Chase Hill Road, Albany, NH 03818
800-426-4147 • 603-447-2181 • Fax 603-447-5726
marc@darbyfield.com

Rooms/Rates
13 Rooms, $140/290 B&B Dbl. Occ; $210/360 MAP Dbl. Occ. before tax and gratuities. Deluxe room/suites, fireplaces, jacuzzi's, A/C & mountain views.
Number of Rooms: 13

Cuisine
Country gourmet dining in a casual setting with mountain views. Choose from 130 bottles of fine wines and a fully stocked tavern. Full country breakfast included; served while watching the birds and maybe even a moose!

Nearest Airport(s)
Portland, ME: 60 miles

Directions
One half mile south of Conway Village off Rte.16, turn on to Bald Hill Road. Go up the hill one mile, and turn right onto Chase Hill Rd. Proceed one mile to inn.

Only 6 miles from North Conway, yet right in the middle of no-where, overlooking the Mt. Washington Valley and White Mountains of New Hampshire, the Darby Field Inn quietly surprises and delights wanderers adventurous enough to leave the beaten path. The Darby Field Inn is much more than just a little bed and breakfast. It is a romantic B&B with fireplace and Jacuzzi rooms and suites, candlelight gourmet dining, a sophisticated wine list, and moonlit sleigh rides. It's a full service country inn for those looking to relax by the fireplace in the living room, on the mountain-view patio, in the fully stocked sunroom Tavern, in our award winning gardens or by the crystal clear, heated swimming pool. The inn also has private nature trails for x-c skiing, snowshoeing, mountain biking or just walking. And, if that's not enough, how about a nice theraputic massage or a rejuvenating yoga class? Whether you are looking for romance, relaxation or a more active adventure, The Darby Field Inn has it all!

AAA ◆◆◆   *Member Since 1981*

8+

"Darby Field Inn was charming and comfortable. A perfect retreat after the rigors of hiking. A wonderful compliment to the magical surroundings. We will send friends."

The Manor on Golden Pond

www.srinns.com/manorongoldenpond
Box T, Rt. 3, Holderness, NH 03245
800-545-2141 Reservations • 603-968-3348 • Fax
603-968-2116
info@manorongoldenpond.com

Innkeepers/Owners
Brian and Mary Ellen Shields

Elegant English
Manor Country Inn

A Love Story began at this English Manor House, and continues with each of our guests pampered in our luxuriously appointed suites. Our suites enjoy working fireplaces where the fire is always laid, oversized Jacuzzis or Air®baths, and steam showers. Many suites have private decks to enjoy magnificent vistas of Squam Lake and the White Mountains. Guests can enjoy massages in our Spa Treatment Room, a tennis match on our clay tennis court, lunch beside our outdoor pool, or the tranquility of our private beach on "Golden Pond." Located in the Lakes Region of New Hampshire activities abound no matter what the season for our guests to explore. Guests awaken to our delectable Gourmet breakfasts each morning. English Afternoon tea is served daily for guests to reminisce their day's adventures. Before dinner enjoy a Manor martini in our "Three Cocks Pub" followed by a dinner in our award-winning Van Horn dining room to finish off a perfect day at the Manor. "Best of New England..." Andrew Harper's *Hideaway Report*.

Rooms/Rates
25 Rooms $200/$475 B&B for two people per night. Open year-round. Carriage house and cottages open seasonally.
Number of Rooms: 25

Cuisine
Full Gourmet Breakfast. Afternoon Tea 4-5:00 p.m. each day. Fine Dining New England Cuisine. Ala Carte Menu plus Chef Tasting menu offered. Dinner by reservation. *Wine Spectator* Award of Excellence wine list. Cozy Three Cocks Pub with Piano Bar.

Nearest Airport(s)
Manchester Airport (1 Hour drive)

Directions
I-93, exit 24, E on Rte. 3, proceed for 4.7 mi., turn R at our sign (Less than two hours from Boston.)

AAA ◆◆◆◆   *Member Since 1995*

12+

"Everything was wonderful! The Inn is beautiful, as is the view, but the service is what made our experience very special..attention to detail incredible."

Innkeepers
Pamela, Ingrid and Glenn Heidenreich

Historic Village Bed & Breakfast Inn

Glynn House Inn

www.srinns.com/glynnhouse
59 Highland Street, Ashland, NH 03217
800-637-9599 • 603-968-3775 • Fax 603-968-9415
theglynnhouseinn@yahoo.com

paii

Rooms/Rates
5 Bedrooms and 8 Suites. High Season - May 26th thru October 30th $139-$259 per night. Low Season - October 31st thru May 25th $139-$229 per night. **Number of Rooms:** 13

Cuisine
Includes full breakfast, afternoon tea, hors d'oeuvres and complimentary wine. Tea, coffee, hot chocolate, soft drinks and bottled water are available throughout the day. Special dietary needs are always accommodated.

Nearest Airport(s)
Manchester

Directions
We are located at Exit 24 on I93. Take Route 3 South and make a left onto Highland Street. The Inn is located 1/4 of mile up on the left.

This beautifully restored 19th Century Inn is located on a quiet tree-lined street in Ashland, New Hampshire. Wake up to coffee, tea or hot chocolate placed outside your door to enjoy whilst getting ready to start your day. Come on down for a gourmet breakfast that will tide you over till late lunch. After breakfast explore the area and return for afternoon tea and refreshments. Before heading out for dinner come and join your hosts for a complimentary glass of wine and hors d'oeuvres.

All of our rooms offer queen size beds and private baths as well as fireplaces, luxurious robes and deluxe amenities. In addition, our suites have a spacious separate sitting area and double whirlpool spas as well as LCD screen televisions.

AAA ◆◆◆   *Member Since 2005*   Mobil ★★★

12+

Colby Hill Inn

www.srinns.com/colbyhillinn

3 The Oaks, P.O. Box 779, Henniker, NH 03242

800-531-0330 • 603-428-3281 • Fax 603-428-9218

innkeeper@colbyhillinn.com

Innkeepers/Owners
Cyndi and Mason Cobb

Traditional Elegant
Colonial Village Inn

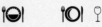

Intimate and romantic country inn located in the charming unspoiled village of Henniker. Enjoy romantic touches including down comforters, plush bathrobes, two-person whirlpools, crackling fireplaces and luxurious linens. 14 romantic guest rooms including two intimate suites with period antiques. All guest rooms have private baths, phones and wireless Internet access. Award winning candlelight dining nightly overlooking lush gardens, antique barns and gazebo. Bountiful breakfasts and candlelight dinners. Genuine hospitality and central New England location make this an ideal getaway spot. Outdoor pool, lawn chess, cross country and downhill skiing, hiking, biking, and tennis all nearby. *Yankee Magazine* Editor's Pick. *Wine Spectator* Award of Excellence. Featured in *The Boston Globe* and *Ski Magazine*. 90 Minutes North of Boston.

Rooms/Rates

$139/$279 depending on season. Some guest rooms have whirlpools/fireplaces. Gourmet breakfast included.
Number of Rooms: 14

Cuisine

Full gourmet breakfast including specialties like pumpkin pancakes w/warm maple cream. Afternoon cookies. Award-winning romantic candlelight dining with full service bar, fine wines & spirits. Dinner avail. nightly for inn guests & public.

Nearest Airport(s)

Manchester

Directions

17 Miles W. of Concord, N.H. 93 N. to 89 N. to Rt. 202/9W (Left exit). Continue on 202/9 & Exit at Rt. 114, Turn L. 1 mile to blinker, turn R, 1/2 mile on Right. 90 min. N. of Boston.

AAA ◆◆◆   *Member Since 1993*   Mobil ★★★

7+

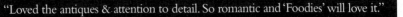

"Loved the antiques & attention to detail. So romantic and 'Foodies' will love it."

Chesterfield Inn

www.srinns.com/chesterfield
Route 9, Box 155, Chesterfield, NH 03443
800-365-5515 • 603-256-3211 • Fax 603-256-6131
chstinn@sover.net

Innkeepers/Owners
Phil and Judy Hueber

Elegant Colonial
Country Inn

Rooms/Rates
15 Rooms, $150/$320 B&B 2
Suites, $200/$225 B&B.Open
year-round except Christmas Eve
and Christmas Day.
Number of Rooms: 15

Cuisine
Full Country Breakfast cooked to
order served daily. Dinner is served
Monday through Saturday in our
candlelit dining room with sweeping views of the Green Mountains.
Room service is available. Wine list
and full bar available.

Nearest Airport(s)
Hartford, CT is a one and a half
hour drive and Boston is a two and
a half hour drive.

Directions
From I-91, take exit 3 to Route 9
E, continue on Route 9 for 2 miles.
Turn L onto Cross Road and R into
driveway.

Serving since 1787 as a tavern, a farm and a museum, the Inn's guest rooms today are spacious. Some have fireplaces, jacuzzi tubs, or outdoor balconies; all have private baths, air conditioning, TV, wireless Internet access, and telephone. Outside, the Inn's 10 acres of gardens and meadow overlook Vermont's Green Mountains. Guests enjoy delicious, innovative cuisine in the candlelit dining room. Chesterfield Inn is a wonderful place to relax in comfortable elegance.

AAA ◆◆◆   *Member Since 1990*

"What a wonderful weekend we had at the Chesterfield Inn! A warm welcome, beautiful room, delicious breakfast and romantic dinner-it was just what we needed."

The Hancock Inn~1789~NH's Oldest Inn

www.srinns.com/hancockinn
33 Main Street, P.O. Box 96, Hancock, NH 03449
800-525-1789 • 603-525-3318 • Fax 603-525-9301
innkeeper@hancockinn.com

Innkeeper/Owner
Robert Short

Traditional Federal Village Inn

AWARD OF EXCELLENCE

Since 1789, the first year of George Washington's presidency, the Inn has hosted rumrunners and cattle drovers, aristocracy, and even a U.S. President. It's seen elegant balls, Concord Coaches, and the first rider of the railroad. Today, the Inn maintains its historic elegance combined with modern day amenities. The town of Hancock, located in the beautiful Monadnock Region of Southern New Hampshire, is considered by many to be one of the prettiest villages in New England, boasting a church with a Paul Revere Bell that rings in each hour, a friendly local general store and many homes that are listed on the National Historic Register. Year-round regional recreation opportunities include hiking, cross country/downhill skiing, swimming, boating and fishing. Visit in any season and find: spring daffodils and real maple sugaring; summer swimming and fishing at Hancock's town beach or music on the village square; fall colors and covered bridges; winter snow...and relaxing by our raging fireplace with a hot toddy!

Rooms/Rates
14 Rooms. $125/$290. Appointed with antiques, TV, phone, AC. 10 with fireplaces, 4 with whirlpools.
Number of Rooms: 14

Cuisine
Amidst the glow of candles and a flickering fireplace you will dine in Colonial splendor. The recipe for our signature dish, Shaker Cranberry Potroast, was requested by *Bon Appetit*. Full bar with 350 wine selections and many single malts. *Wine Spectator* Award.

Nearest Airport(s)
Manchester Airport

Directions
From Boston: I 93N then 101W to Peterborough. R on 202. Turn L onto 123 3 miles to historic Main Street. From NY: I 91 to Brattleboro. Route 9 toward Keene to 123. Turn R to Hancock.

Member Since 1971   Mobil ★★★

"Visiting The Hancock Inn is like taking a step back to a kindler, gentler era."
"Awesome pot roast!!"

The Inn at Crotched Mountain

www.srinns.com/crotchedmountain
534 Mountain Rd., Francestown, NH 03043
603-588-6840 • Fax 603-588-6623
perry-inncm@conknet.com

Innkeepers/Owners
John and Rose Perry
Traditional Mountain
Breakfast Inn

Rooms/Rates
13 Rooms, 3 with fireplaces,
$70/$140 B&B. Open year
round, except first two weeks in
November.
Number of Rooms: 13

Cuisine
Full breakfast daily. Light fare
served in The Winslow Tavern on
Saturday. Wine & liquor available.

Nearest Airport(s)
Manchester, N.H.

Directions
From Boston: I-93N 101W to
114N to Goffstown 13S to New
Boston 136 W to Francestown
47N 2.5 mi. L onto Mt. Rd 1 mi.
From N.Y.: I-91N to Brattleboro
Rt. 9E to 31S 47 4.5 mi. R onto
Mt. Rd. 1 mi.

This 180 year-old colonial house is located on the northeastern side of Crotched Mountain. An awe-inspiring setting and a spectacular view of the Piscatagoug Valley makes all the difference at this out-of-the-way Colonial Inn. Swimming pool, two clay tennis courts, walking and cx ski trails, vegetable and flower gardens supply food and adornment for tables and rooms. Downhill skiing nearby. Light fare served in The Winslow Tavern on Saturday. John and Rose, who have been operating the Inn since 1973, and their three English Cockers, look forward to welcoming you.

Member Since 1981

"We can't ever thank you both enough for your hospitality and thoughtfulness."

Inn by the Bandstand

www.srinns.com/innbythebandstand
4 Front Street, Exeter, NH 03833
877-239-3837 • 603-772-6352
info@innbythebandstand.com

Innkeeper/Owner
Susan Henderson
Managers/Innkeepers
Jim and Vicky Lane
Historic In Town
B&B

The award–winning Inn by the Bandstand is the premier lodging establishment in Exeter, New Hampshire. This bed and breakfast inn is an 1809 historic home located in the heart of downtown Exeter. Only two blocks from the prestigious Phillips Exeter Academy, eight miles to the seacoast and beaches, and 20 minutes from Portsmouth, this charming B&B offers nine antique–furnished guest rooms, all private baths and a delicious full breakfast.

The inn is surrounded by quaint shops, fine restaurants and even an old fashioned movie theatre across the street. You can explore the downtown bookstore, toy store, and our own antique shop plus many fine gift and apparel boutiques. Why not take in a movie at the fully restored Ioka Theater? Stroll around the river walk near the Academy boat house or have a picnic in the park. We also have the American Independence Museum and museum shop, plus historical self-guided tours to broaden your knowledge and interest of this area and its importance in our nation's founding history.

Rooms/Rates
$139/$209 double occupancy rooms. $219 2-room family suites, up to 4 persons
Number of Rooms: 9

Cuisine
Full breakfast

Nearest Airport(s)
Manchester-Boston Regional Airport

Directions
From Interstate 95: Take exit 2 BEFORE the toll booth (route 101 west). Take route 101 west for about 6 miles to exit 11 (Route 108 south). Off the exit ramp turn left (south) on Route 108 for 1 1/2 miles and you will come to a "T" intersection with a light (High Street). Turn right and drive to the center of Exeter. You will see the bandstand on your left with the Inn by the Bandstand on the corner. Parking is available at the rear of the Inn.

AAA ◆◆◆   *Member Since 2006*

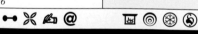

"A wonderful place! Great bed, delicious breakfast... who could ask for anything more?"

New Jersey

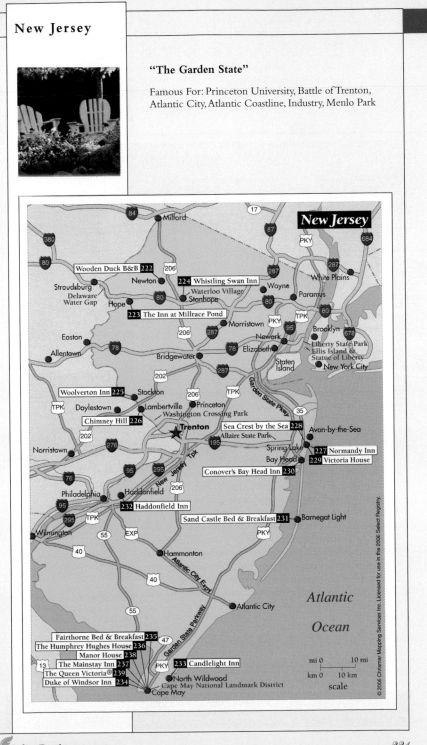

"The Garden State"

Famous For: Princeton University, Battle of Trenton, Atlantic City, Atlantic Coastline, Industry, Menlo Park

New Jersey

- Milford
- 84
- 17
- 87
- PKY
- 684
- 380
- 80
- Wooden Duck B&B 222
- 206
- Newton
- 224 Whistling Swan Inn
- Wayne
- White Plains
- 287
- 287
- Stroudsburg
- Delaware Water Gap
- Hope
- Waterloo Village
- Stanhope
- 80
- 223 The Inn at Millrace Pond
- Morristown
- 206
- 287
- Newark
- Brooklyn
- 678
- Easton
- 78
- Bridgewater
- 78
- Elizabeth
- Liberty State Park
- Ellis Island & Statue of Liberty
- Allentown
- 206
- Staten Island
- New York City
- 202
- 287
- 35
- Woolverton Inn 225
- Stockton
- 206
- Princeton
- TPK
- Doylestown
- Lambertville
- Washington Crossing Park
- Chimney Hill 226
- Trenton
- Sea Crest by the Sea 228
- Avon-by-the-Sea
- Allaire State Park
- Norristown
- 202
- 276
- 195
- Spring Lake
- 227 Normandy Inn
- Bay Head
- 229 Victoria House
- 76
- 95
- 295
- New Jersey TPK
- 206
- Conover's Bay Head Inn 230
- Philadelphia
- Haddonfield
- 95
- 232 Haddonfield Inn
- TPK
- 55
- EXP
- Sand Castle Bed & Breakfast 231
- Barnegat Light
- Wilmington
- 295
- PKY
- 40
- Hammonton
- Atlantic City Expwy
- 40
- 55
- Atlantic City
- *Atlantic Ocean*
- Fairthorne Bed & Breakfast 235
- The Humphrey Hughes House 236
- Manor House 238
- 47
- 13
- The Mainstay Inn 237
- PKY
- 233 Candlelight Inn
- The Queen Victoria® 239
- Duke of Windsor Inn 234
- North Wildwood
- Cape May National Landmark District
- Cape May
- mi 0   10 mi
- km 0   10 km
- scale

© 2006 Chrismar Mapping Services Inc. Licensed for use in the 2006 Select Registry.

The Wooden Duck B&B

www.srinns.com/woodenduck
140 Goodale Road, Newton, NJ 07860
973-300-0395 • Fax 973-300-0395
woodenduckinn@earthlink.net

Innkeepers/Owners
Beth & Karl Krummel
Country Casual
Bed & Breakfast Inn

paii

An oasis of country pleasures! This mini-estate is nestled on 10 acres adjacent to the 1600 acre Kittatinny Valley State Park, abundant with wildlife and hiking trails. All guestrooms have queen bed, private bath, TV/VCR, clock radio, hair dryers, iron and ironing board, telephone, desk, and a comfortable sitting area. Complementary wired and wireless internet available throughout. Deluxe rooms have soaking tub for two, fireplace, private outside balcony. Guests are welcome to use the game room with double hearth fireplace, the inground pool, and video library. The "Guest Kitchen," with complementary snacks, homemade chocolate chip cookies, soda, coffee, and tea, is available 24/7. Nearby are many antique and craft shops, Waterloo Village, Sussex Skyhawks Baseball, golf (6 courses within 10 miles), winter and summer sports, horseback riding, cycling. The Wooden Duck is the only B&B in Northern New Jersey rated 3 star by Mobile Travel Guide. Just 75 minutes to Manhattan. Less than an hour to the Crossings Outlet Mall in PA.

Rooms/Rates
10 rooms, $120/$210 per night/ double Corporate rates Sunday thru Thursday Open all year
Number of Rooms: 10

Cuisine
A full country breakfast featuring variously homebaked breads or muffins, egg dishes, unique French toast, fresh fruit, juice, tea, coffee and more! Guest pantry features homemade cookies, snacks, fruit, hot and cold beverages. Fine and casual dining nearby.

Nearest Airport(s)
Newark Airport, 45 Miles

Directions
From I-80 take Exit 25, following Rte 206 N 7.8 mi. to Goodale Rd. Turn R and proceed 1.5 mi. through the Kitatinny Valley State Park to The Wooden Duck's driveway (#140) on the L.

AAA ◆◆◆   *Member Since 2003*   Mobil ★★★

8+

"If you like B&B's, you will love this one!
Fabulous. Pristine. Serene. Impeccable!"

SelectRegistry.com

Innkeepers/Owners
Cordie & Charles Puttkammer

Traditional Village Inn

🍽️ 🍽️ 🍷

🏮 paii

The Inn at Millrace Pond

www.srinns.com/millrace

313 Johnsonburg Road, P.O. Box 359, Hope, NJ 07844

800-746-6467 • 908-459-4884 • Fax 908-459-5276

millrace@epix.net

Rooms/Rates
17 Guestrooms $145/$185 Fri-Sat, including holidays ($125/$135 Sun-Thurs) Breakfast included Open year-round.
Number of Rooms: 17

Cuisine
Dinner served Mon-Thurs 6-8 Fri & Sat 5-9 Sunday 4-7:30 Luncheon & dinner for groups~Tavern~Wine/liquor served with meals.

Nearest Airport(s)
Lehigh Valley International
Newark International

Directions
From South: 31 to 46W to 519N R at blinker in Hope 1/10M. to Inn. From North, East or West: I-80 exit 12 - 1 mile S on 521 to blinker L 1/10M to Inn.

The Inn building located on 23 acres was an operating grist-mill from 1770 until the early 1950's. Authentically decorated guestrooms with private baths are located in the Gristmill, Mill-race House and Stone Cottage suggesting the quiet elegance of Colonial America. Relax in the ambiance of the parlor. Savor romantic candlelight dinners in the fine dining restaurant. Stroll past the mill's antique water wheel and wine cellar into the tavern offering casual midweek dining beside the walk-in fireplace. An 1830s home from the historic Moravian Village of Hope has been restored into the conference center featuring individual meeting rooms along with library, parlor and fitness area. Perhaps a game of tennis on the private court or a hike nearby is in order. The Delaware Water Gap Recreation Area (a National Park) is 13 miles west of the Inn. Excellent antiquing, a vineyard, golf, and skiing are nearby.

Member Since 1988

☺   🚭 ♿ 🍰 🛅 📂 ❤️ 🍴   @ 🐕   🔲 ◎   ☕

Whistling Swan Inn

www.srinns.com/whistlingswan
110 Main St., Stanhope, NJ 07874
888-507-2337 • 973-347-6369 • Fax 973-347-6379
info@whistlingswaninn.com

Innkeeper
Liz Armstrong

Traditional Village
Breakfast Inn

One of the Top Ten B&B's in the US says the Inn Traveler magazine. Set amidst a spectacular garden on a quiet, tree-lined street the Whistling Swan Inn exudes romance and warmth. This 1905 Queen Anne Victorian features a gracious wraparound veranda where leisurely breakfasts are served on pleasant mornings. Each room embraces you with comfort and warmth with period antiques and modern conveniences; TV/VCR, air conditioning, plus refrigerators, gas fireplaces, and Jacuzzis in our suites.

Whatever the season, a myriad of activities awaits you. After a busy day of hiking, biking, shopping or antiquing relax in a hammock or share pleasant conversations with newfound friends. Enjoy fine dining at one of the area gourmet restaurants, some within walking distance. At day's end, snuggle up with your special someone next to a crackling fire. Sink into your queen-sized feather bed and fall asleep to a movie from our video library.

Rooms/Rates
6 Rooms, 3 Suites $99/$229. Corporate & Gov't Rates. All with private bath (some w/Jacuzzi and fireplaces), Cable TV/VCR, Wireless Internet, Central AC. Open year-round. Special Package & rates available.
Number of Rooms: 9

Cuisine
Full country buffet breakfast, 24-hour complimentary guest bar.

Nearest Airport(s)
Newark, NJ

Directions
Bus & Train via NJ Transit to Netcong. Take Rte 80W to Exit 27B. Take Route 183N to HESS STATION on right, turn left on MAIN ST. Turn left at KING ST-Inn's parking lot is 2nd driveway on RIGHT. For more directions, visit our website. WATERLOO VILLAGE NEARBY.

AAA ◆◆◆   *Member Since 1992*

9+   🚭

"Every detail has been thought of-wonderful ambiance, friendly hosts, and great food! Perfect! Absolutely the best B&B we've ever visited."

Innkeepers/Owners
**Carolyn McGavin and
Bob Haas**

Traditional Village
Breakfast Inn

Woolverton Inn

www.srinns.com/woolvertoninn
6 Woolverton Road, Stockton, NJ 08559
888-264-6648 • 609-397-0802 • Fax 609-397-0987
sheep@woolvertoninn.com

Rooms/Rates
6 Rooms $135/$295; 2
Suites $225/$325; 5 Cottages
$275/$425. Rooms offer featherbeds, fresh flowers, robes, luxury
linens, CD Players.
Number of Rooms: 13

Cuisine
Full gourmet breakfast served by
candlelight in our gardens or in
bed. Signature Dishes include:
apple-cranberry turkey sausage,
Pecan Pancakes, homemade cinnamon buns & fabulous cookies.

Nearest Airport(s)
Philadelphia International

Directions
Philadelphia: I-95, exit 1 to Rte.
29 N to Stockton. R on 523 for
2/10 mi., L on Woolverton Rd.
NY: I-78 W to exit 29 for 287 S,
exit for 202 S for Flemington. Exit
Rte. 29 N. R on 523, L 2/10 mi.

Perched high above the Delaware River, surrounded by 300 acres
of rolling farmland and forest, The Woolverton Inn provides the
seclusion of a grand country estate, yet the activities of New Hope
and Lambertville are just five minutes away. Enjoy the glorious
setting and relaxed elegance of this 1792 stone manor, while feeling as comfortable as you would at your own home in the country. All guestrooms are unique and thoughtfully decorated; they
feature bucolic views, fireplaces, whirlpool tubs and showers for
two, private outdoor sitting areas, stocked refrigerators, and Bose
CD Wave radios. As recommended by *Travel + Leisure, Country
Living,* NBC's *Today in NY* among others.

AAA ◆◆◆   *Member Since 2002*   Mobil ★★★

12+ 🚭 ♿ 💳 🛈 📁 ♥ ✂ @ 🐕 🧺 ◎ ❀ ☕

"A luxury getaway like no other...thank you for a memorable and romantic
Honeymoon! Bravo!"

Chimney Hill Farm Estate

www.srinns.com/chimneyhillfarm
207 Goat Hill Road, Lambertville, NJ 08530
800-211-4667 • 609-397-1516 • Fax 609-397-9353
info@chimneyhillinn.com

Owners
Terry Anne & Richard Anderson

Elegant In Town
Breakfast Inn

On a country road high in the hills above the charming historic riverside town of Lambertville, New Jersey, sits Chimney Hill Farm Estate & The Ol' Barn Inn. This gorgeous fieldstone house and barn, built in 1820, are surrounded by beautiful fields and gardens. The perfect spot for romantic getaways or corporate retreats, Chimney Hill is only 1/2 mi from the antique-filled towns of Lambertville and New Hope. Known for great country-style hospitality, Chimney Hill Farm Estate provides its guests with comfort and elegance. Featured as the cover for *Country Inns, New Jersey Country Roads* magazines, it is a connoisseur's choice—Come visit!

Rooms/Rates
Main Estate House M-Th $135/$155. Fri-Sun $189/$255. Ol'Barn Inn Suites M-Th $189/$275. Fri-Sun $289/$395. **Number of Rooms:** 12

Cuisine
Gourmet country breakfast served by candlelight, a guest butler pantry filled with cookies, goodies and sherry. Excellent Resturuants in Lambertville and New Hope.

Nearest Airport(s)
Philadelphia 45 miles
Newark 42 miles

Directions
Phi: I-95N ext1 (Lambertville) to rt. 29N. Travel 7 mi; turn R onto Valley Rd, L on Goat Hill Rd.-1.5 mi on R. NY: I-78W to I-287S to Rt.202S to Rt.179S (Lambertville ex). At traffic light go straight to 2nd L (SWAN St.) Go to 2nd R. (Studdiford St.) to top.

AAA ◆◆◆   *Member Since 1998*   Mobil ★★★

12+

Owners
The Valori Family

Elegant Victorian
Waterside Breakfast Inn

Normandy Inn
www.srinns.com/normandy
21 Tuttle Avenue, Spring Lake, NJ 07762
800-449-1888 • 732-449-7172 • Fax 732-449-1070
normandy@verizon.net

Rooms/Rates
18 Rooms, high season $145/$295; quiet season $115/225. 2 Suites, high season $395/$375, quiet season $325/$305. Open year-round.
Number of Rooms: 20

Cuisine
Full gourmet breakfast included and served at your own private table. Sumptuous afternoon treats including seasonal fruits and fresh squeezed juice in the summer, homemeade soups in the quiet season. Evening cordials. Fine dining restaurants located nearby.

Nearest Airport(s)
Newark International

Directions
Garden State Pkwy to exit 98. Follow Rte 34 S to traffic circle, 3/4 around to Rte 524 E. Take to ocean, turn R onto Ocean Avenue & then first R onto Tuttle. Fifth house on the L.

A romantic 19th Century inn, the Normandy Inn is on the National Register of Historic Places. Fine antique furnishings adorn this tradionally elegant home which is located just steps from the ocean. Upon visiting the inn, your welcome begins in the spacious double parlors decorated in Victorian splendor. Many guest rooms, each of which are unique, boast cozy fireplaces, Jacuzzis, canopy beds and a peek at the ocean. All rooms include private baths, air conditioning, and telephones. Guests' wake up call is the sound of the ocean as a private table awaits you in the gracious dining room. The Normandy offers a hearty country breakfast, tempting afternoon treats, evening cordials, and prides itself on exceptional service. The Normandy, just 1/2 block to the ocean, is centrally located to cultural and outdoor activities. Mobil and AAA rated, the Normandy makes for the perfect getaway. *New York* Magazine calls it "an antique-laden dreamworld," your inn for all seasons.

Member Since 1996

"Truly a step back in time, this seaside beauty made for the perfect escape!"

Sea Crest by the Sea

www.srinns.com/seacrestbythesea
19 Tuttle Avenue, Spring Lake, NJ 07762
800-803-9031 • 732-449-9031 • Fax 732-974-0403
capt@seacrestbythesea.com

Innkeepers/Owners
Fred & Barbara Vogel

Elegant Waterside
Breakfast Inn

Lovingly restored 1885 Queen Anne Victorian for ladies and gentlemen on seaside holiday. Ocean views, fireplaces, private decks, luxurious linens, DUX beds, whirlpools for two, steam showers, comfort-filled rooms, sumptuous breakfast and afternoon tea, evening cordials. A *Gourmet* magazine "Top Choice." *Philadelphia Magazine* says "Spring Lake's most luxurious inn," one of *Discerning Travelers* top Romantic Inns for 2005. Chosen as one of the country's Top 10 Romantic Inns for 2006 by American Historic Inns. Barbara and Fred Vogel will pamper you with modern amenities and classic hospitality in an atmosphere that soothes your weary body and soul.

Rooms/Rates
8 Rooms and Suites, $310/$490.
All rooms have private baths, whirlpool tubs for two, fireplaces, stocked refrigerators and highspeed wireless Internet. Open all year.
Number of Rooms: 8

Cuisine
Full candlelit buffet breakfast and afternoon tea featuring Sea Crest signature specialties, and evening cordials. Fine restaurants and unique dining nearby. First class Concierge service.

Nearest Airport(s)
Newark Liberty-1 hr.

Directions
From NY and North: GS Pkwy to Exit 98. 34 S to first traffic circle. 3/4 around to 524 E. to Ocean, R 1 block. R again to Tuttle Ave. 4th house on L. From South: Rte I-195 to 34 S, then follow above.

AAA ◆◆◆   *Member Since 1993*

"It doesn't get any better than this," Pam Lanier, noted travel expert & guest.

SelectRegistry.com

Innkeepers/Owners
Lynne and Alan Kaplan

Elegant Victorian
Waterside B&B Inn

Victoria House Bed & Breakfast

www.srinns.com/victoriahouse

214 Monmouth Avenue, Spring Lake, NJ 07762-1127

888-249-6252 • 732-974-1882 • Fax 732-974-2132

info@victoriahouse.net

paii

Rooms/Rates
8 beautifully appointed guests rooms: Jacuzzis, Fireplaces, TV/VCR's/DVD's. High Season $199/$399; Low Season $99/$299.
Number of Rooms: 8

Cuisine
Gourmet-served breakfast with house specialties on the veranda or at tables for two in our dining room. Enjoy afternoon tea and evening cordials & chocolates.

Nearest Airport(s)
Newark, Philadelphia

Directions
From NY, CT, North NJ: GS Pkwy S to ex. 98, to 138E to Rte 35S, 3rd light L Warren Ave. Through next light, turn R on 3rd Ave (Church on L) L on Monmouth Ave. From DC/DE/PA: Rte I-95N/NJ TPKE to 195E to 138E, then follow above dir. NYC/AC 60, Phil 70 miles.

Relax, refresh, renew in our lovingly restored 1882 Queen Anne; the perfect seaside oasis for romantic getaways and business travelers. Enjoy the sea breeze on the veranda or read a book in front of the parlor fireplace. Escape in the distinctive decor of your accommodations; fireplaces, featherbeds, TV/VCRs/DVDs, refrigerator, Jacuzzi for two; all with private baths, air-conditioning, individual temperature control. Stroll our beach boardwalk or around the lake; bicycle our tree-lined streets; or discover a treasure in one of our charming main street shops. Taste our wonderful gourmet breakfasts. Timeless hospitality awaits you. Enjoy our Victorian splendor with modern amenities. A romantic B&B Inn for all seasons. Recently renovated and restored with care. Open all year.

Member Since 1998

12+

"Best B&B experience at the Shore." "Best Breakfast, my compliments to the chef." "My favorite place to stay."

Conover's Bay Head Inn

www.srinns.com/conoversbay
646 Main Ave., Bay Head, NJ 08742
800-956-9099 • 732-892-4664 • Fax 732-892-8748
innkeeper@conovers.com

Owners
The Ramonas Family
Traditional Victorian Village
Breakfast Inn

Discover the antique-filled splendor of Conover's Bay Head Inn, recognized for fine accommodations and hospitality since 1970. Each bed chamber has been uniquely designed for your comfort. Luxurious bed linens are line-dried, starched, and ironed. The aroma of Inn-baked biscuits, muffins or coffee cake and the "feature" of the day will awaken you each morning. Bay Head, with its weathered shingle-style houses, captures the feeling of a late 19th century residential seaside village.

Rooms/Rates
12 Rooms, $165/$320 B&B.
Number of Rooms: 12

Cuisine
Breakfast, afternoon tea. No alcohol license.

Nearest Airport(s)
Newark Airport

Directions
From NY & North Garden State Parkway exit 98 to Rt 34 South to Rt 35 South to Bay Head from PA & S NJ tpke to S 195 East to Rt 34 South to Rt 35 South to Bay Head.

AAA ◆◆◆◆   *Member Since 1996*

"Thank you for making us feel pampered with the wonderful massage, your special linens, a terrific breakfast, but most of all your warm hospitality!"

Sand Castle Bed & Breakfast

Innkeeper/Owner
Nancy Gallimore

Bayfront Bed &
Breakfast Inn

www.srinns.com/sandcastle
710 Bayview Avenue, Box 607, Barnegat Light, Long
Beach Island, NJ 08006
800-253-0353 • 609-494-6555
info@sandcastlelbi.com

Rooms/Rates
5 Rooms $155/$275, depending on season and 2 suites $235/$410. Open April through Thanksgiving
Number of Rooms: 7

Cuisine
Full gourmet breakfast included. Complimentary coffee, tea, snacks, soft drinks available 24 hours. Restaurants next door and within a short drive.

Nearest Airport(s)
Atlantic City, Phila, Newark

Directions
Garden State Parkway exit 63. Take Route 72 East to end. Left onto Long Beach Blvd. Follow 8 miles to Barnegat Light. At 2nd blinking yellow light make left onto 10th Street. Turn right onto Bayview Ave. Sand Castle is 2 blocks down on right.

A truly incomparable experience on Long Beach Island! Spacious suites and luxurious rooms with beautiful bay views, all with fireplace, private entrance, private bath some with jacuzzi, A/C, cable TV/VCR/DVD/CD player, in-room phone with voicemail, current DVD movie library, wireless access, complimentary snacks, 24 hour coffee/tea, soft drinks. Start your day with Nancy Gallimore's sumptuous gourmet breakfast and relaxed hospitality. Enjoy the heated outdoor pool, jacuzzi and exercise room. Take a bike ride or spend a day at our beach, which has been rated one of the top 20 in the USA! The inn provides the bikes and beach gear. Climb the Barnegat Lighthouse and visit the museum. Hike thru the dunes and beach trails. Watersports, fishing, golf, theater, shopping, birdwatching...we have it all nearby. Then celebrate a spectacular sunset on the rooftop deck at the end of a relaxing, fun-filled day. This mini-resort is the perfect romantic escape for couples and companions. Voted top ten "Best Breakfast in the Northeast" by *Inn Traveler* magazine.

Member Since 2003   Mobil ★★★

"My husband and I travel all over. What elegance, what comfort! We both agree this is the best!"

Haddonfield Inn

www.srinns.com/haddonfieldinn
44 West End Avenue, Haddonfield, NJ 08033
800-269-0014 • 856-428-2195 • Fax 856-354-1273

Innkeepers/Owners
Nancy and Fred Chorpita

Elegant Village Bed & Breakfast

This intimate, elegant hotel in historic Haddonfield is just minutes from Philadelphia and the Cooper and Delaware Rivers. The historic village of Haddonfield offers over 200 unique shops and restaurants. The surrounding areas include countless attractions from aquariums to zoos with art, concerts, history, sports and theatre in-between! Each of our lovely guest rooms has a private bath (many have whirlpools), fireplace, TV, phone with free local calls and voicemail, and wireless Internet access. Enjoy a full, gourmet breakfast served on individual tables adorned with candles and fine linens in our firelit dining room. In the warmer months, enjoy breakfast on the large, wrap-around porch in our beautiful residental neighborhood. Packages and extras include tickets for major sporting events in nearby Philly, fine dining and in-room massage. We specialize in business conferences and retreats with special rates for the business traveler.

Rooms/Rates
9 Rooms. $149/$309, depending on room and day of week.
Number of Rooms: 9

Cuisine
Full, gourmet breakfast prepared by our chef.

Nearest Airport(s)
Philadelphia International

Directions
From N: NJ turnpike to exit 4. Rt. 73N to 295S. Take exit 30 and follow Warwick Rd to Kings Hwy. L at next light and then R onto West End. From S: 95N to Walt Whitman Bridge. Exit 168(Audubon). L onto Kings Hwy and L onto West End. From W: I-76 to I-676 to Ben Franklin Bridge. Rt. 70E to Cuthbert Blvd (turn R). L onto Park Blvd which becomes West End Ave.

AAA ◆◆◆   *Member Since 2005*

"What a wonderful place to set up visiting dignitaries!"
"Keeping up the best of B&B traditions."

Innkeepers/Owners
Bill and Nancy Moncrief and Eileen Burchsted

Traditional Village Breakfast Inn

Candlelight Inn

www.srinns.com/candlelight
2310 Central Avenue, North Wildwood, NJ 08260
800-992-2632 • 609-522-6200 • Fax 609-522-6125
info@candlelight-inn.com

Rooms/Rates
7 Rooms, $95/$190; 3 Suites, $130/$250. Some units have double whirlpool tubs, most have fireplaces, & some have both. All rooms have either queen or king beds & all have private baths. Air conditioned. Open year-round.
Number of Rooms: 10

Cuisine
A 3-course, sit-down breakfast with a choice of entrees and afternoon refreshments.

Nearest Airport(s)
Atlantic City (ACY)

Directions
S-bound: G.S. Pkwy to exit 6; Rte. 147 E; L on 2nd Ave.; R on Central Ave.; go to 24th Ave.; Inn is on R. N-bound: G.S. Pkwy to exit 4 into Wildwood. After bridge, L at 6th light (Atlantic Ave.). L at 24th for 1 block.

Come visit a unique part of Wildwoods. Enjoy the quiet elegance reminiscent of another era. The Candlelight Inn is a beautifully restored 1905 Queen Anne Victorian home. We offer rooms and suites with private baths, some with double whirlpool tubs and/or fireplaces. Sit on our veranda where cool ocean breezes delight you, relax anytime of the year in our outdoor hot tub, or warm yourself by a roaring fire in our inglenook. Minutes away are spacious beaches, water sports, lighthouses, antiquing, fine dining, nature activities including a zoo, wetlands and birding, golfing, shopping, history, and a fun-filled boardwalk — something for everyone. Cape May County besides having Islands with great Atlantic Ocean beaches has a Naval Air Station Museum, Historic Cold Spring Village, one of the top ten small zoos in the country, and Leaming's Gardens - the largest garden of 'annuals'

Member Since 2001

"The time spent here was like being 'home away from home,' only better."

The Duke of Windsor Inn

www.srinns.com/dukeofwindsor

817 Washington St., Cape May, NJ 08204

800-826-8973 • 609-884-1355 • Fax 609-884-1887

innkeeper@dukeofwindsorinn.com

Owners
David & Rosann Hague
Innkeeper
Julie McElroy
Historic In Town Breakfast Inn

As you cross the threshold into our expansive foyer, you will immediately sense the romance in this classic Queen Anne Victorian inn. The Duke of Windsor Inn, built in 1896, is among the most authentically restored homes in this historic landmark city. It features a 45-foot tower and a carved oak, open staircase that vaults three stories. The two Tiffany stained glass windows will certainly catch your eye. Renew yourself in the comfort of one of our beautiful guest rooms, furnished with fine antiques, emanating the warmth and elegance of an era gone by. Our location in the heart of the historic district is within a short walking distance to all that Cape May has to offer.

Rooms/Rates
10 rooms, $115/$245, all with private baths and air-conditioning. Open year-round. Private parking on the premises.
Number of Rooms: 10

Cuisine
Included in our rates are scrumptious, gourmet breakfasts served in our grand dining room, and afternoon tea and treats, which can be enjoyed in front of a cozy fire on chilly days, or on our spacious front porch when the weather is warm.

Nearest Airport(s)
Philadelphia

Directions
Garden State Parkway S to the end. Continue straight over bridges, becomes Lafayette St. Turn L at first light. At next light, turn R. Travel 2 blocks on R.

Member Since 2003

12+

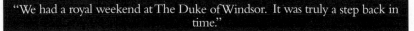

"We had a royal weekend at The Duke of Windsor. It was truly a step back in time."

Innkeepers/Owners
Ed and Diane Hutchinson

Casual Elegant In Town Breakfast Inn

The Fairthorne
www.srinns.com/fairthorne
111 - 115 Ocean Street, Cape May, NJ 08204
800-438-8742 • 609-884-8791 • Fax 609-898-6129
fairthornebnb@aol.com

Rooms/Rates
9 Rooms, $140/$280, Antique furnishings, lace curtains, king or queen beds, TVs/VCR,CD player private baths, some fireplaces and whirlpool baths. Open year-round. Closed only Thanksgiving Eve and Day, Christmas Eve and Day.
Number of Rooms: 9

Cuisine
Full breakfast & afternoon hot tea & coffee on cool days or iced tea & lemonade on summer days. Complimentary sherry. Excellent restaurants a short walk.

Nearest Airport(s)
Philadelphia & Atlantic City

Directions
Garden State Pkwy S to end; continue straight over bridges, becomes Lafayette St. 2nd light, turn L onto Ocean St. 3rd. block on L—111 Ocean Street.

Innkeepers Diane and Ed Hutchinson warmly welcome you to their romantic old whaling captain's home. This 1892 Colonial Revival-style Inn features a gracious wraparound veranda where sumptious breakfasts are served on pleasant mornings and stress-relieving rockers offer afternoon relaxation. The Fairthorne is beautifully decorated in period style without being too frilly or formal. Guestrooms are appointed with a seamless blend of fine antiques and contemporary comforts, including air conditioning, mini-fridges and TV/VCR,CD players plus gas log and electric fireplaces and whirlpool tubs in some rooms. Each day Diane and Ed invite you to gather for tasty snacks and fresh-baked cookies.

Member Since 2001

12+ 🚭 📖 🕐 📂 ✍ @ 🗑 ◎ ❋ 🅑 ☕

"I will savor the memory of your hospitality for years to come. Thanks so much!"

The Humphrey Hughes House

www.srinns.com/humphreyhughes
29 Ocean Street, Cape May, NJ 08204
800-582-3634 • 609-884-4428

Innkeepers/Owners
Lorraine & Terry Schmidt

Traditional Village Breakfast Inn

Nestled in the heart of Cape May's primary historic district, The Humphrey Hughes is one of the most spacious and gracious Inns. Expansive common rooms are filled with beautiful antiques. Relax on the large wraparound veranda filled with rockers and enjoy the ocean view and colorful gardens. Our large, comfortable guest rooms offer pleasant, clean accommodations. All rooms are air-conditioned with cable TV. Our location offers the visitor the opportunity to walk to the beach, restaurants, shops, theatre, concerts, nature trails. A full breakfast and afternoon refreshments are offered daily.

Rooms/Rates
$130/$350 per night, Dbl. Weekday discounts Fall and Spring. All rooms and suites with queen or king beds, TV, Air conditioning. **Number of Rooms:** 10

Cuisine
Delicious and beautifully presented Hot Breakfast (served on the front veranda when weather permits). Elegant Afternoon Tea served in the dining room each day.

Nearest Airport(s)
Atlantic City International

Directions
Take Garden State Parkway S to end. Follow Lafayette Street S. Turn L at second stop light; Ocean Street. The inn is on your Left, the corner of Ocean & Columbia Streets - only one block from the Ocean.

AAA ◆◆◆   *Member Since 1999*

16+

"The Inn is so clean and the food is delicious. We will be back soon."

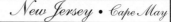

Proprietors
David & Susan Macrae
Innkeeper
Diane Clark

Elegant
Village Breakfast Inn

The Mainstay Inn
www.srinns.com/mainstayinn
635 Columbia Ave., Cape May, NJ 08204
609-884-8690 • Fax 609-884-1498
mainstayinn@comcast.net

Rooms/Rates
9 Rooms, $160/$345 B&B;
3 Suites, $195/$325 B&B;
4 Luxury Fireplace Suites,
$195/$395. Open year-round;
Fireplace suites only Jan. to
mid-March.
Number of Rooms: 16

Cuisine
Breakfast and elegant afternoon
tea. Excellent restaurants a short
walk away. No liquor license.

Nearest Airport(s)
Atlantic City International 45
minutes away

Directions
Take Garden State Pkwy. (S).
In Cape May, Pkwy. becomes
Lafayette St. Take L. at light onto
Madison Ave. Go 3 blocks, R. at
Columbia. Inn on R.

Once an exclusive gambling club, The Mainstay is now an elegant
Victorian inn furnished in splendid antiques. Within a lovely garden setting, the Inn and adjacent Cottage feature wide rocker-
lined verandas, and large, high-ceilinged rooms which are lavishly
but comfortably furnished. The Officers' Quarters is more contemporary with many extras such as whirlpool tubs and fireplaces.
The Mainstay is a landmark within a National Historic Landmark
town, and is but a short walk to restaurants, shops, theater, concerts, nature trails and beaches.

AAA ◆◆◆   *Member Since 1976*   Mobil ★★★

12+ 🚭 ♿ 📖 ⓘ 📂 ♥   @   🧺 ◎ ❄   ☕

"I want you to know how much I enjoyed my time at The Mainstay Inn.
Service, hospitality, and lovely accommodations were far above my expectations!"

Manor House

www.srinns.com/manorhousecapemay
612 Hughes St., Cape May, NJ 08204
609-884-4710 • Fax 609-898-0471
innkeeper@verizon.net

Innkeepers/Owners
Nancy & Tom McDonald

Historic Waterside Breakfast Inn

paii

On a tree-lined residential street in the heart of Cape May's Historic District, Manor House offers guests an exceptionally clean and comfortable turn-of-the-century inn experience. Fluffy robes in the rooms and a generous cookie fairy are but a few of the fun touches found here. Relaxing on the porch, reading in the garden, or roaming the beaches and streets of Cape May occur with little effort. Traditional sticky buns and made-from-scratch full breakfasts and the innkeepers' good humor give the inn its reputation for fine food and character.

Rooms/Rates
9 Rooms, $105/$255 B&B;
1 Suite, $150/$295 B&B.
Open year-round.
Number of Rooms: 10

Cuisine
Bountiful served gourmet breakfast, creative afternoon refreshments and fresh baked cookies in the evening.

Nearest Airport(s)
Philadelphia, Atlantic City

Directions
From Zero-mi. mark on Garden State Pkwy. to Rte. 109 S becoming LaFayette St., turn L. on Franklin for 2 blks to R. on Hughes - 612 Hughes on L.

AAA ◆◆◆   *Member Since 1991*

12+

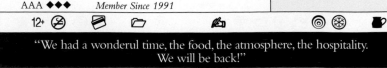

"We had a wonderul time, the food, the atmosphere, the hospitality.
We will be back!"

SelectRegistry.com

Innkeepers/Owners
Doug and Anna Marie McMain

Traditional Victorian Village Bed & Breakfast Inn

The Queen Victoria®
www.srinns.com/queenvictoria
102 Ocean Street, Cape May, NJ 08204-2320
609-884-8702
reservations@queenvictoria.com

Rooms/Rates
23 Rooms: $100/$255. 9 Suites: $145/$485. Weekday discounts Fall, Winter & Spring. Always open. Thanksgiving and Christmas packages.
Number of Rooms: 32

Cuisine
Rates include generous buffet breakfast & afternoon tea with sweets and savories. Complimentary juices, soft drinks, bottled water, coffee and teas. Fresh fruit always available. Fine dining nearby.

Nearest Airport(s)
ACY or PHL

Directions
Garden State Parkway to South end; continue straight over bridges, becomes Lafayette St. 2nd light turn Left onto Ocean St. 3 blocks turn Right onto Columbia Ave. Loading areas for check-in on Right.

A Cape May tradition since 1980, The Queen Victoria is one of America's most renowned bed & breakfast inns. Four impeccably restored 1880s homes are filled with fine antiques, handmade quilts, and many thoughtful extras. The hospitality is warm and the atmosphere is social. Choose from thirty-two inviting and spacious rooms and suites, all with private bath, AC, mini-refrigerator, and TV with DVD. Pamper yourself with a whirlpool tub or gas-log fireplace. For your Victorian enjoyment, rocking chairs fill porches and gardens. Wicker swings carry you back to a quieter time. Bicycles are provided free of charge, as are beach chairs and beach towels. The Queen Victoria is open all year and is located in the center of the historic district, one block from the Atlantic Ocean, tours, shopping, and fine restaurants. Victorian Cape May offers tours, special events, and activities all year including the Spring Music Festival, the Jazz Festival, Victorian Week, and the Food & Wine Festival.

AAA ◆◆◆   *Member Since 1992*   Mobil ★★★

8+ @

"The Queen Victoria is a dream come true! Your hospitality is genuine."
"Our two days at The Queen Victoria were the best two days of my life."

"The Land of Enchantment"

Famous For: Taos, Santa Fe, Pueblos, Adobe, Cliff Dwellings, Carlsbad Caverns (the largest in the world), White Sands National Monument, Ghost Ranch, Ship Rock, Pecos National Historical Park, Pancho Villa State Park, Palace of the Governors (the oldest public building in the country, built in 1610) Desert Flowers, Pottery, Rug-Making, Silver Jewelry, Los Alamos, Uranium.

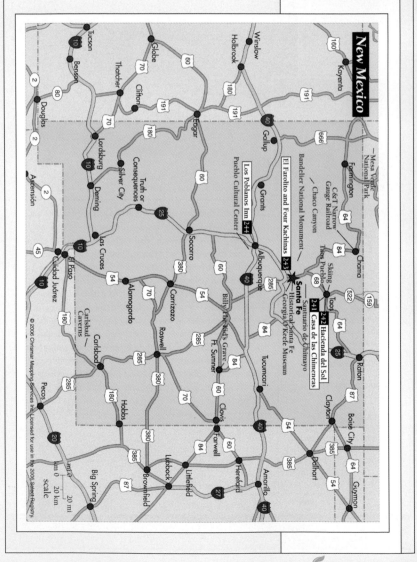

© 2006 Christmas Mapping Services Inc. Licensed for use in the 2006 Select Registry.

Casa de las Chimeneas

Innkeeper
Susan Vernon

Traditional Southwestern
Village Inn

www.srinns.com/casadelaschimeneas
405 Cordoba Road, 5303 NDCBU, Taos, NM 87571
877-758-4777 • 505-758-4777 • Fax 505-758-3976
casa@newmex.com

Rooms/Rates
6 Rooms, $180/$290 MAP;
2 Suites, $325/$615 MAP.
Open year-round.
Number of Rooms: 8

Cuisine
Hearty breakfast with hot entree, evening buffet supper, complimentary in-room bars with juices, sodas, mineral waters and hot beverages. Optional custom picnics.

Nearest Airport(s)
Albuquerque Int'l Sunport

Directions
From Santa Fe (Hwy. 68): turn R onto Los Pandos, go 1 block & turn R on Cordoba at the four-way stop. The inn is the first L off Cordoba. From Colorado (Hwy 522): turn L on Kit Carson Rd., go 1 block & turn R on Montoya. At the four-way stop, go straight. The inn is the first L.

Guests to this AAA Four Diamond inn delight in offerings not often found at small properties. The Wellness Spa, complete with workout room, massage and spa treatment room, sauna and hot tub, entices guests to unwind. A dedicated concierge sees to every guest's need from a menu of possibilities as rich as Taos' multi-cultural history. Special seasonal activities bookable through the inn include hot air ballooning over and into the Rio Grande Gorge, white water rafting, golf, fly fishing, llama trekking, horseback riding, skiing and snowmobiling. A talented kitchen staff prepares two hearty and delicious meals a day. With three scenic byways in Taos County, guests often spend a day enjoying the same views that inspire the many artists that make Taos their home with a lunch packed in a custom backpack. Southwest gardens, to-die-for accommodations and a perfect location near the Historic Plaza complete the picture. The result: delighted guests who leave with refreshed and renewed spirits, eager to return to Taos' *House of Chimneys*.

AAA ◆◆◆◆   *Member Since 1998*

"This, quite possibly, was the most wonderful travel experience we've had. Everything - we do mean everything - was fabulous! Great value for the price."

Hacienda del Sol

www.srinns.com/haciendadelsol
P.O. Box 177, 109 Mabel Dodge Lane, Taos, NM 87571
866–333–4459 • 505–758–0287 • Fax 505–758–5895
sunhouse@newmex.com

Innkeeper/Owner
Dennis Sheehan
Manager
Michelle Marquez

Southwestern
Adobe B&B

The orginal 1804 adobe building once belonged to Mabel Dodge Luhan. This historic Inn has hosted guests such as D.H. Lawrence, Georgia O'Keefe, and Ansel Adams. The Taos Mountain provides a beautiful background to our hacienda which borders 95,000 acres of Taos Pueblo land. Latilla fencing and adobe walls surrounds beautifully landscaped grounds. Though Hacienda del Sol means "House of the Sun" in Spanish, towering cottonwoods, elms, willows and blue spruces shade the hacienda in the summer. Amenities include jacuzzis, outdoor hot tub, wood burning fireplaces and steamrooms. Individually decorated rooms with antiques and hand crafted furniture. Selected by *USA Today* as "One of the 10 most romantic Inns in America."

Rooms/Rates
7 Rooms, $125/$325 B&B. 4 Suites, $190/$540 B&B. Open year round.
Number of Rooms: 11

Cuisine
2-course breakfast w/hot entree. Coffee, hot tea & hot cocoa available all day. Afternoon homemade snacks & fruit available. Experience the local's favorite energetic bistro, the Trading Post Cafe. The beautiful outdoor patio is a great spot to enjoy the culinary expertise of world renowned Chef Rene Mettler.

Nearest Airport(s)
Albuquerque Airport

Directions
From Santa Fe on Hwy 68: 1 mi. N of the Taos Plaza, turn R directly after Southwest Mocassin & Drum onto Mabel Dodge Lane.

Member Since 2003   Mobil ★★★

"The best bed and breakfast at 'the edge of Taos desert.'"

Innkeepers/Owners
Walt Wyss and Wayne Mainus

Southwestern In Town Breakfast Inns

🍽

El Farolito Bed & Breakfast Inn and Four Kachinas Inn

www.farolito.com
514 Galisteo Street, Santa Fe, NM 87501
888-634-8782 • 505-988-1631 • Fax 505-989-1323
innkeeper@farolito.com

paii

Rooms/Rates
12 Rooms, $110/$215; 1 Suite, $195/$250 . Features: TV, phones, fine linens, AC, patios. Fireplaces at ELF and hot tub at 4K.
Number of Rooms: 13

Cuisine
Complete healthy breakfast w/quality home-baked goods, hot entre, fresh fruit, yogurts, & ample accompaniment. Complimentary afternoon light refreshments.

Nearest Airport(s)
Santa Fe & Albuquerque

Directions
From Albq. I-25 N, exit 282. St. Francis N to Cerrillos, R on Cerrillos, R at Paseo de Peralta, To ELF: L at Galisteo to 514. To 4K: R at Webber to 512. From Taos: S on U.S. 84/285, exit to downtown, L on Paseo de Peralta. (See above.)

Surround yourself with the richness of Santa Fe's art, culture and history in two beautiful downtown properties - El Farolito B&B Inn (ELF) and the Four Kachinas B&B Inn (4K). These inns, under the same ownership, offer you award-winning accommodations, showcasing exquisite original Southwestern art and handcrafted furnishings. The rooms are decorated in styles relevant to Santa Fe's rich cultural heritage of native American, Spanish and Anglo inhabitants. Modern amenities also abound including fine linens, rich fabrics, AC, private entrances, TVs, telephones and Internet access. The two inns are conveniently located in the downtown historic district, a short pleasant walk to numerous galleries, shops, museums, world-class fine dining, and the central Plaza. In the warm sunshine, savor a leisurely breakfast on the back portal and relax on your garden patio. At ELF, enjoy a fireside breakfast in the brightly decorated dining room and the coziness of a fireplace in your room. At the 4K Inn, enjoy a warm soak in the spa under the starry night.

AAA ◆◆◆   *Member Since 2001*

☺   ⊘   💳📱📂   📣@   🏙   ❄   ☕

"Quintessential Santa Fe! You create an ambiance that promotes rest and restoration."

Los Poblanos Inn

www.srinns.com/lospoblanos
4803 Rio Grande Blvd. NW, Albuquerque, NM 87107
866-344-9297 • 505-344-9297 • Fax 505-342-1302
info@lospoblanos.com

Innkeepers/Owners
The Rembe Family
Executive Director
Matthew Rembe
Historic Country
Estate Inn

Set among 25 acres of lavender fields and lush formal gardens, Los Poblanos Inn is one the most prestigious historic properties in the Southwest. The Inn was designed by the region's foremost architect, John Gaw Meem, the "Father of Santa Fe Style," and is listed on both the New Mexico and National Registers of Historic Places. Guest rooms are in a classic New Mexican style with kiva fireplaces, carved ceiling beams, hardwood floors, and antique New Mexican furnishings. Guests can relax around the Spanish hacienda-style courtyard or spend hours exploring the property's extensive gardens and organic farm. The buildings feature significant artwork commissioned during the WPA period by some of New Mexico's most prominent artists, including a fresco by Peter Hurd and carvings by Gustave Baumann. Detailed tours highlighting the property's cultural, political, agricultural and architectural history are available to every guest. "One could spend a lifetime at Los Poblanos and never fall out of love." - *Su Casa* Magazine

Member Since 2005

Rooms/Rates
3 Guest Rooms, 3 Suites, $135/$250. Fireplaces, spa services upon request, wireless internet. Open year-round.
Number of Rooms: 6

Cuisine
Complimentary gourmet breakfast buffet w/ fresh organic produce & ingredients from our farm.

Nearest Airport(s)
Albuquerque International Sunport

Directions
From Airport: I-25 N to I-40 W (Gallup Exit 226B). Continue W 3 mi. to Rio Grande Ex. 157A. Turn R and go N 3.3 mi. to 4803 Rio Grande Blvd. From Santa Fe/Taos: I-25 S to Alameda Ex. 233. W on Alameda for 3.2 mi. L on S. Rio Grande Blvd. for 3.8 mi. to property on R.

"Rough-hewn ceiling beams, Saltillo tiles, and traditional kiva fireplaces give Los Poblanos a cozy, comfortable charm." - *Bon Appétit* Magazine

New York

"The Empire State"

Famous For: Statue of Liberty, Ellis Island,
Empire State Building, Times Square,
Metropolitan Museum of Art, Central Park,
Madison Square Garden, Madison Avenue, Wall Street,
Brooklyn Bridge, Catskill Forest, Adirondack Mountains,
Finger Lakes, Hudson River, Niagra Falls, Long Island

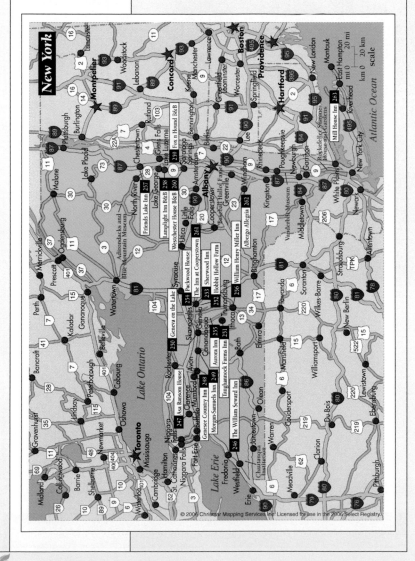

The William Seward Inn

www.srinns.com/williamseward
6645 South Portage Rd., Westfield, NY 14787-9603
800-338-4151 • 716-326-4151 • Fax 716-326-4163
wmseward@cecomet.net

Innkeepers/Owners
Jim & Debbie Dahlberg

Elegant Greek Revival
Country Inn

Although the cultural and educational offerings of the famed Chautauqa Institution are a major attraction, many travelers come specifically to stay at this 1821 antique-filled Inn for rest and relaxation. With its striking Greek Revival exterior, history, fine dining, gracious accommodations and charming wooded setting, the William Seward Inn provides the base for guests to explore the diverse attractions of the area - wineries, antiquing, outdoor activities, skiing, snowmobiling, Roger Tory Peterson Nature Center, Lucy-Desi Museum, etc. The Inn is also known for its special weekends - Birding Weekend, International Wine & Gourmet, Cooking, Victorian Christmas and Women's Escape - which consistently attract repeat visits.

Rooms/Rates
4 Rooms Double Whirlpool, $175/$205 B&B, 2 Rooms Fireplace, $135/$185 B&B, 8 Rooms $80/$140 B&B. Open all year.
Number of Rooms: 14

Cuisine
Dinner available Wed.-Sun., by advance reservation with a single seating at 7 p.m. Guests pre-select their appetizer and main entree from our seasonal menu at least one day in advance of dining. Fine wines and champagnes are available.

Nearest Airport(s)
Jamestown, NY - 30 minutes
Erie, PA - 40 minute

Directions
4 mi. S on Rte 394 from I-90, exit 60. 2.5 hrs. NE of Cleveland, OH; 2.5 hrs. N of Pittsburg, PA; 1.5 hrs. SW of Buffalo, NY; 3 hrs. SW of Toronto, Canada.

AAA ◆◆◆   *Member Since 1992*   Mobil ★★★

10+

"Highlight of our visit was dinner - one of the best we have ever eaten."

Innkeepers/Owners
**Robert Lenz and
Abigail Lenz**

Traditional Village
Inn

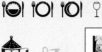

🍴 🍴 🍴 ♈

Asa Ransom House
www.srinns.com/asaransom
10529 Main St. Rt. 5, Clarence, NY 14031
800-841-2340 • 716-759-2315 • Fax 716-759-2791
innfo@asaransom.com

Rooms/Rates
9 Rooms, $98/$175 B&B;
$155/$325 MAP. Full breakfast
included. Closed month of
January.
Number of Rooms: 9

Cuisine
Fine country dining with regional
specialties. Fully licensed - NYS
Wine award. "Best Place to Take
Out-of-Town Guests" award.

Nearest Airport(s)
Buffalo/Niagara - 9 miles

Directions
Traveling E: I-90, exit 49, L on
Rte. 78 for 1 mi. to R on Rte. 5 for
5.3 mi. Traveling W: I-90 exit 48A
& R on Rte. 77 for 1 mi. to R on
Rte. 5 for 10 mi. to Inn.

On the site of the first gristmill built in Erie County (1803),
where guests are romanced in the winter by the glowing fireplaces and spacious grounds full of herbs and flowers in the summer. Many rooms have porches or balconies to view the grounds
or just relax. Experience world-class cuisine and full country
breakfasts with delicious regional accents. Often upon arrival you
will find the aroma of fresh pies and breads lingering in the air!
Clarence is known throughout the east for its antiques and treasures. Explore the bike trails or visit the nearby Opera House,
Erie Canal Cruises, Albright-Knox Art Gallery and Frank Lloyd
Wright's Martin House Complex. Also Niagara wineries, Fort
Niagara, Letchworth State Park and much more. Only 28 miles
from Niagara Falls.

AAA ◆◆◆   *Member Since 1976*   Mobil ★★★

8+ 🚭 ♿ 💳 ⓥ 🗁 ♥   ✍ @ 🐕   🏠 ◎ ✳ 🅢 🍺

"Our favorite place to stay whenever we travel."

Genesee Country Inn Circa 1833

www.srinns.com/geneseecountryinn
948 George Street, Mumford-Rochester, NY 14511
800-697-8297 • 585-538-2500 • Fax 585-248-2488
room2escapeinn@geneseecountryinn.com

Owner
Fran Pullano
Innkeepers
Kim Rasmussen,
Jill Way
Creekside Inn

Step back in time to an era of simple elegance, fine hospitality, and natural beauty. You can escape to our unique water setting with full corporate accommodations like wireless Internet, fax and conference facilities. You can hike the grounds or the nearby Nature Center. Fish to your heart's content in our private Spring Creek or visit the famed Oatka. Our Inn, an 1800s plaster-paper mill, boasts extensive gardens and a dynamic waterfall on the seven acres of natural setting. Enjoy the ambience and the bird-watching! The Genesee Country Inn is just remote enough for you to getaway, but close enough to arts and entertainment to keep you coming back! The Inn is a wonderful location for family reunions, corporate events, and intimate weddings. Romance, Spa and fly-fishing packages are available!

Member Since 1988

Rooms/Rates
10 rooms - 3 Garden $150/$190, 5 Old Mill Rooms $109/$150, 1 Suite $160/$185.
Number of Rooms: 10

Cuisine
Full Country Breakfast Friday-Sunday, continental breakfast Monday-Thursday, tea & coffee available all day.

Nearest Airport(s)
Rochester International Airport

Directions
I-90 Exit 47 to Rte. 19 S. Follow 'Genesee Country Village & Museum' Green signs; turn left onto North Road. At stop sign turn right onto Rte 36S. Follow Rte36S to flashing light, turn right onto George St. Go 2 blocks, the Inn is on the right at 948 George St. From I-390 exit 10, Rte 5W to 36N, left at flashing light onto George St.

"A fine Inn indeed. You are on a par with the better country Inns of England."

Innkeepers/Owners
Julie & John Sullivan
Innkeeper/General
Manager
Brad & Connie Smith

Village Breakfast Inn

Morgan–Samuels Inn

www.srinns.com/morgan-samuels
2920 Smith Rd., Canandaigua, NY 14424
585–394–9232 • 585–721–6656 • Fax 585–394–8044
MorSamBBC@aol.com

Rooms/Rates
5 Rooms, $119/$249 B&B;
1 Suite/Lake Villas $199/$395
B&B.
Number of Rooms: 6

Cuisine
Memorable, extended, candlelit
full gourmet breakfast; dinner
prix fixe by reservation, special
request for eight or more. On day
of arrival we serve hot appetizers,
fruit, cheeses, and soft beverages
served on the Victorian Porch.

Nearest Airport(s)
Rochester International

Directions
I-90 from exit 43 R on 21 to 488;
L 1st R on East Ave. to stop.
Continue 3/4 mi. to Inn on R. The
Inn is located two minutes from
Canandaigua Lake.

Travel the 2,000 foot tree-lined drive to the secluded 1810 English style mansion and sense the difference between ordinary and legendary. The Inn sits like a plantation on a rise surrounded by 46 acres. Four patios, trickling waterfall, tennis court, acres of lawn and gardens canopied by 250 noble trees. Three rooms with French doors and balconies, 11 fireplaces. Tea room with stone wall and 16-foot glass windows, pot-bellied stove. Library, common room, large enclosed porch/dining room, four Jacuzzis, outside hot springs spa Jacuzzi, museum quality furniture, oil paintings. Recognized as one of the "12 Most Romantic Hideaways in the East" by *Discerning Traveler* Magazine.

AAA ◆◆◆◆   *Member Since 1992*

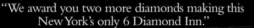

"We award you two more diamonds making this
New York's only 6 Diamond Inn."

Geneva On The Lake

www.srinns.com/geneva
1001 Lochland Road, Route 14, Geneva, NY 14456
800-3-GENEVA • 315-789-7190 • Fax 315-789-0322
info@genevaonthelake.com

General Manager
William J. Schickel

Elegant Wine
Country Resort

Experience European elegance and friendly hospitality in the heart of Finger Lakes Wine Country. Amidst an ambiance of Italian Renaissance architecture, classical sculptures, luxurious suites and Stickley furnishings guests from around the world enjoy vacation getaways, family gatherings, weddings and conferences. Rest, relax and surrender yourself to gracious service and breathtaking surroundings. Candlelight dining with live music. A complimentary bottle of wine and basket of fruit are in your suite on arrival and *The New York Times* is at your door each morning. Complimentary high-speed wireless Internet is available. Glorious formal gardens for lawn games, a 70' outdoor pool, and a boat-house with dock and moorings. Adjacent are Geneva's charming Historic District and the campus of Hobart and William Smith Colleges, both replete with architectural gems. Enjoy magnificent scenic beauty on the Seneca Lake Wine Trail. Golf is nearby. "The food is extraordinarily good." - *Bon Appetit*. "One of the 10 most romantic inns in the United States." - *American Historic Inns*.

AAA ◆◆◆◆   *Member Since 2003*

Rooms/Rates
29 Guest Suites (10 w/ 2 bedrooms). Open year-round. Many 4-Season Vacation Packages offered for a romantic getaway, honeymoon, gala New Year's & more. $217/$1245 per night.
Number of Rooms: 29

Cuisine
Gourmet cuisine is served with a smile in the warmth of candlelight and live music. Breakfast daily and Sunday Brunch. Lunch On The Terrace in summer.

Nearest Airport(s)
Rochester International

Directions
From the North: NY State Thruway Exit #42 then Rt 14 South 7 mi. From the South or NY City: I-86 to Exit #52 then Rt 14 N to Geneva. 1 hour from Rochester, Syracuse or Ithaca Airports.

6+

"Heavenly!! Thank you (and your wonderful staff) for the grandest stay we've ever had!!"

Innkeepers/Owners
Susan and Tom Sheridan

Historic Victorian Waterside Inn

🍽 🍴 ♟

Taughannock Farms Inn
www.srinns.com/taughannock
2030 Gorge Road, Trumansburg, NY 14886
888-387-7711 • 607-387-7711 • Fax 607-387-7721

Rooms/Rates
Main Inn rooms $80/$165. 3 guesthouses $145/$195 per room. Full cottages $140/$450. Seasonal rates for all accommodations.
Number of Rooms: 22

Cuisine
Expanded Continental breakfast—juice, coffee, fruit, breakfast pastries and at least one hot item. 150-seat restaurant. Dinner includes appetizer, salad, entree, dessert. Banquets available.

Nearest Airport(s)
Tompkins Airport

Directions
From Ithaca: Take Rte. 89 N for 9 miles to Gorge Road. Turn L; Inn is on R. From NY State Thruway: Exit 41; Take 318-E to Rte. 5 & 20. Go 1/4 mile; turn R on Rte. 89, S for 34 miles. Inn on R.

Relax and enjoy a bygone era at this Victorian country inn. Majestically situated above Cayuga's waters, the inn offers commanding views of the lake. This Finger Lakes wine region landmark, built in 1873, is known for its gracious hospitality, abundant American cuisine, and charming accomodations. In addition to the five rooms in the Main inn that are furnished with antiques, we also have four guesthouses for a total of 22 rooms. Edgewood, the newest of the four, opened in 2004. All 10 rooms with covered balconies/patios have outstanding views of Cayuga Lake. Four king units feature Jacuzzis. Savor a romantic dinner in the 150-seat fine dining restaurant overlooking the lake. The four-course meal features American cuisine and is complimented by wonderful Finger Lakes wine.

AAA ◆◆◆   *Member Since 2002*

"This place is magical! The inn, the falls, the lake, the wine! I wish I could live here!"

Hobbit Hollow Farm

www.srinns.com/hobbithollow
3061 West Lake Road, Skaneateles, NY 13152
800-374-3796 • 315-685-2791 • Fax 315-685-3426
innkeeper@hobbithollow.com

Proprietor
William B. Eberhardt
Property Manager
Julia Bergan

Elegant Country
Breakfast Inn

Hobbit Hollow Farm has been painstakingly restored inside and out to recreate the casual comfort of an elegant country farmhouse. Hobbit Hollow serves a full, farm breakfast as part of the room price. Overlooking Skaneateles Lake, Hobbit Hollow Farm is situated on 320 acres of farmland with trails and ponds as well as private equestrian stables. Spend time contemplating the lake on our east verandah. Enjoy afternoon tea or coffee and watch the light play on the water in the soft wash of dusk. Rediscover what it means to be truly relaxed in a setting of tranquility. This is the perfect spot for a quiet, romantic getaway.

Rooms/Rates
5 Rooms, $100/$270, elegantly decorated with master-crafted period furniture and antiques. 3 rooms include four-poster beds. Master Suite $250/$270; Lake View $200/$230; Chanticleer $175/$200; Meadow View $150/$170; Twin $100/$120. Open year-round.
Number of Rooms: 5

Cuisine
Full country breakfast. Find excellent dinner and lunches at the Sherwood Inn, Blue Water Grill, and Kabuki.

Nearest Airport(s)
Syracuse (Hancock International)

Directions
Located on the west side of Skaneateles Lake on 41A. Rte 20 (Genesee St.) to 41A South. In less than 2 miles, the stone entrance to Hobbit Hollow Farm will be on the right.

Member Since 1998

"From the moment you pass through the stone pillars, you will feel everyday cares lift away."

Owner
William B. Eberhardt
General Manager
Linda B. Hartnett
Traditional Village Inn

The Sherwood Inn

www.srinns.com/sherwoodinn
26 West Genesee Street, Skaneateles, NY 13152
800-374-3796 • 315-685-3405 • Fax 315-685-8983
info@thesherwoodinn.com

Rooms/Rates
16 Suites and 8 Rooms, $95/$225. Suites have fireplaces/whirlpool baths. All have private baths, telephones & televisions. We are open year-round.
Number of Rooms: 24

Cuisine
Our Tavern serves traditional American fare in a relaxed atmosphere. Our Dining Room offers casual dining in an elegant, yet comfortable setting overlooking Skaneateles Lake. Serving Daily.

Nearest Airport(s)
Syracuse (Hancock International)

Directions
From New York Thruway: Exit Weedsport (exit 40) Rte. 34 S to Auburn. E on Rte. 20, 7 miles to Skaneateles. From the South: 81 N to Cortland, Rte. 41 N to Skaneateles Lake, L (west) on Rte. 20 for 1 mi.

Built as a stagecoach stop in 1807, The Sherwood Inn has always been a favorite resting place for travelers. The handsome lobby with fireplace, gift shop, antiques and orientals offers a warm reception. Each room has been restored to the beauty of a bygone era to create a relaxing harmony away from everyday cares. Our newly renovated dining and banquet rooms are able to accommodate groups of all sizes. In addition to our dining rooms, many of our 24 guest rooms overlook beautiful Skaneateles Lake. Casual lakeside dining and The Sherwood are synonymous, and we have been recognized by the *New York Times, Bon Appetit, Country Living, Harper's Bazaar* and *New Yorker* magazines. Our extensive menu offers American cooking with a continental touch, accompanied by an impressive wine list.

Member Since 1979

"The Sherwood has it all...the rooms, the food, the lobby, the village setting... a perfect getaway!"

Packwood House

www.srinns.com/packwoodhouse
14 West Genesee Street, Skaneateles, NY 13152
877-225-9663 • 315-217-8100 • Fax 315-685-8983
info@packwoodhouse.com

Proprietor
Michael P. Falcone
Property Manager
Julia Bergan
Contemporary
Village Inn

The Packwood House is located in the center of the quaint historic village of Skaneateles on the north shore of Skaneateles Lake, the easternmost of the Finger Lakes. Many of the Packwood's guest suites provide picturesque views of the lake and the village; several feature oversized balconies where guests may sit back and enjoy the view from a unique perspective. The Packwood House is designed to provide all the comforts of home while enjoying the luxury of "getting away." There are many things to see and do, including a scenic boat cruise around the lake, lakeside concerts on summer weekends, and downhill or cross country skiing at nearby trails during the fall and winter months. There is no shortage of activity for guests looking for adventure, and no better place to just sit back, relax and enjoy the scenery.

Rooms/Rates
19 guest suites. $125/$230
Suites feature a sitting area, desk, cable television, hi-speed internet access, and a kitchenette with microwave, refrigerator and coffee-maker.
Number of Rooms: 19

Cuisine
Continental breakfast included. Find excellent dinner and lunches at the Sherwood Inn, Blue Water Grill, and Kabuki.

Nearest Airport(s)
Syracuse (Hancock International)

Directions
From New York Thruway: Exit Weedsport (exit 40) Route 34 S to Auburn. E on Route 20, 7 miles to Skaneateles. From the South: 81N to Cortland, Route 41 N to Skaneateles Lake, L (west) on Rte. 20 for 1 mile.

Member Since 2005

"...comfort and amenities for business or pleasure!"

SelectRegistry.com

Aurora Inn

www.srinns.com/aurorainn
391 Main Street/State Route 90, Aurora, NY 13026
866-364-8808 • 315-364-8888 • Fax 315-364-8887
info@Aurora-Inn.com

Innkeeper
Sue Edinger

Historic Village Inn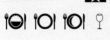

🍴 🍴 🍴 🍷

Rooms/Rates
8 Rooms, 2 Suites. $200/$350
in-season $150/$275 off-season
Number of Rooms: 10

Cuisine
The Inn serves fine American
fare, using the freshest of regional
produce. The menu is frequently
updated to feature new items
throughout the year. Guests enjoy
lakeside indoor or outdoor dining
for breakfast, brunch, lunch or
dinner.

Nearest Airport(s)
Syracuse's Hancock International
Airport, 60 miles

Directions
Situated on the east shore of
Cayuga Lake on State Route 90,
the Aurora Inn is located approx.
30 minutes south of the NY State
Thruway (exit 40 or 41). Call for
specific directions.

On the shores of Cayuga Lake in the heart of Finger Lakes wine country, the Aurora Inn is a beautiful setting for fine dining, comfortable lodging and special events for all seasons.   Elegant décor, fine art and antiques, fireplaces and fresh flowers offer a warm welcome. Its ten luxurious guest rooms are decorated with designer fabrics and furnishings that place an emphasis on comfort. All have well-appointed marble bathrooms with thick towels and terrycloth robes, high-speed Internet access, and flat-panel televisions with DVD players. Most rooms have spacious balconies overlooking the lake or village, and some have inviting fireplaces, deep whirlpool baths, wet bars and other amenities. The Aurora Inn's restaurant is one of the few places in the Finger Lakes to dine outdoors with views of the lake and its spectacular sunsets. Its elegant dining room is warmed by soft music, candlelight and two roaring fireplaces and offers delicious American fare year-round.

Member Since 2005

☺   ♿ 💳 🍷 📁 ♥   ✍ @   📺 ◎

"The Inn is exceptionally well restored, beautifully decorated and staying there was a most gracious experience and of great comfort after a long work day."

William Henry Miller Inn

www.srinns.com/miller

303 North Aurora Street, Ithaca, NY 14850

877-256-4553 • 607-256-4553 • Fax 607-256-0092

millerinn@cnymail.com

Innkeepers/Owners
Lynnette Scofield &
David Dier

Victorian In Town Inn

From the time you enter The William Henry Miller Inn, you will find a home rich in architectural detail with stained glass windows, American chestnut woodwork and working fireplaces. Located just off The Commons, the Inn is in the heart of downtown Ithaca. After a bountiful breakfast, spend the day exploring the best of the Finger Lakes. In the evening, while enjoying our homemade desserts, relax in the common areas or on the Inn's comfortable front porch. Visit us for pleasure or business and learn why The *Yankee Magazine* Travel Guide highlights the William Henry Miller Inn as an Editors' Choice, known for "hospitality and attention to detail."

Rooms/Rates
$115/$210. King/Queen beds. Private baths; some Jacuzzis and fireplaces. High Speed access. Closed Dec. 24 to Jan. 12.
Number of Rooms: 9

Cuisine
Breakfast with choice of two main dishes served during a two hour period. Homemade evening dessert and always available coffee and tea. Wonderful restaurants nearby including the world famous Moosewood.

Nearest Airport(s)
Tompkins County (Ithaca) Airport is just ten minutes away.

Directions
2 blocks from The Commons on the NE corner of Aurora & Buffalo Streets. 10 blocks from Cornell University - 1 mile from Ithaca College.

Member Since 2003

12+

"We felt truly at home!"

Friends Lake Inn

www.srinns.com/friends
963 Friends Lake Road, Chestertown, NY 12817
518-494-4751 • Fax 518-494-4616
friends@friendslake.com

Innkeepers/Owners
John and Trudy Phillips

Traditional Country
Inn

GRAND AWARD DiRoNA

Rooms/Rates
17 Sumptuous guest rooms, all with private baths and lake or mountain views. Rooms with Jacuzzis or Adirondack Rooms with fireplaces available. Rooms range from $325/$475/couple. (MAP)
Number of Rooms: 17

Cuisine
Full country breakfast & candlelight dinner served daily, lunch served on weekends; inquire about conferences, rehearsal dinners, and weddings. Lighter Wine Bar Menu available. Extensive wine collection.

Nearest Airport(s)
Albany

Directions
I-87 (The Northway) to exit 25, follow Rte. 8W for 3.5 miles, turn L at Friends Lake Rd. Bear R at fork, continue for one mile, then turn R. 8/10ths of a mile to Inn, on the R.

Experience the comfort and intimate ambiance of this elegantly restored inn, surrounded by the natural beauty of the Adirondacks. Guest rooms feature antiques, fine fabrics, and featherbeds, most with lake views, Jacuzzis and/or fireplaces. Nationally acclaimed cuisine is served daily in the candlelit Nineteenth Century dining room, complemented by gracious service and a *Wine Spectator* Grand Award-winning wine list. Swim in the lake or the pool, canoe, kayak or fish on Friends Lake. Ski, snowshoe or hike on 32 kilometers of trails.

DiRoNA award of dining excellence.

AAA ◆◆◆◆   *Member Since 1998*   Mobil ★★★★

12+

"Ultimate Distinction" Award – *Wine Enthusiast* Magazine
Dirona dining Award; *Wine Spectator* Grand Award.

The Lamplight Inn Bed & Breakfast

www.lamplightinn.com
231 Lake Ave., P.O. Box 130, Lake Luzerne, NY 12846
800-262-4668 • 518-696-5294 • Fax 518-696-4914
stay@lamplightinn.com

Innkeepers/Owners
Gene & Linda Merlino

Traditional Village Breakfast
Inn

The Lamplight Inn is in the active Saratoga Springs/Lake George area. It was built in 1890 as a Victorian vacation home of a wealthy playboy/lumberman, on the southern edge of the Adirondack Park. The Inn sits on 10 acres surrounded by towering white pines, just a short walk to crystal-clear Lake Luzerne. The Carriage House includes 4 Jacuzzi/fireplace suites w/TV and private deck & one wheelchair-accessible room w/fireplace, TV and private deck. A romantic getaway—a honeymoon location. Memorable full breakfast. Wine and beer, gift shop. 1992 Inn of the Year—*Laniers-Complete Guide to Bed & Breakfast.* Featured in the 1993 Christmas issue of *Country Inns* Magazine.

Rooms/Rates
13 Rooms, 12 with fireplaces, 6 with Jacuzzis. 1 is wheelchair accessible. $95/$239—depending on season and type of room. Open year-round. Closed Christmas Eve & Christmas Day.
Number of Rooms: 13

Cuisine
Memorable full breakfast menu. Wine & beer licensed.

Nearest Airport(s)
Albany, NY

Directions
From the south - NY State Thruway to exit 24 in Albany. After the toll. Take entrance 1N toward Montreal and the Northway (87). Take the Northway to Exit 21 (Lake George/Lake Luzerne). At bottom of ramp make a left on 9N south. Follow 9N south 11 miles. The Inn will be on the right, a block after Lake Luzerne High School.

AAA ◆◆◆   *Member Since 1996*   Mobil ★★★

12+ 🚭 ♿ 💳 ⓘ 📁 ♥   ✍ @   🔲 ◎

"Wonderful staff. Beautiful Inn which is kept above my standards. Lots of privacy."
"The Inn looks like a dream Inn should."

Fox 'n' Hound B&B

Innkeeper/Owner
Marlena Sacca

Historic Mansion
Bed & Breakfast Inn

www.srinns.com/foxnhound
142 Lake Ave., Saratoga Springs, NY 12866
518-584-5959 • Fax 518-584-5959
Innkeeper@FoxnHoundBandB.com

Rooms/Rates
5 Rooms $150/$400
Racing Season $295/$400
Number of Rooms: 5

Cuisine
Guests can expect to find seasonal fresh fruit, ethnic entrees, fresh fruit cobblers, fresh baked scones, strudels, muffins, fresh-brewed coffee, an assortment of specially blended teas, afternoon refreshment. Menu changes daily.

Nearest Airport(s)
Albany International Airport

Directions
I87 take Exit 14 and bear R into Rte 29 to Saratoga Springs. 1st traffic light take a R onto Henning Ave-Rt. 29. Go approx 1 mi. At the light turn L onto Lake Ave (29W). We are at the corner of Lake Ave & Marion Place. Parking lot behind the house.

Visit the historic Saratoga Springs, New York Fox 'n Hound Bed and Breakfast. Conveniently located within walking distance from downtown Saratoga shopping, dining, Saratoga Race Course, Skidmore College and Museums. A restored Victorian Mansion with colonial and Queen Ann architectural detail, that offers comfortable elegance with a cosmopolitan flair, European hospitality with the warmth of home, attention to detail found in the finest resorts, and the convenience of in-town location.

MARLENA'S FRITATTA
For complete ingredients, visit www.FoxnHoundBandB.com

Beat 2 eggs per person; add 2 tbsp. sour cream, 1 to 2 tbsp. grated Jarlsburg cheese. You can also add minced fresh basil, parsley if desired. Pour into oven-proof skillet coated with remaining 1/4 cup olive oil, and place on low burner to brown just a bit. Top with some salsa and bake in a 350° oven on middle shelf. The Frittata is done when the center is firm (approximately 15 minutes depending on the amount of eggs used). Cut into wedges and top with a dollop of sour cream and minced fresh basil if desired.

AAA ◆◆◆   *Member Since 2004*

14+

"A truly special B&B thanks to your warm hospitality. I will enjoy writing about the Fox 'n' Hound- a place I can totally recommend." Katharine Dyson

Westchester House Bed & Breakfast

www.srinns.com/westchesterhouse
102 Lincoln Ave., P.O. Box 944, Saratoga Springs, NY 12866
800-579-8368 • 518-587-7613 • Fax 518-583-9562
innkeepers@westchesterhousebandb.com

Owners/Innkeepers
Bob & Stephanie Melvin

Traditional Victorian
In Town Breakfast Inn

Welcome to the Westchester House - Saratoga's hidden jewel. Nestled in a residential neighborhood of tree-lined streets and surrounded by exuberant gardens this enticing Victorian confection combines gracious hospitality, old-world ambiance and up-to-date comforts. Lace curtains, oriental carpets, high ceilings, the rich luster of natural woods, king-or queen-sized beds, tiled baths and luxury linens provide elegance and comfort. The charm and excitement of Saratoga is at our doorstep. After a busy day sampling the delights of Saratoga, relax on the wraparound porch, in the gardens, or in the parlour, and enjoy a refreshing glass of lemonade. Walk to thoroughbred race track, historic districts, downtown, Spa State Park/SPAC. Close to Skidmore College and Saratoga Battlefield.

Rooms/Rates
King and Queen beds. Customary $135/$225; Special Events $185/$275; Racing Season $255/$445 B&B. Closed December and January.
Number of Rooms: 7

Cuisine
Full cold breakfast incl. fruit salad, platter of cold meat and cheeses. A variety of excellent restaurants within easy walk of the Inn.

Nearest Airport(s)
Albany (commercial)

Directions
From South: 30 mi. N of Albany, I-87 to exit 13N. 4 mi. N to 6th traffic light. R (E) on Lincoln to 102. From North: I-87 to exit 14. R on Union Ave .4 mi. to 3rd traffic light. L (S) on Nelson 1 block to Lincoln. R (W) on Lincoln to 102.

AAA ◆◆◆   *Member Since 1996*

12+

"A little gem that made us feel immediately welcomed. The B&B was immaculate!"

Innkeepers/Owners
Marc and Sherrie Kingsley

Traditional Village Breakfast Inn

The Inn at Cooperstown
www.srinns.com/innatcooperstown
16 Chestnut Street, Cooperstown, NY 13326
607-547-5756 • Fax 607-547-8779
info@innatcooperstown.com

Rooms/Rates
17 rooms each with private bath, A/C, CD/clock radio, hair dryer, iron, wireless Internet access. Televisions/Phones in sitting rooms. Standard rooms: $99/$198, Suite: $190/$325 B&B. Open year-round.
Number of Rooms: 17

Cuisine
Continental breakfast, afternoon refreshments, and fine restaurants within walking distance.

Nearest Airport(s)
Albany, NY or Syracuse, NY

Directions
Cooperstown is 70 mi. W of Albany. From the S, I-88 to exit 17 to Rte 28N, to 16 Chestnut St. From the W I-90 to exit 30 to Rte 28S, to The Inn. From the SE, I-87 to exit 21 to Rte 23W to Rte 145 to Rte 20W to Rte 80W to The Inn.

A stay at The Inn at Cooperstown is a special treat. This award-winning historic hotel is ideally situated to enjoy all that Cooperstown offers. The Inn was built in 1874, fully restored in 1985 and is thoughtfully improved upon every year. Spotless rooms are individually decorated with many charming touches. A relaxing atmosphere enables guests to escape the hectic pace of the modern world. After exploring the lovely village of Cooperstown, visitors unwind in rockers on The Inn's sweeping veranda or enjoy the fireplace in a cozy sitting room. Nearby streets are lined with historic buildings, interesting shops and restaurants. The National Baseball Hall of Fame is just two blocks from The Inn. It is a brief trolley ride to experience another century at The Farmers' Museum, where exhibits, a recreated village and costumed staff depict life over 150 years ago. Nearby, the Fenimore Art Museum displays a premier collection of Native American Indian art, American paintings and folk art. The Glimmerglass Opera, beautiful Otsego Lake and many other treasures are located just beyond the village.

Member Since 1998

"You clearly understand that a good travel experience comes from attention to detail."

Albergo Allegria

www.albergoUSA.com
43 Route 296, P.O. Box 267, Windham, NY 12496-0267
518-734-5560 • Fax 518-734-5570
mail@AlbergoUSA.com

Innkeepers/Owners
Vito and Lenore Radelich

Traditional Mountain Breakfast Inn

Italian for the 'Inn of Happiness,' Albergo Allegria is an 1892 Inn set in the Northern Catskill Mountains. Situated on manicured lawns and country gardens, guests can relax under the 100 year old Oak tree or by the creek that is home to natural wildlife. The Inn's guestrooms offer beauty and history, while the Millenium, Master and Carriage House suites are gracious and inviting with whirlpool and fireplace. A full gourmet breakfast consisting of various frittatas, filled omelettes, Belgian waffles, stuffed French toast, and specialty pancakes are served hot from the kitchen. In addition, a marble side board filled with fresh fruit, homemade muffins, scones, granola and a variety of breads, cereals and juices are offered. Voted '2000 Inn of the Year' by author Pamela Lanier.

Rooms/Rates
14 Rooms, $73/$189 B&B;
8 Suites, $169/$299 B&B.
Guestrooms have down comforters, modern amenities.
Number of Rooms: 22

Cuisine
Hearty, full gourmet breakfast served each morning. 24-hour guest pantry with complimentary soft drinks, hot beverages and sweets. Afternoon tea served on Saturdays. Dinner restaurants nearby.

Nearest Airport(s)
Albany International Airport
50 miles North

Directions
I-87 Exit 21 (Catskill). Take Rte. 23 W for 24 miles. L onto Rte. 296. 1/10 mile on L.

AAA ◆◆◆◆   *Member Since 2001*   Mobil ★★★

☺   🚭♿💳   📁   ✒@   👑◎

"This truly is the Inn of Happiness."

Proprietors
Sylvia and Gary Muller
General Manager
Lee Ellis

Historic Village
Breakfast Inn

Mill House Inn
www.millhouseinn.com
31 North Main Street, East Hampton, NY 11937
631-324-9766 • Fax 631-324-9793
innkeeper@millhouseinn.com

Rooms/Rates
Rooms $200/$650. Suites
$350/$950. Queen or King bed/private bath/gas fireplace.
Number of Rooms: 10

Cuisine
Our guests call Gary's menu "THE breakfast" & there are over 20 reasons why! Among them: crayfish & andouille etouffee, house-cured salmon & goat cheese pizza, chicken sausage & wild mushroom hash, "uncle shorty's breakfast" & "the bb&t sandwich."

Nearest Airport(s)
MacArthur Airport (ISP) 50 miles

Directions
Rte 495 E to Exit 70. Right on Rte 111 S to end. Left on Rte 27 E. Go approx 30 miles into East Hampton Village. Just past Newtown Lane bear left on North Main St. We are on the left directly across from the windmill.

Our historic inn is located in the heart of East Hampton, 'America's most beautiful village.' Surrounded by spectacular ocean beaches, pristine bays, ospreys nesting over sparkling estuaries & quiet country roads, the East End of Long Island is a fisherman's playground, a vintner's paradise & an artist's inspiration. Enjoy foggy mornings, lazy days, blazing sunsets & starry nights. Walk to world-class restaurants, shops, galleries & theatres. Take a scenic drive to all that the Hamptons have to offer – Montauk's fishing boats, Sag Harbor's quaint antique shops, Bridgehampton's wineries & Southampton's magnificent mansions! Curl up on cozy leather sofas, relax in amazingly comfortable Adirondack chairs on our front porch overlooking the Old Hook Windmill, or sneak away for a bit of solitude in our lush gardens. Spacious suites, luxurious baths, fine linens, lofty featherbeds, down quilts & pillows, gas fireplaces, a leisurely breakfast our guests proclaim 'simply the best' & our old-fashioned hospitality assure you a memorable stay.

Member Since 2002

"Finally a place in The Hamptons where I can be truly comfortable. Gary is an amazing chef... Plain breakfast will no longer do. And a good dog fix, too!"

"The Tar Heel State"

Famous For: Blue Ridge Mountains, Smoky Mountains, Outer Banks, Roanoke Island, Cape Hatteras, Kitty Hawk, Tobacco, Textiles, Furniture

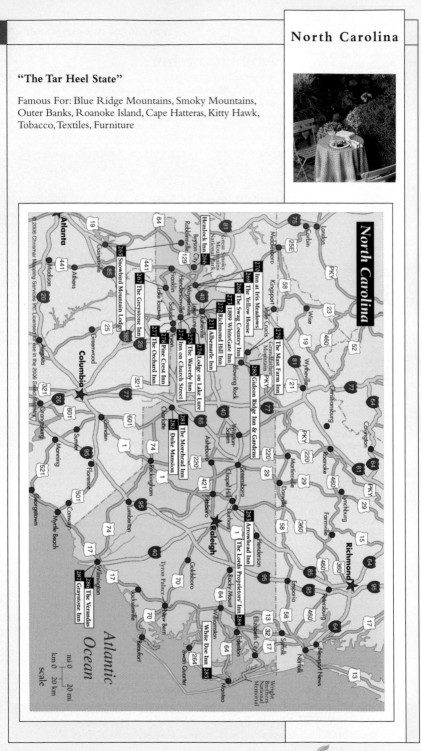

Innkeepers/Owners
Karen & Robert Rankin

Historic Mountain
Retreat/Lodge

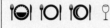

Snowbird Mountain Lodge
www.srinns.com/snowbirdmountain
4633 Santeetlah Rd., Robbinsville, NC 28771
800-941-9290 • 828-479-3433 • Fax 828-479-3473
innkeeper@snowbirdlodge.com

Rooms/Rates
23 Rooms, $170-$350 FAP. In-room fireplaces, air conditioning, whirlpool tubs, steam showers and private hot tubs available.
Number of Rooms: 23

Cuisine
Full gourmet breakfast, packed picnic lunch and four course gourmet dinner.

Nearest Airport(s)
Knoxville, Atlanta

Directions
From Robbinsville take Highway 143 W. 10.5 miles to the Snowbird Mountain Lodge.

High up in Santeetlah Gap, on the Southern border of the Great Smoky Mountains National Park, lies this secluded, rustic yet elegant, historic lodge built of stone and huge chestnut logs. Offering the finest in modern convenience and traditional comfort, Snowbird is the perfect retreat from the pressures of a busy world. The view from the lovely mountaintop terrace is one of the best in the Smokies. An excellent library, huge stone fireplaces, tennis courts and hiking trails on 100 acres of forest with numerous "quiet get-away" spots, offer guests a rare chance to relax. Award-winning gourmet cuisine and a lovely fireside bar with an exceptionally well-stocked wine cellar will have you looking forward to your next meal. Whether it's fly-fishing, hiking, biking, or just relaxing in front of the fire, we can make your next trip to the mountains picture-perfect. It's no wonder that guests have been coming to Snowbird to relax and renew themselves for over 60 years.

Member Since 1973

12+

"...an unspoiled, hidden vacation oasis tucked away in the Southern Appalachians."

Hemlock Inn
www.srinns.com/hemlock
911 Galbraith Creek Road, P.O. Box 2350, Bryson City, NC 28713
828-488-2885 • Fax 828-488-8985
hemlock@dnet.net

Innkeepers/Owners
Mort & Lainey White

Rustic Mountain Inn

High, cool, and restful, Hemlock Inn is beautifully situated on 50 wooded acres on top of a small mountain on the edge of the Great Smoky Mountain National Park. There is a friendly informality at meal times around lazy susan tables. Honest-to-goodness home cooked meals are served family style every day. Enjoy a change of pace, a change of scene, and simple pleasures. Get away from schedules as you walk in the Smokies, ride white-water rapids, fish in one of the beautiful streams, ride the Great Smoky Mountain Railroad, or just sit and relax in a rocking chair on our front porch. Ideal for family reunions.

Rooms/Rates
22 Rooms, $174/$196 MAP; 3 Cottages, $180/$237.
Open Year Round
Number of Rooms: 25

Cuisine
Breakfast, dinner included. Breakfast 8:30 am, daily dinner 6:30 pm Monday - Saturday, and 12:30 Sunday. Genuine home-cooked meals include made from scratch biscuits, rolls and deserts. No alcoholic beverages served.

Nearest Airport(s)
Asheville, NC

Directions
Hwy 74 to exit 69-Hyatt Creek Rd, R on Hyatt Creek 1.5 mi., L on Hwy 19, 1.5 mi to Hemlock Inn sign, turn R at sign, Inn 1 mi on L.

AAA ◆◆◆   *Member Since 1973*

"Hemlock Inn is more than a place...it's an attitude."

SelectRegistry.com

Owner
Reg Heinitsh, Jr.
General Manager
Clark E. Lovelace

Mountain Lake
Resort

The Greystone Inn

www.srinns.com/grey
Greystone Lane, Lake Toxaway, NC 28747
800-587-5351 • 828-966-4700 • Fax 828-862-5689
info@greystoneinn.com

Rooms/Rates
30 Rooms, $280/$550 MAP;
3 Suites, $430/$630 MAP; Includes boats & most recreational activities. Open year-round, except week days Dec./Mar.
Number of Rooms: 33

Cuisine
Includes full breakfast, afternoon tea, hors d' oeuvres, & gourmet dinner. Great wine list; liquor available.

Nearest Airport(s)
Asheville Regional

Directions
*From I-40 in Asheville, I-26E, 9mi, Rte 280S 20mi to Brevard, US-64W 20mi to Lake Toxaway Country Club/Greystone Inn sign. Right turn at entrance & gatehouse, proceed 3.5mi to Inn. Specific directions from other locations available on website.

All of the intimacies of a Four Diamond historic (National Register) inn with the luxurious amenities of a full service resort are combined on North Carolina's largest private mountain lake. Exceptionally romantic, highlights include a pampering spa, championship golf (complimentary certain times of the year) including a Tom Fazio designed golf learning center, guided hikes and full lake activities. Enjoy some refreshing afternoon tea and cakes on the sun porch just before our signature evening champagne lake cruise on our 26-passenger mahogany launch "Miss Lucy." Also included is a sumptuous 7-course gourmet evening meal. Clay tennis courts and fully equipped health and fitness center complement the nearby mountain resort experiences. Modern amenities include Jacuzzi tubs in every room and fireplaces in most. Wireless high-speed internet available throughout most of the campus. Personal guest recognition and exceptional service are our hallmark.

AAA ◆◆◆◆   *Member Since 1991*

Rated one of the best hotels/resorts in the world by both *Travel + Leisure* and *Conde Nast Traveler* magazines.

The Swag Country Inn

www.srinns.com/swagcountryinn
2300 Swag Road, Waynesville, NC 28785
800-789-7672 • 828-926-0430 • Fax 828-926-2036
swaginnkeeper@earthlink.net

Innkeeper/Owner
Deener and Dan Matthews

Rustic Country Inn

Rooms/Rates
12 Rooms $330/$655;
3 Cabins $475/$700; AP. Open
late April to mid-November.
Number of Rooms: 15

Cuisine
A not-to-be-missed hors d'oeuvre
hour precedes superb cuisine
nightly. All 3 meals are included
for two people in the room rate.
We are in a dry county. Guests
are welcome to bring their own
spirits.

Nearest Airport(s)
Asheville, NC and Greenville, SC

Directions
Via Interstate 40: North Carolina
on I-40. Exit #20 onto Hwy. 276 for
2.8 mi. R on Grindstone Rd. At stop
sign turn R onto Hemphill Rd. Four
miles up blacktopped road, L on
Swag Road. 2.5 miles up our gravel
road to the inn at 5,000 feet.

The Swag offers the finest hiking and wilderness experience available in the Great Smokies. This country guest house hotel features unique guest rooms with handcrafted interiors, natural materials of handpicked stone, and hand-hewn century-old logs. 250 unspoiled acres next to the Park sit atop our own ridge at 5,000 feet. *Town & Country* says the meals are "sophisticated." A paradise for nature-lovers seeking the finest amenities in a romantic, natural setting. "It is a soul-stirring experience, a welcome respite from the spiral of urgency and distractions of the world in and beyond the valley below." *USA Today* and American Historic Inns in Feb. 2003 named us "One of the ten most romantic retreats." Conde Nast Traveler, November, 2005, readers choice voted The Swag #34 of the 75 best hotels in the U.S.

Member Since 1991

"The Swag is an experience maker. How can you improve upon The Swag?!?"

The Yellow House on Plott Creek Road

Innkeepers/Owners
Donna & Stephen Shea

Elegant Mountain
Bed & Breakfast Inn ⭐

www.srinns.com/yellowhouse
89 Oakview Drive, Waynesville, NC 28786
800-563-1236 • 828-452-0991 • Fax 828-452-1140
info@theyellowhouse.com

Rooms/Rates
3 Rooms, 7 Suites, $175-$275.
Seasonal Rates and Packages
Available.
Number of Rooms: 10

Cuisine
Gourmet breakfast each morning
served en suite, on private balcony,
verandah or dining room depending
on accommodation; appetizers each
evening. Weekend dinner service.
Picnics available by request.

Nearest Airport(s)
Asheville (AVL) and Greenville/
Spartanburg (GSP)

Directions
From the S, take exit 100
(Hazelwood Ave) off US 23/74.
Proceed to the L for 1 1/2 mi. on
Plott Creek Rd. From the N, exit 100
(Hazelwood Ave) from US 23/74,
turn R on Eagles Nest Rd, L on Will
Hyatt, R on Plott Creek Rd.

A European-style inn of casual elegance, the 19th century Yellow
House accents fine service in a romantic, intimate setting. Located
a mile from the lovely mountain community of Waynesville, NC,
the inn sits atop a knoll 3,000 feet above sea level. Five beautifully landscaped acres of lawns and gardens feature two ponds, a
waterfall, a footbridge and a deck. The Inn offers three rooms and
seven suites, each with luxury linens, private bath, gas fireplace,
coffee service, refrigerator and bathrobes; suites also have wet bar
and 2-person whirlpool tub. Most accommodations include private balcony or patio. The Yellow House offers a quiet rural setting with exceptional views, soothing music, and complimentary
wireless internet service for guests. Minutes from the Blue Ridge
Parkway, Great Smoky Mountains National Park, Pisgah National Forest, Cherokee Indian Reservation, Cataloochee horseback
riding and ski area, and Maggie Valley. Close to four mountain
golf courses and the Biltmore Estate.

AAA ◆◆◆   *Member Since 1998*   Mobil ★★★

12+ ⊘ ♿ 💳   📁 ♥   ✂ 🖼 @   ▨ ◎ ❋ 🅢 ☕

"Our first visit was like a fairy tale. This visit was like a dream come true."

Inn at Iris Meadows

www.srinns.com/irismeadows
304 Love Lane, Waynesville, NC 28786
888-466-4747 • Fax 828-456-3877 • Fax 828-456-3847
info@irismeadows.com

Innkeepers/Owners
George and Becky Fain
Luxury Mountain
Breakfast Inn

Nestled upon five acres of rolling meadows and iris gardens with commanding views of the picturesque town of Waynesville and the surrounding mountains, this stately inn is the perfect destination for romantic getaways, honeymoons, celebrations, and relaxing escapes. Seven lavishly appointed guest rooms – all with fireplaces, private designer baths, large jetted tubs, heavenly king/queen beds, fluffy robes, TV/VCR's, phones, wireless Internet, air conditioning, and intriguing antiques. A meticulously restored turn-of-the-century Greek Revival mansion, Iris Meadows has spacious gathering areas including a library, music room, grand halls with leaded glass doors throughout, intricate wood work, carved mantels, and wraparound porches. Chosen as "one of our new favorites" by the *Atlanta Journal Constitution*'s 2006 "Go Guide" of southern retreats and one of the *Palm Beach Daily Post*'s "Seven Southern Spots to Sit a Spell." Walking distance of 1/2 mile to area shops, galleries, and fine restaurants; just minutes to the Blue Ridge Parkway; a half hour to Asheville.

Rooms/Rates
$225/$275 weeknights; $250/$300 weekends, holidays, & October.
Number of Rooms: 7

Cuisine
A bountiful breakfast is included in room rates. Complimentary beverages, cookies in guest kitchen which includes coffee service, guest refrigerator, microwave.

Nearest Airport(s)
Asheville

Directions
From Asheville I-40W to Exit 27 to US 23/74; 5 miles to Exit 102 to Russ Ave. R at 2nd light to Dellwood Rd; R on Love Lane. From Atlanta, 441 N from Clayton to Dillsboro, NC; US 23/74 to Exit 102, etc. From Knoxville hwy 40 E 75 mi to Exit 20/US 276 to hwy 19; L 4 mi, R on 276/Russ Ave, etc.

Member Since 2006

"We came for a few days and wanted to spend the rest of our lives."

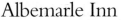

Innkeepers/Owners
Cathy and Larry Sklar

Elegant In Town Breakfast
Inn

🍽️

Albemarle Inn
www.srinns.com/albemarle
86 Edgemont Road, Asheville, NC 28801-1544
800-621-7435 • 828-255-0027 • Fax 828-236-3397
info@albemarleinn.com

Rooms/Rates
$165/$345, B&B. Elegantly appointed period rooms w/claw-foot tubs, fine linens, fresh flowers & turndown service w/chocolates. Rooms w/whirlpool tub, fireplace or private balcony available. Open year round.
Number of Rooms: 11

Cuisine
Full gourmet breakfast at private tables, late afternoon refreshments on the veranda, complimentary beverages.

Nearest Airport(s)
Asheville/Hendersonvillle Airport (AVL)

Directions
From I-26 or I-40: to I-240, Exit 5-B (Charlotte St.). Travel 1 mi. N on Charlotte St. to Edgemont Rd. Turn R on Edgemont & proceed to the end of the street to the inn.

A classic turn-of-the-century Southern mansion on the National Register, the Albemarle Inn offers elegance in a warm and inviting atmosphere. Guests are greeted in the main parlor which glows with recently restored oak wainscoting. An intricately carved staircase leads to period guest rooms, appointed with antiques, fresh flowers, and cozy robes. Morning begins with coffee or tea by the arts & crafts style marble fireplace, followed by a gourmet breakfast on the enclosed, plant-filled sunporch. Late afternoon offers the opportunity to relax on the massive stone veranda overlooking lush gardens while enjoying refreshments and conversation. Near downtown and the Biltmore Estate.

AAA ◆◆◆◆   *Member Since 2002*

12+ 🚭   💳 ⓣ   ✂ 🖊 @   🖼 ◎

"Can't imagine a more perfect stay...snuggly robes, dreamy mattresses & mouthwatering menus. Takes breakfast to an entirely new dimension."

Richmond Hill Inn

www.srinns.com/richmondhill
87 Richmond Hill Dr., Asheville, NC 28806
888-742-4550 • 828-252-7313 • Fax 828-252-8726
reservations@richmondhillinn.com

Innkeeper
Bland Holland

Elegant Victorian
In Town Inn

Romance is encouraged every moment. The 1889 mansion is perched on a hillside, and each room is uniquely decorated and furnished with antiques. Charming cottages surround a croquet court and feature fireplaces and porch rockers. Each of the spacious rooms in the Garden Pavilion offers beautiful views of the Parterre Garden, waterfall, and mansion. Stroll through gardens by the cascading brook. Relax at afternoon tea in the stately Oak Hall. Read in the library. Savor an exquisite dinner in Gabrielle's, our Four Diamond restaurant, featuring an extensive wine list.

Rooms/Rates
33 Rooms and 4 Suites, $215/$595.
Number of Rooms: 37

Cuisine
Full breakfast and afternoon tea included. Gabrielle's fine dining in mansion. The Ambassador's Grille for lunch or Sunday brunch. Extensive wine list & liquor.

Nearest Airport(s)
Asheville Regional Airport

Directions
Take Highway 251 exit on US Highway 19/23, three miles NW from downtown. Follow signs.

AAA ◆◆◆◆   *Member Since 1991*   Mobil ★★★★

12+

Voted Top 3 Country Inns by *Southern Living*

SelectRegistry.com

Innkeepers/Owners
Ralph Coffey and Frank Salvo
General Manager
Steve Guarneri

Historic Breakfast Inn

1889 WhiteGate Inn and Cottage
www.srinns.com/whitegateinn
173 East Chestnut Street, Asheville, NC 28801
800-485-3045 • 828-253-2553 • Fax 828-281-1883
innkeeper@whitegate.net

paii

Rooms/Rates
6 Rooms. $170/$340. Separate Cottage with full kitchen, Spa Suites, on site Orchid Greenhouse, Closest Inn to downtown.
Number of Rooms: 6

Cuisine
Full 3 Course Gourmet Breakfast, Late afternoon refreshments, Complimentary Beverages and Snacks

Nearest Airport(s)
Asheville

Directions
From I-40 or I-26 to I-240 Exit 5B (Charlotte Street) Proceed north on Charlotte; turn LEFT on E. Chestnut Go one block. Turn LEFT onto Central. Turn into the first driveway on the right. Parking is behind the greenhouse in the lower lot.

Romance, elegance and tranquility describe the ambiance at the 1889 WhiteGate Inn and Cottage. The Inn is listed on the National Register of Historic Places, and is minutes from the Biltmore Estate and nestled in The Blue Ridge Mountains. Enjoy a special place for your special moments. Sumptuous breakfasts begin your day. Luxurious spa suites with two-person Jacuzzi tubs and fireplaces set the tone for romance. Wander the stunning award winning gardens or stroll to shops and restaurants in Asheville, less than a five-minute walk.

AAA ◆◆◆   *Member Since 2005*

15+

"It's like waking up to a beautiful dream every morning. A healing place for the mind, body, and soul. The gardens are breathtaking."

Inn on Church Street

www.srinns.com/churchstreet
201 3rd Ave West, Hendersonville, NC 28739
800-330-3836 • 828-693-3258 • Fax 828-693-7263
innonchurch@innspiredinns.com

Innkeepers/Owners
Mike & Rhonda Horton
1920's Art Deco In
Town Boutique Hotel

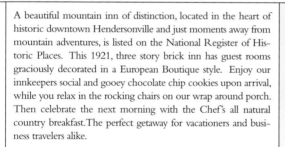

A beautiful mountain inn of distinction, located in the heart of historic downtown Hendersonville and just moments away from mountain adventures, is listed on the National Register of Historic Places. This 1921, three story brick inn has guest rooms graciously decorated in a European Boutique style. Enjoy our innkeepers social and gooey chocolate chip cookies upon arrival, while you relax in the rocking chairs on our wrap around porch. Then celebrate the next morning with the Chef's all natural country breakfast. The perfect getaway for vacationers and business travelers alike.

Relax as our knowledgable staff shows you their Southern hospitality for a memorable experience.

Rooms/Rates
19 guest rooms $99/$129-$169.
2 suites $250, Juniper House $250.
Number of Rooms: 23

Cuisine
Experience our culinary team's award-winning Countryside Cuisine, where we marry all natural products and techniques w/ locally harvested organics. Choose from the Inn's list of over 90 global wines, recent winner of *Wine Spectator* Award of Excellence in 2004.

Nearest Airport(s)
Asheville Airport

Directions
Hwy 26 to exit 49. Follow to downtown Hendersonville. L on Church St. to the corner of Church & 3rd Ave.

Member Since 2003

"We have traveled and dined around the world, and Inn On Church Street's beautiful decor, fabulous food and award winning wine list make it a must visit!"

Innkeepers
**John & Diane Sheiry,
Darla Olmstead &
Debbie Jones**

Traditional Village
Breakfast Inn

The Waverly Inn

www.srinns.com/waverlyinn
783 North Main Street, Hendersonville, NC 28
800-537-8195 • 828-693-9193 • Fax 828-692-101
register@waverlyinn.com

paii

Rooms/Rates
13 Rooms, $159/$199 B&B;
Suite, $225/$250 B&B. Seasonal
& promotional specials appear
regularly on our web site at
www.waverlyinn.com.
Number of Rooms: 14

Cuisine
Full breakfast each morning. A
wide variety of beverages are
available 24 hours a day. Darla's
freshly baked delectables each
afternoon. Evening social hour
5-6 p.m. Guests are welcome to
bring their own spirits.

Nearest Airport(s)
Asheville (AVL)
Greenville-Spartanburg, SC (GSP)

Directions
From I-26, take NC Exit 49B, then
U.S. 64W for 2 mi. into Hendersonville. Bear R onto Rte. 25N for
500 yds. Inn is on Left.

Located in the beautiful Blue Ridge Mountains of Western North
Carolina, the Inn is a short drive from the Biltmore Estate, Blue
Ridge Parkway, Dupont State Forest, Chimney Rock Park, and
the Flat Rock Playhouse. Cited in national publications such as
The New York Times and *Southern Living*, we received high praise in
Vogue Magazine for our "southern breakfast" with your choice of
omelets, french toast, pancakes with real maple syrup, grits, meats,
fresh fruit, farm fresh eggs and egg substitutes. Special touches
like 300 count sheets, Shelbourne mattress pillowtops, robes, free
wireless Internet, and cable TV make our $159-$250 rates a real
value. The Inn is within walking distance of the Mast General
Store, several fine restaurants, exceptional shopping, and antiquing. Two porches with rocking chairs await you. *The New York
Times* suggests that you "arrive early enough to sit outside and
enjoy the descending darkness." Our personal service will make
you happy you chose The Waverly.

"Come experience hospitality as it was meant to be."

Member Since 1991

"Everything from the delicious full breakfast to the comfortable bed was perfect!
We come back every year because of John, Diane, and Darla's hospitality."

e on Lake Lure

www.srinns.com/lakelure
Drive, Lake Lure, NC 28746
789 • Fax 828-625-2421
fo@lodgeonlakelure.com

Hendersonville

792

Innkeepers/Owners
Giselle Hopke

Historic Rustic
Mountain Inn

Along the shores of majestic Lake Lure in the Blue Ridge Mountains, you can golf, hike, boat, fish, ride horses, or just lounge and be spoiled at this elegant seventeen-room getaway with fabulous views, stone fireplaces, terraces and distinctive dining. A wonderful combination of an elegant country inn and a casual bed and breakfast, the Lodge is situated on the hillside to afford a sweeping view of the lake and mountains. The Lodge has recently been brilliantly renovated, with much larger guest rooms, fabulous bathrooms and private decks from many of the rooms. All guest rooms have beautiful private bathrooms and have been individually decorated with country antiques. Many rooms have terraces or balconies overlooking the lake. During the warmer months, swim, boat and fish from our beautiful lakeside dock.

Member Since 2003

Rooms/Rates
17 Guest Rooms. $155/$265, based on single or double occupancy.
Number of Rooms: 17

Cuisine
Price includes a full breakfast, afternoon coffee, tea and pastries, and evening wine and hors d'oeuvres. On Thursday, Friday and Saturday evenings we serve a full-course dinner by reservation only.

Nearest Airport(s)
Asheville Regional

Directions
The Lodge is located on Lake Lure, just off of Highway 64/74A in scenic Hickory Nut Gorge, 30 miles SE of Asheville.

8+

"Exquisite rooms, dining and service have made this our favorite place in the mountains!"

Innkeepers/Owners
Kathy & Bob
Thompson
Charley & Robert
Thompson

Traditional
Mountain Inn

The Orchard Inn

www.orchardinn.com
Highway 176, P.O. Box 128, Saluda, NC 28773
800-581-3800 • 828-749-5471 • Fax 828-749-9805
innkeeper@orchardinn.com

Rooms/Rates
9 Rooms, $125/$195 B&B;
5 Cottages, $175/$425 B&B.
All rooms have private baths,
some with whirlpool and steam
shower. Open year-round.
Number of Rooms: 14

Cuisine
A full breakfast is included in
room rate. Award-winning cuisine
served by reservation Thurs-Sat
evenings. Fine wines and beer
available. Listed as a "Food Find"
by *Southern Living.*

Nearest Airport(s)
Asheville, NC

Directions
Airports Asheville and Charlotte NC
and Greenville SC to I-26. From I-26,
take Exit 59 (old Exit 28)/Saluda NC.
Head WEST up hill 1 mile to Hwy
176. Turn LEFT on Hwy 176, and the
Inn will be 1/2 mile on right.

No matter where you start, The Orchard Inn is a perfect destination. Situated on a 20-acre mountaintop with stunning views, this national historic structure has long been a favorite retreat with its wraparound porches and large, inviting living room with stone fireplace. Guest quarters are furnished with period pieces and antiques. Private cottages feature fireplaces, whirlpools and private decks. Enjoy award-winning cuisine while overlooking the gardens, vineyard and mountains. Walk to waterfalls; hike nearby trails; watch the birds; visit Biltmore Estate, Carl Sandburg's home or local craft galleries; then, experience the peace and tranquility of this gracious retreat.

Member Since 1985

12+

"I feel like I'm letting folks in on a special secret when I tell them about this Inn."

1906 Pine Crest Inn & Restaurant

www.srinns.com/pinecrestinn
85 Pine Crest Lane, Tryon, NC 28782
800-633-3001 • 828-859-9135 • Fax 828-859-9136
select@pinecrestinn.com

Innkeeper/Owner
Carl Caudle

Elegant Historic
Mountain Inn

paii

Wine Spectator
AWARD
OF
EXCELLENCE

Experience a relaxing, intimate retreat nestled in the foothills of the Blue Ridge Mountains in Historic Tryon. Listed on the National Register of Historic Places with 13 consecutive AAA 4-Diamond awards, the Pine Crest Inn is renowned for its excellent foothills cuisine served in a casual environment. Our restaurant has received the *Wine Spectator* Award of Excellence for nine straight years and was named "Best Breakfast in the Southeast" each of the past two years.

Once a favorite of F. Scott Fitzgerald and Ernest Hemingway and known as the "Hidden Gem of Tryon", the Inn's 32 rooms, suites, and cottages are individually decorated, have cable TV, VCRs, & private baths; most have fireplaces.

The Inn's Conference Center combines wireless Internet access with elegant furnishings to provide the perfect place for your executive retreat, seminar or training session. Year-round flower gardens create the ideal setting for weddings, reunions, or a romantic getaway. Inquire about our romance packages, weekly wine tastings, and monthly wine dinners.

AAA ◆◆◆◆   *Member Since 1991*   Mobil ★★★

Rooms/Rates
20 Rooms $89/$199; 8 Suites $179/$349; 4 Cottages $139/$559. Open year-round. Seasonal specials on website.
Number of Rooms: 32

Cuisine
Sumptuous, made-to-order breakfast each day included. The restaurant offers casual fine dining featuring gourmet American cuisine w/ fresh, regional accents & organic ingredients. Award-winning wine list, afternoon tea, & full beverage service.

Nearest Airport(s)
Greenville (GSP), Asheville (AVL), Charlotte (CLT)

Directions
From I-26, exit 67 in Columbus. Follow Hwy 108 4 mi. to Tryon. Go thru town & turn L onto New Market Rd. Go 1/8 mi. & turn L onto Pine Crest Ln.

"We loved the idyllic mountain solitude & beautiful flower gardens, but the impeccable Southern hospitality made our stay!" "Comfort for your soul!"

SelectRegistry.com

Innkeepers/Owners
Sandra Siano
Danielle Deschamps

Rustic Mountain Inn

The Mast Farm Inn

www.srinns.com/mastfarminn
2543 Broadstone Road, P.O. Box 704, Valle Crucis, NC 28691
888-963-5857 • 828-963-5857 • Fax 828-963-6404
stay@mastfarminn.com

Rooms/Rates
8 guest rooms: $145/$250. 7 private cottages: $225/$450.
Number of Rooms: 15

Cuisine
Full 2-course gourmet breakfast included with lodging. Dinner features fresh, organic delightfully creative cuisine. Dining schedule varies seasonally. Fine wines & beer available. Private parties.

Nearest Airport(s)
Greensboro (GSO) or Charlotte (CLT)

Directions
Boone/Blowing Rock/Banner Elk area. From E & S: turn at V.C. sign on 105 betw Boone & Linville. Inn is 2.5 mi from 105 on Broadstone Rd. From W & N: take 194 from 321/421 west of Boone. In V.C., continue STRAIGHT on Broadstone Rd. to the Inn, 1/4 mile on the right.

The Mast Farm Inn is more than a bed and breakfast, with inn rooms, private getaway cottages, fine dining and great wines, organic gardens, and unique gifts completing our historic country appeal. The key to the Inn's success, however, lies in the exceptionally friendly and caring service offered to lodging and dinner guests alike. With inspired restoration and continuing care, the Inn continues to welcome guests, as it did over 100 years ago. Choose from eight guest rooms in our 1880s farmhouse and seven cottages, some restored from original farm buildings. Cottages range in size from cozy ones suitable for a couple to large ones for up to six guests. All are unique spaces. The inn's restaurant is celebrated, enjoyed by lodging guests and locals. The service is attentive, yet relaxed and friendly. Enjoy fireside or terrace dining, depending on the season. The current innkeepers place special emphasis on the environment, creating a "green" inn where recycling, reducing waste, and buying organic produce locally are taken seriously.

Member Since 1988

"...genuine warmth and hospitality...a unique inn that is wonderfully regional...delightful"

Gideon Ridge Inn

www.srinns.com/gideonridge
202 Gideon Ridge Rd., P.O. Box 1929, Blowing Rock, NC 28605
888-889-4036 • 828-295-3644 • Fax 828-295-4586
Innkeeper@gideonridge.com

Innkeepers/Owners
Cindy & Cobb Milner
Elegant Mountain
Inn

Gideon Ridge Inn is ten delightful guest rooms with mountain breezes, French doors and stone terraces. Ceiling fans and wicker chairs. Antiques and good books. Fine breakfasts to linger over. Earl Grey Tea and fresh-baked shortbread cookies to savor. Evening dining with a five-course meal and fine wine list. Bedrooms with warm fireplaces and comfortable sitting areas. Crisp cotton bed linens and well-appointed bathrooms. Suites with whirlpool tubs and massive king beds. And in the library, a piano with a breathtaking view of the mountains. Really...Guests enjoy hiking and walking, the Blue Ridge Parkway, golf at nearby clubs and Blowing Rock Village shops.

Member Since 1990

Rooms/Rates
10 Rooms, including 3 Deluxe Suites, and 3 Terrace Rooms. 9 rooms have fireplaces. 4 have whirlpools. All rooms B&B. $125/$315. Open year-round.
Number of Rooms: 10

Cuisine
Full breakfast included, featuring cornmeal pancakes, blueberry-stuffed French Toast or other signature entrees. Afternoon tea with fresh-made shortbread cookies or scones. Dinner served Tu.-Sat. Five course meal with choice of entree. Full wine list.

Nearest Airport(s)
Charlotte; Greensboro

Directions
US 321, 1.5 mi. S of Village of Blowing Rock, turn on Rock Rd. across from Green Park Inn. 1st L on Gideon Ridge Rd. Go to top of the ridge.

12+

"I always find magical moments at Gideon Ridge Inn... Such elegance and intimacy...The views of the mountains are truly spectacular."

Innkeeper/Owner
Billy Maddalon
Guest Service Manager
Linda Kiss

Classic English
Estate Inn

The Morehead Inn
www.srinns.com/moreheadinn
1122 East Morehead Street, Charlotte, NC 28204
888-MOREHEAD • 704-376-3357 • Fax 704-335-1110
reservation@moreheadinn.com

Rooms/Rates
6 Rooms $130/$160, 6 Suites $179/$219. All rooms are elegantly appointed w/ period antiques & private baths. Open year-round.
Number of Rooms: 12

Cuisine
Full breakfast consists of fresh-baked breads and pastries, waffles, eggs & fresh fruits. Full bar is service available with a substantial wine list.

Nearest Airport(s)
Charlotte-Douglas Int'l

Directions
From I-77 S: Exit at Morehead St. Take L onto Morehead St., Inn is on R, one and one half miles. From I-77 N: take I-277, Exit Kenilworth Ave. Take R onto Kenilworth. Take R onto Morehead St. Inn will be on L, 200 yards.

Located in Charlotte's oldest neighborhood, known as Dilworth, the inn is one mile from the center of the uptown business district. The historic home was built in 1917, by a businessman who required a wonderful place in which to entertain. Today, the inn stands as Charlotte's finest example of Southern hospitality. The Morehead Inn offers six suites and six guest rooms, each with luxurious private baths, color cable TV, and period antiques. All guest rooms have hi-speed and wireless internet access. The inn's public areas feature intimate fireplaces and grand twelve-foot ceilings. Guests may walk or jog the quiet, stately streets of our affluent community, or walk to an array of wonderful dining. Our guests are also afforded complimentary access to the fitness center and pool of the YMCA, which is located five blocks from the inn. A full Southern breakfast is served each morning and your shoes will be shined each evening. You will discover why Charlotteans refer to The Morehead Inn as 'Charlotte's most unique southern estate.'

AAA ◆◆◆   *Member Since 2002*   Mobil ★★★

"Everything was perfect--the room, the breakfast and, most of all, the staff!"
"The Morehead Inn is the only place I'll stay when I'm in the Carolinas."

The Duke Mansion

www.srinns.com/dukemansion
400 Hermitage Road, Charlotte, NC 28207
888-202-1009 • 704-714-4400 • Fax 704-714-4435
frontdesk@tlwf.org

General Manager
Tim Miron

Historic Inn and
Meeting Place

The Duke Mansion, built in 1915 and listed on the National Register of Historic Places, offers 20 unique guest rooms in true Southern splendor with a full breakfast. The rooms are residential in their décor, and appointed with beautiful artwork and furnishings, giving you a breathtaking image of what it was like to be a member of the prestigious Duke family who made The Mansion their home. All rooms have queen or king sized beds, private baths, exquisite linens, luxurious robes, and a gourmet goodnight treat. The Mansion is an integral part of Charlotte's most prestigious and beautiful neighborhood, and is situated on four and a half acres of beautiful grounds. Its professional culinary staff and beautiful public rooms can accommodate family or business celebrations of 10-300 guests. When you select The Duke Mansion, you are supporting a nonprofit where all of the proceeds are used to preserve and protect it.

Rooms/Rates
20 Rooms. $179/$279, including breakfast, plus tax. Special seasonal rates also available.
Number of Rooms: 20

Cuisine
Full-time onsite professional culinary staff featuring New South cuisine.

Nearest Airport(s)
Charlotte-Douglas International Airport, 20 minutes

Directions
From Brookshire Freeway, take 3rd Street exit, turn left. 3rd turns into Providence. Follow Providence to Hermitage Road, turn R. Take second entrance into The Mansion is on the left.

AAA ◆◆◆◆   *Member Since 2005*

"We truly felt like we were guests in an elegant Southern home."

Innkeepers/Owners
Gloria and Phil Teber

Elegant In Town
Breakfast Inn

Arrowhead Inn

www.srinns.com/arrowheadinn
106 Mason Road, Durham, NC 27712
800-528-2207 • 919-477-8430 • Fax 919-471-9538
info@arrowheadinn.com

Rooms/Rates
Rooms & suites in Manor house, Cottage & Log Cabin $150/$295. Whirlpools, steam showers & fireplaces. Corporate & mid-week rates. Specializing in peaceful getaways, small weddings, family gatherings, business retreats.
Number of Rooms: 9

Cuisine
Our delicious homemade breakfasts offer puffed pancakes, blueberry french toast, fresh herbed frittatas, glazed scones, & baked fruits. Our chef/owner will prepare romantic 5-course gourmet dinners.

Nearest Airport(s)
Raleigh/Durham

Directions
Take I-85 to Exit 176 and turn R. Travel 7 mi. on Rt.501 N to Mason Rd and turn L.

Relax in the quiet comfort of our 18th Century plantation home. The Arrowhead Inn rests on six acres of gardens and lawns amid venerable magnolia and pecan trees. Each of our elegant guest rooms, Log Cabin, and Garden Cottage provide a serene respite with the amenities of a fine hotel. The Arrowhead Inn, built circa 1775, has been carefully renovated retaining original moldings, mantelpieces, and heart-of-pine floors. Watch hummingbirds flutter on flowering hibiscus while relaxing with friends on our sun-warmed patio. Drift off for an afternoon nap next to your cozy fireplace. Unwind in your private whirlpool while enjoying fine wine and savory delicacies. Refresh yourself in your soothing steam shower. Awake to the delight of our abundant breakfast. Enjoy fine wines and a dinner feast served in a lovely romantic setting.

AAA ◆◆◆◆   *Member Since 2003*

"Everything was superb–from the furnishings and service to the gourmet food...compliments to you on the right blend of class & warm hospitality!"

The Lords Proprietors' Inn

www.srinns.com/lordsproprietors
300 North Broad Street, Edenton, NC 27932
888-482-3907 • 252-482-3641 • Fax 252-482-2432
stay@edentoninn.com

Innkeepers/Owners
Arch & Jane Edwards

Traditional Village
Inn

The Lords Proprietors' Inn comprises three restored homes on over an acre of grounds in the Historic District of Edenton with sixteen fully equipped and beautifully decorated guest rooms, and two luxury suites. Three spacious parlors with fireplaces, a library, and wonderful big porches are inviting places where guests enjoy our homemade cookies and tea in the afternoon, or a cordial in the evening. The Whedbee House dining room provides the setting for truly fine dining. Chef Kevin's cuisine is sophisticated, with a distinct taste of the region. A gratifying number of guests leave their table saying their supper was one of the very best they have ever enjoyed.

Rooms/Rates
Rates for our sixteen rooms are $155, $170 or $190 plus tax, for double occupancy. The rate for our two suites is $260. Single occupancy rates are available. Special package rates are described on our website.
Number of Rooms: 18

Cuisine
A full country breakfast is served seven days a week, and is included in your rate. A fabulous four-course dinner is served by reservation only Tuesday through Saturday.

Nearest Airport(s)
Norfolk, Virginia (ORF). Approximately 1.5 hours.

Directions
From Raleigh - US 64 E to US 17 N; Norfolk - US 17 S; Washington, DC - I-95 S to US 460-E to Virginia/NC 32 S; Wilmington - US 17 N.

Member Since 1990

"We were wowed by everything here, including the wonderful food! My husband felt that his dessert was the best thing he has ever eaten."

Proprietors
Bebe & Robert Woody
General Manager
Beth Gallagher

Elegant Village Breakfast
Inn

White Doe Inn
www.srinns.com/whitedoeinn
319 Sir Walter Raleigh Street, Post Office Box 1029,
Manteo, NC 27954
800-473-6091 • 252-473-9851 • Fax 252-473-4708
whitedoe@whitedoeinn.com

Rooms/Rates
$175/$280
Number of Rooms: 8

Cuisine
An important part of the Bed & Breakfast experience is the food. The White Doe Inn is pleased to provide outstanding service and a delicious full four-course seated and served breakfast that will delight your palate and be pleasing to the eye.

Nearest Airport(s)
Norfolk International Airport, VA

Directions
Go S on VA-168 to the NC border. Once in NC, US-168 merges into US-158 E. Stay on this road. Follow US-158 E to the Outer Banks. At Mile Post 16 turn W on US-64/264 crossing the George Washington Baum Bridge to Roanoke Island and Manteo.

As one of the most photographed historic homes on Roanoke Island, The White Doe Inn Bed & Breakfast has been welcoming guests since the turn-of-the-century. For years, visitors have admired its beautiful architectural details and old world charm. Now guests come from near and far to experience gracious hospitality in this lovely old home. Located in the heart of the Outer Banks, just minutes from the Atlantic Ocean and its beautiful beaches. The White Doe Inn is listed on the National Register of Historic Places and is noted for its historic and architectural significance. The Inn has been awarded the AAA Three Diamond Rating, and we are also members of the North Carolina Bed & Breakfast Inns and the Professional Association of International Innkeepers.

AAA ◆◆◆   *Member Since 2005*

"This is a place of what the Italians call laniappe, the extra touch, the exquisite detail, they know what you need before you do..."

The Verandas

www.srinns.com/theverandas
202 Nun Street, Wilmington, NC 28401
910-251-2212 • Fax 910-251-8932
verandas4@aol.com

Owners
**Dennis Madsen and
Chuck Pennington**

Elegant In Town
Breakfast Inn

Towering above a quiet tree-lined street in the historic district stands this grand antebellum mansion. Built in 1854, the award-winning Inn is a blend of history, luxury, charm and hospitality. Guest space abounds with wonderful colors, original art, French and English antiques. Four verandas, garden terrace and cupola offer hideaways. Professionally decorated guestrooms have sitting areas, telephone, cable TV, PC jacks. Hand-ironed linens dress comfortable beds. Baths have soaking tubs, showers, marble floors, luxury amenities and robes. French pressed coffee with a gourmet breakfast. Complimentary beverages and snacks and social wine hour. Walking distance to the Riverwalk and restaurants and shopping. High speed wireless internet. Online reservations. Enjoy The Verandas – "An Inn Second to Nun!"

AAA ◆◆◆◆   *Member Since 2001*   Mobil ★★★

12+

Rooms/Rates
8 Corner Rooms, $150/$250, two-night weekends. Open year-round except December 24-26.
Number of Rooms: 8

Cuisine
Included with the room rate is a full gourmet breakfast with French pressed coffee served in our beautiful dining room. Complimentary beverages and snacks are available and white wine is served in tne evening.

Nearest Airport(s)
Wilmington International

Directions
Take I-40 to 74W. Stay on 74W, it bcomes 3rd St,continue 10 blocks, make Rt on Nun. Next corner. On 74/76 - go over drawbridge, make 2nd RT, Front St. N - go 3 blocks, make Rt on Nun. On next corner, on Rt.

 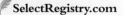

Innkeepers/Owners
Rich & Marcia Moore

Historic
Breakfast Inn

Graystone Inn

www.srinns.com/graystoneinn
100 South 3rd Street, Wilmington, NC 28401
888-763-4773 • 910-763-2000 • Fax 910-763-5555

Rooms/Rates
6 rooms $159/$269. 3 Jr. suites $209/$369. Two night weekends. Open year round.
Number of Rooms: 9

Cuisine
Full gourmet breakfast prepared by chef-owner. Early morning coffee bar. Complimentary beverages. Evening wine.

Nearest Airport(s)
Wilmington International

Directions
I-40E to 74W to downtown Wilmington. Corner of Third and Dock Streets.

The Graystone Inn, one of the most elegant historical structures in Wilmington, is located in the heart of the historic district and just three blocks from shopping, fine dining and the River Walk. The Graystone, originally the "Bridgers Mansion", was built as a private residence in 1905 by Elizabeth Haywood Bridgers and is an excellent representation of the neo-classical revival style. Each elegantly decorated bedroom has its own private bath, telephones with voice mail and data port, WiFi and cable TV. All rooms contain period furnishings, exquisite draperies and fine pima cotton linens, towels and robes. Intricately carved fireplaces grace seven of the nine bedrooms. The Graystone has frequently been used as a set for motion pictures and television and lists many notable personalities among its guests.

AAA ◆◆◆◆   *Member Since 2005*

12+

"Fabulous room, fabulous hosts, fabulous time!"

Ohio

"The Buckeye State"

Famous For: Cincinnati Zoo, Cincinnati Union Terminal,
Taft Museum, Neil Armstrong Air and Space Museum,
Put-in-Bay Village and Perry Memorial
(largest Doric column in the world), Rolling Hills,
Farmlands, Burial Mounds, Steel Mills,
Automobile Factories, Rubber, Plastics, Chemicals

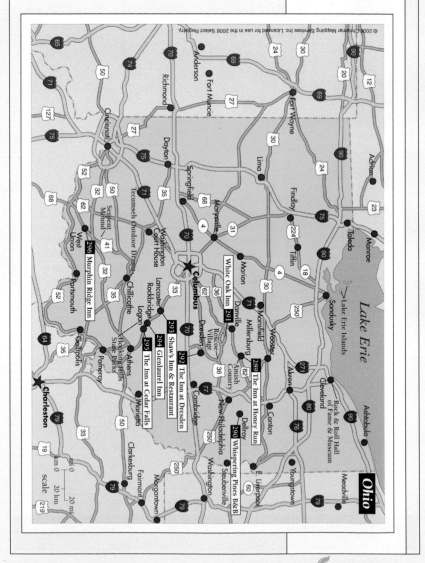

© 2006 Chrismar Mapping Services Inc. Licensed for use in the 2006 Select Registry.

296 Murphin Ridge Inn
293 Rockbridge
294 Glenlaurel Inn
295 The Inn at Cedar Falls
292 The Inn at Dresden
White Oak Inn **291**
289 The Inn at Honey Run
290 Whispering Pines B&B

Lake Erie

288   SelectRegistry.com

Innkeeper/Owner
Phillip T. Jenkins
Managing Partner
Richard Blum

Contemporary
Country Inn

The Inn at Honey Run

www.srinns.com/honeyrun
6920 County Road 203, Millersburg, OH 44654
800-468-6639 • 330-674-0011 • Fax 330-674-2623
info@innathoneyrun.com

Rooms/Rates
43 rooms, $104/$320 Full Service including 3 Guest Cottages and Monarch House VIP Suites. All include Continental Breakfast Buffet. Room amenities include TV/VCR, CD/Clock Radio.
Number of Rooms: 43

Cuisine
Breakfast served daily. Lunch and dinner reservations required. Fine wines, beers and cocktails served in the lounge and dining room.

Nearest Airport(s)
Local airport is 15-minutes away in Millersburg.

Directions
From Millersburg: (3.5 mi.) Rts 62/39 (E) for 2 blocks, L on SR 241 N for 1.9 mi. R (E) on CR 203 for 1.5 mi. From Berlin: (5.5 mi.) Rts 62/39 (W) R on CR 201, L on CR 203 for 2.7 mi.

A prize-winning contemporary Inn located amidst the world's largest Amish community. The Inn at Honey Run provides a chance to recharge batteries and refresh souls. Located on 70 acres of woods and pasture, the Inn offers privacy and serenity in various accomodations. 24 uniquely decorated rooms in its Main Lodge; 12 earth-sheltered Honeycombs with stone fireplaces, patios and shower/whirlpool tubs; 2 guest cottages each with two bedrooms and a honeymoon/anniversary cottage with jacuzzi. Three VIP suites at the Monarch House are perfect for private getaways! Watch birds from picture windows, read by blazing fireplaces, and explore the sights and backroads of Holmes County. Enjoy seasonal educational symposiums, Sunday evening fireside presentations, hike on our private trails or enjoy cocktails in the Pheasant's Nest Lounge. Full Service Executive Conference Center.

Member Since 1984

12+

"WOW! The world and all the stress disappeared the instant I turned into your drive."

Whispering Pines Bed & Breakfast

www.srinns.com/whisperingpines
1268 Magnolia Road, P.O. Box 340, Dellroy, OH 44620
866–4LAKEVU (452-5388) • 330-735-2824
Fax 330-735-7006
whisperingpines@atwoodlake.com

Innkeepers/Owners
Bill & Linda Horn

Picturesque Lakefront
Breakfast Inn

Whispering Pines is located in the gently rolling hills of Carroll County and sits on a hill overlooking beautiful Atwood Lake and its picturesque lush landscape. The lake views will take your breath away and the surroundings are indescribably tranquil. Enjoy a quiet conversation mesmerized by the birds singing and the pines whispering and gather around the warmth of the firepit in the evening. Nine guest rooms with 2-person whirlpool tubs, wonderful views, bedside chocolates and exquisite authentic victorian antiques. Breakfast is served on the enclosed porch overlooking the lake or in the dining room. Spring and fall erupts with a spectacular color show. We offer additional services such as an in-room massage and small weddings and you will discover several first class restaurants in the area for dining. Endless activities with 28 miles of shoreline - a walk/hike in the park, boating, day and night golf, top-notch museums, wineries and the Amish area. Whispering Pines - it's about being together at your dream place on the lake.

Rooms/Rates
9 guestrooms with 2-person whirlpool tub, scenic views, and comfortable reading chairs. Most have fireplace and private balcony. $175/$235.
Number of Rooms: 9

Cuisine
A delicious breakfast of seasonal fruit or warm cobblers, freshly baked breakfast cakes, and a variety of warm entrees served between 9 - 10:30 a.m., earlier upon request. Morning coffee delivered to your room. Afternoon cookies, tea and coffee.

Nearest Airport(s)
Akron/Canton

Directions
I-77 S to exit #103. 800 S then left on 183, right on 542-8 miles to the Inn. I-77 N to exit #81. 39 E to 542 N, 2 miles to the Inn. 90 m from Cleveland/Pittsburgh.

AAA ◆◆◆   *Member Since 2006*

12+

"You have spoiled us so much...we will return. You set yourself apart in so many ways beginning with your warmth on the phone and throughout our stay."

The White Oak Inn

Innkeepers/Owners
Yvonne & Ian Martin

Traditional Country Inn

www.srinns.com/whiteoakinn
29683 Walhonding Rd (SR715), Danville, OH 43014
877-908-5923 • 740-599-6107
info@whiteoakinn.com

Rooms/Rates
10 Rooms and 2 cottages, $110/$215 B&B. Fireplaces and whirlpool tubs in some rooms. Seasonal packages that include dinners available.
Number of Rooms: 12

Cuisine
Generous country breakfast daily. Dinners or romantic dinner baskets by advance reservation. Private wine tastings and wine pairing dinners can be arranged. BYOB.

Nearest Airport(s)
Columbus - 55 miles

Directions
From I71: Rte 36E or Rte 13S to Mount Vernon. Then Rte 36E 13 Mi to Rte 715. The inn is 3 miles East on SR715. From I-77: Rte 36W 35 mi to Rte 206N. 2 mi to Rte 715. The inn is 4 miles W on SR715.

We invite you to visit our turn-of-the-century farmhouse in a quiet wooded country setting. The inn has ten comfortable, antique-filled guest rooms and two luxury log-cabin cottages. Enjoy a candlelit dinner in the inn's dining room, or a romantic dinner basket delivered to your room. Tour local wineries or experience a private wine tasting at the inn. Visit Ohio's Amish area, Roscoe Village, or Longaberger baskets. Hike the local trails, go golfing or canoeing or simply spend your time soaking up the peace and quiet. Let us entertain you at a Murder Mystery, Theater event, Wine Tasting, Nature weekend or Cooking Class. Facilities are available for weddings, retreats, reunions and parties. The inn has received three major awards from *Inn Traveler* Magazine, including "Best Weekend Escape" for 2004 and was featured in Ohio Magazine in 2006 for Best Romantic Getaways. Come join us soon. The cookie jar is always full.

AAA ◆◆◆   *Member Since 1989*

12+

"We loved the peaceful country setting and charm of the inn. The meals were delicious."

The Inn at Dresden

www.srinns.com/innatdresden

209 Ames Drive, Dresden, OH 43821

800-373-7336 • 740-754-1122 • Fax 740-754-9856

info@theinnatdresden.com

Innkeeper/Owner
Patricia Lyall

Village Breakfast
Inn

Tucked away among the rolling hills of southeastern Ohio, The Inn at Dresden provides the perfect setting for a relaxing getaway with family and friends, or a quiet weekend with someone special. Originally built by Dave Longaberger, founder of Longaberger Baskets, this elegant Tudor home offers guests a panoramic view of Dresden and the surrounding countryside. Guests at the Inn enjoy an evening social hour and a full buffet breakfast. Individually decorated rooms feature VCRs, CD players and special ammenities such as wraparound private decks, two person Jacuzzi tubs and gas-log fireplaces.

Rooms/Rates
10 Rooms $85/$170 per night. Each room is individually decorated to depict the area. Many rooms have fireplaces, decks and Jacuzzi tubs.
Number of Rooms: 10

Cuisine
The Inn provides an evening social hour and full breakfast. Menus are available for all restaurants in the surrounding area.

Nearest Airport(s)
Columbus Airport

Directions
The Inn may be reached by SR 60N or Northpointe Dr. from Zanesville, or SR 16 from Newark or Coshocton.

Member Since 2000

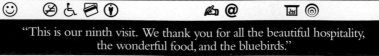

"This is our ninth visit. We thank you for all the beautiful hospitality, the wonderful food, and the bluebirds."

SelectRegistry.com

Innkeepers/Owners
Bruce & Nancy Cork

Classic In Town
Small Hotel

Shaw's Restaurant & Inn

www.shawsinn.com
123 North Broad St., Lancaster, OH 43130
800-654-2477 • 740-654-1842 • Fax 740-654-7032
shaws@greenapple.com

AWARD
OF
EXCELLENCE

Rooms/Rates
Whirlpool Rooms $152/$198
Deluxe Rooms $125 Standard
Rooms $86 Double Occupancy
Full Breakfast is Included in the
Restaurant.
Number of Rooms: 24

Cuisine
Known for Steaks, Prime Rib,
and Seafood. Pasta, Small Plates.
Changing Seasonal Menu--
Holiday Dinners. Wine Spectator
Award of Excellence.

Nearest Airport(s)
Port Columbus Airport

Directions
From Columbus: Rt. 33 East to
Lancaster. Left on Main. Two
blocks, Left on Broad. From
Hocking Hills: Rt. 33 West to
Lancaster. Right on Main, Left
on Broad.

Located on a tree-shaded square in historic downtown Lancaster,
Shaw's has been described as "A unique blend of country freshness and well traveled sophistication". Just minutes from Hocking
Hills, Shaw's Inn offers nine individually decorated theme rooms
with large in-room whirlpool tubs, including the Napa Valley, The
Pearl, The Caribbean, and Louis XIV. Full breakfast in the restau-
rant is included with all rooms. Shaw's Restaurant has a reputation
for New York Strip, Filet Mignon with Bearnaise Sauce, Prime
Rib, and Fresh Seafood. The Chef creates a constantly chang-
ing menu with seasonal items--Spring Lamb, Soft Shell Crab,
Fresh Walleye, 4-pound Lobster, and many others. Add to your
Holiday Festivities with four weeks of Christmas Dinners. Cork's
Bar, serving every day (Sunday after 1:00), has a warm setting of
dark wood and brass. Free High-Speed Wireless Internet Access
Throughout. Nearby attractions include: The Sherman House,
The Decorative Arts Center of Ohio, The Georgian, and The
Ohio Glass Museum.

AAA ◆◆◆   *Member Since 2005*   Mobil ★★★

"...a uniquely pleasant experience...rooms are a delight...staff attentive."
"..fresh and creative menu." "..relaxed environment, yet elegant."

Glenlaurel - A Scottish Country Inn

www.srinns.com/glenlaurel
14940 Mt. Olive Road, Rockbridge, OH 43149-9736
800-809-REST • 740-385-4070 • Fax 740-385-9669
Info@glenlaurel.com

Innkeepers/Owners
Greg & Kelley Leonard
Elegant Old World
Country Breakfast Inn

Sometimes at dinner, the story is told of how Glenlaurel was first imagined—300 years ago in the heart of the Scottish Highlands. Today, the heavily wooded 140-acre estate has the look of the old world, a veil of romance, and a pace of times gone by. Whether in the stately Manor House, the nearby Carriage House, or one of the wee cottages, Glenlaurel defines pampering as lazy kid-less afternoons, sumptuous fine dining for two, hot tub frolics, intimate fireside secrets, sleeping past 7, hearty breakfast choices, & morning walks through our own Camusfearna Gorge ~ with ne'er a soul in sight. As a Scottish Country Inn with Wooded Cottages, we offer the finest amenities for the sophisticated leisure or business traveler who wants the best. Visit our website to learn more about our property, as well as our conference facilities, spa treatments, and intimate wedding ceremonies. The Anniversary Club honors a successful marriage—year after year. Labeled the premier romantic getaway in the Midwest, everybody deserves a wee bit o'Glenlaurel!

AAA ◆◆◆   *Member Since 1998*

Rooms/Rates
3 Suites $189/$239 B&B, 3 Rooms $119/$199 B&B, 7 Crofts $219/$269 B&B, 6 Cottages $269/$319 B&B. Always Open.
Number of Rooms: 19

Cuisine
Dinner is "a private invitation to dine at an estate house in the country" with social hour, greetings from your host, and a candlelit culinary adventure "in the European tradition."

Nearest Airport(s)
Port Columbus 55 minutes

Directions
From N, take 33 thru Lancaster 12 mi to 180 exit, R onto 180, 4.8 mi, L at sign for .5 mi. From W, take 180 thru Laurelville 10 mi. From S, take 33 around Athens 30 mi to 180 exit, L onto 180, 4.8 mi. From E, use 33.

Named one of "our 25 favorite destinations" by *Midwest Living* Magazine in July 2003.

Innkeepers/Owners
Ellen Grinsfelder and
Terry Lingo

Rustic Country Inn ⭐

🍽️ 🍽️ 🍽️ 🍷

The Inn At Cedar Falls
www.srinns.com/cedarfalls
21190 State Route 374, Logan, OH 43138
800-653-2557 • 740-385-7489 • Fax 740-385-0820
info@innatcedarfalls.com

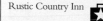

Rooms/Rates
9 Rooms, $99/$129 B&B;
12 Cottages, $149/$219 B&B;
5 Cabins, $169/$269 B&B
Number of Rooms: 26

Cuisine
Watch meals being created in the open kichen. Hearty country breakfasts, delectable lunches, sumptuous dinners by candlelight. Patio dining in the warm months. Enjoy an early beverage at Kindred Spirits, our tavern.

Nearest Airport(s)
Columbus which is 50 miles.

Directions
From Columbus, U.S. Rte. 33S to Logan-Bremen Exit 664S, R on 664, 9.5 miles, L on St Rte. 374, Inn is 1 mile on L. From Cincy, 71N to Washington CH, take 35E to 22E. In Circleville, access 56E to St. Rte. 374, turn L, Inn is 2 1/2 miles on R.

The restored and comfortably rustic 1840 log houses are an open kitchen-dining room, serving the most refined of American cuisine. Antique appointed guest rooms in a barn-like structure have rockers and writing desks and offer sweeping views of meadows, woods and wildlife. We have quaint cottages ideal for two, or secluded, fully-equipped 19th century log cabins accommodating up to four. Casual fine dining for lunch and dinner is served on the patio or the 1840's log cabins. Discover a new degree of relaxation as you escape into a sanctuary of natural beuaty and personal discovery at the Spa At Cedar Falls. We offer renewing experiences with lasting effects.

The rugged and beautiful Hocking Hills State Parks with glorious caves and waterfalls flanks the Inn's 75 acres on three sides. Casual and avid hikers will enjoy Old Man's Cave, Cedar Falls, Ash Cave and Conkle's Hollow. A variety of cooking classes, wine tastings, and hikes are scheduled year round. Call for a calendar of events and off season rates and specials.

AAA ◆◆◆   *Member Since 1989*

☺   🚲 ♿ 💼 🎨 📂 ❤   ✂ 🎒 @ 🐕   🎱 ◎ ❄   ☕

"Could there be any better place to recharge and reconnect?" "The Inn made magic happen." "Meals were delicious and beautifully served."

Murphin Ridge Inn

www.srinns.com/murphinridge
750 Murphin Ridge Rd., West Union, OH 45693
877-687-7446 • 937-544-2263 • Fax 937-544-8151
murphinn@bright.net

Innkeepers/Owners
Sherry & Darryl
McKenney
Innkeeper
Brittany Seaman
Traditional Country
Inn and Restaruant

Selected by *National Geographic Traveler* as one of the top 54 Inns in the U.S. and achieving a prestegious spot on the National Geographic Geotourism MapGuide—this prize-winning Inn welcomes you to 142 acres of four-season beauty. The Inn showcases the Guest House with spacious rooms, some with fireplaces or porches, and nine romantic cabins, as shown above, each with fireplace, two person whirlpool, two person shower and porch. All are decorated with David T. Smith Early American and Shaker reproduction furniture. The 1828 farmhouse features four dining rooms with original fireplaces, and gift shop. Enjoy award winning regional cuisine, in season, gathered from the Inn's gardens. View the Appalachian foothills, enjoy the night sky by the bonfire, and visit local Amish Shops, the Edge of Appalachia Preserve, the Serpent Mound State Memorial, and the Highlands Nature Sanctuary. The Inn has an outdoor pool, hiking, bird-watching, tennis, lawn games and more. Golf is nearby. Perfect for retreats, reunions, and conferences.

Rooms/Rates
19 rooms and cabins $107/$240
Number of Rooms: 19

Cuisine
Award-winning country inn fine dining. Full breakfast. The chef and staff make dining a charming experience that brings guests back time and again. Selected fine wine and premium beer available in the Dining House. Inn Guests Dine Nightly.

Nearest Airport(s)
Cincinnati/Northern Kentucky Int'l

Directions
FROM CINCINNATI: SR 32E., Right on Unity Rd. 2-1/2 mi. to Stop Sign turn Left on Wheat Ridge Rd. 2-7/10 mi. to Left on Murphin Ridge Rd. FROM COLUMBUS: SR 23 to 32W. Left on 41S to Right on Wheat Ridge Road at Dunkinsville. 1-1/2 mi. to Right on Murphin Ridge.

AAA ◆◆◆   *Member Since 1992*

"R&R for the soul! Great hosts, accommodations, food, and trails worthy of frequent visits."

Oklahoma

"The Sooner State"

Famous For: Will Rogers Memorial, Alabaster Caverns
State Park, National Cowboy Hall of Fame,
Pioneer Woman Statue, Cattle Ranching,
Oral Roberts University, Oil,
Plastics, Rubber, Cotton.

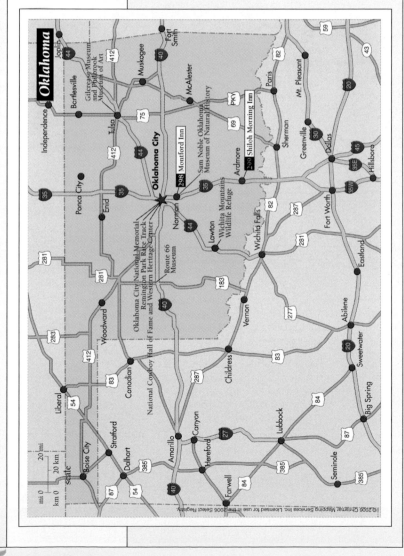

Oklahoma

Oklahoma City

298 Montford Inn

299 Shiloh Morning Inn

Joplin, Independence, Bartlesville, Muskogee, McAlester, Fort Smith, Tulsa, Ponca City, Enid, Norman, Lawton, Wichita Falls, Woodward, Liberal, Stratford, Boise City, Dolhart, Amarillo, Canyon, Hereford, Farwell, Childress, Vernon, Lubbock, Seminole, Abilene, Sweetwater, Big Spring, Eastland, Fort Worth, Greenville, Sherman, Paris, Mt. Pleasant, Dallas, Hillsboro, Ardmore, Canadian

Gilcrease Museum and Philbrook Museum of Art

Sam Noble Oklahoma Museum of Natural History

Wichita Mountains Wildlife Refuge

Oklahoma City National Memorial
Remington Park Race Track
Route 66 Museum
National Cowboy Hall of Fame and Western Heritage Center

scale
20 mi
20 km
mi 0
km 0

© 2006 Christmas Mapping Services Inc. Licensed for use in the 2006 Select Registry

Montford Inn & Cottages

www.srinns.com/montford
322 W. Tonhawa, Norman, OK 73069
800-321-8969 • 405-321-2200 • Fax 405-321-8347
innkeeper@montfordinn.com

Innkeepers/Owners
**Phyllis & Ron Murray,
William & Ginger
Murray**

Traditional In Town
Breakfast Inn

Celebrating their 11th year of operation, the Murrays welcome you to the award-winning Montford Inn and Cottages. With its ten uniquely decorated rooms in the main house, and six incredible cottage suites, the Montford Inn has everything the discriminating inngoer is looking for in lodging. Located in the heart of Norman's Historic District, this Prairie-style inn envelops travelers in a relaxing atmosphere. Antiques, family heirlooms and Native American art accent the individually decorated guest rooms and suites. Awaken to rich coffees and a gourmet country breakfast served in the beautifully appointed dining room or in the more intimate setting of the suites. Relax in private hot tubs. Escape in luxurious whirlpool bathtubs. Unwind in elegant cottage suites. Stroll through beautiful gardens. Find your heart... at the Montford Inn and Cottages! Featured in *Southern Living, Country, Holiday*, Fodor's, and *Oklahoma Today.*

Rooms/Rates
10 Rooms, $95/$169 B&B;
6 Cottage Suites, $199/$229
B&B. Open year-round, main inn closed Christmas Eve & Christmas Day. Cottage suites open all year.
Number of Rooms: 16

Cuisine
Gourmet Breakfast served in cottages and dining room. Complimentary wine and refreshments early evening.

Nearest Airport(s)
Will Rogers World Airport in Oklahoma City

Directions
20 minutes S of Oklahoma City. From I-35, take Main St., Downtown exit 109. Turn L on University (about 2.2 miles from I-35). Go 2 blocks, turn R 1/2 block on Tonhawa.

AAA ◆◆◆   *Member Since 1997*   Mobil ★★★

"Thank you so much for your warm hospitality. Our experience at Montford Inn rivals any five-star hotel we've stayed in. You have created a gem."

Innkeepers/Owners
Bob & Linda Humphrey

Luxury Bed & Breakfast Inn

Shiloh Morning Inn & Cottages
www.srinns.com/shilohmorning
2179 Ponderosa Road, Ardmore, OK 73401
888-554-7674 • 580-223-9500 • Fax 580-223-9615
innkeepers@shilohmorning.com

paii

Rooms/Rates
5 luxurious suites and 4 very private cottages. $149/$289. Two night minimum on weekends. Some holidays three night minimum. Closed Thanksgiving and Christmas.
Number of Rooms: 9

Cuisine
Three course gourmet breakfast at tables for two in the dining room is included. Dinner by advance reservation available for intimate in-room dining on Fridays & Saturdays. In-room complimentary soft drinks, juices, bottled water, coffees, and teas. Late afternoon wine & cheese available on weekends.

Nearest Airport(s)
Dallas (DFW)

Directions
Map sent with reservation

Oklahoma's premier country inn, Shiloh Morning Inn is located on 73 beautifully wooded acres, just minutes off I-35, yet a world away. Uniquely designed suites and cottages offer large luxurious baths, king beds, fireplaces, TV/VCR/DVD, private hot tubs or jetted tubs for two, and a private balcony, patio, or deck. Guests choose from an extensive library of movies and books. Walking trails are dotted with hammocks and park benches. Wildlife abounds. Privacy is a number one priority. Two new cottages take luxury to a new level. Roadrunner Hideaway is so secluded, its occupants are furnished with a personal golf cart. They will enjoy watching deer, or soaking in a hot tub on a deck cantilevered into the trees. The Villa at Shiloh is a two story cottage for the ultimate quixotic experience including an upstairs jetted tub for two, a spa shower, and a downstairs outdoor room with hot tub. The perfect romantic getaway for couples seeking the quiet seclusion of a rural countryside, Shiloh Morning Inn is truly a "Place of Peace & Rest."

Member Since 2004

"Shiloh Morning Inn is the Gold Standard for what a B&B should be."

"The Beaver State"

Famous For: The Oregon Trail, Mount Hood,
Flowers, Lumber, Wineries, Rose Festival, Crater Lake,
Painted Hills National Monument, Columbia River
Gorge, Coast Range, Cascade Range, Redwoods,
John Day Fossil Beds National Monument,
Hart Mountain National Wildlife Refuge

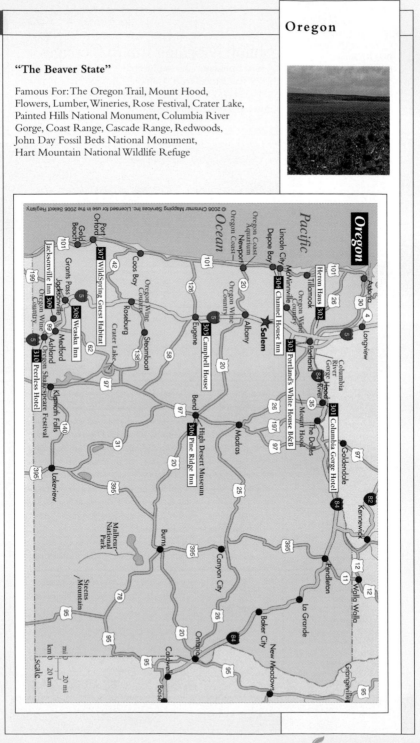

© 2006 Christus' Mapping Services Inc. Licensed for use in the 2006 Select Registry

SelectRegistry.com

Columbia Gorge Hotel

Owners
Boyd and Halla Graves

Elegant Waterside
Hotel

www.srinns.com/columbiagorge
4000 Westcliff Drive, Hood River, OR 97031
800-345-1921 • 541-386-5566 • Fax 541-386-9141
cghotel@gorge.net

AWARD
OF
EXCELLENCE

Rooms/Rates
$179/$350, 2 rooms with gas fire-places, 5 with electric fireplaces. Rates include nightly champagne and caviar service and the five-course "World Famous Farm Breakfast." Well-behaved dogs welcome with a $35 charge.
Number of Rooms: 39

Cuisine
Exceptional Northwest continental dining, 'World Famous Farm Breakfast'®. Outdoor dining on the terrace (seasonal). *Wine Spectator* Award of Excellence winner.

Nearest Airport(s)
Portland International Airport (PDX) is an hour away.

Directions
One hour E of Portland on I-84. Take exit 62, turn L. Take next L, hotel on R.

At the top of a 210-foot waterfall, overlooking the majestic Columbia River Gorge, the Columbia Gorge Hotel, 60 miles east of Portland, has a national reputation for fine cuisine, warm service and elegant surroundings. In the heart of the Columbia Gorge National Scenic area, this historic property has been lovingly restored and boasts 39 fully-appointed guest rooms, an award-winning dining room, full-service lounge, outdoor seating, and exquisite wedding and meeting facilities on 6 beautifully landscaped creek-side acres. Overnight stays include a champagne and caviar hour and the 5-course "World Famous Farm Breakfast." Well-behaved dogs gladly accommodated.

AAA ◆◆◆   *Member Since 1998*   Mobil ★★★

12+

"Oregon's Finest Country Inn" *Northwest Travel Magazine*
"...so dazzling that a visit becomes mandatory" *Portland Oregonian*

Heron Haus
www.srinns.com/heronhaus
2545 NW Westover Road, Portland, OR 97210
503-274-1846 • Fax 503-248-4055
julie@heronhaus.com

Owner
Julie Beacon Keppeler

Elegant In Town
Breakfast Inn

This elegant three-story turn-of-the-century tudor sits high in the hills, offering accommodations for both the business traveler and romantic getaways for couples. Each room has sitting areas, work areas, phones with computer hook-ups, and TVs; all have fireplaces. All have queen or king-sized beds. The baths offer special extras—one has a spa on a windowed porch; another has a shower with seven shower heads. Off-street parking is provided. Two and one half blocks down the hill is the Nob Hill area with boutiques, specialty shops, and some of the best eating places in Portland.

Rooms/Rates
6 Rooms, all with fireplaces, TV, sitting areas, phones, wireless/DSL hook-up, work areas, parking, AC: $95/$185 Single; $135/$350 Double. Open year-round.
Number of Rooms: 6

Cuisine
Continental breakfast.

Nearest Airport(s)
Portland Airport - 20 minute drivelite-rail access

Directions
On website.

Member Since 1994

"An inviting sitting garden provides a quiet and relaxing getaway for the weary visitor."

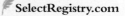
SelectRegistry.com

Innkeepers/Owners
Lanning Blanks and
Steve Holden

Historic In Town
Mansion

Portland's White House B&B
www.srinns.com/portlandswhitehouse
1914 NE 22nd Ave., Portland, OR 97212
800-272-7131 • 503-287-7131 • Fax 503-249-1641
pdxwhi@portlandswhitehouse.com

Rooms/Rates
$125/$225. Spa suites include
Champange, Moonstruck
Chocolate gift box and flat screen
televisions.
Number of Rooms: 8

Cuisine
Always vegeterian breakfast with
meats served on the side. Bread
Pudding French Toast, Crab
Cakes Eggs Benedict, Oregon
Blueberry Muffins, Pear Ginger
Scones. Full Espresso bar.

Nearest Airport(s)
Portland International Airport,
within 20 minutes.

Directions
From 1-5 take Weidler to 22nd,
N to NE Hancock. Hgwy 84 to
Lloyd Center, R at light, R on
Multnomah to 22nd, N to NE
Hancock.

Situated in Portland's North East Historic Irvington District,
Portland's White House was built as a summer home in 1911 by
Robert Lytle, a wealthy lumber baron. The house was billed as
the most expensive home built in the district for the period. This
Greek Revival Mansion boasts a lifestyle of past years with 14
massive columns, circular drive and fountain to greet you. Summer days show impressive hanging baskets and wonderful flowers to warm your senses. Restored to its original splendor by
Lanning and Steve with sparkling European Chandeliers, formal
linened Dining Room, Large Parlor, grand staircase, magnificent
leaded glass windows, gilt-gold ceilings, Trompe loiel and Grande
Ballroom. Extensive collections of European and Continental
Porcelains, 18th and 19th Century oil paintings. Guest rooms are
appointed with period antiques, paintings, king or queen feather
beds and exquisite linens. Fresh local Breakfast, utilizing SLOW
FOODS, is served in the Main Dining room by candle light.

AAA ◆◆◆   *Member Since 2004*   Mobil ★★★

"Be prepared to get spoiled rotten. Everything about this place is decadent,
from the breakfast to the big beds to the bath amentities."

Channel House Inn

www.srinns.com/channelhouse
35 Ellingson Street, P.O. Box 56, Depoe Bay, OR 97341
800-447-2140 • 541-765-2140 • Fax 541-765-2191
cfinseth@channelhouse.com

Owners
Carl & Vicki Finseth
Innkeeper
Bart Barrowclough

Contemporary Village
Breakfast Inn

Rooms/Rates
3 Oceanfront Rooms $225/$260;
9 Oceanfront Suites, $240/$320.
Number of Rooms: 14

Cuisine
Buffet-style breakfast featuring
fresh-baked goods is served
in our oceanfront dining room.
Enjoy a morning repast while
having one of the best views on
the coast. We have a significant
wine selection available and there
are many fine restaurants nearby.
The friendly staff will attend to
your every need.

Nearest Airport(s)
Portland International (PDX)
- 2.5 Hours

Directions
Just off Hwy 101, one block South
of Depoe Bay's only Bridge. Turn
West onto Ellingson Street, 100
feet to our parking lot.

Nestled in the Oregon Coast's magnificent scenery, Channel House combines the comforts of a first-class hotel with the congeniality of a small country Inn. Imagine fresh ocean breezes, sweeping panoramic views, powerful surf, truly unbelievable sunsets and whales within a stone's throw. Perched on an oceanfront bluff, guestrooms have an understated natural elegance and contemporary decor, including whirlpools on oceanfront decks and gas fireplaces. The friendly staff will attend to your every need. One of the West Coast's most renowned and romantic inns, it has been listed by Harry Shattuck among "a baker's dozen of world's (sic) most delectible hotels" and by *Sunset Magazine* as one of the 20 best Seaside Getaways on the West Coast.

Member Since 1997

"Too many accolades to count. Relax & enjoy the peace and tranquility, listen to the sound of the ocean and enjoy a truly unforgettable experience."

Proprietor
Myra Plant
General Manager
Lydia Lindsay

Elegant In Town
Country Inn

Campbell House, A City Inn

www.campbellhouse.com
252 Pearl Street, Eugene, OR 97401
800-264-2519 • 541-343-1119 • Fax 541-343-2258
campbellhouse@campbellhouse.com

Rooms/Rates
12 Rooms, $92/$189; 5 Luxury FP/Jacuzzi $239/$269; 2-room Luxury Suite FP/Jacuzzi, $289/$349; 1 Guest Cottage $245/$289 w/2 rooms $345.
Number of Rooms: 19

Cuisine
The Dining Room offers an ever-changing dinner menu utilizing the freshest local ingrediants. Complimentary full breakfast. Dinners from $16/$55. Room Service available.

Nearest Airport(s)
Mahlon Suite/Eugene Airport

Directions
From Airport: Hwy. 99 becomes 7th Ave, L on High, L on 5th, R on Pearl. From I-5, take I-105 to Eugene (exit 194B), to Coburg Rd (exit 2), stay L, merge onto Coburg Road, cross over River, take the second R (6th Ave), R on Pearl.

Built in 1892 and restored in the tradition of a fine European hotel, the Campbell House is surrounded by beautiful gardens. It is located in the historic district, within walking distance of downtown, restaurants and the theater. Hike Skinner's Butte or use over ten miles of riverside jogging and bicycle paths. Elegant guest rooms have private bathrooms, hidden TV with VCR, telephones and luxury amenities. Luxury rooms feature gas fireplaces, four-poster beds and Jacuzzi tubs. Enjoy complimentary wine in the evening and a full breakfast with newspaper in the morning. The Dining Room serves dinner Thursday through Saturday during winter months and nightly during the summer months. "Top 25 Inns in the nation," *American Historic Inns*. Weddings, receptions, meetings.

AAA ◆◆◆◆   *Member Since 2003*   Mobil ★★★★★

"A change in pace, place and a break in routine,
for the weary business traveler."

Pine Ridge Inn

www.srinns.com/pineridge
1200 SW Century Drive #1, Bend, OR 97702
800-600-4095 • 541-389-6137 • Fax 541-385-5669
pineridge@empnet.com

Owners
Judith & Don Moilanen
Innkeeper
Addie Rehberg

Elegant Boutique
Hotel/Inn

In an area known for its natural beauty, Pine Ridge Inn is distinguished by its spectacular location above the scenic Deschutes River Canyon. Cozy suites feature king sized poster or library beds, valuted ceilings, and living room areas. Enjoy an evening turndown with refresh service including ice, bottled waters and a homemade pillow treat. The Inn's spa suites feature two person Jacuzzi spa tubs in the bathing area and living room with decks overlooking Deschutes Canyon and trendy Old Mill District. Combining the ambiance of a small country inn and the amenities found only in a select number of luxury boutique hotels, Pine Ridge Inn offers unequaled comfort.

Rooms/Rates
13 Mini-suites $145/$185
7 Suites $210/$250/$325
Number of Rooms: 20

Cuisine
Afternoon wine and local brewed beer with seasonal snacks. The daily breakfast consists of a casual and friendly buffet of fruits, juices, homemade granola and hot porridge, bread goods and a plated hot special.

Nearest Airport(s)
RDM 15 miles

Directions
From HW 97, take Bend Parkway, Exit #138 onto Colorado Ave. Follow to 2nd traffic circle & take 3rd R onto Century Dr. Take the first L and an immediate L into drive.

Member Since 2004

12+

"Anyone who changes their personal commitments to accommodate others shows a service level above and beyond."

Innkeepers/Owners
**Dean & Michelle
Duarte**

Secluded Boutique Resort

🍽️

WildSpring Guest Habitat
www.srinns.com/wildspring
92978 Cemetery Loop, PO Box R, Port Orford, OR
97465
866-333-WILD • 541-332-0977 • Fax 775-542-1447
michelle@wildspring.com

Rooms/Rates
$179/$249 double; $55 ad-
ditional/person. Open all year.
Number of Rooms: 5

Cuisine
An opulent extended continental
breakfast buffet; each day we ask
our guests what they would enjoy
the following morning. Organic
fruits. Dairy-free available. On Sat.
nights, indulge in our signature
homemade hot fudge sundae bar.

Nearest Airport(s)
United or Alaska Air connect into
Crescent City, CA, 1 hour S and
North Bend OR, 1 hour N. Hertz at
both. Or fly into Eugene, a 3-hour
drive or Portland, 4.5 hours.

Directions
Take Cemetery Loop off Hwy
101 in Port Orford, 60 mi. N of
California.

The great outdoors now comes with an equally great indoors. A
small luxury resort overlooking the ocean on the south Oregon
coast, WildSpring Guest Habitat™ is unique. On five acres of
old Native American grounds, it offers luxurious accommodations and facilities in a naturally beautiful setting. Our goal is
to make you feel like a privileged guest in a private estate. Stay
in elegant cabin suites in the woods. Relax in the Guest Hall
with spectacular views of the ocean; help yourself to a cup of tea
and whale-watch on its expansive deck. Immerse in the steamy
open-air slate hot tub/spa overlooking the ocean. Wander the
walking labyrinth, find a hammock or secluded alcove. Take a
nap under the trees. Enjoy an in-cabin massage. Sleep to the
sound of wind through the trees and wake up to deer outside
your window. A short walk to look for agates and driftwood
along the beach, in a lovely small town with art galleries, hiking
trails, historical sites and a lighthouse. The best of the south coast...
without the crowds.

Member Since 2006

13+ 🚭 ♿ 💳   📂 ♥   ✂️ 🎨 @ 🐕   📷 ◎   🦅

"This seems a truly magical place...an environment that puts my soul at
peace. I can't remember the last time I have slept so well or felt so pampered."

Weasku Inn

www.srinns.com/weaskuinn
5560 Rogue River Hwy., Grants Pass, OR 97527
800-493-2758 • 541-471-8000 • Fax 541-471-7038
info@weasku.com

Owner
Vintage Hotels
Director of Operations
Charmaine Brown

Historic Waterside Retreat/
Lodge

The Weasku Inn was recently named as 'One of the country's greatest inns' by *Travel + Leisure,* and rests on the banks of the famous Rogue River, in southern Oregon. This secluded fishing lodge was a favorite vacation spot of Clark Gable during the 1920s and '30s. A complete remodeling took place in 1998, restoring the Inn to its former glory. The warm log exterior, surrounded by towering trees and 10 private acres, provides a tranquil setting ideal for an intimate getaway or corporate retreat. The lodge houses five guestrooms, and there are an additional 12 riverside cabins. A wine and cheese reception and deluxe continental breakfast are served each day.

Rooms/Rates
5 Lodge Rooms, $160/$285; Jacuzzi Suites, $305; 12 River Cabins with fireplaces, $205. Open year-round.
Number of Rooms: 17

Cuisine
Complimentary wine and cheese reception and continental breakfast are provided each day. BBQ on lodge deck for minimum fee, weekends May-September. Several restaurants are within minutes.

Nearest Airport(s)
Medford Airport

Directions
Located 51 miles north of the California and Oregon border. Take I-5, exit 48. Turn W, go across the bridge to the stop sign. Rogue River Hwy. Turn R. Go 3 miles. The Inn is on your Right.

Member Since 2001

"Top 25 Great American Lodges" - *Travel + Leisure*

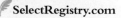
SelectRegistry.com

Jacksonville Inn

www.jacksonvilleinn.com
P.O. Box 359, Jacksonville, OR 97530
800-321-9344 • 541-899-1900 • Fax 541-899-1373
jvinn@mind.net

Innkeepers/Owners
Jerry and Linda Evans

Elegant In Town
Inn

Rooms/Rates
8 Rooms, $149/$189 B&B;
4 Honeymoon Cottages,
$250/$450 B&B.
Number of Rooms: 12

Cuisine
Restaurant with International
Cuisine; Both formal and bistro
dining; Sunday Bunch; Patio
Dining;Wine and Gift Shop featuring
over 2,000 wines.

Nearest Airport(s)
Medford Airport (5 miles)

Directions
From I-5 N - Exit 40: S on Old
Stage Road, follow signs to Jacksonville. L on California Street.
From I-5 S - Exit 27: L on Barnett
Road, R on Riverside Avenue, L
on Main Street to Jacksonville, R
on California Street.

The Inn offers its guests luxury and opulence, and its honeymoon cottages cater to romance and privacy of special occasions. Each has a king-sized canopy bed, whirlpool tub, steam shower, entertainment center, wet bar, fireplace, sitting room, computer with high-speed internet accessibility, and private patio with lovely surrounding gardens and waterfall--perfect for intimate weddings, receptions, and private parties. Nestled in a National Historic Landmark town, the Inn was featured on CNN and the Learning Channel's "Great Country Inns." Its restaurant is one of Oregon's most award-winning restaurants and features a connoisseurs' Wine Cellar and private catering. Five-star Diamond Academy Award of the Restaurant Industry. Recipient of "Readers' Choice Award--Best Restaurant" by Medford's *Mail Tribune* newspaper five consecutive years.

AAA ◆◆◆   *Member Since 2003*   Mobil ★★★

"A destination for relaxing and pampering."

Peerless Hotel and Restaurant

www.srinns.com/peerlesshotel
243 Fourth Street, Ashland, OR 97520
800-460-8758 • 541-488-1082 • Fax 541-488-5508
reservations@peerlesshotel.com

Innkeeper/Owner
Crissy Barnett

Historic In Town Hotel

🍽️ 🍽️ 🍽️ 🍷

AWARD
OF
EXCELLENCE

An intimate luxury inn built in 1900 and listed on the National Register of Historic Places, The Peerless today offers uncompromising style and service. Located in Ashland's Historic Railroad District, just steps from downtown and Oregon Shakespeare Festival. Uniquely and whimsically decorated with hand-painted murals, fine art and an eclectic mixture of furnishings from New Orleans to Hawaii. Guests are pampered with Italian bed linens, English silk and cotton towels, AVEDA bath products, spa tubs, and a sumptuous complimentary breakfast. The restaurant creatively interprets flavors of the Pacific Northwest and offers a *Wine Spectator*'s Award of Excellence wine list.

Rooms/Rates
6 Rooms, $78/$242 (not including 8% lodging tax). Rates include breakfast, coffee service, morning newspaper, nightly turndown service, handmade Peerless chocolates & Lobby port wine service. Packages available.
Number of Rooms: 6

Cuisine
Creative interpretation of sustainable seasonal Pacific Northwest cuisine to perfection. Wine Spectator's Award of Excellence. Dinner from 5:00 June-Oct: Tues-Sun. Nov-May: Tues-Sat Reservations: 541-488-6067 (Breakfast 8:30-9:30 a.m.)

Nearest Airport(s)
Medford Airport

Directions
Ashland's Historic Railroad District.

Member Since 2003

12+ 🚭 ♿ 🧳 ⓘ 📁 ❤️   ✍️ @   ◎

"Thank you for the 'The Peerless' fix." Parents of two-year-old twins.

Pennsylvania

"The Keystone State"

Famous For: Liberty Bell, Declaration of Independence, Articles of Confederation, Constitution, Gettysburg Address, Valley Forge National Historical Park, Poconos, Hershey Chocolate World, Amish Homestead, Steel, Pumpkins, Glass

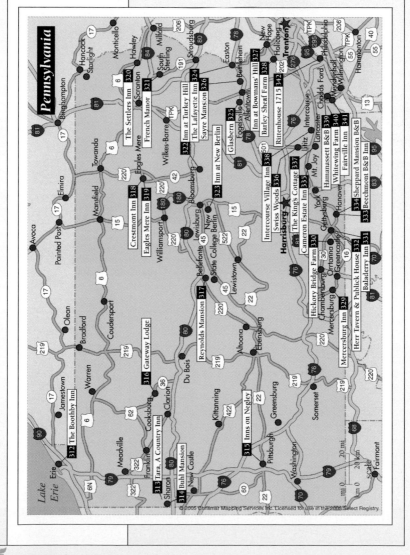

The Boothby Inn

www.srinns.com/boothby
311 West Sixth Street, Erie, PA 16507
866-266-8429 • 814-456-1888 • Fax 814-456-1887
info@theboothbyinn.com

Innkeepers/Owners
Wally and Gloria Knox

Historic Breakfast Inn

Rooms/Rates
$110/$160 with Midweek and corporate discounts of $20 per room and AAA 10% discounts on the full rates. Some rooms have a gas-log fireplace or a Jacuzzi tub. **Number of Rooms:** 4

Cuisine
A full gourmet breakfast is included. A guest galley at the end of the hall is stocked with refreshments and snacks all free to guests.

Nearest Airport(s)
Erie International Airport is only 20 minutes away.

Directions
Easily accessible from I-79 or I-90 and located on W. 6th Street (Alt. Rte #5). Detailed directions available on the website or from the Innkeepers.

Swing open the door of this Victorian era home and thrill to the rich oak paneled hallway with its impressive stairway. Notice the three stained glass windows that grab the sunlight and shine on the portrait of Gloria Boothby, namesake of the Inn. Settle down in the living room awash with natural light and pale yellow walls, or sit in front of a fireplace in the adjoining library filled with old and treasured family books. Enjoy the large dollhouse built as an exact replica of a family home in Springfield, Illinois, or curl up with a book in the Shakespeare room, so called because of the tiles around the fireplace of different Shakespeare plays. Outside on warm mornings, you may have breakfast served to you in the garden patio with a fountain's quiet soothing sounds, or stroll through the perennial garden. You may also sit on the comfortable front porch and watch the world go by! The rooms are luxurious, restful and quiet. This is a sanctuary for the vacationer and business traveler.

AAA ◆◆◆   *Member Since 2005*   Mobil ★★★

12+

@

"Details! Details! Details! Your attention to the needs of the guests is extraordinary...A lovely, well-appointed and comfortable home. Bravo!"

Innkeepers/Owners
Donna & Jim Winner
General Manager
Deborah DeCapua

Elegant Waterside
Country Inn

Tara – A Country Inn

www.srinns.com/taracountryinn
2844 Lake Road, Clark, PA 16113
800-782-2803 • 724-962-3535 • Fax 724-962-3250
info@tara-inn.com

Rooms/Rates
Gone With The Wind Getaway
Packages (MAP) $250-$425.
B&B $195-$350. Corporate and
Off-Season Rates Available.
Number of Rooms: 27

Cuisine
Ashley's Gourmet Dining Room
offers the finest in 7-course white-
glove and candlelight service
while Stonewall's Tavern boasts
a casual atmosphere with a wide
array of hearty dinner selections.

Nearest Airport(s)
Pittsburgh, PA Cleveland, OH

Directions
From I-80 take Exit 4-B to Sharon/
Hermitage Follow Rt. 18 North
– drive 7 miles to exit PA 258.

Inspired by the greatest movie of our time, Gone With the Wind,
Tara recreated is in a real sense an embodiment of the Old South.
Tara – although located in the "North" – offers you a lasting im-
pression of Southern Hospitality and a chance to enjoy the luxuries of days gone by. Tara is a virtual museum of Civil War and
Gone With the Wind memorabilia and antiques. Indulge in our
magnificent guest rooms complete with fireplaces and Jacuzzis
and enjoy the finest in gourmet or casual dining. Tara offers an
extensive wine list and an expertly stocked lounge. Afternoon
Tea is a daily opportunity for houseguests to mingle and enjoy.
Take a leisurely swim in either our indoor or outdoor heated
pools, or stroll through formal gardens overlooking the beautiful
450-acre Shenango Lake. Celebrating 20 years of award-winning dining and overnight accommodations, Tara is the ultimate
in World Class Country Inns, devoted to guests who expect the
exceptional and appreciate the best.

AAA ◆◆◆◆   *Member Since 2005*

12+

"The owners have succeeded in capturing the essence of the grand mansion
that was the cynosure of *Gone With The Wind*." Dallas Morning News.

Buhl Mansion Guesthouse & Spa

www.srinns.com/buhlmansion
422 East State Street, Sharon, PA 16146
866-345-2845 • 724-346-3046 • Fax 724-346-1702
info@buhlmansion.com

Owners
Jim and Donna Winner
General Manager
Laura Ackley

Elegant Victorian In
Town Breakfast Inn

Rooms/Rates
Castle Escape Packages
$300/$450; Spa Packages and
Off-Season Rates available.
Number of Rooms: 10

Cuisine
Champagne & Welcome Tray
await in each room. Afternoon
Tea served daily, Champagne
Reception served Fri & Sat.
Rates include 25% discount at
Ashley's Gourmet Dining Room
or Stonewall's Tavern both at
nearby Tara-A Country Inn (Limo
provided on weekends).

Nearest Airport(s)
Pittsburgh, PA Cleveland, OH

Directions
From I-80: Exit 4-B to Sharon/
Hermitage; N on Rt.18 for 3 mi.;
L on E. State St. for 3 mi. Buhl
is on L.

Buhl Mansion Guesthouse & Spa, one of America's top-rated B&Bs, offers the ultimate in luxury, pampering & unsurpassed hospitality. Listed on the National Register of Historic Places, this 1890 Romanesque castle is steeped in history & romance. After years of neglect & abuse, the opulent home of Steel Baron Frank Buhl is now lovingly restored & offers grand memories of a lifetime as guests experience the life of America's royalty in our lavishly appointed guestrooms with fireplaces and Jacuzzis. The full-service spa offers the epitome of indulgence with dozens of massage, body treatment, facial, nail, & beauty services from which to choose as well as a sauna, steam room & monsoon showers. Indulge each morning with breakfast in bed or dine in the picturesque breakfast room. Perfect for romantic getaways, indulgent spa escapes, exclusive executive retreats & castle weddings.

Member Since 2002

"Here in the westernmost part of Pennsylvania sits one of the most elegant, romantic properties in the United States." *The Washington Post*

Proprietor
Elizabeth Sullivan

Historic Urban
Luxury Inns

Inns on Negley

www.srinns.com/innsonnegley
703 and 714 South Negley, Pittsburgh, PA 15232
412-661-0631 • Fax 412-661-7525
info@theinnsonnegly.com

Rooms/Rates
Luxury Suites: $195/$235. King Suites: $170/$195. Queen Suites: $150/$180. Suites are beautifully appointed with private baths, luxurious linens, fireplaces, jacuzzis, personal robes, high speed Interent, cable television, & private phones.
Number of Rooms: 16

Cuisine
Room rate includes gourmet breakfast for two. Breakfast includes homemade baked goods, fresh fruit, yogurt, homemade cereals and granola, and hot savory or sweet entrees.

Nearest Airport(s)
Pittsburgh International Airport (20 miles)

Directions
Call Innkeeper for Directions.

The Inns on Negely are beautifully restored period homes located in the heart of Pittsburgh's charming and historic Shadyside area. Each of the sixteen guest rooms are custom designed with exquisite antiques, period furnishings, and a careful attention to detail. The Inns are just one block from Walnut Street and Ellsworth Avenue, which offers the finest and most unique shopping, dining, and entertainment experiences in Pittsburgh. Guests can linger and enjoy the tranquil atmosphere over refreshments while the innkeepers assist with plans to enjoy Pittsburgh. Whether guests plan a full day of activities, business meetings, or a day of total relaxation, The Inns on Negley can accomodate every guest preference.

Member Since 2006

10+ 🚭 ♿ 💳 🏷️ 📁 ♥ ⟷ ✂️ 🖊️ @ 🖼️ ◎ ✦

"During my visit to the university, the Inns on Negley met my every need. The rooms are sensational and the food is even better!"

Gateway Lodge – Country Inn

www.srinns.com/gatewaylodge
14870 Route 36, P.O. Box 125, Cooksburg, PA 16217
800-843-6862 • 814-744-8017 • Fax 814-744-8017
info@gatewaylodge.com

Innkeepers
Joe and Linda Burney

Rustic Log Cabin Inn,
Restaurant & Spa

Pennsylvania's 2004 Innkeepers of the Year. Amid some of the most magnificent forest scenery east of the Mississippi, this rustic log cabin inn has been awarded one of the top 10 best inns in the U.S. is also *Money* Magazine's Top Travel Pick. The Inn features two large stone fireplaces, home-cooked meals by candlelight, indoor heated pool and sauna, afternoon tea, nightly turn-down, AC. 22 Suites with king/queen-beds, each with a two-person fireside whirlpool tub. Seven historic rooms with double beds, seven Cottages with fireplaces. Customized small weddings, retreats and meetings. Conference complex. Spa and Gift shop. Gateway buildings are non-smoking.

Rooms/Rates
7 small historic Rooms, $95/$125; 8 Cottages, $145/$215; Suites, $225/$250 Ep. Mid-week and weekend packages. Closed Thanksgiving and Christmas day.
Number of Rooms: 39

Cuisine
Breakfast,lunch, dinner served daily, featuring homemade french toast, catfish and omelets to Prime Rib,steak & lobster tail.Over 300 selective wines to choose from.

Nearest Airport(s)
DuBois Regional

Directions
I-80 E:Exit 78(Brookville)R on Rte.36 N,17 miles.Lodge on R.I-80 W: Exit 62(Clarion)L on Rte.68,go thru 4 stop lights to Main St. continue 10 mi.to Rte 36 At stop sign turn R,go S 4 miles cross river Go 1/2 mile farther,Lodge is on L.

AAA ◆◆◆   *Member Since 1983*

"The in 'INN' if you're looking for a way to escape from stress and pressure of everyday life.""To say that guests are pampered is an understatement."

Innkeepers/Owners
Charlotte and Joseph Heidt, Jr.
Innkeepers
Joseph Heidt III
Victorian Village
Breakfast Inn

Reynolds Mansion

www.srinns.com/reynoldsmansion
101 West Linn Sreet, Bellefonte, PA 16823
800–899–3929 • 814–353–8407 • Fax 814–353–1530
innkeeper@reynoldsmansion.com

Rooms/Rates
6 Suites, $125/$300. Spacious rooms feature private baths with showers, fireplaces, Jacuzzi or steam shower, air conditioning, TV/VCR/DVD. Open year-round. Closed December 24 and 25.
Number of Rooms: 6

Cuisine
Full breakfast included. Walk to fine dining at the Wine Spectator award winning Gamble Mill Tavern. Complimentary Brandy.

Nearest Airport(s)
University Park (SCE)

Directions
I-80 exit 161. Take Rte. 220 S. toward Bellefonte to 550. Go right at bottom of ramp and follow 550 into town. At 3rd light, turn right onto Allegheny St. At 2nd light turn left on Linn. Enter through iron gates on right.

Escape to the Reynolds Mansion and enter a romantic atmosphere of Victorian elegance and luxurious comfort. Enjoy a game of pool in the billiard room or curl up by the fire in the snuggery with your favorite book. Relax in four common rooms, each with a unique wood-carved and tiled fireplace. Built in 1885, the mansion is a blend of the Gothic, Italianate and Queen Anne styles. Interior details include a marble vestibule, classic mirrors, Eastlake woodwork, stained glass windows and inlaid parquet floors. Come and experience the architectural wonders of Bellefonte's Victorian days. Flyfish in "Class A" trout streams, attend top-notch concerts and legendary sporting events. Go antiquing or golfing. If you are looking for a romantic getaway, or a retreat from the stress of daily life, come visit us. A warm welcome awaits you. The Reynolds Mansion has been featured on the cover of "County Victorian" and voted "Best in the US near a University." Penn State is only 10 miles away.

Member Since 2001

12+

"A night or two at The Reynolds Mansion
is a week's worth of vacation relaxation."

Crestmont Inn

www.srinns.com/crestmontinn

Crestmont Dr, Eagles Mere, PA 17731

800-522-8767 • 570-525-3519 • Fax 570-525-3534

crestmnt@epix.net

Innkeepers/Owners
Elna & Fred Mulford

Traditional
Mountain Inn

Rooms/Rates
$108/$268 per night Bed & Breakfast. MAP Rates are available. Economy Rooms, Suites, Whirlpool Suites, and Family Suites each with private bath, Cable TV/HBO and telephone. **Number of Rooms:** 15

Cuisine
Traditional country breakfast included. Fine dining and casual dinners available weekends in off season and 6 nights per week in season. Cocktail lounge with fine selection of spirits, wine and beer.

Nearest Airport(s)
Williamsport, PA

Directions
From Interstate 80, exit 232 to 42(N) for 33 miles to Eagles Mere Village. Turn left onto Lakewood Ave, then first right onto Crestmont Drive.

The Crestmont Inn is nestled in the woods on the highest point in Eagles Mere, a quiet historic mountaintop town surrounded by a pristine lake, State Parks and State Forests. Our Restaurant is well known for delicious cuisine, romantic fireplaces, original art and warm hospitality. Our suites include king or queen beds, large private baths with clawfoot tubs, whirlpool tubs, spacious sitting areas with cable TV/HBO, fireplaces and refrigerators. Our family suites can accomodate 4 to 6 people. Enjoy nature walks, hiking, biking, tennis, lake activities, cross country skiing, ice skating, antiquing, shopping or simply relax. Crestmont Inn "Romance and Nature at its Best"!

Member Since 1989

"Your hospitality made us feel like treasured friends visiting in your home."

Innkeepers
**Matthew Gale and
Barbie Gale**

Traditional Victorian
Mountain Inn

Eagles Mere Inn
www.srinns.com/eaglesmere
Box #356 Corner of Mary & Sullivan Avenues
Eagles Mere, PA 17731
800-426-3273 • 570-525-3273 • Fax 570-525-3904
relax@eaglesmereinn.com

Rooms/Rates
16 rooms/3 suites $169/$279
includes five course Gourmet
Dinner & Breakfast for two.
Number of Rooms: 19

Cuisine
Selected as a "Top Ten" Pennsylvania Inn, our experience is in 3-and
4-star restaurants. Meals included
in rates. We have the area's best
reputation for excellent 5-course
candlelit gourmet dinners. Wine
List. Enjoy cocktails, beer & wine
in our Pub. We serve ample full
Country breakfasts.

Nearest Airport(s)
Williamsport Regional Airport (IPT)

Directions
Print directions from our website. I-
80 to Exit #232 to Rt# 42N. I-99/15
take Rt. 220 east to Rt. 42N. From
Rt 6 go south on 220 to 42S. In
Eagles Mere turn on Mary Avenue.

Eagles Mere, 'the last unspoiled resort,' sits on a mountain with a
pristine lake surrounded by giant hemlock, rhododendron, and
mountain laurel. Restored in 2000, we are the last full service
Historic Inn remaining from the 1800s. Incredible waterfalls,
sunsets, hiking trails, birding, covered bridges, fishing, golf, tennis
and swimming. Featured by numerous travel writers. Guests
enjoy genuine hospitality and personal attention. We loan our
bikes, xc skis and canoe. If you want a quiet, relaxing place to
spend time together while enjoying warm hospitality and gourmet meals, visit our web site or call for reservations. "The LAST
UNSPOILED RESORT" now waits for you!

Member Since 1993

"Wonderful Food; Accomodating Staff; Ultimate Relaxation;
A Nature Photographer's Dream"

The Settlers Inn at Bingham Park

www.srinns.com/settlersinn
4 Main Ave., Hawley, PA 18428
800-833-8527 • 570-226-2993 • Fax 570-226-1874
settler@thesettlersinn.com

Innkeepers/Owners
Jeanne and Grant Genzlinger

Traditional Village Inn

The Settlers Inn is a place to gather. Relax, play & rejuvenate at this artfully restored arts & crafts inn. Stroll the extensive grounds & discover colorful flower & herb gardens, a quiet reflecting pond, or sit along the banks of the meandering Lackawaxen River.

Guestrooms are thoughtfully appointed with your comfort in mind. Luxurious European linens, fireplaces, whirlpool tubs & rosemary-infused bath amenities invite travelers to pamper themselves. High speed wireless Internet, available at no additional cost, provides the flexibility to stay connected with friends, family or business associates.

The cornerstone of the inn is the chef-owned farm-to-table restaurant highlighting artisan breads & menus influenced by the season. The Dining Room & Chestnut Tavern reflect the style of William Morris carried throughout the building. After a day of hiking or cross-country skiing, bask in the warmth of the bluestone fireplace. Summer offers dining alfresco on the terrace overlooking the grounds & The Potting Shed, a gift shop in the garden.

Member Since 1992   Mobil ★★★

Rooms/Rates
21 Rooms and Suites, $125/$250 B&B. Open year-round.
Number of Rooms: 21

Cuisine
The seasons and cultural history of the area shape both our ever-changing menu and the preparation of each dish which highlight products of local farmers and producers. In addition to the dining room, the Chestnut Tavern is the perfect place for conversation and a flavorful microbrew. In season, alfresco dining is available on our Terrace overlooking the gardens.

Nearest Airport(s)
Scranton (AVP) Allentown (ABE)

Directions
I-84 West to Exit 26. Route 390 N to Rt. 507 N. At light, turn left onto Rt. 6 West. 2 1/2 miles to the Inn.

Visit this Inn's website at www.thesettlersinn.com

Innkeepers/Owners
The Logan Family

Elegant French Chateau
Mountain Inn

The French Manor
www.srinns.com/frenchmanor
P.O. Box 39, 50 Huntingdon Drive, South Sterling, PA 18460
877-720-6095 • 570-676-3244 • Fax 570-676-8573
info@thefrenchmanor.com

Rooms/Rates
6 Rooms, $155/$245 B&B; 9 Suites, $230/$325 B&B. 8 Suites w/ fireplace & Jacuzzi. Rates are per couple.
Number of Rooms: 15

Cuisine
Gourmet breakfast. Room service available. Nouvelle & authentic French cuisine for dinner, semi-formal attire. An extensive wine list is available & top-shelf liquors.

Nearest Airport(s)
Scranton/Wilkes-Barre & Lehigh Valley International

Directions
From NY & NJ: I-80 W to PA exit 307. Follow 191 N 28 miles, to South Sterling, turn L on Huckleberry Rd; From PA tpke (NE Extension): take exit #95, 80E to 380N to Exit #8 for Route 423 N for 8 mi to Route 191 N, 2 miles and turn L on Huckleberry Rd.

An enchanting storybook stone chateau, the French Manor is nestled on 45 acres overlooking the beautiful Pocono Mountains. Old world charm and elegant furnishings are seamlessly joined with all the modern conveniences. Guests can enjoy luxurious suites with fireplace, Jacuzzi, and private balconies. Every guest is welcomed with complimentary sherry, cheese and fruit plate, and pampered with turndown service with Godiva chocolates. Our fine French restaurant features authentic and Nouvelle French cuisine served in our "Great Hall" where a wonderful vaulted ceiling and magnificent twin fireplaces create a romantic setting. Travelers can also enjoy our midweek 'Enchanted Evening' package or a special weekend throughout the year. Massage Therapy is available upon request in the privacy of your own room or suite. Enjoy miles of trails for hiking, mountain biking, picnicking, snowshoeing, and cross-country skiing. Nearby Sterling Inn offers additional amenities such as an indoor pool, hot tub, nature programs, tennis, and winter sports.

AAA ◆◆◆◆   *Member Since 1991*

"Absolutely perfect in every detail."

The Inn at Turkey Hill

www.srinns.com/turkey
991 Central Road, Bloomsburg, PA 17815
570-387-1500 • Fax 570-784-3718
info@innatturkeyhill.com

Innkeeper/Owner
Andrew B. Pruden

Traditional Country
Inn

From romantic couples looking for a weekend diversion, corporate travelers seeking a tranquil place to rest, to visiting celebrities and dignitaries seeking quiet anonymity, the Inn is a casually elegant and comfortably appointed escape of charm and class. Among the rolling hills and farmlands of rural Pennsylvania, The Inn at Turkey Hill is considered "an oasis along the interstate." Just a moment off Interstate 80 and minutes from downtown Bloomsburg, guests are treated to a hospitable atmosphere of towering trees and friendly ducks waddling about the courtyard. Rejuvenate yourself in one of our guest rooms attractively furnished with reproduction pieces or give in to the alure of a whirlpool bath and fireplace or take advantage of some of our amenties such as complimentary high speed Internet and DVD/CD players. An award winning restaurant is located on the property featuring creative, world class cuisine and a critically acclaimed wine list along with a friendly and accommodating staff. A warm welcome awaits you.

Rooms/Rates
14 Standard rooms $109/$120; 2 Inn rooms $115/$125 5 Stable Rooms $145/$179; Deluxe King $165/$205; King Supreme $172/$225.
Number of Rooms: 23

Cuisine
Complementary continental breakfast including hot entree. Afternoon refreshments. American-Continental cuisine featured nightly. Full service tavern.

Nearest Airport(s)
Wilkes-Barre

Directions
Conveniently located at Exit 236 of I-80. Traveling W on I-80, take Exit 236A. At the 1st traffic light, turn L, & the Inn will be on your L. Traveling E on I-80, take Exit 236. Turn L at the off-ramp stop sign. Turn L at the 1st light. The Inn is

AAA ◆◆◆   *Member Since 2002*   Mobil ★★★

"How nice to find an enclave of good taste and class." Art Carey, *Philadelphia Inquirer* "Exquisite flavors seem to be the trademark." *Times Leader*

The Inn at New Berlin

Innkeepers/Owners
Nancy & John Showers

Traditional Village Inn

www.innatnewberlin.com
321 Market Street, New Berlin, PA 17855
800-797-2350 • 570-966-0321 • Fax 570-966-9557
stay@innatnewberlin.com

AWARD
OF
EXCELLENCE

Rooms/Rates
11 rooms in 2 historic buildings, $139/$209 B&B. Whirlpool, fireplace & suite rooms available.
Number of Rooms: 11

Cuisine
Gabriel's Restaurant: dinner Wed. through Sun., brunch Sat.& Sun.Contemporary American cuisine. *Wine Spectator* Award of excellence.

Nearest Airport(s)
Harrisburg

Directions
In central PA, exit 210A (Lewisburg) off I-80. Rt 15 south 11 miles to Rt 304W 8 miles to New Berlin. (OR) Rt 15 north from Harrisburg to Selinsgrove exit Rt 35. In Selinsgrove, R on Market St and L on Rt 522. R on Rt 204W 9 miles to New Berlin. The Inn is a stone's throw from the intersection of Rts 204 & 304.

The *Philadelphia Inquirer* purports, "A luxurious base for indulging in a clutch of quiet pleasures." A visit to central Pennsylvania wouldn't be complete without a stay at The Inn at New Berlin. In the heart of the pastoral Susquehanna Valley, this romantic getaway offers an abundance of life's gentle pursuits. Bike country roads and covered bridges less traveled; explore charming downtowns and mountain hiking trails; shop antique coops, Amish quilt shops, and artist's galleries. Meanwhile, back at The Inn, Innkeepers Nancy and John Showers invite guests to relax on The Inn's front porch, savor an exquisite meal and a glass of fine wine, and rediscover the nourishing aspects of simple joys and time together. The Inn offers gracious accommodations in two restored historic homes, casual fine dining at Gabriel's Restaurant, and a treasure trove for shopping at Gabriel's Gifts. Guests relay they depart feeling nurtured and relaxed, and most of all inspired...especially after indulging in The Inn's massage and yoga offerings.

AAA ◆◆◆   *Member Since 1997*   Mobil ★★★

"A feast for the soul. Your chef is a treasure and your gift shop is dangerous. An uptown experience in a rural setting!"

The Lafayette Inn

www.srinns.com/lafayette
525 W. Monroe St., Easton, PA 18042
800-509-6990 • 610-253-4500 • Fax 610-253-4635
lafayinn@fast.net

Innkeepers/Owners
**Paul and Laura
Di Liello**

Traditional In Town
Breakfast Inn

paii

Our elegant mansion, built in 1895, is situated in a beautiful historic neighborhood near Lafayette College. Eighteen antique filled guest rooms welcome travelers visiting the Lehigh Valley's many attractions. The suites feature fireplaces and whirlpool tubs for that special getaway. The inviting parlor coddles visitors and plays host to business meetings and social gatherings. The wraparound porch and tiered patio call out to those longing to relax with a cup of coffee and a good book. The entire inn has wireless high-speed internet access, so, go ahead, borrow our laptop and surf the net or check your e-mail. Sure, it's OK to have a second brownie! Whether visiting the colors of the Crayola Factory with the kids, riding the historic, mule-drawn canal boats, hot air ballooning above the countryside, exploring underwater diving excitement, or just lounging and rejuvenating, The Lafayette Inn makes a great base for your getaway.

Welcome to our inn!

Rooms/Rates
18 Rooms/Suites $125/$250. Antique-filled rooms, private baths, TV/VCR, phones. Premier rooms and suites with gas fireplaces, whirlpool or soaking tubs, balcony. The entire inn is high-speed wireless. Open year-round.
Number of Rooms: 18

Cuisine
Full breakfast daily, complimentary soft drinks, coffee, fruit, and pastries available all day. Excellent restaurants within walking distance. No liquor license.

Nearest Airport(s)
Lehigh Valley International

Directions
I-78, Easton exit North to Third St. toward Lafayette College. Up hill to corner of Cattell and Monroe Sts.

AAA ◆◆◆   *Member Since 2000*

"What a great place for our weekend.
And the orange marmalade croissant French Toast...!!"

Owner
Al Granger

Traditional Country
Inn

Glasbern

www.srinns.com/glasbern

2141 Pack House Road, Fogelsville, PA 18051

610-285-4723 • Fax 610-285-2862

innkeeper@glasbern.com

Wine Spectator

AWARD
OF
EXCELLENCE

Rooms/Rates
Four rooms, $130/$225. Six whirlpool rooms, $140/$250. Fifteen whirlpool/fireplace rooms, $150/$325. Ten whirlpool/fireplace suites, $225/$450. One whirlpool/ fireplace cottage, $250/$475
Number of Rooms: 36

Cuisine
Breakfast and dinner in Barn dining room year round. Breakfast buffet and entree selections from kitchen. Seasonal as well as classic year-round choices available daily. Fully licensed.

Nearest Airport(s)
Lehigh Valley Int'l, 15 miles

Directions
From I-78 take Rt. 100 (N) for .2 mi. to L. at light for .3 mi. to R. on Church St. (N) for .6 mi. to R. on Pack House Rd. for .8 mi. to the Inn.

At the edge of Pennsylvania Dutch Country, a 21st Century Country Inn has evolved from a 19th Century family farm. You are welcome to explore our many pastures, gardens, and greenhouses that flourish amidst 100 acres of paths, streams, and ponds. Inside, whirlpools and fireplaces enhance most guest rooms. All have private baths, phones, high-speed Internet access, TVs and DVDs. Some luxury suites include wet bars, Jacuzzi shower systems and CD music systems. Canine-friendly suites available with limitations for our four-legged friends. For the physically ambitious guest, an outdoor pool, bicycles, hiking trails and an indoor fitness center are available. Contemporary American Cuisine is offered under the Barn's timbered cathedral ceiling. Much of the food comes from the gardens and pastures of the Inn. The magic of Glasbern provides a romantic glimpse of the past, with an invitation to enjoy the pleasures of today.

Member Since 2002

12+

"Unbeatable-so relaxing and warm-we'll be back."

Proprietors
Jeanne and Grant Genzlinger
Innkeeper
Carrie Ohlandt

Historic In Town Inn

Sayre Mansion
www.srinns.com/sayremansion
250 Wyandotte Street, Bethlehem, PA 18015
877-345-9019 • 610-882-2100 • Fax 610-882-1223
innkeeper@sayremansion.com

Timeless Elegance in a Distinguished Guest House. The Inn offers luxury and comfort in eighteen guest rooms each preserving the architectural details of the Mansion. Amenities include: fine linens, private baths, highspeed wireless internet access and voicemail telephones. Robert Sayre's Wine Cellar offers guests an opportunity to sample a selection of wine. Personal Service is the cornerstone of the guest experience. The Asa Packer Room, our unique conference center is ideal for business meetings. Gatherings and special events are held in a pair of elegant parlors, each with its own fireplace. Century old trees adorn the two acres of picturesque grounds which provide a beautiful setting for outdoor affairs under our tent covering a 30 by 60 patio area.

Rooms/Rates
18 rooms and suites, $150/$250
B&B Open Year-Round.
Number of Rooms: 18

Cuisine
Breakfast highlights homemade artisan breads, pastries, house specialties including french pudding, stratas and quiche, fresh juices and coffee ground to order. Excellent restaurants serving lunch and dinner are located within one mile of the Inn.

Nearest Airport(s)
Lehigh Valley International Airport is a five minute drive.

Directions
Located within blocks of Lehigh University, St. Lukes Hospital and Historic Bethlehem. See the website for door-to-door driving directions.

Member Since 2003

"Most enjoyable!"

Innkeepers
Lynne and Mike Amery

Elegant Colonial Manor
Country Inn

The Inn at Bowman's Hill

www.srinns.com/bowmanshill
518 Lurgan Road, New Hope, PA 18938
215-862-8090 • Fax 215-862-9362
info@theinnatbowmanshill.com

paii

Rooms/Rates
4 rooms $295/$355. 2 suites
$395/$455. Seasonal rates may
vary. Rooms feature king-size
featherbeds, whirlpools, fireplaces
and robes ... some rooms with
verandas.
Number of Rooms: 6

Cuisine
3-course gourmet breakfast
included. Full-English breakfast or
gourmet choices. Light afternoon
snacks. 24-hour tea & coffee
service.

Nearest Airport(s)
Trenton Mercer or Philadelphia Int'l

Directions
Exit 51 on I-95 toward New Hope.
7 miles TL onto River Rd. 2 miles
TL onto Lurgan Rd. Inn is 1/4 mile
on left. From New Hope 2 1/2 miles
S on River Rd. TR onto Lurgan Rd.
See above.

Award-winning luxury, romance and privacy on a manicured 5-acre estate adjacent to Bowman's Hill Wildflower Preserve ... and yet just minutes from the "action" in downtown New Hope. Selected in 2006 as one of the "Top 10 Most Romantic" Inns in the nation, this exclusive retreat offers just two suites and four rooms, all with king-size featherbeds, DVD players, high speed Internet access and flatscreen TV's. Beautifully appointed, modern bathrooms feature heated whirlpools for two, separate showers and heated towel racks. Our two-person Manor Suite shower has 11 jets ... enter at your own risk! The dramatic Tower Suite features cathedral ceilings, master bedroom, bathroom, sitting room and private entrance. Other amenities include seasonal swimming pool, hot tub and orchid room/conservatory. In-room massage and facials available by licensed beauticians and therapists from the upscale Solebury Club and Spa, and room rates include complimentary day passes to their facilities.

Member Since 2006

"World class elegance." "An amazing retreat."
"How do you go elsewhere after this experience?"

Barley Sheaf Farm Estate & Spa

5281 Old York Road (Rte 202), Holicong,
Bucks County, PA 18928
215-794-5104 • Fax 215-794-5332
info@barleysheaf.com

Innkeeper/Owner
Christine Soderman

Elegant Country
Breakfast Inn

An exclusive destination estate spa in historic Bucks County, once the home of Pulitzer-prize winning playwright George S. Kaufman, is surrounded by 100-acres of pasture and woodland views. Sixteen luxurious suites in the 1740 manor house, the guest cottage, and 19th Century barn feature whirlpool tubs, fireplaces, feather beds, full body steam showers, sunrooms, wet bars private balconies and terraces. The spa offers exceptional all-natural custom blended products and services in private in-suite treatment rooms. The elegant estate has trellis gardens, an antique French gazebo, pond, a junior Olympic-size pool and fitness center. A gourmet brunch is presented in the conservatory and on the terrace. Wine and cheese are offered in your suite upon arrival, a fully stocked courtesy wet bar, flat-screen TV and Bose CD. Centrally located near New Hope and Peddler's Village shops, antiquing, museums, fine restaurants and outdoor activities. Available for conferences and weddings with event planners on staff. French, German and Swedish spoken

Rooms/Rates
16 luxurious suites, $250/$750 Open year round. Activities: Spa, New Hope shops, antiquing, museums, art galleries, Delaware River outdoor activities.
Number of Rooms: 16

Cuisine
Full gourmet brunch, afternoon snack, dining can be arranged in advance, fine restaurants close by. Guests are welcome to bring their own spirits.

Nearest Airport(s)
Philadelphia Airport (PA) and Newark Airport (NJ)

Directions
On Rte 202/263 between New Hope and Doylestown, 0.5 mi SW of Lahaska, 4 miles south of New Hope.

Member Since 1982

12+

"A living masterpiece...Barley Sheaf Farm Estate & Spa."

Innkeepers/Owners
Lisa and Jim McCoy

Traditional Village Inn

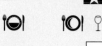

Mercersburg Inn
www.mercersburginn.com
405 South Main St., Mercersburg, PA 17236
717-328-5231 • Fax 717-328-3403
Lisa@mercersburginn.com

Rooms/Rates
$140/$325 B&B. 3 w/fireplaces, 1 w/clawfoot whirlpool tub, 2 w/Jacuzzi & TV, 3 w/antique baths. Kings and Queens. Open year round except Christmas Eve & Christmas Day.
Number of Rooms: 17

Cuisine
Full gourmet breakfast, afternoon tea and scones on weekends, evening refreshments. Fine dining, seating from 5:30 till 8:30 p.m. Thurs. Fri. and Sat. and 5:00 till 8:00 p.m. on Sunday. Reservations are recommended. Full bar service.

Nearest Airport(s)
BWI, Dulles

Directions
I-81, PA exit 5 (Greencastle), W on 16; twelve miles to historic Mercersburg. Located at junction of 16 and 75.

In 1909, Ione and Harry Byron had a magnificent dream, to build a home that brought comfort and entertainment to those that entered. From that dream, the 24,000 sq. ft Prospect, with 11 ft ceilings throughout, was born. The mahogany-paneled dining room and the sun-filled enclosed porch invite our guests to a culinary experience that will not be soon forgotten. The double-curving staircases lead you to our luxuriously appointed guest rooms. Draw yourself a nice warm bath in one of our antique soaking tubs, dry off with the softest of towels, slip on a fine robe, and drift away to sleep on your feather-bed. Awake in the morning to the smell of fresh baked morning goods, and our delicious 3-course breakfast. If the season permits, stroll through the flower and herb gardens that appoint the 5.5 acre property. If golfing, hiking, fly-fishing, or skiing are on your to-do-list, let our staff make the arrangements for you. All these activities and more are only a few minutes from the Inn. We look forward to having you in our home.

Member Since 1998   Mobil ★★★

7+

"Absolutely Wonderful! Great food, great service! The Inn and our room was so elegant. We felt so at home. Thank you for a beautiful and relaxing stay."

Hickory Bridge Farm

www.srinns.com/hickory
96 Hickory Bridge Road, Orrtanna, PA 17353
800-642-1766 • 717-642-5261 • Fax 717-642-6419
hickory@pa.net

Innkeepers/Owners
Robert and Mary Lynn Martin

Traditional Country Breakfast Inn

A quaint country retreat offering 5-bedroom farmhouse (circa 1750's) accommodations (some with whirlpool baths), and four private cottages with fireplaces along a mountain stream. Dinner is served in a beautiful restored Pennsylvania barn decorated with hundreds of antiques. All meals are farm-fresh & bountiful. Full breakfast is offered to overnight guests at the farmhouse and is taken to their cottages on Sunday morning. The farm is located 9 miles west of Gettysburg, Pennsylvania, on 75 beautiful acres–a wonderful place to relax while visiting Gettysburg or antiquing in the nearby area. Featured in *Taste of Home* magazine. Serving guests since 1977.

Rooms/Rates
9 Rooms, Cottages and Farmhouse, $95/$155 B&B.
Open year-round.
Number of Rooms: 9

Cuisine
Fine country dining in a beautiful restored Pennsylvania barn—Friday, Saturday, and Sunday. No spirits are served; you may bring your own.

Nearest Airport(s)
Harrisburg

Directions
Gettysburg, Rte 116 W to Fairfield and R 3 mi N to Orrtanna. Or Rte 997 to Rte 30 E for 9 mi turn S at Cashtown for 3 mi.

AAA ◆◆◆   *Member Since 1976*

12+ 🚭 ♿ 💳   @   🛏 ◎ ✺

"What a special retreat from life's demands!" Thank you." K. Shull

Innkeeper/Owner
Suzanne Lonky

Traditional Country
Breakfast Inn

 paii

Baladerry Inn at Gettysburg

www.srinns.com/baladerry
40 Hospital Road, Gettysburg, PA 17325
800-220-0025 • 717-337-1342
baladerry@blazenet.net

Rooms/Rates
10 Rooms, $135/$235 B&B;
$20 extra person in room. Open
year-round. Smoking permitted
outdoors only. No pets.
Number of Rooms: 10

Cuisine
Full country breakfast. Guests
are welcome to bring their own
spirits.

Nearest Airport(s)
Harrisburg

Directions
From U.S. 15, exit at Taneytown
Road. N 1 mile, R at Blacksmith
Shop Road, R onto Hospital Road.

Baladerry Inn is located five minutes from downtown Gettysburg on four acres at the edge of the Gettysburg Battlefield near Little Round Top. This brick Federal-style home (circa 1830), served as a field hospital during the War Between the States. A large two-storied great room dominated by a massive brick fireplace is both a dining and gathering area. A brick terrace provides an outdoor area for breakfasting and for socializing. A garden gazebo offers tranquil privacy. Private and spacious, the Inn is an excellent choice for history buffs, leisure travelers, bicyclists, small business meetings, weddings and reunions.

AAA ◆◆◆   *Member Since 1998*   Mobil ★★★

10+ ⊘ ▭   ♥   ✍ @   ▥ ◎ ✳

"Beautiful site and accomodations. Great breakfast.
We love it. A warm place like home."

Herr Tavern & Publick House

www.srinns.com/herrtavern
900 Chambersburg Rd., Gettysburg, PA 17325
800-362-9849 • 717-334-4332 • Fax 717-334-3332
info@herrtavern.com

Innkeeper/Owner
Steven Wolf

Historic Country Inn

Located in the western outskirts of Gettysburg, the Tavern sits atop a ridge overlooking the Gettysburg Battlefield. The Main House, built in 1815, has a storied past becoming the first Confederate hospital during the battle. It is beautifully restored and proudly listed in the National Register of Historic Places. Guestrooms include queen beds, gas fireplaces and private Jacuzzi baths. Each room is tastefully decorated in its own unique character. Extensive *Wine Spectator* award winning wine list and premium spirits served from our full service bar. All guests enjoy a sumptuous breakfast. Elegantly appointed dining rooms have fine German china and glassware. A private downstairs dining room is available within full view of windowed wine cellar.

Rooms/Rates
16 rooms $109/$209. Open year-round.
Number of Rooms: 16

Cuisine
Fabulous seasonal French influenced menu. Private Dining & Banquet facilities.

Nearest Airport(s)
Harrisburg Airport

Directions
From Gettysburg square, Proceed on Route 30 west, 1.7 miles. Tavern is on left at Herr's Ridge Rd.

AAA ◆◆◆   *Member Since 2004*   Mobil ★★★

12+

"...we can't say enough to truly explain how happy we are with the beautiful room and excellent staff."

Innkeepers/Owners
Kathryn and Thomas White

In Town Breakfast Inn

The Beechmont Bed & Breakfast Inn
www.srinns.com/beechmont
315 Broadway, Hanover, PA 17331
800-553-7009 • 717-632-3013 • Fax 717-632-2769
innkeeper@thebeechmont.com

paii

Rooms/Rates
3 suites, $139/$169. 4 rooms, $99/$129. Corporate rates Mon-Thur. All rooms have A/C, TV & telephones. Some w/ fireplaces & whirlpools. Open year round.
Number of Rooms: 7

Cuisine
Sumptuous breakfast. Help yourself cookie jar. Complimentary soft drinks and bottled water. Excellent restaurants nearby.

Nearest Airport(s)
Baltimore Washington Int'l (BWI)

Directions
From Baltimore: I-695 to I-795 to MD 30/PA 94. Turn R at the square on Broadway (PA 194). Inn is 3.5 blocks from square on the R; guest parking in the rear of the inn. From DC: I-495 to I-270 to Rt. 15 N to Rt. 116 E.

Located on a tree-lined street of stately historic homes, The Beechmont has welcomed business and leisure travelers since 1986 with exceptional hospitality and thoughtful extras designed to meet your needs. Strolling through the garden guests are awed by its centerpiece, a 130-year-old Magnolia tree. A well-stocked library and parlor offer a backdrop for relaxed conversation, while well-appointed, spacious guest rooms assure a comfortable stay. High speed wireless internet access is available, or use our guest internet station. Guests often explore Gettysburg (just 14 miles west of Hanover), and roam through numerous antique malls, enjoy golf outings on championship courses, and discover vibrant fall colors in the hills of southern Pennsylvania. The innkeeper's sincerest wish is for The Beechmont to be a memory that lingers joyously long after your visit has ended.

Member Since 2003   Mobil ★★★

6+

"Friends couldn't treat us better." "Wonderful time. Breakfast was great!"

The Sheppard Mansion
www.srinns.com/sheppardmansion
117 Frederick St., Hanover, PA 17331
877-762-6746 • 717-633-8075 • Fax 717-633-8074
reservations@sheppardmansion.com

Innkeeper/Owner
Kathryn Sheppard-Hoar
General Manager
Timothy Bobb
Historic In Town
Inn

paii

Nestled in the heart of Hanover's Historic District stands a grand 3-story brick and marble Mansion surrounded by lush gardens. Built in 1913 by Mr. and Mrs. H.D. Sheppard, co-founder of The Hanover Shoe, the Mansion now operates as an elegant full service Inn and event facility. Featuring the original furnishings and restored with modern amenities, the Mansion features numerous parlors, bedrooms and suites with oversized soaking tubs in the private marble baths--all for our guests' enjoyment. Days can be spent exploring nearby Gettysburg, antique hunting or touring Lancaster, Baltimore, Washington, DC or Hershey. Want to relax instead? Have a massage and lounge around the house. Complete your pampered experience with an exquisite meal in our Dining Room, serving French-inspired cuisine Wednesday through Saturday nights. Check our website for lodging and dining packages.

Member Since 2002

Rooms/Rates
9 rooms and suites, King, Queen and Twin Beds, $140/$350 per night. 2 BR Guest Cottage on property available weekly. Corporate rates available. All rooms have private baths, A/C, Data Port, TV, Telephones and in-room coffee.
Number of Rooms: 9

Cuisine
Full gourmet breakfast included. Fine dining offered Wed. thru Sat. nights featuring a seasonal menu of French-inspired cuisine.

Nearest Airport(s)
BWI 1hr, MDT 1hr

Directions
1 block S of Center Square in Hanover, @ intersection of Frederick St. (Rt 194) & High St. (Rt 116). Minutes from US Rt 15, I-83, I-270, I-795 & PA Turnpike.

12+

"Sinking into the cloud-like beds provided our best night's sleep ever!"

Innkeepers/Owners
Randy Wagner
John Jarboe

Elegant Country
Inn

Cameron Estate Inn & Restaurant
www.srinns.com/cameronestate
1855 Mansion Lane, Mount Joy, PA 17552
888-422-6376 • 717-492-0111 • Fax 717-653-8596
info@cameronestateinn.com

Rooms/Rates
16 guest rooms & suites and a 2 bedroom cottage, some w/fireplaces & Jacuzzi tubs. Private baths, A/C. $119/$249. Open year round. Corporate Rates.
Number of Rooms: 18

Cuisine
Complimentary daily served breakfast. Fine Dining Wed-Sun. Contemporary American Cuisine w/ full liquor license.

Nearest Airport(s)
Harrisburg (MDT) Philadelphia (PHL) Baltimore (BWI)

Directions
Midway between Harrisburg & Lancaster, Hershey & York. Detailed directions online at http://www.cameronestateinn.com/directions.htm

The Cameron Estate Inn is the former summer estate of Secretaries of War to Lincoln and Grant. It is the largest historic Inn in the Pennsylvania Dutch and Hershey regions of the Susquehanna Valley. This grand 1805 Federal style mansion is secluded on 15 acres of lawn and woodland with two trout streams and provides the perfect venue to relax and unwind in an unspoiled country setting. Step back in time and let us pamper you with our historic, yet sumptuous guest accommodations featuring authentic European antiques and Ralph Lauren linens. Allow us to tantalize you with our refined culinary expertise, a full liquor license and our extensive wine list. For brides, grooms and their families, the Inn provides an elegant outdoor wedding venue. Well-situated out-of-the-way location ideal for exploring Lancaster, Hershey, Harrisburg, York, day trips to Gettysburg or Longwood Gardens, and all major tourist activities that include Amish/Pennsylvania Dutch, Lancaster, Hershey Park and Spa, golfing, theaters, fine dining, museums, antiquing, hiking and biking. Physically located midway between Hershey and Lancaster, but truly located....A WORLD AWAY! Visit us on the web at www.cameronestateinn.com.

Member Since 2005

"What a treasure! Lovely house, beautiful guest rooms, charming hosts! The restaurant rivals any in New York or Philly. Highly Recommended! Simply the best!"

Swiss Woods

www.srinns.com/swisswoods
– 500 Blantz Road, Lititz, PA 17543
800-594-8018 • 717-627-3358 • Fax 717-627-3483
innkeeper@swisswoods.com

Innkeepers/Owners
Werner and Debrah Mosimann

Traditional Swiss Style
Country Breakfast Inn

Surrounded by meadows and gardens, Swiss Woods is a quiet retreat on 30 acres in Lancaster's Amish country. All rooms feature patios or balconies, some with lake views, and are decorated with the natural wood furnishings typical of Switzerland. Fabulous breakfasts, complemented by our own blend of coffee, are served in a sunlit common room. Convenient to Lancaster's famous farmers markets and wide variety of activities, Hershey is also just a short drive. After a day of antiquing, shopping or visiting quilt shops, enjoy the views of extraordinary gardens, landscaped with a wide variety of annuals and perennials. Take a relaxing hike through the woods, watch the birds, or enjoy a drink on the garden swing with a good book and a sweet treat from our kitchen. In winter settle in to read next to the inn's handsome sandstone fireplace. We offer a quiet, restful place for you to reconnect and refresh. German spoken.

Rooms/Rates
6 Rooms (2 with Jacuzzi), all with patios and balconies. $135/$190.1 suite $170/$190
Number of Rooms: 7

Cuisine
Inn breakfast specialties may include garden fritatta, freshly-baked breads from old world recipes, honey apple french toast, or a potato quiche. The afternoon boasts sweets on the sideboard. Don't miss the biscotti!

Nearest Airport(s)
Harrisburg & Philadelphia

Directions
From Lancaster: 11 miles N on 501 thru Lititz. L on Brubaker Valley Rd 1 mi to lake. R on Blantz Rd. Inn is on the L. From NYC: Rt 78/22 West to exit 13-Bethel. S on Rt 501 1 mile beyond Brickerville. R on Brubaker Valley Rd. 1 mi to lake.

AAA ◆◆◆   *Member Since 1993*   Mobil ★★★

"Truly a haven of rest" ... "Spectacular--I didn't want to leave!" ... "beautiful grounds!"

Innkeepers/Owners
Janis Kutterer and Ann Willets

Historic In Town
Breakfast Inn

The King's Cottage, A Bed & Breakfast Inn
www.srinns.com/kingscottage
1049 East King Street, Lancaster, PA 17602-3231
800-747-8717 • 717-397-1017 • Fax 717-397-3447
info@kingscottagebb.com

Rooms/Rates
7 rooms, 1 Honeymoon Cottage: Fireplaces, Whirlpools, Hot Tub, DVD/VCR, Wireless High Speed Internet, Business rates available. Closed at Christmas. $150/$260
Number of Rooms: 8

Cuisine
Gourmet breakfast with fresh local fruit & meats. Dietary restrictions accomodated with advance notice. Near many fine & casual restaurants. 24 hr. guest kitchen w/ice, bottled water, snacks, coffee, tea.

Nearest Airport(s)
Harrisburg, PA - 35 minutes.

Directions
Rt. 30 to Walnut St. exit. At second light turn L. At 2nd stop sign turn L. Go 1 block & turn R onto Cottage Ave. Inn is last building on R. Parking: turn R before white wall.

In the midst of historic Lancaster, The King's Cottage is an oasis of comfort and hospitality. The elegant decor, original crystal chandeliers and romantic fireplaces will warm your heart. Each luxurious room is fit for royalty with polished hardwood floors, canopied, brass or carved beds, antique armoires, private baths with soaking tub or whirlpool. After a gourmet breakfast, visit scenic Amish farmlands, tour historic sites or shop for handmade quilts, crafts or antiques. Relax with afternoon refreshments while we make plans for fine dining or dinner with an Amish family for you. Listed on National Register. Awarded 'Top 10 Most Romantic Inn' by American Historic Inns. We provide business travelers a refreshing alternative to hotels with complimentary wireless high speed Internet access, full gourmet or continental breakfast times to fit your schedule, late check in, billing options, corporate rates, massage room on site and resident nationally certified massage therapist.

Member Since 1995   Mobil ★★★

16+

The Inn & Spa at Intercourse Village

www.srinns.com/ivbbs
Rt 340 - Main St - Box 598, 3542 Old Philadelphia
Pike, Intercourse, PA 17534
800-664-0949 • 717-768-2626
innkeeper@inn-spa.com

Innkeeper/Owner
**Ruthann & Elmer H.
Thomas, CHA**

Historic Village Inn

🍽

paii

Surround yourself in luxury, comfort and pleasures for the body and spirit at our inn and spa. Enjoy elegance in a quiet village setting that entreats you to a place of peace, beauty and comfort. Travel through time as you enter the 1909 Victorian Inn filled with period furnishings and antique treasures. Its refinement and sophistication deliver high-class accoutrements for those of discerning tastes. If upscale country is more your style, then reserve one of our rustic Country Homestead suites with private entrances and over 400 sq. ft. of space to relax in and forget the world around you. Our suites include ensuite baths, jet tubs, steam showers, sitting areas with love seats, fireplaces, wet bars and many other special treats which await you. For the ultimate escape in luxury, for divine romance and relaxation, find yourself engulfed in sumptuous grandeur in our Grand Suites complete with Jacuzzi and fireplace. Arise to a full five course gourmet candlelit breakfast and then indulge yourself in a delightful diversion to our on-site spa.

Rooms/Rates
All suites have king/queen beds, ensuite bath, gas log fireplace, loveseat, microwave, refrigerator, coffee maker, CTV, CD player, phone, data port, wi-fi, & AC. Grand Suites $279/$379 Homestead Suites $169/$239 Victorian Rooms $149/$199
Number of Rooms: 9

Cuisine
5 course gourmet candlelit breakfast, prepared by our chef & served on fine English china in our formal dining room.

Nearest Airport(s)
Harrisburg 1 hr, Philadelphia 1 1/2 hrs, Baltimore 1 1/2 hrs.

Directions
Located on Pa Rte 340 in the Historic Village of Intercourse. 11 mi. E of Lancaster, Pa.

AAA ◆◆◆◆   *Member Since 2005*

18+ Ⓧ 💳 ❤ ✂ @ 🎲 ◎ ❄ ☕

"For your Serenity, enjoyment and relaxation, OUR NEW SPA offers therapeutic massages, spa pedicures, signature manicures, & deep cleansing facials."

Hamanassett Bed & Breakfast

**Innkeepers/Owners
Ashley and Glenn Mon**

Elegant Country
Breakfast Inn

www.srinns.com/hamanassett
115 Indian Springs Drive, P.O. Box 366, Chester Heights,
PA 19017
877-836-8212 • 610-459-3000
stay@hamanassett.com

Rooms/Rates
Rooms and Suites: $140/$225.
Carriage House: $350/$500.
Weekly rates available.
Number of Rooms: 8

Cuisine
Full gourmet breakfast. Special
diets accommodated if notified in
advance. Guest pantry stocked
with complimentary soft drinks
and snacks, microwave oven,
refrigerator, and wine cooler.

Nearest Airport(s)
Philadelphia International, Baltimore Washington International

Directions
From Route 1, turn onto Darlington Road, left onto Indian Springs
Drive. Bed and Breakfast is at the
top of the hill on the right. See
web site for detailed directions.

Voted one of the most romantic bed and breakfasts in North
America, Hamanassett is a grand 1856 English country house
located in the Brandywine Valley of Pennsylvania. With six spacious bedrooms and suites, each is individually decorated and features en suite baths, original hardwood floors, antique furniture,
queen or king beds, TV/VCR, robes, and gorgeous views of the
wooded grounds.

Enjoy a game of pool in the billiards room, sip a glass of sherry in
the elegant living room or light-filled solarium, or enjoy a quiet
moment on the terrace or beside the koi pond with waterfall.
Our candlelight breakfast is always a special occasion, served on
antique china and silver. There is also a charming two story carriage house on the estate for those traveling with small children or
dogs or for those who just want a little extra privacy.

Although quietly elegant, there are no formalities. We provide
personal service and Southern hospitality. Hamanassett is near all
Brandywine Valley attractions and Philadelphia -- but a world
away.

Member Since 2005

12+

"We came to the area because of Longwood Gardens and Hamanassett turned
out to be the highlight."

Inn at Whitewing Farm

www.srinns.com/whitewingfarm
P.O. Box 98, Kennett Square, PA 19348
610-388-2664 • Fax 610-388-3650
info@whitewingfarm.com

Innkeepers/Owners
Edward & Wanda DeSeta
Manager/Pastry Chef
Cathleen L. Ryan

Elegant Country
Breakfast Inn

Whitewing Farm is a 1700s Pennsylvania farmhouse with greenhouses, flower gardens, a barn and carriage house, all situated on 43 rolling acres in historic southern Chester County. Whitewing Farm is adjacent to Longwood Gardens. Breakfast is served in our recently renovated Haybarn. Refreshments are also available 24 hours in the Haybarn Gathering Room where guests can relax and mingle in the library, or read a book in front of the fire during the winter months. Guests are welcome to play tennis or a round of golf on our 10 hole chip-and-putt course, or relax in the pool or heated Jacuzzi. All rooms have marble-floored private baths and are decorated in Hunt Country Elegance.

Rooms/Rates
7 Rooms $135/$199, 3 Suites with fireplaces $235/$279. Open year-round.
Number of Rooms: 10

Cuisine
Full country breakfast, afternoon tea. Guests are welcome to bring their own spirits.

Nearest Airport(s)
Philadelphia

Directions
9 1/2 mi N on Rte 52 from I-95 (exit 7) Wilmington DE at Rte 1 turn L 8/10 mi to red lt. Turn N on Rte 52 1 1/3 mi to Valley Rd to Whitewing Farm.

AAA ◆◆◆   *Member Since 1998*

"...the farm is so much more than we expected."

Fairville Inn

Innkeepers/Owners
Noel and Jane McStay

Traditional Country
Breakfast Inn

 paii

www.srinns.com/fairville
506 Kennett Pike (Rte. 52), Chadds Ford, PA 19317
877-285-7772 • 610-388-5900 • Fax 610-388-5902
info@fairvilleinn.com

Rooms/Rates
13 Rooms and 2 Suites, $150/$250
B&B Open year-round.
Number of Rooms: 15

Cuisine
Full breakfast (Mon-Fri 7-9 am)
(Sat., Sun. and holidays 8-10 am)
of refreshing beverages, cereal, fruit,
yogurt, homemade 'sweets,' and hot
selection(s) of the day. From 4-5
cheese, crackers, and homemade
cookies compliment our afternoon
tea. Guests are welcome to bring
their own wine or spirits. Special
diets upon request.

Nearest Airport(s)
Philadelphia International airport,
28 miles from the Inn.

Directions
Located on Rte. 52, 8 miles N of
I-95 (exit 7 Wilmington DE.), 1 1/2
mi. S of U.S. Rt. 1 (Mendenhall/
Longwood Gardens area), PA.

Located in the heart of the Brandywine Valley, the Fairville Inn,
listed on the National Register of Historic Places, echoes the pastoral scenes of the Wyeth Family paintings. The allure of the Brandywine Valley, which reaches from all directions in Chadds Ford,
comes primarily from the enchanting landscape and the close
proximity to distinguished museums, such as Winterthur, Longwood Gardens, and the Brandywine River Museum. Accented
with barn wood, beams, and occasional cathedral ceilings, the Inn
is the embodiment of elegant comfort. Most rooms feature rear
decks/balconies overlooking acres of gentle grassy meadows rolling toward a serene pond. Rooms in the Main House (circa 1857),
Carriage House, and Springhouse have a private bath, satellite
TV, telephone, and individually controlled heat/air conditioning.
Most rooms have a canopy bed. Eight rooms with fireplaces in
season. Fresh flowers gracefully welcome you. Your room has all
the comforts of a country house inn! The inn is suited for adult
family gatherings. Tea served daily.

AAA ◆◆◆   *Member Since 1995*   Mobil ★★★

15+ Ⓢ ♿ 💳 Ⓥ   ✂ 🔌 @   🛏   ❄   ☕

"There are very few innkeepers who make their guest feel at home as you
have. Splendid in everyway! We'll be back. Delightful and elegant."

Rittenhouse1715, A Boutique Hotel

www.srinns.com/rittenhousesquare
1715 Rittenhouse Square Street, Philadelphia, PA 19103
877-791-6500 • 215-546-6500 • Fax 215-546-8787
reservations@rittenhouse1715.com

General Manager
Harriet Seltzer

Elegant Urban
Townhouse

One of Philadelphia's most exclusive and luxurious hotel accommodations, Rittenhouse1715 (formerly the Rittenhouse Square Bed & Breakfast) embraces its fresh, innovative look with a distinct new name. Rittenhouse1715 guarantees impeccable service infused in a locale of refined and sophisticated style. Intimate surroundings, unique design, a dedication to detail, and the highest standards of hospitality will define this boutique hotel experience at Rittenhouse1715. Located off Philadelphia's world-renowned Rittenhouse Square, Rittenhouse1715 is a boutique hotel of 16 stately rooms outfitted in the finest furnishings and decorated with exquisite artwork and fabrics. The highlight of this property is the grand presidential suite where a sleek spiral staircase transcends from the loft, king-size bedroom down to an elegant black and green-hued living space complete with comfortable couches, powder room, bar and large screen television. Each morning in the Parisian-like breakfast room, artisan breads and pastries from Philadelphia's finest bakeries are served. Upscale boutiques, alluring galleries and gourmet restaurants line the pristine neighborhood.

Member Since 2002

Rooms/Rates
Prices from $239/night for Standard Room to $599/night for Presidential Suite. Closed Christmas Eve and Christmas Day.
Number of Rooms: 16

Cuisine
Lavish European Continental Breakfast; Complimentary Wine Reception every evening. Turndown service includes chocolates and bottled water.

Nearest Airport(s)
PHL

Directions
Rittenhouse1715 is located in the Rittenhouse Square section of Philadelphia. We are on a small street located between Locust and Spruce Streets; between 17th and 18th Streets. We are a few steps away from Rittenhouse Square. Visit website for detailed directions.

12+

"The attention to detail is breathtaking. We loved our stay and recommend to everyone. Staff and all amenities were top notch."

"Little Rhody"

Famous For: Jazz Festivals, Seaside Victorian Mansions, "Mile of History," Cliff Walks, Beaches, Sailing

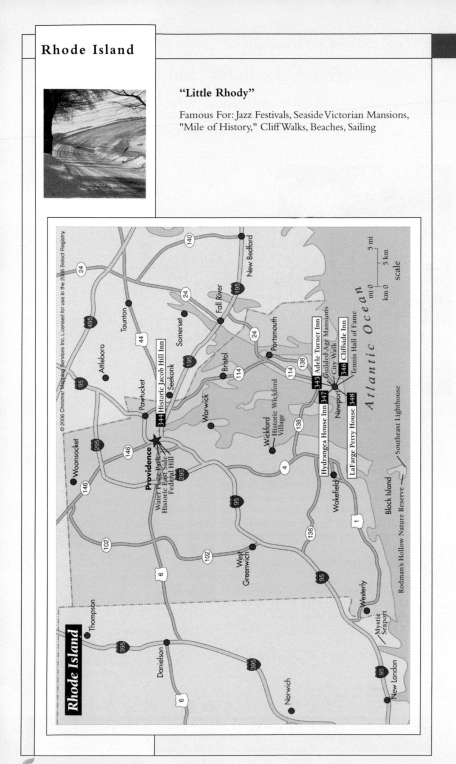

Rhode Island

© 2006 Christma! Mapping Services Inc. Licensed for use in the 2006 Select Registry

Providence
Water Place Park
Historic East Side
Federal Hill

344 Historic Jacob Hill Inn

345 Adele Turner Inn
Guilded Age Mansions
City Walk

346 Cliffside Inn
Tennis Hall of Fame

347 Hydrangea House Inn

348 LaFarge Perry House

Newport

Historic Wickford Village

Rodman's Hollow Nature Reserve

Block Island

Southeast Lighthouse

Atlantic Ocean

scale
mi 0 ... 5 mi
km 0 ... 5 km

New Bedford
Fall River
Portsmouth
Bristol
Somerset
Taunton
Attleboro
Pawtucket
Seekonk
Warwick
Woonsocket
Wakefield
West Greenwich
Westerly
Mystic Seaport
New London
Norwich
Danielson
Thompson

Historic Jacob Hill Inn

www.srinns.com/jacobhill
P.O. Box 41326, Providence, RI 02940
508-336-9165 • 888-336-9165
host@jacobhill.com

Innkeepers/Owners
Bill and Eleonora Rezek

Traditional Country
Breakfast Inn

Located on a peaceful country estate, just a ten-minute drive from downtown Providence, The Convention Center, Brown University or the Historic East Side. Built in 1722, Jacob Hill has a long history of hosting America's most prominent families, including the Vanderbilts. Recently updated rooms are spacious, all with private bathrooms; most have Jacuzzi tubs. King-and queen-sized canopied beds blend with hand-picked antiques, period wall coverings and Oriental rugs. The gleaming wood floors mirror the romantic flames from the original fireplaces. The elegant surroundings are complemented by the genuine warm hospitality that will make you feel at home. Central to several major day trip attractions: Newport, Boston, Plymouth Cape Cod, and Mystic.

Awarded "Best Hotels on the Web 2004" and Best Guest accommodations 2005" "Ten best Urban Inns" Forbes.com. "Room of the Year" *North American Inns* Magazine.

Rooms/Rates
12 unique guestrooms, w/private bathrooms $199/$459. Phones, TV, AC, Internet Access. Open year-round. Pool, tennis, billiard room w/large plasma TV, meeting room, & gazebo to view the beautiful sunsets. Spa services. **Number of Rooms:** 12

Cuisine
Award-winning breakfast, complimentary beverages, chocolate chip cookies and cheese plate on arrival. Many fine restaurants nearby for lunch and dinner.

Nearest Airport(s)
Providence T F Green

Directions
From I-95: exit 20 Rte. 195 E Mass. exit 1 Seekonk Rte 114A. Turn L follow to Rte 44 E. Turn R follow 2.5 mi. Turn L on Jacob St.120 Jacob St. Seekonk, MA.

AAA ◆◆◆◆   *Member Since 2000*

12+

"Attention to every detail, exceptional service, delicous breakfast and elegant decor."

Adele Turner Inn

Innkeeper/Owner
Winthrop Baker

Elegant Victorian
In Town Bed &

www.srinns.com/adeleturner
93 Pelham Street, Newport, RI 02840
800-845-1811 • 401-847-1811 • Fax 401-848-5850
reservations@legendaryinnsofnewport.com

Rooms/Rates
13 Guest Quarters on 3 Floors: 10 Deluxe Rooms, 3 Luxury Suites $150/$510.
Number of Rooms: 13

Cuisine
Morning in-room coffee service. Multi-course breakfast. Afternoon tea service. Daily wine & food events. Dining & wine tasting in the elegant parlor or in warmer weather on the veranda & outside tables.

Nearest Airport(s)
TF Green Providence, RI

Directions
NY: 95N to Rte. 138E, first exit off Newport Bridge to America's Cup, 3rd light L on Memorial, 2nd light L on Bellevue, 1 block L on Pelham. Boston: 95S to Rte. 24S to 138S to Memorial.

This elegant and romantic Victorian sits quietly tucked away in one of Newport's most historic neighborhoods, filled with two and three-century old homes on the first gas-lit street in America. The inn has been named one of America's "Top 10 Most Romantic" and is on the National Historic Register. Built in 1855, it is framed by 27 magnificent arched windows. All guest quarters have fireplaces, king or queen beds, fine linens, antiques and artwork, TV, DVD or VCR, CD. Some rooms have Newport Harbor views, whirlpools for two, or steam bath. Perhaps the most unique room in Newport is the inn's Harborview Spa room. French doors open out onto a private rooftop deck and hot tub, with commanding, panoramic views of Newport Harbor and Narragansett Bay. Guests enjoy daily wine and food events and tasting menus, pairing the best regional wines with artisan cheeses and other fine foods. The inn also provides an acclaimed afternoon tea, twice daily housekeeping and evening turndown. Adele Turner is centrally located just two blocks from Newport's picturesque harbor and downtown restaurants, shops and famous mansions.

Member Since 2002

13+

"THE Place to Unwind," Britain's *Sunday Mirror*; "As Romantic as a Valentine," *Yankee Magazine*; "Sumptuous," Frommer's; *Country Living* "Inn of the Month."

Cliffside Inn

www.srinns.com/cliffsideinn
2 Seaview Avenue, Newport, RI 02840
800-845-1811 • 401-847-1811 • Fax 401-848-5850
reservations@legendaryinnsofnewport.com

Innkeeper/Owner
Winthrop Baker
Inn Manager
Daniel Coggins
Elegant Victorian
Oceanside Luxury Inn

The celebrated Cliffside Inn, home of former legendary artist Beatrice Turner, has earned a worldwide reputation as one of America's favorite boutique luxury Inns. Seamlessly blending today's most luxurious amenities--whirlpools, steam baths, fireplaces, grand beds, fine linens, LCD TVs--with exquisite design and decoration, this elegant Victorian Manor House is a one-of-a-kind place, in a unique setting near Newport's renowned Cliff Walk, beaches and Gilded Age Mansions. Beatrice Turner painted more than 3,000 works at Cliffside at the turn of the 19th century—more than 1,000 of which were self-portraits. Her remarkable story has been told by the New York Times, ABC-TV, Discovery Channel, and LIFE magazine among others. Some 100 surviving artworks are displayed throughout the Inn. Cliffside is also well known for having some of the most luxurious bathing salons and suites in New England, and a stunning collection of antique beds. Named one of the 20 Great Tea Rooms of America, afternoon tea is not to be missed.

Rooms/Rates
Manor House - 13 Rooms: 5 Luxury Suites, 8 Deluxe Rooms. Seaview Cottage: 3 Luxury Suites. $175/$600
Number of Rooms: 16

Cuisine
In-room morning coffee service. Multi-course breakfast. Legendary Newport Afternoon tea (named one of America's 20 best) features seasonal menu of tea sandwiches, scones, Devon Cream & curds, tarts, other sweets & savories.

Nearest Airport(s)
TF Green Providence

Directions
From NY: 95 N to RI exit 3 for Rte. 138, follow into Newport. America's Cup Blvd to Memorial Blvd. R on Cliff Ave. L on Seaview Ave. From Boston: 93 S to Rt. 24 S to 114 S to 214 S to Newport. L on Cliff Ave. L on Seaview.

AAA ◆◆◆◆   *Member Since 1997*

13+

Top In-Room Spa Service AAA; "Top 4 Most Romantic," New England Travel&Life; Frommer's Top RI Inn; Fodor's Choice; "Luxury&Artistic Intrigue," *Boston Globe*

Innkeepers/Owners
**Grant Edmondson &
Dennis Blair**

Village Breakfast
Inn on Mansion

🍽️

Hydrangea House Inn

www.srinns.com/hydrangea
16 Bellevue Avenue, Newport, RI 02840
800-945-4667 • 401-846-4435 • Fax 401-846-6602
hydrangeahouseinn@cox.net

paii

Rooms/Rates
$265/$475 year round. Quiet
Season Specials.
Number of Rooms: 9

Cuisine
Expect to find more than the
usual continental breakfast. We
will serve you our own special
blend of fresh ground House
Coffee, home-baked breads &
granola--as well as our incredible
raspberry pancakes perhaps or
seasoned scrambled eggs in puff
pastry. Be assured, a Hydrangea
House breakfast will last the day
& energize you for your Newport
experience.

Nearest Airport(s)
Providence Airport(PVD)30 mins.

Directions
From the S: 95N to 138E to
Newport. From the N: 95S to 4S
to 138E to Newport.

The *Boston Globe* writes, "In a city renowned for its lodging, Hydrangea House is not to be missed!" Enter a world of grace, elegance and style where the intimate charm of Hydrangea House is complemented by its prestigious Bellevue Avenue address where once lived the Vanderbilt's, the Astors and the Dukes. Its proximity to the magical gilded mansions, recreational harbor, important historic sites, fine dining and extraordinary shopping means you can walk to almost everything right from our front door. All nine rooms and suites are individually decorated with a dramatic use of color, sumptuous fabrics and trims and elegant furnishings. The two-level Dudley Newton Suite is decorated in the lush tones of gold, greens and reds and has the added luxury of a two person spa tub, two-person marble shower and steam bath, flat screen "mirror" television and CD player. Complimentary high speed Internet, long distance and local telephone calling is available from each room. Winner of *Yankee* Magazine "Editors Choice" 2006 award.

AAA ◆◆◆◆   *Member Since 2005*

12+

"I have never felt warmer hospitality like I experianced at this inn. Kudos!"
"Quiet sophistication in the 'City by the Sea'."

La Farge Perry House

www.srinns.com/lafargeperryhouse
24 Kay Street, Newport, RI 02840
877-736-1100 • 401-847-2223
mknerr@lafargeperry.com

Owner
Jeanie Shufelt
Innkeeper
Midge Knerr
Luxury Bed and Breakfast
Inn

La Farge Perry House is a Victorian-era Luxury Inn, with a choice location on a quiet street within walking distance to all of the major sights of Newport. Named after the famed stained glass artist John La Farge and his wife Margaret Perry La Farge, a direct descendant of Commodores Oliver and Matthew Perry, the Inn has six rooms, all of unique appeal and each with its own panache. Common areas, a formal living room, a casual cozy kitchen with separate sitting room and a large fireplace complement a welcoming porch that extends across the front of the house with white wicker furniture. Formal gardens in the backyard, where you may sip iced tea or lemonade and sample our signature golden coconut macaroons, lend a touch of elegance to a sunny summer afternoon. The dining room is exquisite with original murals of Newport. The Innkeeper has lived and worked in Newport for more than 20 years, and delights in advising on places to see, eat and enjoy in this city-by-the-sea.

Rooms/Rates
$225/$395 mid-week; $325/$495 weekends
Number of Rooms: 6

Cuisine
Breakfast is served at the grand table in the main room or at one of our bistro tables in the sun room. Featuring Eggs Benedict on Sundays to a roster of cooked to order delights during the week as well as fresh fruit and homemade pastries. Afternoon tea with signature golden coconut macaroons will greet you as return from beach, sailing, mansion hopping.

Nearest Airport(s)
TF Green Providence, RI

Directions
Sent with confirmation letter.

AAA ◆◆◆   *Member Since 2006*

"Thank you for making our honeymoon so special. We feel it is our duty to spread the word about the Inn. You took wonderful care of us!"

"The Palmetto State"

Famous For: Congaree Swamp National Monument, Hilton Head Island, Myrtle Beach, Plantations, Charleston, Blue Ridge Mountains, Fort Sumter, Tobacco, Corn, Peaches, Cotton, Textiles

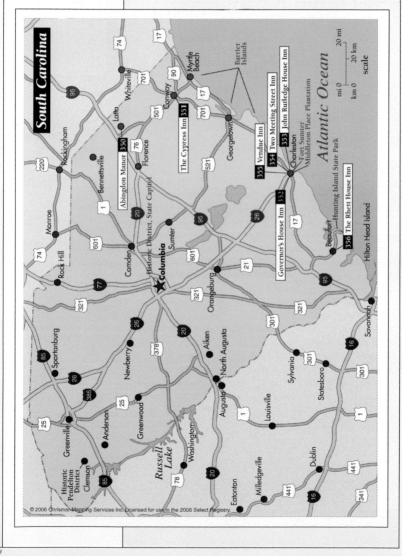

South Carolina

Atlantic Ocean

Barrier Islands

20 mi
20 km
scale
mi 0
km 0

74
17
701
90
Myrtle Beach
Whiteville
Conway
17
701
95
Rockingham
Loris
501
Georgetown Two Meeting Street Inn
John Rutledge House Inn
220
Bennettsville
76
Florence
521
Charleston
Fort Sumter
Middleton Place Plantation
1
Abingdon Manor **350**
The Cypress Inn **351**
355 Vendue Inn
354
353
Hunting Island State Park
Monroe
20
95
26
The Rhett House Inn **356**
601
Camden
Sumter
601
17
Beaufort
74
Rock Hill
Historic District, State Capitol
Governor's House Inn **352**
Hilton Head Island
321
77
★ Columbia
Orangeburg
21
95
321
26
378
Aiken
301
Sylvania
301
16
Savannah
Spartanburg
85
Newberry
20
North Augusta
301
Statesboro
301
26
385
25
Greenwood
Augusta
Louisville
1
1
25
Anderson
Washington
Dublin
441
Greenville
Russell Lake
78
20
341
Historic Pendleton District
Clemson
85
Eatonton
Milledgeville
441
16

© 2006 Chrisman Mapping Services Inc. Licensed for use in the 2006 Select Registry

Abingdon Manor
www.abingdonmanor.com
307 Church Street, Latta, SC 29565
888-752-5090 • 843-752-5090
abingdon@bellsouth.net

Innkeepers/Owners
Michael & Patty Griffey
Classic Country Inn

Offering luxury accommodations and fine dining in the Carolinas and Georgia close to I-95, Abingdon Manor is the overnight destination for travelers on the East Coast. Halfway between New York and Palm Beach, the Inn offers superior lodging, extraordinary cuisine and impeccable service. One of only a select few properties in South Carolina to be awarded a AAA 4-diamond rating annually for both the Inn and Restaurant, Abingdon Manor offers the amenities of a small luxury hotel in an opulent National Register mansion. Located in a historic neighborhood in a quaint turn of the century village, the Inn features three acres of landscaped grounds. For destination travelers, the Inn offers a variety of packages including cooking school weekends, historic touring, antiquing, nature-based activities and private country club golf. Food writers and critics consistently rank the restaurant as one of the best in the Carolinas. Abingdon Manor offers a refined, yet comfortable, atmosphere for the discriminating traveler.

Rooms/Rates
7 spacious rooms, $165/$205. All rooms offer cable TV, working fireplaces, individual temperature control
Number of Rooms: 7

Cuisine
4 diamond-rated cuisine. Elegant full breakfast included at individual tables from 7:45 to 9:00am. The one-seating, reservations-only dinner is at 7:30pm. Full liquor and wine service. Guests may peruse the Inn's wine selections displayed in the library.

Nearest Airport(s)
Florence, Myrtle Beach

Directions
Interstate I-95 exit 181A, 1 mile E to Rte. 917. 5 mi. to 1st light (Marion St.), L for 2 blocks and R onto Church St. Abingdon Manor is at the end on the L.

AAA ◆◆◆◆   *Member Since 2005*   Mobil ★★★

12+

"There isn't a better place to stay anywhere on the East Coast."
Alexander Ix, *Croquet News*

Innkeepers/Owners
Hugh & Carol Archer
George & Anne Bullock

Traditional In Town
Breakfast Inn

🍽️

The Cypress Inn
www.srinns.com/cypressinn
16 Elm Street, Conway, SC 29526
800-575-5307 • 843-248-8199 • Fax 843-248-0329
info@acypressinn.com

Rooms/Rates
$120/$215 B&B. Open year-round. Corporate Rates.
Number of Rooms: 11

Cuisine
A wonderful hot breakfast is served each morning. There are fine restaurants within walking distance. A small guest refrigerator is stocked with lemonade, sodas, bottled water. Complimentary sherry, cookies and other treats.

Nearest Airport(s)
Myrtle Beach

Directions
From Hwy. 501: Take Bus. 501. W on 3rd Ave. L on Elm St. Inn is on L. From Charleston, SC: Use Hwy 701. R on Elm St. Inn is on L. From Wilmington, NC: Use Hwy. 90 R on Bus. 501. L on 3rd Ave. L on Elm St. Inn is on L.

Overlooking the Waccamaw River, tucked away in the historic town of Conway, this luxury Inn is near, but distinctly apart from the golf mecca of Myrtle Beach. Located 2 blocks from the downtown area of Conway, the Inn is within walking distance of charming shops, restaurants, art galleries and stately live oak trees. Eleven unique guestrooms offer comforts such as en-suite private baths with Jacuzzis, plush robes, individual heat/air, TV/VCR with video library, high speed internet (Wi-Fi) & some fireplaces. We also have an on-site massage therapist. The Inn offers the privacy of a hotel with the personal service of a bed and breakfast. Enjoy the pristine beaches of the South Carolina coast or the peacefulness of an ancient river; an outstanding sculpture garden, or live theater shows. Many extras such as massages, fresh flowers, Godiva chocolates or walks along the Waccamaw River. In addition to being a charming destination, the Inn is great for those traveling north or south along the southeastern coast. For the discerning traveler.

Member Since 2001   Mobil ★★★

10+ 🚭 ♿ 💳 ⓘ 📂 ♥   ✂️ 🎨 @   🧺 ◎ ❄️   ☕

Governor's House Inn

www.srinns.com/governorshouse
117 Broad Street, Charleston, SC 29401
800-720-9812 • 843-720-2070 • Fax n/a
governorshouse@aol.com

Innkeepers/Owners
Karen and Rob Shaw

Elegant In Town
Breakfast Inn

Governor's House is a magnificent National Historic Landmark (circa 1760) reflecting the Old South's civility and grandeur. Praised by one national publication as "Charleston's most glamorous and sophisticated inn," the former Governor's mansion is the perfect blend of historic splendor and romantic elegance. The mansion's original living rooms, dining room, nine fireplaces, Irish crystal chandeliers, and sweeping southern porches delight guests from around the globe. Harmonize these aristocratic pleasures with luxuries like whirlpool baths, wetbars, high speed Internet and individually controlled room environments, and the result is refined gentility.

During the American Revolution, Governor's House was the home of Edward Rutledge, youngest signer of the Declaration of Independence. Today, the Inn has been acclaimed as "a flawless urban hideaway" by *Southern Living*. *www.governorshouse.com*

Member Since 2000

Rooms/Rates
Governor's House offers 11 elegant guest rooms and suites. Rates are $249/$549 in season. Rates include gracious Southern breakfast, afternoon tea, private parking and WI-FI internet access.
Number of Rooms: 18

Cuisine
Southern breakfast, Low country afternoon tea. Premier restaurants nearby.

Nearest Airport(s)
Charleston

Directions
From I-26 or Hwy 17 S take Meeting St. 2.0 miles S to Broad. Turn right. Inn is on left 1 block past King St. From Hwy 17 N or James Is., cross Ashley River, then go right on Lockwood Blvd. S until it becomes Broad (sharp left curve). Inn is on the right, past third light.

12+

"I'm not easily impressed, but I was overwhelmed with your glorious Inn."
"A magical, mystical place."

SelectRegistry.com

Owner
Richard Widman

Elegant In Town
Breakfast Inn

John Rutledge House Inn
www.srinns.com/johnrutledge
116 Broad Street, Charleston, SC 29401
800-476-9741 • 843-723-7999 • Fax 843-720-2615
kleslie@charminginns.com

Rooms/Rates
16 Rooms, $190/$315 B&B;
3 Suites, $330/$385 B&B.
Open year-round.
Number of Rooms: 19

Cuisine
Continental breakfast included,
full breakfast available. Afternoon
tea with refreshments.

Nearest Airport(s)
Charleston International

Directions
From Charleston Visitor's Ctr.: (R)
on John St., then (L) on King St.,
1 mile then (R) on Broad St. The
John Rutledge House Inn is 4th
house on right.

Built in 1763 by John Rutledge, a signer of the U.S. Constitution, this antebellum home is now an elegant B&B Inn. Located in the heart of the Historic District, the Inn is a reminder of a more gracious time. Guests enjoy afternoon tea, wine and sherry in the ballroom where patriots, statesmen and presidents have met, evening turn-down service with chocolates at bedside and pastries delivered to the room each morning. A charter member of Historic Hotels of America, designated a National Historic Landmark.

AAA ◆◆◆◆   *Member Since 1992*

2004 Gold List - "World's Best Places to Stay" - *Conde' Nast Traveler*

Two Meeting Street Inn

www.srinns.com/twomeetingstreet
2 Meeting Street, Charleston, SC 29401
843-723-7322
innkeeper2meetst@bellsouth.net

Innkeepers/Owners
**Pete and Jean Spell,
Karen Spell Shaw**

Elegant In Town Breakfast
Inn

Rooms/Rates
9 Guest Rooms, $175/$375 B&B;
Victorian Rooms with 12' ceilings,
canopy beds, and private baths.
Closed 3 days for Christmas.
Number of Rooms: 9

Cuisine
A gracious continental breakfast;
afternoon tea; evening sherry. No
bar in the Inn.

Nearest Airport(s)
Charleston International Airport
12 miles from downtown.

Directions
From I-26, exit Meeting
Street/Visitor Center. A left-hand
exit. When Meeting Street dead
ends into the park, we are the last
house on the Left.

Two Meeting Street Inn is the city's oldest inn welcoming guests for over half a century located in the heart of the historic district. The Queen Anne Mansion was given as a wedding gift by a bride's loving father in 1890. Elegant from head to toe, the inn features a carved English oak stairwell and Tiffany windows, as well as the Spell's collection of antiques and silver. The softly curved, two tiered verandahs overlook the manicured landscaped garden and Charleston's harbour. Guests enjoy a Southern continental breakfast and gracious afternoon tea in the dining room or on the piazza. "Never have we stayed in a place so beautiful or so lovingly cared for, nor have we ever felt as pampered. Thank you for making our stay both comfortable and memorable."

Member Since 1992

12+ ⊘

People's choice for the City's Best Bed and Breakfast in Charleston City Paper -
Seventh Year. Featured in *Southern Living* Magazine, October 2004.

General Manager
Pierre Estoppey

Historic In Town Inn

Vendue Inn

www.srinns.com/vendueinn
19 Vendue Range, Charleston, SC 29401
800-845-7900 • 843-577-7970 • Fax 843-577-2913
info@vendueinn.com

Rooms/Rates
40 Rooms, $169/$239; 25 Suites, $259/$299. Period decor; suites have fireplaces, large marble baths. Open year-round.
Number of Rooms: 65

Cuisine
Complimentary full, Southern breakfast buffet. The Rooftop Bar and Restaurant serves lunch and dinner 7 days. Outside dining available; entertainment. The Library Restaurant is open Tuesday through Saturday from 5:00 PM until 10:00 PM.

Nearest Airport(s)
Charleston

Directions
I-26 E to East Bay Exit. Continue S on East Bay approximately 3 miles. L onto Vendue Range. Check-in is halfway down the block on R at 19 Vendue Range.

From the moment you enter the Vendue Inn, you will know you are somewhere special. Located in Charleston's French Quarter, the Vendue Inn is a place rich in the European elegance of early Charleston. Antiques and eighteenth century reproductions decorate each charming guest room and suite. There is, however, more to the Vendue Inn than the world within your room. Charleston's finest shopping and restaurants, as well as historical sights and the waterfront are within walking distance. The Vendue Inn Rooftop Bar and Restaurant, a favorite with locals, offers a view of Charleston Harbor, as well as dramatic views of historic Charleston. Join us in the newly re-opened Library Restaurant, located on the first floor.

Member Since 2002

Recipient of the Carolopolis Award, recognizing "sensitive rehabilitation of historic buildings."

The Rhett House Inn

www.srinns.com/rhetthouse
1009 Craven Street, Beaufort, SC 29902
888-480-9530 • 843-524-9030 • Fax 843-524-1310
info@rhetthouseinn.com

Owners
Steve & Marianne Harrison

Elegant Greek Revival
In Town Breakfast Inn

Located in historic Beaufort. The Rhett House Inn is a beautifully restored 1820s plantation house, furnished with English and American antiques, oriental rugs, fresh orchids, fireplaces and spacious verandahs. Lush gardens provide the perfect setting for weddings and parties. Our town was the film site for "Forrest Gump," "Prince of Tides," "The Big Chill" and "White Squal." History-laden Beaufort, Charleston and Savannah offer rich exploring.

Rooms/Rates
17 Rooms $175/$315, 8 with fireplaces and whirlpool baths. Open year-round.
Number of Rooms: 17

Cuisine
Breakfast, afternoon tea, evening hors d'oeuvres, picnic baskets, desserts.

Nearest Airport(s)
Savannah/Hilton Head International Airport

Directions
From the North, take I-95 to Exit 33, then follow the signs to Beaufort. From the South, take I-95 to exit 8 and follow the signs.

AAA ◆◆◆◆   *Member Since 1991*   Mobil ★★★★

5+

"Beautiful rooms, lovely grounds, exquisite desserts – what an enchanting place."

Tennessee

"The Volunteer State"

Famous For: Cumberland Gap National Historic Park, Cumberland Caverns, Fall Creek Falls, Grand Ole Opry House, Great Smokey Mountains, Graceland, Guinness World Records Museum, Country Music Hall of Fame, Tennessee Valley Authority, Zinc, Marble

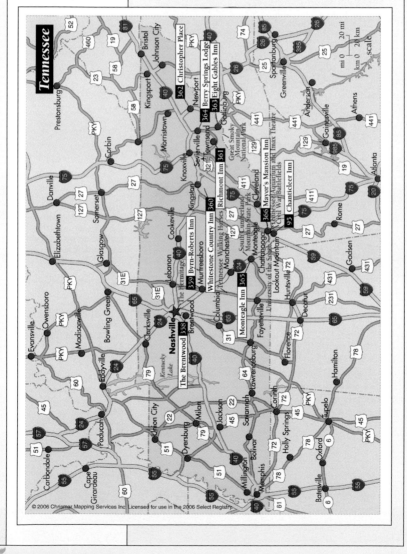

The Brentwood, A Bed & Breakfast
www.srinns.com/thebrentwood
6304 Murray Lane, Brentwood, TN 37027-6210
800-332-4640 • 615-373-4627 • Fax 615-221-9666
info@brentwoodbandb.com

Innkeeper/Owner
Ly Anne & Dick Thorman
Elegant Country Breakfast
Inn

The luxurious Brentwood estate is located in one of the finest sections of greater Nashville. The drive over the stream, through the trees and up to the white columns welcomes you to our "Classic Hospitality." The casual elegance of the interior and eclectic combination of traditional furnishings, family and European antiques and objects 'd arte creates an atmosphere of quiet relaxation. Private decks overlook the rolling hillside and fireplaces warm the cool evenings. Private tours of Civil War sites, Grand Ole Opry, Country Music Hall of Fame, The Ryman, The Hermitage and Antebellum mansions can be arranged.

Rooms/Rates
Rooms $135/$165, Suites $175/$250. All suites have custom Jacuzzi tubs, some with fireplace and decks. Data ports, DSL, TV, phone, VCR library, terry robes.
Number of Rooms: 6

Cuisine
Full breakfast & afternoon refreshments. Special dietary menus w/ notice. Minutes from fine dining & the historic attractions of Nashville, Belle Meade & Franklin.

Nearest Airport(s)
Nashville Int'l - 20 Minutes

Directions
From Nashville on I-65 S @ Exit 71 on Concord & turn R. At Franklin Road turn R. At Murray Lane turn L & proceed 1 mi. past Granny White Pike. The Brentwood Sign is on your R.

Member Since 2003

12+

"Where Classic Hospitality Lives!"

Byrn-Roberts Inn

Innkeepers/Owners
David & Julie Becker

Elegant In Town
Breakfast Inn

paii

www.srinns.com/byrn-roberts
346 East Main Street, Murfreesboro, TN 37130
888-877-4919 • 615-867-0308 • Fax 615-867-0280
byrnrobert@aol.com

Rooms/Rates
$150/$245: King beds, private baths, TV, VCR, DVD, CD, cable, phone & Wi-Fi.
Number of Rooms: 5

Cuisine
Full 3 course Gourmet Breakfast plus complimentary beverage & snack bar. Guests welcome to bring spirits. Fine dining restaurants within 4 blocks of the Inn.

Nearest Airport(s)
Nashville-Jet service
Murfreesboro-Prop service

Directions
Located south and east of the Nashville airport. Take I-24 to Exit 78B. Travel E 2 miles. Turn R on NW Broad St. Go 1 block, turn L on W Main St. Circle around the Courthouse. Go R on E Main St. We are on the R 3 blocks from the Courthouse.

This elegantly restored 12,000 square foot (Circa 1900) mansion is nestled in the Historic District of a quaint college town 30 minutes SE of Nashville. Byrn-Roberts Inn offers you the best of both worlds: a quiet haven yet in the shadows of Nashville's glamour! All of the guests rooms have luxurious linens, fresh flowers, yummy bed time chocolates, private baths including showers (in addition some w/double whirlpools) plus working fireplaces and in-room thermostats. You will also find breath taking beauty in the original woodwork and 11 fireplaces. Enjoy a scrumptious breakfast, extensive gardens, Koi pond and a magnificent waterfall. Walk 4 blocks to quaint shops and restaurants for dinner. As you stroll to dinner, a self guided walking tour will provide architectural history of the renovated homes on East Main Street. Activities (but, not limited to) include: National Park Civil War sites, antebellum homes, museums, golf, bike riding, Jack Daniel's Distillery, Fall Creek Falls, Franklin, Chattanooga and Tennessee Walking Horse Country!

Member Since 2002

12+

"Such wonderful, caring hospitality and remarkable attention to detail!
It is a haven and a sanctuary!"

Whitestone Country Inn

www.srinns.com/whitestone
1200 Paint Rock Rd., Kingston, TN 37763
888-247-2464 • 865-376-0113 • Fax 865-376-4454
moreinfo@whitestoneinn.com

Innkeepers/Owners
Paul Cowell and Jean Cowell

Elegant Waterside Inn

A spectacular 360 acre Country Estate with views of the Smoky Mountains provides you with a serene combination of natural woods and landscaped gardens. Whitestone's rolling hillsides and peaceful surroundings are guaranteed to soothe your soul and calm your spirit. We serve three lavish meals a day and you can nibble on home baked cookies and other delectable treats anytime. Many of our rooms are equipped with the sensuous delight of waterfall-spa showers and private decks. You will be surrounded by 5,400 acres of wildlife-waterfowl refuge and 39,000 acre Watts Bar Lake with opportunities for birding, fishing, kayaking, canoeing, paddle-boating or just rocking on our many porches and swinging in our hammocks. This is the perfect place for vacations, retreats, meetings, weddings or honeymoons. Whitestone Country Inn is one of only six AAA, four-diamond inns in Tennessee, and was named one of the '10 Most Romantic Inns in America!' Find a Sanctuary for your Soul.

Rooms/Rates
21 Rooms/Suites, $160/$270 per night. Each room and suite has fireplace, king bed, spa tub, TV/VCR, and refrigerator.
Number of Rooms: 21

Cuisine
The very best classic cuisine. Enjoy elegant meals in one of our three dining rooms, two overlooking the lake. For between-meal snacks, sample from the cookie jars in our great room.

Nearest Airport(s)
Knoxville, Mcghee/Tyson airport

Directions
From I-75, exit 72. Turn W on Hwy 72, go 9 mi. R on Paint Rock Rd., just after Hwy. 322 jct. Entrance is 4 mi. on R. - From I-40, exit 352. S on Hwy 58. Go 6 mi. to L on Hwy 72E, then 5 mi. to L on Paint Rock Rd. 4 mi.

AAA ◆◆◆◆   *Member Since 2000*

12+

"Just a brief note to say that at Whitestone we found a true 'Sanctuary of the Soul.' Your hospitality has demonstrated extraordinary grace."

Innkeeper
Nancy Schimmick
Innkeepers/Owners
Susan and Jim Hind

Elegant Mountain Inn

Richmont Inn

www.richmontinn.com
220 Winterberry Lane, Townsend, TN 37882
866-267-7086 • 865-448-6751 • Fax 865-448-6480
richmontinn@aol.com

Rooms/Rates
9 Rooms, $145/$185, 5 Luxury Suites $245/$260 King beds/spa tubs/firepl/balconies/fridge/coffee
Number of Rooms: 14

Cuisine
Full French and Swiss style breakfasts. Also complimentary gourmet desserts and flavored coffees by candlelight. Evening dinners by reservation - classic four course Swiss fondue. Fine wines and imported beers.

Nearest Airport(s)
Only 30 mins. from McGhee Tyson (Metro Knoxville) airport.

Directions
Enter Townsend (near mile marker 26), from Maryville on US 321 N. 1st R on Old Tuckaleechee Rd., R on next paved rd.(Laurel Valley),.8 mi. thru stone gate, crest hill, turn left at sign.

Escape to the Great Smoky Mountains and refresh your body and soul. Relax in our historic Appalachian cantilever barn, elegantly furnished with 18th Century English antiques and French paintings. Breathtaking views, private balconies, spa tubs and wood-burning fireplaces. Ten minutes to the Great Smoky Mountains National Park entrance, activities include: hiking, biking, fishing, picnicking, and wildflower walks. Our new Heritage Center showcases the history and culture of mountain people. Richmont Inn - Rated "Top Inn" by *Country Inns* and awarded grand prize by *Gourmet* for our signature dessert. "...just might be the most romantic place in the Smokies"—*Southern Living*. "A wonderful place to recharge your batteries"—*Country*. "Appalachia with style," selected as "one of the top 25 authentic hotels across the United States"—*National Geographic Traveler*. "Romantic getaway"—*HGTV*.

Member Since 1997

10+ 🚭 ♿ ① 🗂 ♥ ✂ 🏠 @ 🧺 ◎ ⑤

Selected by National Geographic Traveler Magazine as "one of the top 25 authentic hotels across the United States."

Christopher Place, An Intimate Resort

www.srinns.com/christopherplace
1500 Pinnacles Way, Newport, TN 37821
800-595-9441 • 423-623-6555 • Fax 423-613-4771
stay@christopherplace.com

Innkeeper/Owner
Marston Price

Elegant Mountain Inn

paii

Secluded in the scenic Smoky Mountains on a 200-acre private estate, Christopher Place is the ideal inn for a romantic, relaxing getaway. An elegant setting is coupled with friendly, unpretentious service and unspoiled, panoramic views. The hosts know your name and greet you with a warm smile. You can fill your days with activities, or with none at all, as the inn is centrally located to most of the sights and attractions of the Smokies and offers many resort amenities of its own. Rooms and Suites are spacious and romantically appointed. Casual fine dining with an extensive wine list completes your romantic retreat. Special requests are encouraged. Voted the area's Best B&B. Named one of the 10 most romantic inns in America and one of the 12 best locations for a fantasy B&B wedding.

Rooms/Rates
4 Rooms, $175; 4 Suites, $275/$330. Most have double whirlpools, woodburning fireplaces and/or scenic views.
Number of Rooms: 9

Cuisine
Hearty mountain breakfast served at your leisure. Picnics. Intimate 4-course candlelit dinners by reservation at tables set for two in our exquisite dining room overlooking the mountains. Some seats available to non-inn guests. Light afternoon snacks available.

Nearest Airport(s)
Knoxville

Directions
I-40 to exit 435. Go S 2 mi. on Hwy 32. Turn R on English Mountain Rd. Go 2 mi. Turn R on Pinnacles Way. Follow to the top.

AAA ◆◆◆◆   *Member Since 2000*

"Thanks for providing a place for people to experience life the way they wish it was."

Owners
The Binning Family

Casually Elegant
Mountain Inn

Eight Gables Inn

www.srinns.com/eightgablesinn
219 North Mountain Trail, Gatlinburg, TN 37738
800-279-5716 • 865-430-3344 • Fax 865-430-8767
inquiries@eightgables.com

Rooms/Rates
10 Rooms $140/$230; 9 Suites $210/270. Luxurious rooms, TV/VCR/CD, some w/King beds, fireplaces, Jacuzzis.
Number of Rooms: 19

Cuisine
Full served breakfast; Picnic baskets available for intimate excursions; Homemade soups, sandwiches & desserts served Tues- Fri in Magnolia Tea Room Cafe; 3 and 4 course candlelight dinners on Tues, Thur & Sat - RSVP; Afternoon English Tea.

Nearest Airport(s)
Knoxville TN

Directions
From Hwy. 441, one mi. N of Gatlinburg, turn on Little Smoky Road. Go to stop sign, road turns into North Mountain Trail (sign posted). First drive on L.

Eight Gables Inn, The Smoky Mountains' Premier Country Inn, offers 19 luxurious rooms and suites. All rooms have private baths, cable TV, feather top beds, plush bathrobes, telephones, personal amenities and several feature the warmth of fireplaces and whirlpool tubs. Our rates include a full served breakfast, afternoon tea and evening desserts. Elegant candlelight dinners and High Tea are available by reservation. Conveniently located on the drive between Gatlinburg and Pigeon Forge, our peaceful setting lends itself to a casual elegance and relaxing charm. Eight Gables is easily accessible to all the area attractions and Knoxville is just 30 miles away.

AAA ◆◆◆◆   *Member Since 2002*   Mobil ★★★

10+

"An excellent getaway from the everyday world! Your Inn has nourished both body and soul!"

Berry Springs Lodge

www.srinns.com/berrysprings
2149 Seaton Springs Road, Sevierville, TN 37862
888-760-8297 • 865-908-7935
info@berrysprings.com

Innkeepers/Owners
Patrick & Sue Eisert
Elegant Mountain
Retreat/Lodge

Perched on a 33 acre secluded scenic ridge top in the Great Smoky Mountains, this lodge offers the perfect picture of solitude and romance. Take a leisurely walk down to the bass or catfish ponds and try your luck. Ride bikes, play horseshoes, relax in a hammock or just sit back and enjoy the beautiful views of the Smoky Mountains from your rocking chair on the main deck of the lodge. With this remote setting, one would not guess the lodge is within a 15-minute drive of most area destinations, including Gatlinburg, Pigeon Forge and Sevierville. Named best inn for mountain views and rest and relaxation.

Rooms/Rates
9 rooms. $149/$209, 2 Suites $229/$249. Includes breakfast and evening desserts. King Beds, Fireplace, Whirlpool Tubs TV/VCR/CD. Open year-round. **Number of Rooms:** 11

Cuisine
Country gourmet breakfast. Lunch & dinner picnic baskets are available upon advanced request. Local restaurants within 15 minutes. Nightly signature desserts.

Nearest Airport(s)
Knoxville

Directions
Interstate 40 exit #407.Go 8 miles turn left on Rt 411. Go 1.2 miles right at Middle Creek road. Go 3.9 miles left on Jay Ell Rd. Go 1.6 right McCarter Hollow Rd go 1/4 mile left on Seaton Springs Road. Lodge is first drive on left.

AAA ◆◆◆   *Member Since 2005*

12+

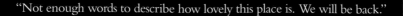

"Not enough words to describe how lovely this place is. We will be back."

Monteagle Inn

www.srinns.com/monteagleinn
204 West Main Street, P.O. Box 39, Monteagle, TN 37356
888-480-3245 • 931-924-3869 • Fax 931-924-3867
suites@monteagleinn.com

Innkeeper/Owner
Jim Harmon
Bed and Breakfast
& Retreat Center

Rooms/Rates
$160/$185. All suites have spacious private baths & are furnished w/luxurious white bed & bath linens including coverlets, fluffy towels, down/feather & poly pillows. All room phones have data ports for private Internet connections.
Number of Rooms: 13

Cuisine
The Inn utilizes their extensive herb and vegetable gardens to create their high acclaimed "mountain gourmet" breakfast which will satisfy the most discriminating tastes.

Nearest Airport(s)
Chattanooga-45 miles

Directions
Conveniently located less than/ mi. from I-24 between Nashville & Chattanooga.

The Monteagle Inn is situated atop the Cumberland Plateau just minutes away from The University of the South, hiking trails, antique shops, & superb restaurants. Picturesque balconies, a spacious front porch & garden courtyards provide outdoor relaxation. You are greeted by warm Mediterranean colors & soft music as you enter the foyer. Living areas are outfitted with overstuffed furnishings washed by accent lighting & graced with special antiques, which invite you to experience the mountaintop & all its seasons. The Inn's large living room with 4 distinct sitting areas encourages you to curl up on one of the oversized sofas with a good book. A welcoming fire in the cool months makes even the most relaxed guest lazier. Indoor entertainment options include cable TV, movies on the VCR, a game of chess on the antique French game board, or books from the library nook. Hot cookies & flavored teas ward off the munchies. The spacious dining room, which seats 70, is filled with light from windows on 3 sides. Provencal linens grace the windows & tables. Brightly-patterned Italian urns, bowls, & dishes serve as a backdrop for breakfast specialties. The perfect place for business retreats, family reunions & wedding functions or just an escape from the busy world.

Member Since 2006

10+

"Gracious host, inviting atmosphere, excellent attention to detail, comfortably and beautifully furnished."

Mayor's Mansion Inn

www.mayorsmansioninn.com
801 Vine Street, Chattanooga, TN 37403
888-446-6569 • 423-265-5000 • Fax 423-265-5555
info@mayorsmansioninn.com

Owners
Gene & Carmen Fenn Drake
General Manager
Linda Davis
Inn Princess
Savannah, Chocolate Lab
Elegant In Town
Inn

Entering the Fort Wood neighborhood, Chattanooga's premier historic district, you are immediately greeted by a magnificent mansion, built in 1889 by the city's Mayor. Picture majestic oaks sheltering this massive stone Victorian treasure that carries a prestigious award for historical preservation from The National Trust. Find yourself exploring lazy porches, 16-foot ceilings, carved pocket doors, hand-painted murals, as well as breathtaking mountain views. Hidden among the treasures of yesteryear, you suddenly discover subtle modern conveniences of 300-gallon soaking tubs, televisions, VCRs, and modem connections. Most importantly, you will rest easy always knowing our dedicated hospitality team eagerly awaits every opportunity to make your stay as unforgettable as your surroundings.

Rooms/Rates
4 Suites, $195/$275; 7 Rooms, $150/$175. Open all year.
Number of Rooms: 11

Cuisine
Full breakfast, dinner served on Friday and Saturday evenings by reservation. Many fine restaurants a short distance away. Wines, liquors, brews, and spirits available.

Nearest Airport(s)
Chattanooga Metro Airport

Directions
From Atlanta or Knoxville I-75 to I-24W. 27N to exit 1C. 1mile straight, R on Palmetto St. 1 block to Inn. From Nashville I-24E to 27N, then same.

AAA ◆◆◆◆ *Member Since 1996*

12+

"Thank you for your grand southern hospitality. Grounds are immaculate and the service is outstanding. This is the finest B&B in which we have ever stayed."

SelectRegistry.com

Texas

"The Lone Star State"

Famous For: The Alamo, San Antonio Missions National Historic Park, Enchanted Rock, Big Bend National Park, Padre Island National Seashore, Marfa Lights, Guadalupe Mountains National Park, Lyndon B. Johnson Space Center, Armadillo, Oil, Cattle, Cotton

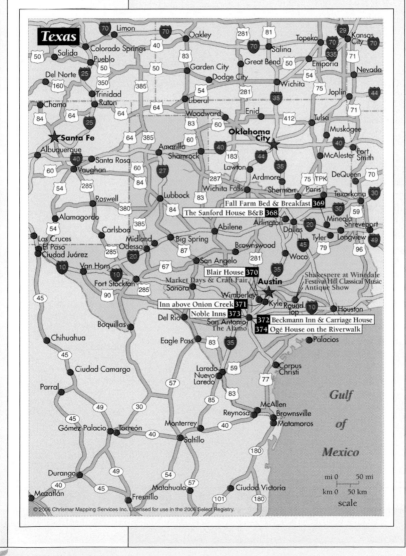

The Sanford House Inn & Spa

www.srinns.com/sanfordhouse
506 N. Center St., Arlington, TX 76011
817-861-2129 • 817-861-3624 • Fax 817-861-2030
info@thesanfordhouse.com

Director
Cheryl Allgood
Owners
Drs. J. Bergstrom & J. McDonald
French Country
Inn & Spa

The Sanford House Inn and Spa is located in the heart of the Dallas Fort Worth metroplex. There are 7 luxurious rooms and 4 secluded cottages with private baths and whirlpool tubs. The Grand Courtyard is ideal for events up to 200 people. We will take care of all the details for weddings, executive retreats, and receptions for small or large groups. All Sanford House meals are meticulously prepared by our gourmet chef and dining is available by reservation for individuals and groups, large or small. Located in central Arlington, just minutes from DFW Airport, Six Flags and The Ballpark in Arlington, The Sanford House Inn & Spa is only a short drive away from the museums and other attractions of Dallas and Fort Worth.

Rooms/Rates
7 Rooms, 4 Private Cottages. Rates from $125/$250.
Number of Rooms: 11

Cuisine
Full Gourmet Breakfast is included with your stay. Lunch is served daily from 11:30-1pm Monday - Friday. Fine dining is available for small or large groups with reservations.

Nearest Airport(s)
DFW Airport

Directions
From Dallas: Take I-30 W to Cooper St. Go S on Cooper to Sanford St. Turn L and go E to Center St. From Fort Worth: Take I-30 E to Cooper St. Go S on Cooper to Sanford St. Turn L on Sanford St. and go E to Center St. Located on the corner of Center and Sanford.

AAA ◆◆◆   *Member Since 2003*

"....the accomodations were superb. The staff was attentive and the dining incredible. I'll be back again."

Innkeepers/Owners
Mike and Carol Fall

Traditional Country
Breakfast Inn

Fall Farm, A Fine Country Inn
www.srinns.com/fallfarm
2027 F.M. 779, Mineola, TX 75773-3287
877–886–7696 • 903-768-2449 • Fax 903-768-2079
info@fallfarm.com

Rooms/Rates
2 Rooms/3 Suites $135/$175. Cottages $200/$250. Guest House $400. Conference Ctr. $175. Elegantly appointed rooms with comfortable sitting areas, fine linens and lovely views. Open year-round.
Number of Rooms: 5

Cuisine
Full gourmet breakfast, afternoon refreshments, fresh fruit, cold drinks. Complimentary evening wine. Fine and casual dining in and around Mineola.

Nearest Airport(s)
Tyler or Dallas

Directions
Mineola is approx. 80 mi. from both Dallas and Shreveport. From I-20, take Hwy 69 N to Mineola. When Hwy 69 forks, take Hwy 37 N for 6 mi. and turn L on FM 779. Fall Farm is 2 mi. on L.

Escape to this tranquil, ten-acre retreat in the scenic piney woods of East Texas and be drawn into a luxurious country farmhouse with unique personality, reflecting Mike and Carol's history and welcoming spirit. The inviting atmosphere conveys a familiar feeling of home, yet transforms you with beautifully decorated rooms filled with color and whimsical details. Enjoy the sparkling pool in the afternoon, as well as stargazing in the soothing spa after dark. Professional massages are available in the spa room, a perfect way to end the day. A bountiful breakfast assures that no one leaves hungry. Quiet moments and total relaxation are inevitable...our hospitality awaits!

Member Since 2000

16+

"Every room and view is a warm profusion of color and pattern."

Blair House
www.srinns.com/blairhouse
100 W. Spoke Hill Drive, Wimberley, TX 78676
877-549-5450 • 512-847-1111 • Fax 512-842-1147
info@blairhouseinn.com

Innkeepers/Owners
Mike and Vickie Schneider

Traditional Southwestern Country Inn

Conveniently located just minutes from the Wimberley Square, Blair House Inn is situated on 22 peaceful acres featuring breathtaking hill country vistas. Meticulous service, warm hospitality, delectable food and luxury amenities provide the ultimate in comfort. This inviting inn is light and airy and features one of the best art galleries in Wimberley. A pool and whirlpool spa set in the hillside allows for spectacular views while relaxing. Blair House also provides spacious and attractive common areas including a living room with a fireplace, a television/game room, a library, plus a front porch with beautiful sunset views and a patio by the herb garden. Guests can enjoy a massage, use the sauna, hike the grounds, venture out on one of the bicycles or just nap in a hammock. Rated third nationwide as "Best Evening Cuisine" and "Best B&B for Relaxing and Unwinding," by *Inn Traveler* Magazine and the "Best Breakfast in Texas" – *Southern Living*.

Rooms/Rates
3 rooms, main house, $142/$167. 8 rooms or executive suites, $185/$280. All uniquely decorated guest rooms have luxurious linens, lovely views, satellite TV/VCR/CD/some DVD, and private baths, most with whirlpool tubs. Open year-round
Number of Rooms: 11

Cuisine
Full breakfast, evening dessert, 5-course, fixed menu gourmet dinner on Saturday evenings. Complimentary beverages.

Nearest Airport(s)
Austin/San Antonio

Directions
From Austin take I-35 S to Kyle Exit; continue W to Wimberley; 1.6 miles S of Wimberley Square on E side of Ranch Road 12.

AAA ◆◆◆   *Member Since 1998*   Mobil ★★★

14+ ⊘ ♿ ▭ ▱   ✂ ✍ @   ≋ ▣ ◎

"We have spent just 48 hours with you. We thank you now
for a lifetime of wonderful memories."

Owners
John and Janie Orr
Innkeeper
Amy Dolan

Elegant Texas
Country Inn

The Inn Above Onion Creek

www.srinns.com/onion
4444 W. FM 150, Kyle, TX 78640
800-579-7686 • 512-268-1617 • Fax 512-268-1090
info@innaboveonioncreek.com

Rooms/Rates
10 rooms, incl. 2 suites & cottage: $215/$450. All w/fireplace & porch, 6 w/whirlpool bath. Breakfast & dinner included in room rate. 15% discount Sun-Thur.
Number of Rooms: 10

Cuisine
Upscale cuisine served in a casual rustic dining environment. Full breakfast served from 8:30-10:00 each morning. Three-course dinner served at 6:00 each evening. Complimentary coffee, tea, cold drinks, homemade cookies and fruit.

Nearest Airport(s)
Austin Bergstrom

Directions
25 mi. SW of Austin. Exit 213 off I-35 and head W. to last stop sign in Kyle. Turn R with W. FM 150 and travel 5.3 mi.

The Inn Above Onion Creek is a replica of a late 1800s homestead set on a 100-acre Hill Country plot with panoramic views. The Inn was built to remember the past with all of the present day amenities, each of the ten rooms meticulously decorated to tell its own story about its namesake. The first of two buildings is built of rustic cedar with sawn cedar posts, while the second building is finished in white stone and supported by white pillars. The entire Inn features classic antique pieces, comfortable furnishings and feather beds. The character of the Inn as a whole is unlike anything else, providing a tranquil setting that makes it easy to unwind and appreciate the surrounding beauty. The Inn sits about five miles from the closest town and one mile off any main road. Included in each night's stay is a full breakfast and a three-course dinner, prepared using the freshest seasonal ingredients available. Hosted by a friendly staff, The Inn Above Onion Creek is the Hill Country's answer to southern hospitality.

Member Since 2003   Mobil ★★★

"...beautiful sunrises and sunsets, rolling hills, flowers, butterflies, wildlife... excellent food and service...simply magnificent!"

A Beckmann Inn and Carriage House

www.srinns.com/beckmanninn
222 E. Guenther Street, San Antonio, TX 78204
800-945-1449 • 210-229-1449 • Fax 210-229-1061
beckinn@swbell.net

**Innkeepers/Owners
Paula & Charles
Stallcup**

Historic In Town
Breakfast Inn

Experience gracious hospitality at its very best, in a beautiful Victorian home and carriage house in the picturesque, downtown, King William Historic District. The perfect location for business or leisure travel accommodations. The "hidden treasure" of San Antonio, across from the landscaped Riverwalk and minutes to the Alamo by trolley. The wonderful wraparound porch welcomes guests to spacious antique filled rooms, ornately carved queen size beds, private bathrooms, robes, TVs, phones, refrigerators, hair dryers, and irons/ironing boards. A gourmet breakfast, with a breakfast dessert, is served in our formal dining room with china, crystal and silver.

Rooms/Rates
5 rooms $109/$179. Open year-round.
Number of Rooms: 5

Cuisine
Full gourmet breakfast, with a breakfast dessert.

Nearest Airport(s)
San Antonio International

Directions
From airport, take 281 South to 37 South, exit Right on Durango, Left on South St. Mary's St., then immediately take Right on King William St., Left on E. Guenther Street.

AAA ◆◆◆   *Member Since 1997*   Mobil ★★★

12+ 🚭   💳 ① 📁 ❤️   ✍️ @   📺   ❄️

"Warm and personal hospitality, gourmet breakfast,
artisitcally served, best location!"

Owners
Liesl and Don Noble
Senior Innkeeper
Megan Macdaniel
Elegant In Town
Breakfast Inn

Noble Inns
www.srinns.com/nobleinns
107 Madison Street, San Antonio, TX 78204
800-221-4045 • 210-225-4045 • Fax 210-227-0877
stay@nobleinns.com

Rooms/Rates
7 Rooms, $139/229; 2 Suites, $189/279. Special weekday & corporate rates.
Number of Rooms: 9

Cuisine
The Jackson House features a full gourmet breakfast, afternoon refreshments, evening sherry. Pancoast Carriage House features an expanded continental breakfast and full kitchens en suite.

Nearest Airport(s)
San Antonio International

Directions
From airport to Jackson House: US 281 S to Durango/Alamodome exit downtown. R on Durango. L on S. St. Mary's. R on Madison to #107. To PCH: same as above, then continue R on Turner. L on Washington. Enter gates at 202 Washington.

Don and Liesl Noble, sixth-generation San Antonians, invite guests to experience the rich history and ambiance of San Antonio. Noble Inns comprise The Jackson House (JH) and Pancoast Carriage House (PCH), two 1890s-era historic landmarks, located four houses apart in the King William Historic District. Both provide Victorian elegance with modern luxuries and superior amenities for the discerning business or leisure traveler, and are just off the Riverwalk near all downtown sites, including the Alamo, convention center and Alamodome. All rooms include private marble bath, gas fireplace with antique mantel, antique furnishings and elegant fabrics. Complimentary high-speed internet (wired and/or wireless), color cable TV w/HBO, private phone w/ voice mail, custom guest robes, and central air conditioning. Gardens feature two pools and heated spa. Two-person whirlpool tub in bath, canopy bed, and transportation in our classic 1960 Rolls Royce Silver Cloud II are available.

AAA ◆◆◆◆   *Member Since 2001*   Mobil ★★★

"Your inn is gorgeous!—our room cozy, spacious bath, delightful spa, delicious breakfast!"

Inn on the Common

www.srinns.com/innonthecommon
P.O. Box 75, 1162 N. Craftsbury Road
Craftsbury Common, VT 05827
800-521-2233 • 802-586-9619 • Fax 802-586-2249
info@innonthecommon.com

Innkeepers/Owners
Jim and Judi Lamberti,
Vermont Innkeeper of
the Year 1994

Elegant Country Inn

Dreaming of a classic Vermont country inn experience? Visit Inn on the Common in scenic Craftsbury Common, one of the state's most photographed hill towns. Profiled on NBC's famous *Today Show*, the Inn has been showcased in many national and international publications. Nestled in the Northeast Kingdom's pristine countryside, this jewel of an inn offers a quiet, sophisticated retreat from today's hectic lifestyle. Surrounded by manicured gardens and the legendary Green Mountains, the Inn's lovely campus is home to three meticulously restored Federal houses. Guestrooms feature private baths, hand-stitched quilts, beautiful artwork and heirloom antiques. This is THE vacation getaway that you'll be telling all your friends and family about! Come stay a while, enjoy our gracious hospitality and superb customer service, and take home a wealth of warm, happy memories! Skiers: Our area offers some of the best cross-country skiing in the East. Corporate, groups and weddings welcome. Check our website for specials. Gift Certificates available.

Rooms/Rates
16 Rooms. $135/$299 B&B (for one or two people per night including refreshments and full breakfast). Dinner Meal Plan (4 courses) additional, available Wed.-Sun. Rates adjusted seasonally. Rooms available with wood-burning fireplaces and/or whirlpool tub.
Number of Rooms: 16

Cuisine
On-site Trellis Restaurant offers innovative country cuisine. Guests enjoy a full country breakfast, candle-lit romantic dining, afternoon refreshments and our complete wine cellar.

Nearest Airport(s)
Burlington, VT

Directions
Call or visit
www.innonthecommon.com.

AAA ◆◆◆   *Member Since 1976*   Mobil ★★★

9+

"After an incredible scenic drive, we pulled into the Inn and it was just...'wow.' It feels like how life is supposed to be...beautiful, tranquil, inspiring."

Innkeepers
Kim Borsavage

Victorian In Town
Bed & Breakfast Inn

🍽️

Lang House on Main Street

www.srinns.com/langhouse
360 Main Street, Burlington, VT 05401
877-919-9799 • 802-652-2500 • Fax 802-651-8717
innkeeper@langhouse.com

Rooms/Rates
11 Rooms, $135/$225.
Number of Rooms: 11

Cuisine
Gourmet Breakfast.

Nearest Airport(s)
Burlington International (BTV)

Directions
Located on Main Street (Rte 2), approx. 1.5 mi. from I-89 and just E of Rte 7. From I-89, exit 14W, Rte 2, which turns into Main Street. As you come down the hill into Burlington, the Lang House is on your R, just before the traffic light. Coming from across the Lake via the Lake Champlain Ferry, take a L at the 1st light onto Battery St. At the 1st traffic light, take a R & head up Main Street (or Route 2 E). We are located approx. 1/2 mi. up Main, on the L side of the street.

Built as a private residence in 1881, the Lang House was converted in 2000 to an 11-room bed and breakfast inn. The renovation preserved the house's historic nature and added a number of contemporary amenities. The Lang House features qualities guests expect in a 19th c. Victorian home--antiques, soaring ceilings, stunning woodwork, stained glass windows, and the rosette pattern repeated throughout the house. The inn is situated in Burlington's Hill Section, which is known for its remarkable residential architecture and proximity to the University of Vermont and Burlington restaurants, shopping and cultural and waterfront venues. The Lang House innkeepers and staff provide genuine hospitality and personalized attention to leisure and business travelers.

Member Since 2003

☺ 🚭 ♿ 💼 🍷 🗂 ❤ @ ◎

"We love the Lang House! Our room was lovely, the food great and the staff were the best. Thanks for making this such a memorable trip for us."

Willard Street Inn

www.srinns.com/willardstreet
349 South Willard Street, Burlington, VT 05401
800-577-8712 • 802-651-8710 • Fax 802-651-8714
info@willardstreetinn.com

Innkeepers/Owners
Katie and Larry Davis
General Manager
Carrie Davis

In Town Bed and
Breakfast Inn

Burlington's first historic inn is located in the city's prestigious hill section. This 3 story Georgian/Queen Anne Revival-style mansion was built in 1881 as a private residence and has been lovingly restored. Tall double front doors with antique brass handles open to welcome you into the beautiful cherry paneled foyer with its 11 feet high ceiling and striking staircase.

All 14 guest rooms, each with private bath, are individually decorated with authentic and reproduction antiques. The decor is both elegant and comfortable. In many, the view of Lake Champlain and Adirondack Mountains takes center stage. Classic breakfasts, prepared by our chef and featuring Vermont products and items fresh from our garden, are served with a delightful dash of the unexpected in our sunny marble-floored solarium. Outside, stroll down the twin marble staircases and visit our 1.5 acres of lawn and English gardens filled with herbs and flowers. A short walk takes you to the University of Vermont, Champlain College, Lake Champlain's waterfront and Church Street's fine restaurants and shopping.

Member Since 2002

Rooms/Rates
14 Rooms including 2 suites, $125/$225. Private baths, AC, cable TV, wireless Internet. Antiques, lake views and gardens. Open year-round.
Number of Rooms: 14

Cuisine
Full breakfast served from 7:30-10:00 AM daily. 3 different choices daily: egg entree, sweet entree, & our homemade granola. Daily in-room snack plate with: cookies, Lake Champlain Chocolates & dried fruit.

Nearest Airport(s)
Burlington

Directions
From I-89: take Exit 14 W. Follow Rte. 2W for 1.5 mi. Turn L onto S. Willard St. (also Rte. 7S). We are 1/2 mi. down, on the R side.

12+

"A lovely place to forget what day it is. Casual, comfortable elegance galore! Inn-credible!"

Stone Hill Inn

Innkeepers/Owners
Amy and Hap Jordan

Elegant Contemporary
Mountain Breakfast Inn

www.srinns.com/stonehill
89 Houston Farm Road, Stowe, VT 05672
802-253-6282 • Fax 802-253-7415
stay@stonehillinn.com

paii

Rooms/Rates
All rooms offer a king bed and fireside Jacuzzi for two. LCD TV & DVD/VCR. $275 to $395 B&B, depending on season.
Number of Rooms: 9

Cuisine
A memorable, full country breakfast with 3 daily choices is served from 7:30 to 10:00 AM in the sunny, window-walled breakfast room with tables set for two. An evening hors d'oeuvre and 24-hour soft drinks included. BYOB if you wish.

Nearest Airport(s)
Burlington, VT

Directions
From I-89, take exit 10. Follow Rte 100 North for 10 miles to Stowe. At the 3-way stop, turn left on Rte 108. Go 3 miles. Turn right on Houston Farm Rd. It's the first driveway on the left.

Designed and built by the innkeepers, the Inn was created to be a peaceful, romantic, one-of-a-kind getaway. Relax in your bubbling, fireside Jacuzzi for two--every room has one--along with many other thoughtful touches and indulgent amenities. Schedule a massage by the fireplace in the privacy of your room, or outside in our spectacular summer perennial gardens. In winter, glide down the hill on the toboggan, or borrow some snowshoes to explore our wooded trail. Stowe has long been known as the 'Ski Capital of the East,' but this scenic mountain village offers so much to do year-round. After dinner at one of 50 local restaurants, return to the Inn for billards, games, and puzzles by the huge stone fireplace, or select a movie from the movie library (popcorn provided!). This is truly a place for couples who treasure their time together. Chosen one of the Twelve Best B&Bs in North America, Forbes.com. Recommended by the *New York Times, Boston Globe, Montreal Gazette, Washington Post,* and *USA Today.*

Member Since 2002

"The food at the Stone Hill Inn is the best we have had at an inn..."
– *The Boston Globe*

Heart of the Village Inn

www.srinns.com/heartofthevillage
5347 Shelburne Road, Shelburne, VT 05482
877-808-1834 • 802-985-2800 • Fax 802-985-2870
innkeeper@heartofthevillage.com

Innkeepers/Owners
Pat Button

Traditional Village Breakfast
Inn

Located in the heart of Shelburne Village, this 1886 historic inn welcomes guests with elegance and warmth. The Inn has retained its prominence as one of the centerpieces of the Village, and is listed on the National Register of Historic Places. There are five Inn rooms and four Carriage Barn rooms—each elegantly decorated with a mix of period furnishings – armoires, comfortable beds, plus linens and a sunny view of Shelburne Village. Each room has a private bath, air conditioning, phone service, cable television and a cozy reading chair. The Inn's large living room, library and wrap around porch provide comfortable chairs to relax in and enjoy morning coffee, afternoon tea, or a glass of wine. Walk to Shelburne Museum. Shelburne Farms, downtown Burlington, and the airport are closeby.

Rooms/Rates
4 king/twins $170/$190; 3 queens $160/$180; 1 queen suite $225/$245; 1 queen room $130/$150. TV, telephone, AC, private baths, 3 w/clawfoot tub, 1 Jacuzzi. Corporate rates available.
Number of Rooms: 9

Cuisine
Early AM coffee & tea. Full breakfast featuring home made granola, yogurt, fresh fruit, baked goods & unique hot entree each day. Fresh baked cookies. Wine & cheese.

Nearest Airport(s)
Burlington VT

Directions
From I-89, ex. 13; S on Rt 7; 4.7 mi. to the inn. From I-87, exit 20; Rt 9 to Rt 149 to Ft Ann, NY; Rt 4 to Rt 22A N to Vergennes, VT; Rt 7 N to Shelburne.

Member Since 2002

"Beautiful, comfortable Inn - a warm welcome from a gracious hostess and breakfast-to-die for."

Innkeepers/Owners
Brian & Leslie Mulcahy

Elegant Federal
Country Inn

Rabbit Hill Inn
www.rabbithillinn.com
48 Lower Waterford Rd., Lower Waterford, VT 05848
800-76-BUNNY • 802-748-5168 • Fax 802-748-8342
info@rabbithillinn.com

Rooms/Rates
Classic Rooms: $195/$230B&B / Superior Rooms w/fireplace: $255/$290 B&B / Luxury Rooms w/whirlpool & fireplace: $330/$390 B&B. All offer queen or king beds, plush robes, CD players and many fine amenities.
Number of Rooms: 19

Cuisine
Full country breakfast and afternoon tea & pastries included. Enjoy a multi-course gourmet candlelit dinner in our romantic dining room. Beer, wine, and spirits available in our Snooty Fox Pub.

Nearest Airport(s)
Manchester, NH/Burlington, VT

Directions
From I-91 (N or S), exit 19 to I-93 S. Exit 1 R. on Rte. 18 S 7 mi. to Inn. From I-93 N, exit 44, L on Rte. 18 N, 2 mi. to Inn.

Even time could not change this 1795 Country Inn classic ~ an enchanting romantic hideaway in a tiny hamlet set between a river and the mountains. Our Inn features elegant and uniquely styled guest rooms, most with fireplaces, many with double whirlpool tubs and private porches. We are recognized for award-winning candlelit dining, pampering service, attention to detail, and warm hospitality unlike you have ever experienced from staff and ever-present innkeepers. Rabbit Hill Inn has been repeatedly voted one of America's Best Inns by travel writers, guidebooks, and magazines. Come experience for yourself why Rabbit Hill Inn is "a paradise for the senses, vacation for the soul!"

AAA ◆◆◆◆   *Member Since 1990*   Mobil ★★★

14+

"...accommodations are incredible, meals are amazing... this just might be the most romantic place on the planet." Zagat's 2005

The Inn at Round Barn Farm
www.srinns.com/roundbarn
1661 East Warren Road, Waitsfield, VT 05673
802-496-2276 • Fax 802-496-2276
lodging@theroundbarn.com

Innkeepers/Owners
**AnneMarie DeFreest &
Tim L. Piper**

Elegant Historic Country Bed
& Breakfast

We invite you to our elegant, romantic Bed & Breakfast Inn, surrounded by lush green hillsides, flower-covered meadows, graceful ponds, and extensive perennial gardens. This idyllic pastoral scene, in the heart of the Sugarbush/Mad River Valley, has offered a serene peaceful escape for travelers since 1987. The interior of the Inn is memorable; the restoration impeccable. Reconstructed timbers, refurbished floors covered in oriental rugs, walls awash in a palette of rich tones, warm, relaxing gathering rooms, and soothing music create an unpretentious atmosphere. Gracious and friendly Innkeepers await your arrival. In winter, our meadows and woodlands are covered in snow. Snowshoe trails and snowshoes are available for our guests to experience the magic of our Vermont winter wonderland.

Rooms/Rates
12 Rooms, 1 Suite $165/$325.
Guest rooms are tasteful & luxurious, comforts of home, none of the demands...canopied beds, whirlpool tubs, fireplaces
Number of Rooms: 12

Cuisine
The Inn at the Round Barn Farm takes pride in serving creative breakfasts made with the best seasonal and local ingredients. Dinner is enjoyed at one of 15 area restaurants within 10 miles.

Nearest Airport(s)
Burlington Airport (BTV)

Directions
I-89 S exit 10, Rte. 100 S 14 mi. L on Bridge St., through covered bridge, R at fork up 1 mile. I-89 N exit 9, Rte. 100B 14 mi. L on Bridge St., through covered bridge, R at fork, up 1 mile.

AAA ◆◆◆   *Member Since 2000*   Mobil ★★★

15+ 🚭 💳 📂 ❤ ⊶ ✍ @ ≋ 🖼 ◎ ❋ ⑤

"Round Barn is the most peaceful and nourishing place on earth!"
"Enchanting views!"

Swift House Inn

Innkeepers/Owners
Dan & Michele Brown

In Town Village Inn

www.srinns.com/swifthouseinn
25 Stewart Lane, Middlebury, VT 05753
866-388-9925 • 802-388-9925 • Fax 802-388-9927
info@swifthouseinn.com

AWARD
OF
EXCELLENCE

Rooms/Rates
20 Rooms in three buildings $100/$285. Many with fireplaces and two person whirlpool tubs. All with telephone, individually controlled AC/heat, and cable TV. Sauna, steam shower, and conference room.
Number of Rooms: 20

Cuisine
Full Breakfast. Dinner served 4 nights a week; changing menu prepared with many local Vermont products. Full bar service and extensive wine list, *Wine Spectator* Award.

Nearest Airport(s)
Burlington International Airport, 35 miles

Directions
The Inn is located on Stewart Lane just off of Route 7, 2 blocks N of the village green.

Life's most memorable moments are spent with loved ones in exceptional places. The Swift House Inn is just such a place. Located in historic Middlebury, Vermont, this 20-room former governor's mansion offers the essence of New England warmth. Inside, candlelit dinners await you. Large, comfortable rooms offer modern amenities in period decor. Relax. Sip a glass of wine by the fire, or ponder your favorite book in the library while the kids explore the garden or sled on a nearby hill. Every window frames a picture of country tranquility, yet shops, museums, and Middlebury College are a short walk away. The Inn's three buildings are on five acres with extensive lawns and fabulous gardens. Enjoy hiking just out the back door or in the nearby Green Mountains. Bike the Champlain Valley or participate in the many water activities on nearby Lake Champlain. Numerous ski areas are just a short drive.

AAA ◆◆◆   *Member Since 2005*

"Exceptional food, wonderful service..."

The Maple Leaf Inn

www.srinns.com/mapleleaf
PO Box 273, 5890 Vermont Route 12, Barnard, VT 05031
800-516-2753 • 802-234-5342
mapleafinn@aol.com

Innkeepers/Owners
Gary and Janet Robison

Elegant Country Breakfast
Inn

We welcome you to refresh your spirit and restore your soul in this pastoral corner of Vermont. Nestled snugly within sixteen acres of maple and birch trees, our Victorian-style farmhouse was lovingly designed and built by the innkeepers. Each spacious guest room has its own personality and charm with delicate stenciling, stitchery, and handmade quilts. Individually controlled central heating/air-conditioning, heated bathroom tile floors and a pillow library all help to add to your personal comfort. Upholstered chairs and good reading lights are provided. Woodburning fireplaces are set daily for your convenience and a collection of romantic videos awaits your viewing. An honor bar with snacks, sodas and bottled water is available at any time and room service, including delectable treats, beer and wine, may be ordered as well. "Nook and Cranny Gift Shelf". Memorable gourmet breakfasts are prepared fresh each morning and served at individual candlelit tables for two. Evening turn-down service is offered. Come share our dream.

Rooms/Rates
7 Rooms $130/$270 B&B.
Spacious guest rooms with king beds, luxurious private baths with whirlpools, TV/VCR with premium satellite service, telephones, woodburning fireplaces, spa robes, hair dryers, air-conditioning. Open all year.
Number of Rooms: 7

Cuisine
A gourmet three-course breakfast is served at individual candlelit tables for two, and light afternoon refreshments are served in the parlor at check-in. Beer and wine available.

Nearest Airport(s)
Burlington, VT

Directions
From Woodstock, VT: 9 miles N on Rte. 12. Inn sits back in woods on R, just before school.

AAA ◆◆◆◆ *Member Since 2002* Mobil ★★★

"When couples stay at the Maple Leaf Inn, they fall in love again ... what guests leave behind are tales of romance." *The Boston Globe*

Innkeepers/Owners
Steven and Lauren Bryant

Traditional
Mountain Resort

The Mountain Top Inn & Resort

www.srinns.com/mountaintopinn
195 Mountain Top Road, Chittenden, VT 05737
800-445-2100 • 802-483-2311 • Fax 802-483-6373
stay@mountaintopinn.com

Rooms/Rates
29 Luxury and Classic Lodge Rooms $150/$745; 5 Pet friendly Cabins $195/$485; Private Chalets $275/$2600; Rates include Vermont country breakfast. Open year round.
Number of Rooms: 34

Cuisine
Highlands Dining Room offers innovative cuisine. Highlands Tavern features casual bistro fare. Seasonal outdoor terrace. Children's menu.

Nearest Airport(s)
Rutland - 20 min.; Burlington, VT - 1.5 hrs; Albany, NY - 2hrs

Directions
Easy access from Interstate 91 & 89. From Rts 4 or 7 follow signs for The Mountain Top Inn & Resort. 11 miles from Killington or Rutland. Visit the website for directions.

Offering breathtaking natural beauty, every season for every experience, The Mountain Top Inn & Resort is surrounded by the Green Mountain National Forest and set amidst 350 acres overlooking a pristine, recreational lake. In the tradition of a mountain lodge, our guests enjoy breathtaking views, innovative dining, warm hospitality and endless outdoor adventures. Distinctive seasonal packages entice couples, families, cross country skiers, equestrian enthusiasts and nature lovers to visit the luxury Resort. Located in Central Vermont, a short drive from Killington or Rutland, this four-season destination has something for everyone. In summer enjoy horseback riding, hiking, private lake-front sandy beach, scenic pontoon boat rides, canoes, kayaks, fly-fishing, claybird shooting, mountain biking, and tennis. Winter's transformation creates 80km of nordic ski and snowshoe trails; as well as horse drawn sleigh rides, ice skating, and dog sledding. Casual, yet refined, the furnishings throughout dazzle with sophistication and comfort.

Member Since 1987

"For the ultimate in Neiman Marcus fantasy fulfillment, head to the Mountain Top Inn." *Ski* Magazine

Fox Creek Inn

www.srinns.com/foxcreek
49 Dam Road, Chittenden, VT 05737
800-707-0017 • 802-483-6213 • Fax 802-483-2623
foxcreek@sover.net

Innkeepers/Owners
Alex and Ann Volz

Traditional Country Inn

Just the way you have always pictured a Country Inn. Here is the Vermont for which you have been searching. There are a myriad of activities: hiking, biking and water sports in Summer and alpine and XC skiing in Winter. Relaxing in front of a fireplace or sitting on the front porch with a glass of wine, these are the times when memories are made. Once the home of William Barstow, you can easily imagine the family entertaining their friends, the Fords, Firestones, and his partner, Thomas Edison. By earning our share of awards for food, wine and innkeeping, we have kept that tradition of entertaining alive. See the difference between eating and dining. This is backwoods elegance at its best.

Rooms/Rates
9 Rooms, all w/private baths:1 w/fp+fp in Dbl Jacuzzi; 2 w/fp + Jacuzzi; 3 w/Jacuzzi; 2 w/full bath; 1 w/Dbl. Jacuzzi; $160/$295 B&B; $190/$409 MAP.
Number of Rooms: 9

Cuisine
Enjoy a full Vermont country breakfast and a candlelit 4-course dinner. Choose from our ever-changing menu, featuring the freshest ingredients. Full bar & an award-winning wine menu with over 175 labels, many older vintages.

Nearest Airport(s)
Burlington

Directions
Chittenden is 10 mi. NE of Rutland, VT. From Rutland take Rt. 7N or Rt. 4E and follow the state hospitality signs.

Member Since 1998

"Terry and I loved staying at Fox Creek. We felt like we were guests in your home."

SelectRegistry.com

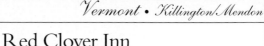

Innkeepers/Owners
Bill Pedersen and
Tricia Treen Pedersen

Traditional Mountain
Inn

Red Clover Inn

www.srinns.com/redcloverinn
7 Woodward Road, Killington/Mendon, VT 05701
800-752-0571 • 802-775-2290 • Fax 802-773-0594
innkeepers@redcloverinn.com

Rooms/Rates
6 rooms with fireplace, 4 double &
1 single whirlpools, 7 with TV, all
air conditioned. $145/$290, Foliage/Holidays: $205/$350
Number of Rooms: 14

Cuisine
Candlelit gourmet dining
complemented by fine wine from
award-winning list. Full bar. Hearty
country breakfast served in a sunlit
breakfast room. Special events and
celebrations welcome.

Nearest Airport(s)
Rutland State Airport (10 mi);
Lebanon, NH; Burlington, VT;
Albany, NY

Directions
From Killington take Rte 4 West 5
miles to Woodward Rd., turn Left;
from Rutland take Rte 4 East 5 miles,
to Woodward Rd., turn Right - 1/4
mile to Inn on Left.

Down a tree-lined country road in the Green Mountains, this rambling 1840s farmhouse estate on 13 acres offers warmth, pampering by caring staff and attentive innkeepers, and exceptional gourmet fare complemented by an award-winning wine list. Rooms are attractively furnished with thoughtful attention to detail; some offer whirlpool tubs for two, gas fireplaces and all have majestic mountain views. From the Inn, explore quaint villages and pastoral beauty or choose from many seasonal activities; Killington Resort Area is only 5 miles away; take in a round at Green Mountain National Golf Course or other fine courses nearby; explore Woodstock, Vermont; or hike the Appalachian Trail. Later, dine leisurely and sumptuously from an extensive menu featuring the freshest dairy, produce and game that Vermont offers. Restaurant has been awarded *Wine Spectator* Award of Excellence since 1995.

AAA ◆◆◆   *Member Since 1998*   Mobil ★★★

12+ 🚭 ♿ 💳 🌙 📁 ❤   ✏ @ 🐕 📷   🧺 ◎ ❄

"What a comfortable taken-care-of stay..."

Crisanver House

www.srinns.com/crisanverhouse
1434 Crown Point Road, Shrewsbury, VT 05738
800-492-8089 • 802-492-3589 • Fax 802-492-3480
info@crisanver.com

Innkeepers/Owners
Carol & B. Michael Calotta

Historic Country Inn

🍽️ 🍽️ 🍽️ 🍷

Central to historic places, great shopping, cultural events and year round sports, this Circa 1800s Historic Register Farmhouse is totally renovated and redecorated in classic country style with original art, oriental rugs, and antiques to create comfort and charming elegance. At 2000 ft. amid 120 acres, spectacular panoramic views, a rolling tapestry of the Green Mountains and brilliantly colorful sunsets. Cottage suite luxuries-king bed, marble baths, his/her spun glass sinks, Jacuzzi, ceiling fans and heated towel bars, fireplaces. Great fun fills your days: tennis, shuffleboard, croquet, hiking, large pristine pond, ping pong, darts, TV, VCR movies, board games, books, magazines and the porch. Meander the gardens savoring the fresh aromas. A foliage spectacle with its breathtaking colors beckons in autumn, while the Inn glows from within amidst a winter wonderland. Crisanver House is everything you imagine a Country Inn should be: sublime setting, fine accommodations, delicious food--gourmet breakfast, afternoon tea, Inn-baked cookies, biscotti, beverages, fruit and bedtime truffle--magnificent views, unobtrusive attentiveness and warm hospitality.

Rooms/Rates
6 rooms/3 suites: $115/$295. Private baths, robes, European bath products, clock, radio/CD, CDs, daily papers, flowers. Closed Apr/Nov.
Number of Rooms: 9

Cuisine
Menu of the day dinner service with linen, Wedgewood china, music, candlelight and fresh flowers. Hikers picnic lunch.

Nearest Airport(s)
Rutland - 10 minutes
Burlington Int'l - 2 hrs.

Directions
7N or S to 103: 91S to 4W to 7S to 103: 91N to 103N: 87 to 787E to NY 7E to VT 7N to 103: From 103 to Lincoln Hill Rd to Crown Point Rd. Pickup @ Rutland Airport or train station.

AAA ◆◆◆   *Member Since 2005*

"We've stayed at over 55 B&B's–But you are our TOPS! BRAVO - You are our new #1!"   See our website for other guest comments.

October Country Inn

Innkeepers/Owners
Edie and Chuck Janisse

Traditional Farmhouse
Country Inn

www.octobercountryinn.com
P.O. Box 66, 362 Upper Rd., Bridgewater Corners, VT 05035
800-648-8421 • 802-672-3412 • Fax 802-672-1163
oci@vermontel.net

Rooms/Rates
$110/$175 Dbl. B&B. Dinner, $25.00 per person.
Number of Rooms: 10

Cuisine
Full country breakfast. Internationally-themed dinners cooked to gourmet standards and served family-style. Beer and wine license.

Nearest Airport(s)
Manchester, NH

Directions
From Woodstock, follow Rte. 4 westward about 8 miles. Go 1/10 mile past Country Store at junction of Rte. 100A, turn right on Bridgewater Center Rd., and right again on Upper Rd. From Rutland, follow Rte. 4 eastward about 20 miles. Just before the Long Trail Brewery, turn left on Bridgewater Center Rd., and right on Upper Rd.

Loved for its hospitality and relaxed atmosphere, Chuck and Edie's converted nineteenth century farmhouse between Woodstock and Killington offers warmth and intimacy in the finest innkeeping tradition. The scents of baking muffins, fresh herbs and homemade desserts fill the inn as Chuck works magic in French Country, Mexican, Italian, Greek, and even American cuisines. Swim in the pool, bicycle, hike, ski, shop, sight-see or simply relax by the fire—then dine by candlelight. Away from the crowds, yet close to Killington, Okemo, Woodstock, Weston, and Dartmouth. Bridgewater Corners and October Country Inn are always just around the corner.

Member Since 1992

"What a wonderful place! We love the laid back atmoshpere, delicious food, and cozy feel. A great place to come 'home' to on a cold Vermont night."

Juniper Hill Inn

www.srinns.com/juniperhill
153 Pembroke Road, Windsor, VT 05089
800-359-2541 • 802-674-5273 • Fax 802-674-2041
innkeeper@juniperhillinn.com

Owner
Ari Nikki
General Manager
Robert Dean
Traditional Country Inn

Ascend a winding driveway canopied by ancient pines to a restored Colonial Revival mansion surrounded by acres of lawns and gardens. Experience incomparable views of Lake Runnemede and Ascutney Mountain from our new spectacular 1,800 sq. ft. terrace surrounded by lush gardens and flanked by our crystal clear pool! History and elegance abound creating a peaceful retreat for you to enjoy. Finely appointed guest rooms feature antiques, decanters of sherry, chocolates, robes, hair dryers, CD players. Many guest rooms also include fireplaces, private balconies or porches. Attention to detail and the fine, but comfortable, dining are additional reasons Juniper Hill is awarded a Romantic Hideaway destination by *The Discerning Traveler* and featured in the *Boston Globe*, Newsday, and many others. Near popular Vermont/New Hampshire locations including Woodstock, Quechee, Dartmouth College. Enjoy golfing, skiing, canoeing, horse or sleigh rides, bicycling, croquet, shopping, historic sites or simply relax, restore, revive, rekindle!

Rooms/Rates
$105/$285 B&B. Many rooms w/ fireplaces, porches or balconies, queen beds, antiques, woods, garden or mountain views, all individually air conditioned.
Number of Rooms: 16

Cuisine
Full country breakfast menu plus daily special, afternoon refreshment from 3-5 PM. Single 7PM seating for 4-course dinner, advance reservation only, Tues-Sat. Self-serve warm beverages 7-10 PM.

Nearest Airport(s)
Manchester, NH

Directions
From I-91 North: Exit 9. R (L from I-91 S) onto Rte. 5 S. Proceed 2.7 mi., R onto Juniper Hill Rd, stay L at fork. Driveway on R at crest of hill.

AAA ◆◆◆   *Member Since 2002*   Mobil ★★★

12+

"Perfection relized!" "Attention to detail and charming innkeepers." "We travel all over the world and give JHI Five Stars!" "Spectacular! We'll be back"

Innkeepers/Owners
Jim and Cathy Kubec

Elegant Victorian Village
Breakfast Inn

The Governor's Inn

www.thegovernorsinn.com
86 Main Street, Ludlow, VT 05149
800-468-3766 • 802-228-8830
innkeeper@thegovernorsinn.com

Rooms/Rates
7 Rooms, $149/$264 B&B; 1 Suite, $249/$309 B&B. Includes Afternoon Tea and Full Breakfast. Dinner available Sat. Ski packages. Air conditioned. Open year-round, except 2 wks in Apr., 2 wks in Nov., and Dec. 23 - 26.
Number of Rooms: 8

Cuisine
Full, hot breakfast, afternoon tea and sweets. Extensive tea menu. Prix fixe dinner on Saturdays. Full beverage service. Specially prepared Vermont country picnics by request.

Nearest Airport(s)
Hartford - 125 miles;
Boston - 144 mile

Directions
Ludlow is located at intersection of VT Rte. 100 & VT Rte. 103. Inn is south on Main St. (Rte 103), just off village green.

From the moment you step into this late Victorian country home, you are surrounded by the gracious elegance and warm hospitality befitting its first owner, Vermont Governor William Stickney. Enjoy afternoon tea, sweets, and tea sandwiches served in the parlor with its extraordinary slate fireplace, polished woodwork, and oriental rugs. Retire to your cozy bed chamber, warmed by a gas fireplace in cooler weather or air conditioned during warmer months. Read or watch TV, relax in the whirlpool. Awake to a bountiful breakfast – perhaps apple cinnamon pancakes or our Cuckoo's Nest souffle - served with antique china, silver, and crystal. Culinary Magic Cooking Seminars are held on premises. Walk to village restaurants, shops, and galleries. Near Okemo Mountain, downhill and cross-country skiing, maple houses, cheese factory, golf, hiking, antiquing, summer theater, bicycling, Weston Priory. Take along one of Cathy's gourmet picnics as you explore Vermont.

Member Since 1987   Mobil ★★★

"Everything about the inn says 'relax and enjoy'...and we did! Incredible gourmet breakfast!"

Inn at Water's Edge
www.srinns.com/watersedge
45 Kingdom Road, Ludlow, VT   05149
888-706-9736 • 802-228-8143 • Fax 802-228-8443
innatwatersedge@mail.tds.net

Innkeepers/Owners
Bruce & Tina Verdrager

Historic Waterside Inn

Situated on Echo Lake and the Black River, this 150 year old Victorian estate has been thoroughly restored and now boasts all the charm and ambiance of a truly unique Victorian Inn. The Inn exudes the endless enthusiasm of the innkeepers to create the feeling of a bygone era along with the warmth and comfort of being home. Located minutes from skiing and golfing at Okemo and Killington mountains, the Inn is only a short drive to the attractions of Manchester, Weston and Woodstock. Our library, gathering room and English pub all have fireplaces and comfortable seating for guests to enjoy. Each of our 11 guest rooms has a private bath, most with Jacuzzi bathtubs and fireplaces. Whether relaxing in our outdoor hot tub, swimming off our private beach, canoeing or biking, the Inn offers year-round activities. The Inn is also completely air-conditioned and handicapped accessible.

Rooms/Rates
$125/$250 B&B. $175/$300 MAP. Golf packages from $125/ppdo include 18 holes of golf, lodging, breakfast & 4-course dinner. Ski packages from $100/ppdo include adult lift ticket at Okemo Mt., lodging, breakfast & 4-course dinner. Reservations 60 days in advance.
Number of Rooms: 11

Cuisine
Full country breakfast. Afternoon refreshments. 4-course candlelit Dinner. Beer, wine & spirits available in Doc's English Pub & in the Dining Room.

Nearest Airport(s)
Bradley Springfield (Hartford)

Directions
4 mi. N of Ludlow Village on Rte 100 at Echo Lake between Okemo & Killington Resorts.

AAA ◆◆◆◆   *Member Since 2003*

"Our 4-course dinner is not to be missed. A real Gem, don't change a thing!"

Innkeepers/Owners
Linda & Jim McGinnis

Traditional Village
Inn

Barrows House
www.srinns.com/barrowshouse
3156 Route 30, PO Box 98, Dorset, VT 05251-0098
800-639-1620 • 802-867-4455 • Fax 802-867-0132
innkeepers@barrowshouse.com

Rooms/Rates
$120/$260 B&B double occupany
for 18 double sized rooms and 10
suites, nine with fireplaces and
two with whirlpool tubs.
Number of Rooms: 28

Cuisine
Dining is relaxing and informal.
The menu is Regional American
in style with Continental influence.
The quality of your meal will
impress especially in a village
of less than 1,000 people. A
speciality of the Inn is Maine Crab
Cakes, Chesapeake Style.

Nearest Airport(s)
Albany, NY

Directions
Boston: 3 hours
New York: 4 hours
Montreal: 4 hours

Barrows House is a collection of nine white clapboard buildings on 12 groomed acres in the heart of the picture-book Vermont village of Dorset. Guests have a choice of 28 rooms and suites in nine different buildings, each with a history and style of its own. All rooms and suites have as a minimum their own private bath, king or queen bed, expanded cable TV, air conditioning and private telephones. Nine also have fireplaces and two have whirlpool tubs. Dining at Barrows House is an informal and delicious adventure in American regional cuisine in our three dining rooms. Whether with iced tea in the gazebo or English garden or mulled cider in front of a warm fire and historic stenciling, Barrows House extends its welcome. Weddings and family reunions are done with a very personal touch.

Member Since 1974

"Soft beds, wonderful food, beautiful place, best hosts
—I wish I could come here every day!"

1811 House

www.1811house.com
3654 Main Street, PO Box 39, Manchester, VT 05254
800-432-1811 • 802-362-1811 • Fax 802-362-2443
stay@1811house.com

Innkeepers/Owners
Marnie and Bruce Duff
Innkeepers/Owners
Cathy and Jorge Veleta

Elegant Village Breakfast
Inn

Located in the heart of historic Manchester Village, the 1811 House is listed on the National Register of Historic Places. Carefully restored to its original Federal period style, the 1811 House offers unequaled ambiance with English and American antiques and decor. The inn is fully air conditioned and the 13 guest rooms offer warmth and detail with wood-burning fireplaces, oriental rugs, fine paintings and canopied beds. The British style pub, featuring a collection of over ninety single malt scotch whiskies, along with a large selection of wines, beers and liquors, is the perfect place to relax. A delicious, made-from-scratch, full breakfast is served every morning in the dining room with fine china and sterling silver place settings. The seven acres of grounds, with terraced gardens and a pond, invite you to stroll around and enjoy the exceptional views of the Green Mountains. Elegant, but casual, the 1811 House is the vacation destination you deserve for that romantic Vermont getaway.

Rooms/Rates
11 Rooms, 2 Suites $210/$280 B&B. Open year-round except week prior to Christmas and Christmas Day.
Number of Rooms: 13

Cuisine
Elegant full breakfast, award-winning cookies and complimentary sherry. British Pub featuring over 90 single malts, 30 different beers, wine by the glass and premium liquors and cordials.

Nearest Airport(s)
Albany, New York - one hour and 15 minutes

Directions
In Manchester Center, at junction of Rtes. 11/30 and 7A, go south on Historic Rte. 7A, approximately 1 mile. The 1811 House is on the left.

Member Since 1998

16+

"The location, the ambience, the breakfast, and most of all the welcoming innkeepers and staff made our brief stay above all words and expectations."

The Inn at Ormsby Hill

Innkeepers/Owners
Ted and Chris Sprague

Elegant Historic Country
Bed & Breakfast

www.srinns.com/ormsbyhill
1842 Main Street, Historic Route 7A, Manchester, VT 05255
800-670-2841 • 802-362-1163 • Fax 802-362-5176
stay@ormsbyhill.com

Rooms/Rates
10 Rooms, all with fireplace and Jacuzzi for two, $215/$335 B&B. Peak season premiums apply. Open year-round. See website for specials.
Number of Rooms: 10

Cuisine
Nationally-acclaimed breakfasts served in the magnificent Conservatory with its wall of windows facing the mountains. "...a breakfast that'll knock your socks off..." *Yankee Magazine's Travel Guide.* "...perhaps the best breakfasts in Vermont," says *New England Travel.*

Nearest Airport(s)
Albany, New York

Directions
In Manchester Center, at junction of Routes 11/30 and 7A, take Historic Route 7A South. The Inn is approximately 3 miles on the left.

A distinguished, romantic, luxurious, tranquil retreat. Surround yourself with a spectacular setting. Be pampered in bed chambers with canopies, fireplaces, air-conditioning, and slim-line digital flat-screen televisions. Luxurious bathrooms with Jacuzzis for two and some with two-person steam saunas. Imagine having a massage in front of your fireplace with a choice of beverage and a tray of goodies placed in your room for you to enjoy. Indulge in "...the attention to detail, the romantic ambiance..." *Colonial Homes.* A patio, porch and gazebo, with breathtaking views of the Battenkill Valley and Green Mountains. A restored manor house, c. 1764, so serene you will never want to leave. Renowned for comfort, heartfelt hospitality, and profound attention to detail. "...arguably one of the most welcoming inns in all of New England." *Lonely Planet.*

AAA ◆◆◆◆   *Member Since 1996*

12+ 🚭 ♿ 💳 Ⓟ   ✍ @   🛏 ◎ ✳ Ⓢ ☕

"...a romantic bed-and-breakfast of the highest caliber."
Andrew Harper's *Hideaway Report*

West Mountain Inn

www.srinns.com/westmountain
144 West Mountain Inn Road, Arlington, VT 05250
802-375-6516 • Fax 802-375-6553
info@westmountaininn.com

Innkeepers/Owners
The Carlson Family

Traditional Mountain Inn

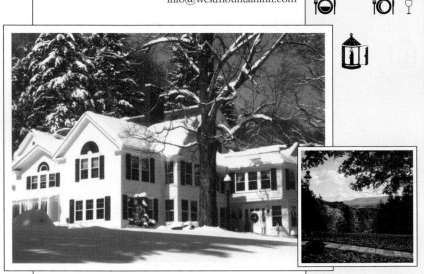

Nestled on a mountainside overlooking the historic village of Arlington and the Green Mountains beyond, the century-old West Mountain Inn has been welcoming travelers with warmth and hospitality for over a quarter of a century. Visitors are treated to spacious antique-filled guest rooms and common areas, 150 woodland acres with beautiful views, gardens, a labyrinth, and llamas providing space to relax and renew the body and spirit. Miles of hiking trails and the Battenkill River provide seasonal outdoor activities. A hearty country breakfast and an elegant 6-course dinner in front of an open hearth complement your stay. The Inn also offers private dining and meeting rooms for unique celebrations of weddings, birthdays, anniversaries, reunions or business meetings.

Rooms/Rates
12 Rooms, 3 Suites, 3 Townhouses $149/$304 B&B, $224/$379 MAP. Service charges included in all rates.
Number of Rooms: 20

Cuisine
A full country breakfast and elegant 5-course dinner are prepared daily. Seasonal menus focus on local VT products and organic produce. Weddings and rehearsal dinners a specialty. Full bar, premium beers and exceptional wine list.

Nearest Airport(s)
Albany, NY

Directions
Vermont Route 7 N, exit 3, L off ramp, take access road to end, R on Rte. 7A into Arlington. One mile then L on Rte. 313 for .5 mile, L on River Rd., green bridge over river, Inn's driveway on the L, Inn at top of driveway.

Member Since 1984   Mobil ★★★

"A wonderful ambiance where the warmth extends beyond the fireplace."

SelectRegistry.com

Innkeepers/Owners
Jennifer and Ed
Dorta-Duque

Elegant Country
Village Inn

AWARD
OF
EXCELLENCE

Three Mountain Inn

www.srinns.com/threemountaininn
3732 Main Street Route 30/100, P.O. Box 180, Jamaica, VT 05343
800-532-9399 • 802-874-4140 • Fax 802-874-4745
stay@threemtn.com

Rooms/Rates
15 Rooms. $145/$345.
Number of Rooms: 15

Cuisine
This historic 1790 culinary
landmark, offers an elegant
dining experience, showcasing
Contemporary Vermont Fresh
Cuisine. The dining rooms, with
wood burning fireplaces, are set
in two intimate but casual rooms
decorated with timeless elegance.

Nearest Airport(s)
Hartford/Springfield

Directions
Jamaica is located on VT Rt 30, 1/2
hr. NW of Brattleboro (I-91, Exit 2).
Take Rte 30, North to Jamaica. The
Inn is on the right. From Manchester, take VT Rte 11/30 make right
to continue on Rte 30, continue on
Rte 30 towards Jamaica, the Inn is
on the left.

The mission of Three Mountain Inn is all about you. We await
the opportunity to exceed your expectations. Our 18th Century
origins are evident in the hand hewn beams and wide "King's
Wood" in the Main House. The 21st Century is also evident in
our amenities, Vermont-fresh cuisine in our AAA Four Diamond-
rated restaurant, extensive wine menu that has been awarded the
Wine Spectator Award of Excellence, and our well-stocked pub.
Three Mountain Inn is convenient to all of Vermont. Hiking,
skiing, summer theater and the Vermont Symphony are seasonal
events, while fresh air, starry nights, and mountain views are available year-round. Most of all, our staff is devoted to the fulfillment
of desires you never knew existed.

AAA ◆◆◆◆   *Member Since 1982*

12+

"Perfect hosts, wonderful rooms with a beautiful Vermont setting."
"Jamaica Vermont...Vermont as one hoped it would be..." *Travel + Leisure*

Windham Hill Inn

www.srinns.com/windhamhill
311 Lawrence Drive, West Townshend, VT 05359
800-944-4080 • 802-874-4080 • Fax 802-874-4702
windham@sover.net

Innkeepers/Owners
Marina & Joe Coneeny
Elegant Country
Inn

Windham Hill Inn, a "...place that touches your soul." sits on 160 acres at the end of a Green Mountain hillside country road, surrounded by rock-wall bordered fields and forests, and breathtaking views. Friendly innkeepers and staff welcome you to this country estate with its sparkling rooms, memorable gourmet meals, extensive and award winning wine list, relaxing ambiance and closeness to nature. Relax in four elegantly furnished common rooms with wood-burning fireplaces, a 1911 Steinway grand piano and extensive CD library. Guest rooms feature antiques, locally crafted furnishings, hardwood floors and oriental rugs. Most rooms have soaking or Jacuzzi tubs, gas fireplaces or Vermont Castings stoves. Some have private decks. Centrally air-conditioned throughout. Close to abundant Southern Vermont events and activities. A true destination property, the Inn is "....as good as it gets, especially if you're in search of a romantic getaway." *Frommers* 2004.

Member Since 1989

Rooms/Rates
21 Rooms, $195/$380 B&B; Peak season premiums apply. Open year-round except the week prior to the 27th of December during the Christmas season, and the first two weeks of April.
Number of Rooms: 21

Cuisine
Full breakfast and afternoon refreshments. Light Lunch avail. Dinner by reservation every evening. Wine and liquor available. Winner *Wine Spectator* award for the past 7 years.

Nearest Airport(s)
Hartford (Bradley Intl. 1.5 hrs)

Directions
I-91 N to Brattleboro exit 2, follow signs to Rte. 30, 21.5 miles NW to West Townshend. Turn R opposite Post Office onto Windham Hill Rd., 1.3 miles, follow sign to Inn.

12+

"Everything you would think a Vermont Inn should be!"

Innkeepers/Owners
Debbie and Bruce Pfander

Elegant Country Inn

🍽 🍽 🍷

Four Columns Inn
www.srinns.com/fourcolumns
P.O. Box 278, 21 West Street, Newfane, VT 05345
800-787-6633 • 802-365-7713 • Fax 802-365-0022
innkeeper@fourcolumnsinn.com

Wine Spectator
AWARD
OF
EXCELLENCE

Rooms/Rates
$150/$385 includes full breakfast. Special Packages in some seasons. 11 rooms with fireplaces, 9 suites with whirlpool/soaking tubs. Open year round.
Number of Rooms: 15

Cuisine
Chef Greg Parks has led the culinary team for over 25 years. Awards: James Beard Foundation, Wine Spectator. Dinner nightly except Tues. Extensive wine list.

Nearest Airport(s)
Bradley, Logan, JFK

Directions
I-91 to VT Exit 2. Turn L at end of ramp. Go 1/2 mile, turn L on Cedar St. Go to the 3rd stop sign. Turn L on VT Rte.30 N. Go 11 mi. to Newfane. Village Green on the L-Inn is just behind Courthouse.

The Four Columns Inn was lovingly built in 1832 by Pardon Kimball to replicate the childhood home of his southern wife. Today that home is an elegant country inn with 15 delightful guest rooms ranging from six charming traditional rooms to nine beautifully refurbished suites, all featuring private baths, individual heat and air conditioning, period antique furnishings, complimentary telephone usage, and afternoon tea and cookies. Gas fireplaces are the focal point in eleven rooms, and the suites deliver grand scale bathrooms with spa tubs and separate showers. Select rooms also offer high speed internet access, and televisions with DVD players plus a huge library of complimentary movies. A hearty country breakfast, complete with a selection of morning newspapers, is included for all house guests. And not to be missed is dinner in the Inn's fine dining restaurant, where Chef Greg Parks has a well earned reputation for his creative regional cuisine. Situated on the historic Newfane Green unchanged since the 1830s, the property includes 150 acres of rolling hills, an inviting stream, ponds and exquisite gardens. Guests will enjoy the lovely pool and rustic hiking trails in summer, plus access to all the seasonal outdoor activities in Southern Vermont only a short distance away. "Why go anywhere else"? - Sandra Soule

Member Since 2000

6+ 🚭 🛏 🕐 📁 ♥ ✂ 🛥 @ 🐕 〰 🏞 ◎

"If romance requires a stage set, Four Columns is the theater of choice!"
Country Home "Quintessential New England!" *Daily Candy*

Deerhill Inn

www.srinns.com/deerhill

14 Valley View Road, P.O. Box 136, West Dover, VT 05356
800-993-3379 • 802-464-3100 • Fax 802-464-5474
innkeeper@deerhill.com

Innkeepers/Owners
**Chef Michael Allen &
Stan Gresens**

Elegant Mountain
Inn

Once chosen "one of the most romantic places in the world," Deerhill Inn is nestled on a hillside overlooking the quintessential Vermont village of West Dover with panoramic views of the Green Mountains. Perfectly located in the middle of Southern Vermont, Deerhill has access to the best of Vermont and Northern Massachusetts. Museums, theaters, antiquing, shopping, hiking, boating, and of course skiing. Fourteen uniquely decorated guest rooms (including *Country Inn* Magazine's Room of the Year) with private baths, designer linens, microfiber robes, private porches and complimentary full country breakfast. Three comfortable sitting rooms, art gallery, gift shop, secluded "grotto" pool, lush gardens and the "amazing" cuisine of Chef Michael Allen complete the experience. Chef-owned and operated and only four hours from Manhattan and two and a half from Boston.

Rooms/Rates
13 rooms, 1 suite $135/$335. Special packages and off-season discounts. Open nearly all year, except late April/early May. **Number of Rooms:** 14

Cuisine
Full, made to order, Country breakfast; the "amazing" Modern American Cuisine of Chef Michael Allen; and a *Wine Spectator* awarded, New World wine list. Chosen one of the 25 best Chef-Owned Inns in the U.S. by *Conde Nast Traveler* April 1999. Full liquor license.

Nearest Airport(s)
Albany, NY - 1.5 hours
Hartford, CT - 2 hours

Directions
From I-91, Vt. exit 2 (Brattleboro); to Rte. 9W 20 miles to Rte. 100N 6 miles to Valley View Road, up hill 200 yards.

Member Since 1999

12+

"Beautiful, charming, great touches everywhere – food incredible – just what we were looking for!! Thank you!!"

SelectRegistry.com

Virginia

"The Old Dominion"

Famous For: Blue Ridge Mountains, Mount Vernon,
Monticello, Arlington National Cemetery, Skyline Drive,
Manassas National Battlefield Park, Colonial Williamsburg,
Jamestown Settlement, Virginia Beach, Yorktown,
Booker T. Washington National Monument,
Appomattox Court House, Chesapeake Bay,
Rock of Ages Natural Bridge, Shenandoah National Park

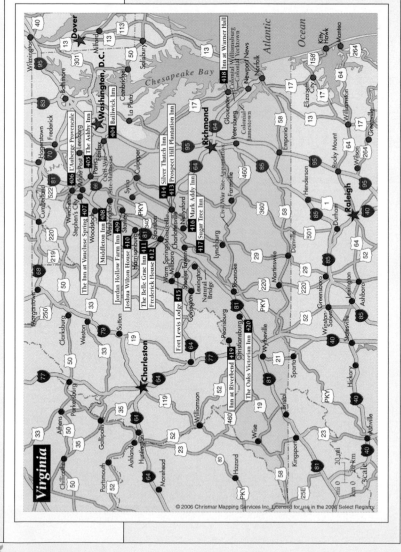

© 2006 Chrismar Mapping Services Inc. Licensed for use in the 2006 Select Registry

The Bailiwick Inn

www.srinns.com/bailiwick
4023 Chain Bridge Road, Fairfax, VA 22030
703-691-2266 • Fax 703-934-2112
theinn@bailiwickinn.com

Owner/Propreitor
Bonnie W. McDaniel
General Manager
Jackie Bowens
Elegant Federal
Style Downtown

This charming, elegant National Register Inn is located only 15 miles from Washington D.C. in historic Old Town Fairfax, Virginia. Luxurious guest chambers patterned after famous Virginians, with feather beds, antiques, Frette bathrobes, fireplaces, whirlpools, mini-bars, dataport phones, afternoon tea, turn-down service and gourmet breakfast. Enjoy fine dining; breakfast, lunch, dinner and Sunday brunch at the Inn in its award-winning restaurant, Christina's at The Bailiwick. The Inn is a wonderful place for weddings, corporate retreats, or romantic getaways. The Bailiwick has received many national awards including *Country Inns* Magazine Top 12 Inns. Featured on Food Network, Travel Network, Discovery Channel and Romancing America.

Rooms/Rates
11 Guestrooms, $170/$230; 1 Suite, $355. Afternoon tea and gourmet breakfast included in room rate. Open year-round. Packages available.
Number of Rooms: 11

Cuisine
Christina's at The Bailiwick serves creative Continental cuisine w/ French and American accents in an intimate setting. Full bar service & extensive wine list available. Sunday brunch.

Nearest Airport(s)
Dulles

Directions
I-66 to exit #60, Rte 123 S Chain Bridge Road toward Fairfax. Pass Main Street, Rte 236, the Inn is on the next L corner at intersection of Sager & Chain Bridge. Free parking behind building.

AAA ◆◆◆   *Member Since 2003*

15+

"Beautiful room, lovely inn, delicious food and above all, gracious service. Food is to die for. We loved it!"

Innkeeper/Owner
Jackie and Charles Leopold
General Manager
Deborah Cox

Traditional Village Inn

🍽️ 🍽️ 🍽️ 🍷

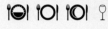

The Ashby Inn & Restaurant

www.srinns.com/ashby
692 Federal St., Paris, VA 20130
866-336-0099 • 540-592-3900 • Fax 540-592-3781
celebrate@ashbyinn.com

Rooms/Rates
6 guest rooms at the Main Inn, $145/$185 and 4 guest rooms at the School House, $250. Sun.-Thurs. discounts on all rooms. Closed Jan 1, July 4, Dec. 24 & 25.
Number of Rooms: 10

Cuisine
Full country breakfast inclusive for our inn guests. Dinner is available Wednesday-Saturday offering traditiional American cuisine. Sunday afternoon brunch. On-site special events. Wine and liquor available.

Nearest Airport(s)
Winchester Regional Airport
Washington/Dulles International

Directions
From Wash DC Rte 66 W to exit 23 - Rte 17 N, 7.5 miles L on Rte 701 for .5 miles or Rte 50 W thru Middleburg, L just after light at Rte. 17.

This 1829 Inn finds its character in the small village of Paris and its heart in the kitchen. The menu is guided more by tradition than trend—with great attention paid to seasonal foods like asparagus, shad roe, softshell crabs and game. Much of the summer produce, herbs and flowers come from its gardens. Guest rooms furnished in period pieces (half with fireplaces and balconies) have views stretching beyond the formal perennial gardens to the hills of the Blue Ridge. The four dining rooms are as intimate as they are distinct - from an enclosed porch, to a converted kitchen with walnut beams and fireplace, to a cozy room with booths set against faux painted walls and striking paintings. Summer dining on the covered patio overlooking the lawn attracts a wide Washington following.

Member Since 1988

12+ 🚭 💳 🍷 📁 ❤️ @ 🎦

"Back here in paradise. Warm, elegant, exceptional. Don't change a thing."

L'Auberge Provencale

www.srinns.com/lauberge
P.O. Box 190, 13630 Lord Fairfax Highway
White Post, VA 22663
800-638-1702 • 540-837-1375 • Fax 540-837-2004
cborel@shentel.net

Innkeepers/Owners
Alain & Celeste Borel

Elegant Country
Inn

paii

AWARD
OF
EXCELLENCE

Essence of Provence in the Shenandoah Valley. Come dine and dream in this eclectic and sophisticated Country Inn with it's nationally renowned "Cuisine Moderne Provencal" by Chef/ Owner Alain Borel and his team of chef's. Transport yourself to the South of France, where every meal is a special and unique occassion. The three intimate dining rooms, each with their delightful decor, offer just the right setting for a 5-course dinner and cheerful gourmet breakfast. The inn exudes the ambience of French Country with warm faux painted walls, Provencale fabrics and antiques. Orchards, herbs, flowers, and vegetables grown by the innkeepers. Charming elegant guest rooms and suites, are all romantic. Perfect for honeymoons and special getaways. Our Villa La Campagnette offers a swimming pool, luxury suites and privacy. The two inns set in Virginia Hunt country, offer a special experience for discerning guests, with exquisite food and courteous attentive service. Weddings and rehearsal dinners. An inn where Great Expectations are quietly met.

Rooms/Rates
6 Charming French Country Rooms, $155/$245; 7 Romatic Suites, $275/$325. Closed first three weeks of January. Some with Fireplaces, steam showers and Jacuzzi.
Number of Rooms: 13

Cuisine
Elegant Five Course Dinners with Provencale flair served Wed. thru Sunday, breakfast of one's dreams, gourmet picnics and the best bistro brunch on Sunday Full extensive wine list of French Chateaux and American Wines, liquor.

Nearest Airport(s)
Dulles

Directions
1 hour W of DC Beltway. One mile S of Rt. 50 on Rt. 340, Inn is on the R. 45 minutes west of Dulles Airport. 10 miles east of Winchester in the Shenandoah Valley.

Member Since 1988   Mobil ★★★

12+

"If you're not happy about life after a meal here you haven't got a pulse." *Washington Post*
"5 hearts, my top prize for Romance." *Washingtonian*

Innkeepers/Owners
Barry & Neil Myers

Traditional Country Inn

The Inn at Vaucluse Spring

www.srinns.com/innatvauclusespring
231 Vaucluse Spring Lane, Stephens City, VA 22655
800-869-0525 • 540-869-0200 • Fax 540-869-9546
mail@vauclusespring.com

Rooms/Rates
12 Rooms/Suites: $145/$230
B&B. 3 Private cottages:
$250/$285. Beautifully furnished,
queen or king beds, all have
fireplaces, 14 with Jacuzzis, some
water/mountain views.
Number of Rooms: 15

Cuisine
Full 3-course breakfast served daily.
A 3-course 'Southern Comfort'
Friday night supper and a romantic
4-course Saturday dinner are available by advance reservation. Wine
and beer available.

Nearest Airport(s)
Dulles International

Directions
From I-66W, take exit 1B to I-81N. Go
1 mile to exit 302. Turn L on Rte 627,
go .5 mile. Turn R on Rte 11, go 2
miles. Turn L on Rte 638, go 3/4 mile
to Inn on L. Follow signs to check-in.

Set amidst 100 scenic acres in the rolling orchard country of the
Shenandoah Valley, this collection of six guest houses is the perfect country retreat. Experience the elegance of the gracious 200
year old Manor House or the warmth and charm of an 1850s
log home. For the ultimate in peace and privacy, stay in the old
Mill House Studio at the water's edge, the Gallery Guest House
with views of the meadow, or the Cabin by the Pond. Relax beside Vaucluse Spring's cool, crystal clear waters. Savor the region's
bounty at the delicious breakfasts and weekend dinners. Ideally
located for enjoying nearby activities.

Member Since 2000   Mobil ★★★

11+

Southern Living Magazine says "Perhaps The Inn at Vaucluse Spring was our
best total experience. The best news? This place is an unbelievable value."

Middleton Inn

www.srinns.com/middletoninn
176 Main Street, P.O. Box 254, Washington, VA 22747
800-816-8157 • 540-675-2020 • Fax 540-675-1050
innkeeper@middletoninn.com

Proprietor
Mary Ann Kuhn
Historic Estate &
Breakfast Inn

Middleton Inn is AAA's highest rated bed and breakfast in the Mid-Atlantic and in "Little" Washington, Virginia, where it is a pleasant stroll on a village street to dinner at the world renowned restaurant of the Inn at Little Washington.

Middleton's 1850s elegant manor house and original outbuildings–summer kitchen, smokehouse and slaves' quarters–sit high on a grassy knoll on a 6-acre estate in the Historic District.

Only 67 miles from "Big" Washington, DC, the inn provides a rural, tranquil setting with horses grazing in the paddocks while sterling silver trays carrying complimentary wine and cheese are served to guests sitting on the front porch, enjoying the spectacular views of the Blue Ridge Mountains. The inn has four elegantly appointed bedrooms in the manor house and an historic, romantic cottage. Working fireplaces are in all the rooms. Enjoy a scrumptious, complimentary four-course breakfast served on fine china and silver in the beautifully restored dining room.

The inn is owned and operated by journalist Mary Ann Kuhn.

AAA ◆◆◆◆   *Member Since 2006*

Rooms/Rates
4 rooms, $195/$375 and 1 guest cottage, $350/$475. Rates vary depending on room, season, day of week. Call for rates or visit Web site.
Number of Rooms: 5

Cuisine
Scrumptuous 4-course breakfast on fine china and silver and afternoon wine/hors d'oeuvres included. Walk to dinner at Inn at Little Washington or drive to other fine dining.

Nearest Airport(s)
Dulles, Reagan National

Directions
From I66 W take Exit 43A to Gainesville. Follow 29 S to Warrenton, Take 211 W for 23 mi. to Washington, Va. At first stop sign turn L onto Main St for 2 1/2 blocks.

12+

"There are 5 B&Bs in the village. The most deluxe is Middleton Inn where no expense was spared on detail and comfort." *The Washington Post*

Jordan Hollow Inn

Innkeeper
Angela Fernandes

Traditional Country
Inn

www.jordanhollow.com
326 Hawksbill Park Road, Stanley, VA 22851
888-418-7000 • 540-778-2285 • Fax 540-778-1759
jhf@jordanhollow.com

Rooms/Rates
$190/$250 B&B; All rooms have fireplaces, hydro-thermo massage spas, whirlpool baths or soaking tubs. Closed Jan. 2 - Feb. 11.
Number of Rooms: 8 Suites, 6 Rooms and 6 Luxury cabins

Cuisine
Full restaurant dinner, breakfast, American Regional features Virginia wines and local produce (including our own "Inn-grown"). Picnic Baskets Available for Lunch. Extensive Wine List and full service bar available.

Nearest Airport(s)
Dulles, Reagan National

Directions
Luray, VA Rte. 340 Business S for 6 mi. to L onto VA Rte. 624 L on VA Rte. 689 continue .5 mi. & R on VA Rte. 626 for .25 mi. to Inn on R.

Surround yourself with spectacular mountain views, history, peace and serenity at our over 200 year-old farm. Located in the Shenandoah Valley, at the base of the Blue Ridge Mountains; you can relax in a rocking chair on a sunporch outside your room, or in front of a cozy fire. Meander through our beautiful gardens, explore the valley, vineyards, Civil War sites, historic villages, or take a hike on the five miles of trails onsite or in the nearby national park and forest. Begin and end each day with fabulous meals in our restored 1700s farmhouse restaurant. Outdoor porch and deck dining seasonally with outstanding views! As we are a horse farm, you may bring your own horse if you like. We have 150 gorgeous acres for you to enjoy!

Member Since 1985   Mobil ★★★

"Unpretentious and Totally Relaxing" "Great Hospitality!"
"What a Gem!" "Super Food!"

Joshua Wilton House Inn and Restaurant
www.srinns.com/joshuawilton
412 S. Main St., Harrisonburg, VA 22801
888-294-5866 • 540-434-4464 • Fax 540-432-9525
info@joshuawilton.com

Innkeepers/Owners
Sean Pugh, Ann Marie Coe and Mark Newsome

Historic Victorian In Town Inn

Located in an elegantly restored Queen Anne Victorian, Joshua Wilton House offers guests an oasis of quiet charm and gracious living in the heart of the Shenandoah Valley. The home is within walking distance of historic downtown Harrisonburg and the campus of James Madison University. The Inn features five non-smoking bedrooms that have been decorated and furnished with beautiful antiques and reproductions. All rooms have one queen size bed, private baths, individually controlled thermostats, telephones, clock radios and hair dryers. Premium AVEDA amenities and luxurious terry cloth bathrobes are provided for your use during your stay. High-speed wireless internet service is available throughout the house. The first floor lounge is tastefully decorated and furnished with roomy high-backed leather chairs, a perfect place for a cocktail before dinner or a brandy by the fire after dinner.

Member Since 1985

Rooms/Rates
5 Rooms, $75/$150 B&B.
Number of Rooms: 5

Cuisine
The Restaurant offers an exquisite a la carte menu that changes with the seasons and an award-winning wine list. Featured are the food products of many small local farms and producers who supply our kitchen with high quality ingredients that simply cannot be found elsewhere. During the warmer months, seating is available on the outdoor brick patio. The restaurant is open from 5:00 PM, Tuesday through Saturday.

Nearest Airport(s)
Dulles - Washington, D.C.

Directions
412 S. Main St. I-81, exit 245, W on Port Rd. to Main St. N approx. 1 mi. To Joshua Wilton House located on R.

12+

"The best overnight we've ever had in a B&B."

Innkeeper/Owner
Michael Organ
General Manager
Dawn Pryor

Traditional Victorian
In Town Inn

The Belle Grae Inn and Restaurant
www.srinns.com/bellegrae
515 West Frederick St., Staunton, VA 24401-3333
888-541-5151 • 540-886-5151 • Fax 540-886-6641
bellegrae@adelphia.net

Rooms/Rates
13 Rooms, $139/$199; Suites, $169/239 B&B, MAP available. Honeymoon Hideaway, $199. Open year-round.
Number of Rooms: 13

Cuisine
Breakfast served daily at 9:00 AM. Dinner served Fri and Sat 5:30-9:00 PM. "Tapas" menu available daily for Inn guests and Friends. Full ABC available.

Nearest Airport(s)
Shenandoah Valley Regional (Weyers Cave) or Charlottesville

Directions
I-81 exit 220, 222 or 225. Follow signs to Woodrow Wilson Birthplace. W on Frederick St. (RT 250W and 254W) to 515 W. Frederick (red brick mansion on R). Circle block for registration and off-street parking.

This Italianate Victorian house is the centerpiece of numerous restored 1890s homes transformed into comfortable lodging rooms in a quaint, architecturally rich residential district in Historic Staunton. The graciously furnished rooms, bistro bar, Azalea Courtyard and garden paths leading to the guest houses create a tasteful small hotel ambience. The Inn is an easy walk to the shops and museums, and an easy drive to Colonial and Civil War History. Dining is a must at Belle Grae if you are staying over the weekend! The American Shakespeare Center is within walking distance.

AAA ◆◆◆   *Member Since 1990*   Mobil ★★★

12+

"Very private...personalized attention by staff and service...so Southern!"
"Fine dining, tasteful lodging..."

Frederick House

www.frederickhouse.com
28 North New Street, Staunton, VA 24401
800-334-5575 • 540-885-4220 • Fax 540-885-5180
stay@frederickhouse.com

Innkeepers/Owners
**Karen Cooksey &
Denny Eister**

Traditional In Town
Breakfast Inn

Frederick House's five beautifully restored 19th Century residences offer 23 spacious rooms and suites in award winning buildings. The buildings date from 1810 and offer guests an escape into the relaxed atmosphere of a bygone era. All rooms are individually decorated with antiques and period furniture. All offer private bathrooms, cable TV, telephone, internet access, alarm clocks, hair dryers and bathrobes. Frederick House is located in culturally rich historic downtown Staunton, the oldest city in the Shenandoah Valley. Staunton's historic downtown includes over 60 shops, restaurants, museums, galleries, concerts, the American Shakespeare Center's Blackfriars Playhouse, Woodrow Wilson Presidential Library, Mary Baldwin College and Stuart Hall. For that leisurely getaway, park your car and enjoy strolling downtown. From the Frederick House, explore the historical, cultural, and recreational opportunities that surround Staunton in the Shenandoah Valley. Visitors are always amazed at the variety of options to explore.

Rooms/Rates
12 Rooms, $95/$165; 11 Suites, $140/$225. "Shakespeare Theater Package" and "Drama, Dining, Heritage & Shopping Pleasures Package" available year-round. Other packages available. Open year-round.
Number of Rooms: 23

Cuisine
11 Restaurants available within walking distance; Fine Dining, Seafood, Steaks, American, Italian, Mexican, Ribs, Gourmet Deli, Southern Home Cooking, Casual and Coffee Shops.

Nearest Airport(s)
Shenandoah Valley Regional Airport or Charlottesville

Directions
From I-81 exit 222 follow Rt 250 West. Turn right on Coalter St. Take first left after the railroad overpass. Turn right on New St.

AAA ◆◆◆   *Member Since 1997*   Mobil ★★★

"You are TOPS! We were made to feel very welcome. The rooms were choc-full of antiques and felt like going back in time to a slower pace of life. Lots to do."

Innkeepers/Owners
The Sheehan family
since 1977

Elegant Plantation
Country Inn

🍴 🍴 🍴 🍷

🏮 paii

Prospect Hill Plantation Inn
www.srinns.com/prospecthill
Box 6909, Charlottesville, VA 22906
800-277-0844 • 540-967-0844 • Fax 540-967-0102
Innkeeper@prospecthill.com

Rooms/Rates
12 rms/suites from $195/$545 B&B, $295/$595 dbl MAP all-incl. pkgs w/gratuities.
Number of Rooms: 12

Cuisine
Elegant Continental-American cuisine. Wine and snacks on arrival, pre-dinner wine reception, 5-course candlelight dinner, full country breakfast-in-bed (or in dining room). All gratuities included with MAP pkgs.

Nearest Airport(s)
Charlottesville-Albemarle or Richmond Int'l

Directions
From C'ville (15 mi) East via I-64, exit 136 at Zion Crossroads. From Wash, DC (approx 100 mi) I-66 West to Hwy#29 S, to Hwy#15 South just past I-64, turn Left on Hwy#250E go 1 mile, left on Poindexter Rd, go 3 mi to Prospect Hill on left.

Award-winning country inn and restaurant on historic 1732 plantation located just 15 miles East of Charlottesville, VA. Romantic candlelight dining daily with all gratuities included in MAP package rates. 12 rooms and suites featuring breakfast-in-bed, working fireplaces, double Jacuzzis in eight rooms, swimming pool, gazebo on 40 acres of manicured grounds in the serenity of the coutryside near Jefferson's "Monticello," excellent wineries, and many other historic sites. Selected many times over the past 29 years as one of America's most romantic getaways. MAP Lodging Package rates include pre-dinner wine reception, candlelight dinner at table for two, full country breakfast-in-bed, and all gratuities. B&B, meeting, and other special rates available. Go to www.prospecthill.com for descriptions, rates, virtual tours of all rooms, sample menus.

Member Since 1979   Mobil ★★★

😊 🚭   💳💲📂❤   ✂📠@   ≋ 🏰 ◎ ✳ Ⓢ ☕

Silver Thatch Inn

www.srinns.com/silverthatch
3001 Hollymead Drive, Charlottesville, VA 22911
800-261-0720 • 434-978-4686 • Fax 434-973-6156
info@silverthatch.com

Innkeepers/Owners
Jim and Terri Petrovits

Traditional Colonial
Suburban Inn

This historic inn began its life as a barracks built in 1780 by Hessian soldiers captured during the Revolutionary War. As wings were added in 1812 and 1937, it served as a boys' school, a tobacco plantation, and a melon farm. It has been providing gracious lodging in antique-filled guest rooms and elegant candlelit dining since the 1970s. Relax and unwind in our intimate pub. Enjoy contemporary cuisine from our menu and wines from a list which has consistently won the *Wine Spectator* Award of Excellence and the *Wine Enthusiast* Award of Unique Distinction.

Rooms/Rates
7 Rooms, $155/$190 B&B. Open year-round.
Number of Rooms: 7

Cuisine
Breakfast for houseguests; Sunday Brunch; Dinner served Tues. - Sat., specializing in contemporary cuisine, featuring local produce when available and eclectic sauces. Open to the public. Great English Pub, outstanding selection of wine and spirits.

Nearest Airport(s)
Charlottesville/Albemarle Regional Airport, 2 miles.

Directions
From S: 6 miles N of intersection of US 29 & US 250 bypass, turn R on North Hollymead Dr. From N: 1 mile S of Airport Rd., turn L on North Hollymead Dr.

AAA ◆◆◆   *Member Since 1986*   Mobil ★★★

"I wanted to stay forever."

Innkeepers/Owners
John and Caryl Cowden

Rustic Mountain
Full-Service Inn

Fort Lewis Lodge
www.srinns.com/fortlewislodge
603 Old Plantation Way, Millboro, VA 24460
540-925-2314 • Fax 540-925-2352
ftlewis@tds.net

Rooms/Rates
13 Rooms, $175/$190 MAP; 3
Family Suites, $190 MAP; 3 Log
Cabins, $225/$275 MAP. Open
April–early November.
Number of Rooms: 19

Cuisine
Full dinner and breakfast included
in the daily room rate. Evening
meals offer a vibrant mix of fresh
tastes, just plucked vegetables
and interesting menus. The aroma
of hickoy smoke rising from the
grills will leave you yearning to
hear the dinner bell.

Nearest Airport(s)
Roanoke, VA (1.5 hrs.);
Charlottesville, VA (2 hrs.)

Directions
From Staunton, Rt. 254 W to Buffalo
Gap; Rt.42 to Millboro Spgs.; Rt. 39
W for .7 mi. to R onto Rt. 678, 10.8
mi. to L onto Rt. 625, sign on L.

Centuries old, wonderfully wild, uncommonly comfortable. A
country inn at the heart of a 3200-acre mountain estate. Outdoor activities abound with miles of river trout and bass fishing,
swimming, extensive hiking trails, mountain biking, and magnificent vistas. Fort Lewis is a rare combination of unpretentious
elegance and unique architecture offering a variety of lodging
choices where every room has a view. Three "in the round" silo
bedrooms, three hand-hewn log cabins with stone fireplaces, and
Riverside House are perfect for a true country getaway. Evenings
are highlighted by contemporary American-style cuisine served
in the historic Lewis Gristmill. Like most country inns, we trade
in a change of pace, romance and exceptional fare. But over the
years, we've come to understand that Fort Lewis has an asset that
very few others have. Our wilderness - the mountains, forests,
fields and streams and all the creatures that call this their home.

AAA ◆◆◆   *Member Since 1990*

"The mountains, the river, the stars ... it's my Shangri-la."

The Mark Addy

www.srinns.com/markaddy
56 Rodes Farm Drive, Nellysford, VA 22958
800–278–2154 • 434–361–1101 • Fax 434–361–2425
info@mark-addy.com

Innkeeper
Leslie Tal

Mountain Breakfast Inn

Sincere hospitality based on a family legacy of gracious living awaits refreshed spirits on the sunrise side of the Blue Ridge. Vested on a verdant knoll, the inn is surrounded by magnificent mountain views and pathways redolent of lavender. History buffs explore Mr. Jefferson's country. Hot air ballooning, hiking the highest waterfall east of the Mississippi, or skiing, challenge the adventurous. Serenity awaits in the hammock or luxuriating in a Jacuzzi, or stargazing from one of five porches that envelop the home. The memorable magic of our chef edifies local bounty and harvest with classic technique and contemporary regional inspiration. We want you to be our guest!

Rooms/Rates
5 Rooms $100/$135 B&B; 5 Deluxe Rooms $135/$195 B&B. Jacuzzis, guest kitchen with complimentary snacks, beverages. Open year round.
Number of Rooms: 10

Cuisine
Full breakfast, with an a la carte dinner menu available Wednesday through Saturday. Sunday Brunch. On/off-site catering for weddings and special affairs. Visit our website for cooking classes and special events.

Nearest Airport(s)
Charlottesville, Lynchburg

Directions
From I-64, Exit 107; turn W onto Rte. 250. After 5 miles, turn S on Rte. 151. Follow 10 miles. Turn R on Rodes Farm Drive (Rte. 613 W), first drive on R.

Member Since 2002

12+

"The most gracious hospitality we have experienced in years.
The cuisine was excellent!"

Innkeepers/Owners
Jeff & Becky Chanter

Rustic Mountain Inn

Sugar Tree Inn

www.sugartreeinn.com
P.O. Box 10, Hwy 56, Steeles Tavern, VA 24476
800-377-2197 • 540-377-2197 • Fax : please call
innkeeper@sugartreeinn.com

Rooms/Rates
9 Rooms, $150/$185; 1 Luxury Cabin, $245; 2 Suites, $170 & $185; includes our full country breakfast for 2. Creek House with 2 bedrooms, bath & full kitchen, $175 excluding breakfast.
Number of Rooms: 12

Cuisine
Gourmet four course dinners with a selection of entrees available Wednesday ~ Saturday by reservation.

Nearest Airport(s)
Roanoake

Directions
From I-81: Exit 205. E on Hwy 606 to Steeles Tavern. Turn L on Hwy 11 and then immediately R on Hwy. 56. Go up the mountain approx. 4.5 mi. to our sign. From Blue Ridge Parkway: (MP 27) W on Hwy. 56 approx. 3/4 mi. to our sign.

Recently featured as one of *Washingtonian* Magazine's "Most Romantic Inns" and called "Mountain Magic" by *Hampton Roads* Magazine! High above the Shenandoah Valley in the Blue Ridge Mountains, less than a mile from the Blue Ridge Parkway, is our haven of natural beauty. Set on twenty-eight wooded acres at 2800 feet, Virginia's Mountain Inn is a place of rustic elegance, peace and tranquility. Enjoy our 40-mile views, which are complimented by spring wildflowers, cool summer nights and brilliant fall colors. Each elegantly rustic room has a WOODBURNING FIREPLACE, incredibly comfortable bed, private bath, coffee maker, CD player, and is decorated with a colorful country quilt. A full breakfast is served in our glass-walled dining room and you can savor our fine evening dining by reservation.

AAA ◆◆◆   *Member Since 1998*

12+

"What a Mountain Inn should be: elegantly rustic, historic but comfortable, convenient but worlds away.... our B&B experience to date."

Inn at Warner Hall

www.srinns.com/warnerhall
4750 Warner Hall Road, Gloucester, VA 23061
800-331-2720 • 804-695-9565 • Fax 695-9566
info@warnerhall.com

Innkeepers / Owners
Theresa and Troy Stavens

Historic Waterfront
Country Inn

paii

Old world charm and new world amenities create the perfect balance between luxury and history in this beautifully restored romantic waterfront retreat. Established in 1642 by George Washington's Great, Great Grandfather, Warner Hall beckons guests to relax and enjoy. Comfortable elegance, fabulous food and attentive, friendly service are the essence of Warner Hall. Spacious guest rooms combine sumptuous antiques, fabrics and art with modern conveniences. Many rooms offer fireplaces, Jacuzzis or steam showers – all have spectacular views. Experience Chef Eric Garcia's delicious cuisine paired with a bottle of fine wine. Explore the historic triangle of Williamsburg, Yorktown and Gloucester, or simply relax at the Inn's charming boathouse. Ideally situated at the head of the Severn River surrounded by 500 acres of fields and forest, Warner Hall resonates with tranquility and southern hospitality.

National Register of Historic Places. Recommended by *Travel + Leisure*, *Hampton Roads Magazine*, *Virginian Pilot* and *Free Lance Star*.

Member Since 2006

Rooms/Rates
$150/$220 Mon.-Thurs.
$170/$245 Fri-Sun.
Number of Rooms: 11

Cuisine
Extraordinary breakfasts included. Chef's Tasting Dinners Fri./ Sat., or by special reservation. Cocktail and wine bar. Gourmet supper baskets Sun–Thurs. Box lunches daily.

Nearest Airport(s)
Nearest Airports Richmond / Norfolk

Directions
I-64 to Williamsburg area. Follow signs for Colonial Pkwy/Yorktown. Exit Rt. 17 N. Cross York River, proceed 6.5 mi. Turn R onto Rte. 614/Featherbed Lane. Go 2.3 mi. and turn R onto Warner Hall Rd/Rt. 629. Go 1 mi. Inn on R.

8+

"All we can say is "WOW"!... Unbelievable food & hospitality...What a beautiful, romantic place...something magical. We WILL be back!"

Innkeepers/Owners
Linda and Lynn Hayes
Assistant Innkeeper
Eric Hanson

Contemporary
Mountain Inn

🍽️ 🍽️ 🍽️

Inn at Riverbend
www.srinns.com/innatriverbend
125 River Ridge Drive, Pearisburg, VA 24134-2391
540-921-5211 • 540-599-6400 • Fax 540-921-2720
stay@innatriverbend.com

Rooms/Rates
7 rooms $130/$240. Closed
Thanksgiving week.
Number of Rooms: 7

Cuisine
Full plated breakfast featuring
fresh local ingredients. Guests
welcome to bring their own
spirits. Early hiker, birder or
business breakfast available.
Picnic and candlelight dinner with
prior reservation. Fine Dining at
"The Bank Food and Drink" just
3 mi. away.

Nearest Airport(s)
Roanoke-ROA

Directions
Located between 1-81 and 1-77,
2 mi. off Hwy 460. Exit 460 Business at Ripplemead/Pearisburg, to
1st light (Walmart) and turn L. L
again at Virginia Hts, to Riverbend
Dr. L at River Ridge.

Newly constructed in 2003, Inn at Riverbend sits on 13 acres on a hilltop overlooking the oldest river in the United States, the New River. Designed to view the mountains and river from the great room, TV room and each guestroom; spacious, decks and terraces provide plenty of space to enjoy the panoramic views, bird watch and even spot a deer or two in the lower meadow. The distant sound of the train sets the tone for a restful sleep. Perfect for romantic getaways, outdoor enthusiasts, retreats and family gatherings. All rooms feature private baths, large closets, pressed sheets, robes, satellite TV, wireless Internet and luxury amenities. Enjoy afternoon refreshments, the endless cookie jar, weekend evening social hour with the other guests, turn-down service and a sumptuous breakfast. Just two miles from the Appalachian Trail. Let us help plan a hike, a trip down the river or a picnic at the Cascades Waterfalls! Dinner is available Friday, Sunday and Monday.

Member Since 2005

13+ 🚭 ♿ 💳 🕐 📁 ♥ ✂️ 📷 @ 🧺 ◎ ❄️ ☕

"Almost heaven, Inn at Riverbend...What a place! What a view!"

The Oaks Victorian Inn

www.srinns.com/theoaksinn
311 East Main St., Christiansburg, VA 24073
800–336–6257 • 540–381–1500 • Fax 540–381–3036

Owners and Hosts
Lois and John Ioviero

Elegant Victorian
Village Breakfast Inn

Warm hospitality, comfortable, relaxed elegance and memorable breakfasts are the hallmark of The Oaks, a century-old Queen Anne Victorian on the National Register of Historic Places. Set on Christiansburg's highest hill in the beautiful mountain highlands of Southwest Virginia, The Oaks delights and welcomes leisure and business travelers from around the world. Surrounded by lawn, perennial gardens and 300 year-old oak trees, the inn faces Main Street, once part of the Wilderness Trail blazed by Daniel Boone and Davey Crockett. Fireplaces and beautiful private baths with Jacuzzis for romantics. Private telephones, wireless DSL, cable TV, DVD/VCR and stocked refrigerators in all rooms. Discover the historic places of the New River, Roanoke and Shenandoah Valleys, the majestic grandeur of the Blue Ridge Parkway. Visit Virginia's wine industry or search for antiques, collectibles and crafts. The region provides the best in recreational attractions–bike trails, hiking, boating and golf...or just relax on the world class porch!

Rooms/Rates
7 Rooms, $150/$200 B&B; $99 Corp. rate Sun. though Thu., Sgl. Only. Extended stay suites/7 days + (EP) (check rates). Open year-round.
Number of Rooms: 7

Cuisine
3-course breakfast by candlelight, excellent restaurants for dinner nearby.

Nearest Airport(s)
Roanoke, 30 miles

Directions
From I-81 Exit 114 (Main St.) just 2 miles on the corner of E Main & Park. From Blue Ridge Pkwy.: Take Rt. 8 (MP165) west 28 miles to The Oaks. Also near US 460. 38 miles north of I-77 and I-81 Interchange.

AAA ◆◆◆◆   *Member Since 1993*   Mobil ★★★

12+ 🚭   💳 ① 🗁 ♥ ⊶ ✗ 🖎 @   🗺 ◎

"Thank you for all you do to make our stay so pleasant. The best breakfast we've ever had."

Washington

"The Evergreen State"

Famous For: Mount St. Helens, Redwoods, Olympic National Park, Grand Coulee Dam, Space Needle, Pike Place Market, Puget Sound, San Juan Islands, Mount Rainer, Kettle Falls, Cascade Mountains, Apples, Jets, Hi–Tech.

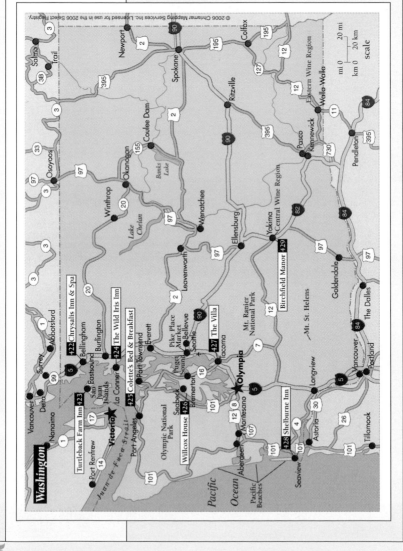

© 2006 Christmas Mapping Services Inc. Licensed for use in the 2006 Select Registry

422 Chrysalis Inn & Spa
423 Turtleback Farm Inn
424 The Wild Iris Inn
425 Colette's Bed & Breakfast
426 Willcox House
427 The Villa
428 Shelburne Inn
429 Birchfield Manor

Chrysalis Inn & Spa

www.srinns.com/chrysalis
804 10th St., Bellingham, WA 98225
888-808-0005 • 360-756-1005 • Fax 360-647-0342
info@thechrysalisinn.com

Innkeepers/Owners
J. Michael and Lisa Keenan
Operations Manager
Julia Stiner
Contemporary
Waterside Inn

Situated on Bellingham Bay, just blocks from Historic Fairhaven, The Chrysalis invites guests to relax and unwind. From the moment you enter you sense a special place as you view the bay from the floor to ceiling windows in the living room. Enjoy the shops and restaurants in Fairhaven, stroll along the waterfront in Boulevard Park or just relax on your windowseat and watch the activity on the bay. Our spa offers massages, facials, hydrotherapy tub treatments, body treatments, manicures and pedicures, all designed to rejuvenate the body, mind and soul. Perfect for small business meetings and retreats, we can accomodate groups up to 45 in our two meeting rooms, and we offer on site catering.

Rooms/Rates
34 Deluxe Rooms, $169/$209, 9 Suites, $209/$289. All have fireplaces, window seats, 2 person tubs. Breakfast is included.
Number of Rooms: 43

Cuisine
Fino is our full service wine bar and restaurant featuring classic foods and wines of Europe. Lunch and dinner daily, room service and outdoor dining.

Nearest Airport(s)
Bellingham Airport

Directions
Bellingham is 90 miles north of Seattle and 50 miles south of Vancouver BC, Canada. Take exit 250 off of I-5 and head west to stop light at 12th St. (about 1.2 miles). Turn right on 12th and proceed approximately 1/2 mile to Taylor, turn left. Turn right on 10th.

AAA ◆◆◆   *Member Since 2003*

"What a way to celebrate life." "We love it here."
"Beautiful, indulgent, wonderful."

Innkeepers/Owners
William C. & Susan C. Fletcher

Traditional Country Breakfast Inn

Turtleback Farm Inn and Orchard House
www.srinns.com/turtlebackfarm
1981 Crow Valley Road, Eastsound, WA 98245
800-376-4914 • 360-376-4914 • Fax 360-376-5329
info@turtlebackinn.com

Rooms/Rates
11 Rooms. $100/$245 B&B.
Open year-round.
Number of Rooms: 11

Cuisine
Full breakfast, beverages anytime, fruit, freshly baked treats and complimentary sherry. Picnic baskets prepared. Luncheons and dinners catered for private parties. BYOB.

Nearest Airport(s)
Eastsound - 4 miles

Directions
From Orcas Ferry Landing: Follow the Orcas Road N 2.9mi, turn L, .9 mi to first R, continue N on Crow Valley Road 2.4 mi. to Inn.

THE FARMHOUSE and ORCHARD HOUSE is located on Orcas Island, the loveliest of the San Juan Islands. This graceful and comfortable Inn is considered one of the most romantic places in the country. Highlighted by a spectacular setting, the Inn is a haven for those who enjoy breathtaking scenery, comfortable accommodations and award-winning breakfasts. The island offers unique shopping, fine dining and varied outdoor activities: hiking, swimming, sea-kayaking, whale watching, sailing, fishing, birding, golf and bicycling. Turtleback Farm Inn is the perfect spot for the discriminating traveler to experience a step back to a quieter time.

Hideaway Report, "1000 PLACES TO SEE BEFORE YOU DIE."

AAA ◆◆◆   *Member Since 1991*   Mobil ★★★

"A marvel of bed and breakfastmanship full of tasteful personal touches and tender care. You are a model by which other innkeepers could use.."

The Wild Iris Inn

www.srinns.com/wildiris
121 Maple Avenue, P.O. Box 696, LaConner, WA 98257
800-477-1400 • 360-466-1400
info@wildiris.com

Innkeepers/Owners
Stephen & Lori Farnell
Contemporary
Village Inn

The award winning Wild Iris Inn and LaConner, Washington, an outstanding year-round destination, are a short drive from Seattle and Vancouver, British Columbia, but "miles" away. The Inn's convenient location is perfect for your exploration of the Pacific Northwest; located just 20 minutes from the ferry terminals that lead to the San Juan Islands, Victoria, BC and points beyond. Each season brings wonderful changes to LaConner. In winter, swans and snow geese cover the fields in a sea of white. The farmlands are brightly colored with daffodils in March, world famous tulips in April, iris in May, and dahlias in August. In summer, whale watching cruises leave LaConner each day and follow magnificent orcas in the North Puget Sound. The highlight of your stay, however, will be the hospitality, service and amenities of The Wild Iris Inn. Guest suites feature spa tubs, fireplaces and decks facing the Cascade Mountains, as well as all of the amenities you would expect from a Select Registry property.

Rooms/Rates
12 Guest Suites w/King beds, spa tubs, fireplaces & private decks $149/$199 B&B. 5 Casual Guest Rooms w/King beds and 1 with 2 twin beds $109/$129 B&B. Open Year Round.
Number of Rooms: 18

Cuisine
A full breakfast including fresh baked goods, homemade granola, hot entrees and fresh fruits is served each morning at tables for two. In-room and early departure breakfast options.

Nearest Airport(s)
Seattle & Vancouver

Directions
By Land: 1 hour N of Seattle. 1 1/2 hours S of Vancouver, BC. 9 mi. W of I-5. By Sea: 20 min. from the San Juan Islands & Victoria, BC ferry in Anacortes.

Member Since 2003

"This is an amazing place. The attention to detail and warm hospitality made us feel truly pampered. We loved everything about our stay!"

Colette's Bed & Breakfast

Innkeepers/Owners
Lynda & Peter Clark

Luxury Oceanfront Estate

🍽️

www.srinns.com/colettes
339 Finn Hall Road, Port Angeles, WA 98362
877-457-9777 • 360-457-9197 • Fax 360-452-0711
colettes@olypen.com

Rooms/Rates
Luxury King Suites $175/$375
Number of Rooms: 5

Cuisine
Our chef has created an exciting variety of culinary delights. Enjoy your multi-course, gourmet breakfast served with a panoramic view of the Strait of Juan de Fuca and the San Juan Islands.

Nearest Airport(s)
Seattle and Port Angeles

Directions
Two hours from Seattle via the Bainbridge ferry. Hwy 305 to 3 to 104 to 101 around Sequim. Travel 4.8 miles past the Sequim Ave. exit, R on Kitchen-Dick Road. Drive 1.5 miles to Old Olympic Hwy, turn L drive 2.5 miles to Matson road and turn R. Drive .5 to Finn Hall Road and turn L, drive .9 miles.

Colette's is a breathtaking 10 acre oceanfront estate nestled between the majestic Olympic Range and the picturesque Strait of Juan de Fuca. This unique area is the gateway to Olympic National Park, a world of fog-shrouded coast with booming surf, wave-manicured beaches, spectacular alpine country and sweeping vistas in every direction. Each perfect day at Colette's starts with a gourmet multi-course breakfast. Luxurious King Suites with magnificent oceanfront views, romantic fireplaces, and indulgent two-person Jacuzzi spas rejuvenate guests at the end of the day. Stroll through Colette's 10 acre outdoor sanctuary which includes enchanting gardens, towering cedars and lush evergreen forest. Fodor's Pacific Northwest - "Top Choice" for the Olympic Peninsula - considered the very best. Karen Brown's Guide Pacific Northwest - "Top Pick". Best Places to Kiss Pacific Northwest "Highest Rating" - 4 Kisses.

AAA ◆◆◆   *Member Since 2003*

Fodor's Pacific Northwest "Top Choice" - considered the very best.
Best Places to Kiss Pacific Northwest "Highest Rating" - 4 Kisses.

Willcox House Country Inn

www.srinns.com/willcox
2390 Tekiu Rd. NW, Seabeck, WA 98380
800-725-9477 • 360-830-4492 • Fax 360-830-0506

Innkeepers/Owners
Cecilia and Phillip Hughes

Elegant Waterside Inn

With spectacular views of Hood Canal and the Olympic Mountains, this waterfront Country House Inn is situated in a forest setting beween Seattle and the Olympic Peninsula. The historic 1930s mansion estate offers beautiful gardens with fish ponds. Walk our oyster-laden saltwater beach. Enjoy the peace and serenity. Period pieces and antiques are featured in guest rooms, the great room, billiard room, pub, library, theater, and dining room. *Country Inns* magazine award: One of the top twelve inns in North America. Featured on *Great Country Inns* T.V. series. Golfing, birding, and hiking nearby.

Rooms/Rates
5 Rooms, $149/$229 B&B. Open year-round.
Number of Rooms: 5

Cuisine
Breakfast, afternoon wine and cheese included. Dinner available. Complimentary hot beverages. Large selection of wine and beer.

Nearest Airport(s)
Seattle

Directions
17 miles W of Bremerton on Hood Canal, near Holly.

AAA ◆◆◆   *Member Since 1993*

12+

"A jewel within an emerald forest."

SelectRegistry.com

Innkeepers/Owners
Kristy and Aaron House

Historic In Town
Breakfast Inn

🍴

The Villa
www.srinns.com/thevilla
705 N. 5th Street, Tacoma, WA 98403
888-572-1157 • 253-572-1157
villabb@aol.com

Rooms/Rates
6 Rms/Suites, K/Q, $135/$235 B&B. Fireplaces, TV/CD/stereos, soaking/spa tubs, separate showers, private verandahs, mountain/water views, phones/dataports.
Number of Rooms: 6

Cuisine
3-course breakfast 7, 8, 9 AM weekdays, 8:30, 10 AM weekends. Complimentary fine wines, ale, pop, cookies & snacks all day. Award-winning waterfront restaurants nearby.

Nearest Airport(s)
Sea-Tac Airport

Directions
From I-5 N or S, take exit 133, I-705 N. Exit to Schuster Pkwy, then exit to Stadium Way. At first light R on Stadium Way; at next light R on Tacoma Ave. N; then L on N 5th St., 1 block on R.

Beautifully appointed and spotless, this Italian Renaissance mansion on the Historic Register is attractively furnished in Italian Country decor. The Villa overlooks the peaceful Stadium Historic District with views expanding to Puget Sound and the majestic Olympic Mountains. Amenities include European linen sheets, Egyptian cotton robes and plush towels. Artistically landscaped, The Villa features heritage rose gardens. Truly a place to relax your body and revive your spirit, yet located centrally to the most popular NW attractions. 1/2 hour from Seattle Airport. Rated 'excellent' by *Mobil, NW Best Places* and *Best Places to Kiss NW*. Full business services.

Member Since 2000   Mobil ★★★

12+ 🚭 ♿ 💳 ⓘ 📁 ♥ ⊶   ✍ @   📺 ◎

Shelburne Inn & China Beach Retreat

www.srinns.com/shelburne

P.O. Box 250, 4415 Pacific Way, Seaview and Ilwaco, WA 98644
800-INN-1896 • 360-642-2442 • Fax 360-642-8904
innkeeper@theshelburneinn.com

Innkeepers/Owners
David Campiche and Laurie Anderson

Traditional Victorian Village Inn

An unspoiled 28-mile stretch of wild Pacific seacoast is just a short walk through rolling sand dunes from this inviting Country Inn, built in 1896. Art Nouveau stained glass windows and period antiques highlight the Inn. A sumptuous gourmet breakfast featuring the best of the Northwest is complimentary. Innovative cuisine and a discriminating wine list have brought international recognition to the restaurant and pub. Discover the western end of the Lewis and Clark trail and our China Beach Retreat with national historic sites and Discovery Trail, paralleling the majestic Pacific Ocean. New Audibon Cottage is the jewel in the crown.

Selected as 'Best Bed & Breakfast in the Northwest', *NW Palate* Readers' Favorites. Selected as one of the 'West's Best Small Inns,' by *Sunset* Magazine, February, 2001. Featured in the January 2003 issue of Martha Stewart *Living*. ★★★ 1/2 *NW Best Places*. 100 Best Hotel/Restaurants, 2006 *USA Today*. 'Breakfast at the Shelburne is like art to the Louvre.' *St. Louis Post*.

Member Since 1988

Rooms/Rates
13 Rooms, $135/$175 B&B; 2 Suites, $195 B&B. Additional off-site waterside B&B; two Rooms $199; 1 Suite $229. Audibon Cottege: $279.
Number of Rooms: 18

Cuisine
Gourmet Regional Cuisine features the best seasonal and local ingredients. Restaurant and Pub offer lunch and dinner featuring fine NW wines, microbrewed beer and liquor. Innkeepers' Breakfast served daily and offers creative preparations to choose from.

Nearest Airport(s)
Portland International

Directions
From Seattle, I-5 (S) to Olympia, Hwy. 8 & 12 to Montesano & Hwy. 107 then 101(S) to Seaview; From OR coast, U.S. 101N across Astoria Bridge L. to Seaview.

"This was our first B&B experience and we felt like we started at thr top."
"Best breakfast in the Pacific Northwest." "An oasis of civility."

Birchfield Manor Country Inn

Innkeepers/Owners
The Masset Family

Traditional Country Inn

www.srinns.com/birchfieldmanor
2018 Birchfield Road, Yakima, WA 98901
800-375-3420 • 509-452-1960 • Fax 509-452-2334
birchfield@ewa.net

Rooms/Rates
$119/$219 B&B.
Number of Rooms: 11

Cuisine
Award-winning Northwest cuisine in a casual relaxed atmosphere.

Nearest Airport(s)
Yakima Airport approx. 7 miles

Directions
I-82 to Yakima, exit 34. Go E 2 miles, turn R (south) on Birchfield Road. First house on R.

Yakima's true Country Inn only two miles from town. We offer a relaxing getaway with award-winning multi course dinners prepared by professional chef/owners served in the casual warm atmosphere of a gracious home. Park-like grounds surround the outdoor pool. Choose from the extensive selections of Washington wines from our *Wine Spectator, Wine Enthusiast* and Northwest Wine Press award winning list—and you may find your favorite winemaker at the next table! Most rooms w/fireplace, two-person tub, panoramic views. We can personalize a tour of local wineries, direct you to roadside stands for fresh fruit and vegetables, or you may talk to Brad or Tim for tee times at the local golf courses.

AAA ◆◆◆   *Member Since 1993*   Mobil ★★★

12+ 🚭 ♿ 💳   📁   ✒ @   ≋ 🖼 ◎

"Restaurant of the Year" Award – Washington Wine Growers Association

"The Mountain State"

Famous For: Appalachian Mountains, Monongahela
National Forest, White Sulphur Springs, Harper's Ferry
National Historical Park, Smoke Hole Caverns,
Apple Butter Festival, Grave Creek Burial Mounds,
Country Music, Coal, Oil, Gas

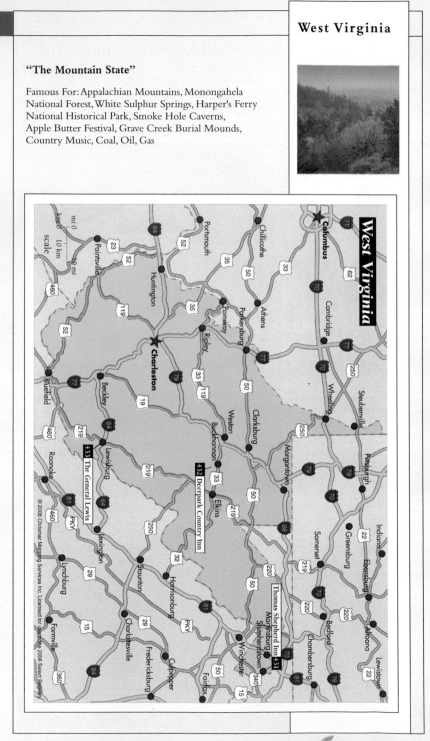

West Virginia

Columbus

Charleston

†33 The General Lewis

†32 Deerpark Country Inn

Thomas Shepherd Inn †31

© 2006 Christmas Mapping Services Inc. Licensed for use in the 2006 Select Registry

Thomas Shepherd Inn

Innkeepers/Owners
Jeanne Muir & Jim Ford

Traditional In-Town
Breakfast Inn

www.srinns.com/thomasshepherdinn
300 W. German Street, P.O. Box 3634
Shepherdstown, WV 25443
888-889-8952 • 304-876-3715
info@thomasshepherdinn.com

Rooms/Rates
$110/$165-lower rates apply
Mon-Thurs & off-season. Rates
double occupancy; 2-night min
stay on Saturdays & holidays.
Senior & corp discounts available
most weekdays.
Number of Rooms: 6

Cuisine
Full homemade breakfast daily
w/fruit, entree, meat, baked goods;
early beverage service with
signature spice biscotti. Walk to
several restaurants.

Nearest Airport(s)
BWI & Dulles airports-70 miles.

Directions
Corner of German & Duke Streets
at 4-way stop sign-intersection
of Routes 230, 45 & 480. See
website/call for area directions.
Parking beside & behind Inn.

We invite you to stay in our bed & breakfast inn, with six "inviting, well kept and beautifully decorated" guest rooms with private baths and air conditioning. Built in 1868, the Inn has offered hospitality to guests for over 20 years. Relax in front of the living room fireplace or on the back porch overlooking the garden and start your day with a generous homemade breakfast.

Shepherdstown, a hidden gem for weary urbanites, is less than two hours from Washington, DC, or Baltimore. The town has a vibrant cultural scene, ranging from premiere plays at the Contemporary American Theater Festival, to independent movies at the Opera House, to music and crafts festivals featuring local and nationally-known artists. Unique shops with artisan crafts and over a dozen restaurants serving flavorful meals fill the historic buildings on German Street. Rich American history is only a few minutes away at Antietam Battlefield or Harpers Ferry. Biking, hiking and rafting abound along the C&O Canal Path or on the Potomac or Shenandoah rivers.

Member Since 2006

12+ ♿ 💳 ⎆ @ 🗼 ✺

'You didn't miss a thing-the room was lovely, bed very comfortable-breakfasts
were more than ample & quite delicious. Hope to return some day.'

Deerpark Country Inn

www.srinns.com/deerpark
P.O. Box 817, Buckhannon, WV 26201
800-296-8430 • 304-472-8400 • Fax 304-472-5363
deerpark@deerparkcountryinn.com

Owners
Liz and Patrick Haynes

Traditional Country
Inn

Liz and Patrick Haynes invite you to surround yourself with 100 acres of rejuvinating country ambiance that reflects a by-gone era. The inn includes an 18th Century log cabin, a post-Civil War farm house and a newly constructed Victorian wing. Detailed period architecture is featured throughout. About 400 feet from the inn is the two story lodge, a 19th Century log cabin with attached wing, offering three gracious bedrooms, a fireplace as large as a man is tall, and french doors that open onto two wrap around porches...perfect for watching fireflies or shooting stars or snowflakes falling on deep pine forests. All the rooms and suites of both buildings are richly furnished with fine antiques and collectibles, ferns and fresh flowers and crisp cotton linens; each presents its own personality as well as central air, private bath and other amenities. Mist rises from the pond that invites you to fish under the watchful eye of resident mallards and clannishly arrogant geese. Let us design a special getaway package for you.

Member Since 1999

Rooms/Rates
DBL occupancy, 4 Rooms and 2 Suites. $125/$185. B&B, private baths, phone, A/C, TV, VCR/DVD. Open year-round.
Number of Rooms: 6

Cuisine
Gourmet breakfast daily. Full bar (honor system) on premises. Dinner service by request 8 or more persons. Several fine dining restaurants in the area. Catered events on site-weddings and reunions.

Nearest Airport(s)
Buckhannon Airport

Directions
From I-79: Exit 99, US 33-E, go 4 miles past Buckhannon, turn R at Keesling Mill SIGN, turn left on 151-E. When on 151-E, turn L and travel .7 mile to Heavener Grove Rd., turn R. 1.3 miles to Deerpark sign on R.

"A great discovery! Worth every inch of a 500 mile trip."

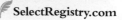

Innkeepers/Owners
The Morgan Family

Traditional Village Inn

The General Lewis Inn
www.srinns.com/generallewisinn
301 East Washington St., Lewisburg, WV 24901
800-628-4454 • Fax 304-645-2601
info@generallewisinn.com

Rooms/Rates
23 Rooms, $99/$150 EP;
2 Suites, $148/$168 EP. Open
year-round. Romantic Getaway
packages available December
through March. Holidays and
special events not available for
reduced rates.
Number of Rooms: 25

Cuisine
Breakfast, lunch and dinner.
Wine and liquor available.

Nearest Airport(s)
Greenbrier Valley Airport
Lewisburg, WV, 15 mins. away.

Directions
I-64, Lewisburg exit 169, 219
South for 1.5 miles to 60 East,
turn left and we are three blocks
up on the right.

Come rock in a chair on the veranda of the Inn. On chilly days, dream by the fireplace, solve one of the puzzles or play a fascinating game. Enjoy Memory Hall's display of old tools for home and farm which the first family members began collecting even before they opened the Inn. Cat and dog live here. Antiques furnish every room, including canopy, spool and poster beds. Lewisburg offers antique shops, fine arts and crafts, live year round theater and music with the unique flavor of a town named as one of the best small arts towns in America. The dining room in the 1834 wing features Southern cooking. Enjoy your dining experience with specialty foods, hot homemade bread and desserts, a full service bar and wine list. Lewisburg has been designated by the National Trust for Historic Preservation as one of the "12 Most Desirable Vacation Destinations" (2004). We're located on the Midland Trail, a national scenic byway and the site of the 1862 Battle of Lewisburg. The Inn has been owned and operated by the same family since 1929.

AAA ◆◆◆   *Member Since 1973*   Mobil ★★★

"...a country guest house...enjoy the lovely common areas with antiques everywhere..." Frommer's

"The Badger State"

Famous For: Wisconsin Dells, Apostle Islands
National Lakeshore, Lake Superior, Mirror Lake State Park,
House on the Rock (a 1940s retreat built on a 60-foot rock
outcropping overlooking a 450 ft drop) Dairy, Beer,
Cranberry Fest, Fresh Water Fishing.

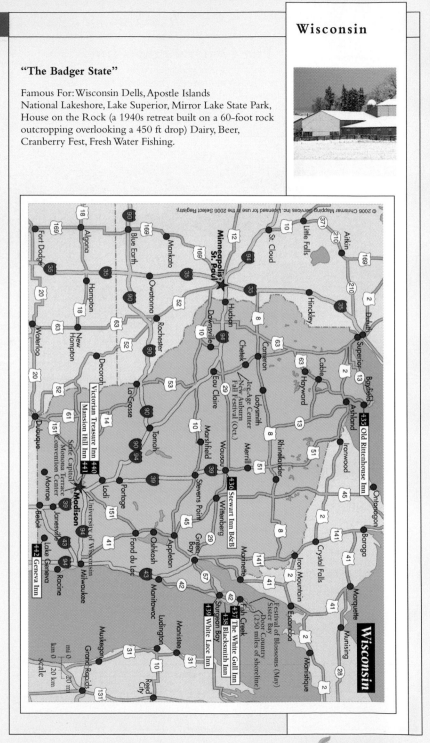

© 2006 Christmas Mapping Services Inc, licensed for use in the 2006 Select Registry.

Minneapolis/St. Paul

Duluth

Superior

Madison

Milwaukee

Victorian Treasure Inn
Mansion Hill Inn #40 #41

State Capitol
Monona Terrace
Convention Center
University of Wisconsin

Lake Geneva Inn #42

Stewart Inn B&B #36

Old Rittenhouse Inn #35

The White Gull Inn #37
Blacksmith Inn #38
White Lace Inn #39
Sturgeon Bay
Fish Creek #42

Festival of Blossoms (May)
Sister Bay
Door Country
(250 miles of shoreline)

New Auburn
Fall Festival (Oct.)
Ice-Age Center

Innkeepers/Owners
Jerry & Mary Phillips

Elegant Victorian
Village Inn

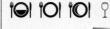

Old Rittenhouse Inn
www.rittenhouseinn.com
301 Rittenhouse Ave., P.O. Box 584, Bayfield, WI 54814
888-560-4667 • 715-779-5111 • Fax 715-779-5887
Gourmet@RittenhouseInn.com

Rooms/Rates
10 rooms $109/$199 B&B; 14 rooms/suites with whirlpools $139/$299 B&B; 1 Cottage, $299 B&B; All rooms have private baths. Most have fireplaces, many with lake views.
Number of Rooms: 25

Cuisine
Serving a creative regional menu. Bayfield peninsula's freshest ingredients combined with flavorful sauces, seasonal specialties, and gourmet artistry. Serving breakfast, lunch and dinner. Featured in *Gourmet Magazine*, and *Bon Appetit*.

Nearest Airport(s)
Madeline Island - 4 miles

Directions
Duluth E on Hwy 2 for 60 miles, to N on Hwy 13 for 21 miles. Located on Rittenhouse Avenue and Third Street in the heart of Bayfield.

Victorian lodging and dining, with guestrooms in two historic Queen Anne-style mansions, guesthouse and private cottage all located within Bayfield's 52 block historic district. A stay at the Old Rittenhouse Inn combines romance and elegance with gourmet cuisine and comfortable lodging. Guestrooms are beautifully appointed with antique furnishings. Amenities include wood burning fireplaces, private baths, breath-taking views of Lake Superior, and luxurious whirlpools. Open all year offering romantic winter get-aways, wine, beer, martini, and margarita weekends, wassail dinner concerts, mystery weekends, antiques weekends, life-coaching weekends, chocolate weekends and spring theatre weekends.

AAA ◆◆◆   *Member Since 1980*

Voted Wisconsin's Most Romantic Inn by the readers
of *Wisconsin Trails Magazine.*

The Stewart Inn Bed and Breakfast

www.srinns.com/stewartinn
521 Grant Street, Wausau, WI 54403
715-849-5858 • Fax 715-845-3692
innkeeper@stewartinn.com

Innkeepers/Owners
Paul and Jane Welter
Downtown
Historic Mansion

Located in the historic downtown Wausau River District, the Stewart Inn offers upscale accommodations in an authentic National Register Arts and Crafts masterpiece. Public rooms on the first floor of this Prairie Style mansion retain the incredible architectural detail created 100 years ago by Chicago architect, George W. Maher, a contemporary and associate of Frank Lloyd Wright. The second floor serves as an exclusive five-room boutique hotel where the owners take pride in providing guests with the highest level of personal service. Each of the newly renovated guest rooms has an extraordinary ensuite bath and tasteful combination of modern amenities and historic charm, sure to please even the most discriminating travelers. The Inn is fully equipped for the business traveler and offers a comfortable, secure alternative to conventional lodging. Restaurants, shops, museums, and entertainment are all within walking distance. If you're traveling with a dog, you'll find the accommodations extremely pet-friendly.

Rooms/Rates
$150/$195 weekdays, $170/$215 weekends. Business rates available. Closed April. All rooms have private bath, steam shower, air conditioning, premium bedding, cable TV/DVD/CD, desk, telephone, wireless Internet.
Number of Rooms: 5

Cuisine
Full gourmet breakfast, afternoon wine and cheese, evening cookies and milk.

Nearest Airport(s)
Central Wisconsin Airport

Directions
From I39/Hwy 51 take Exit 192, to Hwy 52 East. Go 2 miles and cross the Wisconsin River. Turn left (North) on 1st Street and go 4 blocks to Grant Street. Turn right (East) and go 4 1/2 blocks to 521 Grant Street.

AAA ◆◆◆ *Member Since 2005*

"You remain our standard for B&B and Inn stays, and we have yet to find anything close. Your hospitality made the marvelous setting even better."

Innkeepers
Andy & Jan Coulson

Traditional Village
Inn

White Gull Inn
www.srinns.com/whitegullinn

4225 Main Street, P.O. Box 160, Fish Creek, WI 54212
800-625-8813 • 920-868-3517 • Fax 920-868-2367
innkeeper@whitegullinn.com

Rooms/Rates
6 Rooms, $140/$205; 7 Suites, $205/$265; 4 Cottages (1,2 and 4 bedroom), $219/$425. Includes full breakfast. Winter and Shoulder Season Packages. Open year-round.
Number of Rooms: 17

Cuisine
Hearty full breakfast included, lunches daily, and dinner from the menu or traditional Door County fish boil served nightly. Wine and beer available. Dining room open to the public.

Nearest Airport(s)
Austin Straubel Field, Green Bay (75 miles)

Directions
Milwaukee I-43 for 98 mi. to Green Bay, then Rte. 57 N for 39 miles to Sturgeon Bay; N on Rte. 42 for 25 mi. to Fish Creek, L at stop sign for 3 Blks.

Established in 1896, this white clapboard Inn is tucked away in the scenic bayside village of Fish Creek, on Wisconsin's Door Peninsula. Turn of the century antiques, fireplaces and meticulously restored and exquisitely decorated rooms and cottages provide a warm, hospitable atmosphere. Renowned for hearty breakfasts, sumptuous lunches and candlelit dinners, the Inn is famous for its traditional Door County fish boils, featuring locally caught Lake Michigan whitefish cooked outside over an open fire. Close to summer stock theater, music festivals, art galleries, antique stores and every imaginable recreational activity, from golf to wind surfing, from hiking to cross country skiing.

AAA ◆◆◆   *Member Since 1979*   Mobil ★★★

"The room is lovely – fireplace, Jacuzzi, shower, sitting room. Restaurant is magnificent."

Blacksmith Inn On the Shore

www.srinns.com/blacksmith
8152 Highway 57, Baileys Harbor, WI 54202
800-769-8619 • 920-839-9222 • Fax 920-839-9356
relax@theblacksmithinn.com

Owners
**Joan Holliday and
Bryan Nelson**

Traditional Waterside
Breakfast Inn

Awaken to the sound of waves lapping the shore as the morning sunlight glistens on the water. Linger over breakfast on our sun-washed porch. Kayak in summer, snowshoe the harbor edge in winter. Step out our door to hike the nearby Ridges Wildlife Sanctuary. Bike a sleepy backroad to explore Cana Island Lighthouse. Bask in your whirlpool as you take in the warm glow of the fire. Stroll to nearby village restaurants and shops. Revel in an extraordinary view of the harbor any time of year. Complete privacy with all the amenities including, water views, balconies, in-room whirlpools, fireplaces, canopied beds, fine linens, down pillows, TV/DVD/CD with in-house DVD library, individually controlled heat & air conditioning, free wireless internet, ipod docks, phones with data ports, in-room refrigerators and a bottomless cookie jar! Door County offers art galleries, antiquing, music, theater and miles and miles of shoreline. Romance & relaxation are yours at the Blacksmith Inn On the Shore, located in the heart of the Door County Peninsula.

Rooms/Rates
May through Oct., Rooms $195/$245, Cottage $255/$425; Nov. through April, Rooms $125/$225. All rooms have whirlpool, fireplace, & balcony w/view of the harbor. Open year round.
Number of Rooms: 15

Cuisine
Guests enjoy a homemade continental breakfast from the balcony overlooking the harbor. 'There is nothing simple about the view that beckons each guest every morning.'—Jill Cordes, Food Network.

Nearest Airport(s)
Green Bay

Directions
From Airport; Hwy 172 E 8 mi. to Hwy 43 N, 5 mi. to Hwy 57 N, 63 mi. to the inn at the north end of the village on the shore.

Member Since 2002

"To fall asleep to the sound of that water is heavenly!"

Innkeepers/Owners
Dennis & Bonnie Statz

Traditional In Town
Breakfast Inn

White Lace Inn

www.srinns.com/whitelaceinn
16 N. 5th Ave., Sturgeon Bay, Door County, WI 54235
877-948-5223 (toll free) • 920-743-1105
Fax 920-743-8180
romance@whitelaceinn.com

Rooms/Rates
13 Rooms, \$120/\$195; 5 Suites, \$200/\$235. Late October-Mid June, Weeknights, Rooms \$70/\$130, and Suites \$150/\$160. Open year-round. Breakfast is included.
Number of Rooms: 18

Cuisine
A delicious full breakfast is served to our guests daily. Afternoons and evenings include hot cider, hot cocoa, lemonade, and homemade cookies.

Nearest Airport(s)
The Green Bay airport is a one hour drive.

Directions
Hwy. 42 or 57 N to Sturgeon Bay. Bus. Rte. 42/57 into town across Historic Bridge. Left on 5th Ave., 1/2 block on 5th Ave. to Inn on right.

Romance and relaxation in Door County begin as you follow winding garden pathways to your beautifully appointed room or suite. Four lovingly restored historic homes are nestled in a friendly old neighborhood and bordered by a white picket fence. Guest rooms and suites are furnished for a special getaway and feature period antiques, down comforters on wonderfully ornate beds, oversized whirlpools and inviting fireplaces. Fifteen rooms have a fireplace, twelve rooms have a whirlpool and nine of our rooms/suites have both a fireplace and whirlpool. Mornings start with a delicious full breakfast served in the sunlit parlor of the Main House. Bonnie, Dennis and their staff invite you to enjoy the hospitality that has made their Inn a Door County tradition. We've had over 900 small weddings performed at White Lace Inn - usually in the Gazebo. DoorCountyNavigator.com's User's Choice Award, Best B&B in Door County, 2003. Top 10 Romantic Inns of America, 1998, 2004 & 2005, American Historic Inns.

AAA ◆◆◆   *Member Since 1988*   Mobil ★★★

12+ 🚭 ♿ 💳   ♥   ✍ @   ⬚ ◎ ✳   ☕

"This Whimsical Victorian Inn doesn't merely pamper its guests, it envelops them in comfort..expected amenities are here, but the unexpected set it apart."

Victorian Treasure Inn

www.srinns.com/victoriantreasure
115 Prairie Street, Lodi, WI 53555
800-859-5199 • 608-592-5199 • Fax 608-592-7147
innkeeper@victoriantreasure.com

Innkeepers/Owners
Renee and Eric Degelau

Elegant Victorian Village
Bed & Breakfast Inn

The Victorian Treasure Inn is a Madison, Wisconsin area bed and breakfast tucked away in the scenic Wisconsin River Valley. Come visit for a romantic getaway as you discover 'One of America's Top Ten Most Romantic Inns' as awarded by American Historic Inns. Gracious hospitality and casual elegance in two 1890s National Registry Victorian homes and a 1928 Craftsman bungalow featuring eight romantic, individually decorated guest rooms with private baths—including luxurious whirlpool fireplace suites with wet bars and entertainment centers including TV's, VCRs and DVDs. Caring owner-innkeepers fuss over details - meticulous accommodations, luxurious amenities, attentive service. Enjoy a gourmet full breakfast and complimentary evening reception. The inn is conveniently located in the heart of South-Central Wisconsin, four miles west of I-90/94, between Madison, WI and the Wisconsin Dells. Close to hiking, biking, skiing and wineries. Limousine service provided for dinner package and available for nominal fee to local attractions. Airport pickup available. Wine tours nearby.

AAA ◆◆◆◆   *Member Since 1998*

Rooms/Rates
8 Rooms; 7 Suites with whirlpools and fireplaces, $119/$279. Includes full 3-course gourmet breakfast & daily wine/cheese reception featuring Wisconsin cheese & wine. Romance & Honeymoon Pkgs.
Number of Rooms: 15

Cuisine
Enjoy a memorable, full gourmet breakfast as featured on PBS *Country Inn Cooking with Gail Greco*. Complimentary evening wine & Wisconsin cheese reception provided.

Nearest Airport(s)
Dane County Airport (Madison)

Directions
20 miles NW of Madison on I-90/94, Exit Hwy 60/Lodi West four miles to Main Street/Hwy 113, continue straight on 60 one block, first Right turn is Prairie St.

"Eric and Renee know how to please their guests. We have been to many 'Select Registry' Inns, but this one is tops!" Ginny and Bob, Villa Rico, Georgia

SelectRegistry.com

General Manager
Patricia Guttenberg

Elegant In Town Inn

Mansion Hill Inn
www.srinns.com/mansionhill
424 N. Pinckney Street, Madison, WI 53703
800-798-9070 • 608-255-3999 • Fax 608-255-2217

Rooms/Rates
11 Rooms including 3 Suites,
$145/$345 B&B.
Number of Rooms: 11

Cuisine
Many fine restaurants within walking distance. Complimentary refreshments, including wine tasting every evening. Continental-plus breakfast delivered to your door on a silver tray each morning of your stay.

Nearest Airport(s)
Dane County Regional Airport

Directions
Hwy. 151 to State Capitol, turn R on Wisconsin, 4 blocks to R on Gilman 1 block to R on Pinckney.

Elegance, luxury and charm await you at The Mansion Hill Inn. The Inn's warm hospitality has made it a favorite of business and leisure travelers alike. Lovingly restored and lavishly decorated, Mansion Hill Inn is the American Automobile Association's only 4 diamond rated guest residence in Madison. A masterpiece of Romanesque Revival style built in 1857, it abounds in fine architectural detail and period furnishings. Each of the eleven guest suites and rooms are individually and exquisitely decorated to provide the best of antique ambience and contemporary amenities. Many rooms have marble fireplaces and balconies as well as views of the State Capitol building. The Inn is conveniently located on a quiet corner in the heart of downtown Madison and boasts sumptuous accommodations, awesome amenities, and a stellar location! There's not a sweeter spot in all of Madison, close to the campuses of The University of Wisconsin, Madison Area Technical College and Edgewood College as well as being walking distance to State Street and the Capitol, Overture Center for the Arts, Monona Terrace and all of Madison's best restaurants! The inn offers optional "Sweet Dreams" turndown service every night. Valet parking is also available.

Member Since 1997

12+

"Madison's most gracious and intimate seclusion..."

The Geneva Inn

www.srinns.com/genevainn

N2009 S. Lake Shore Dr., Lake Geneva, WI 53147

800-441-5881 • 262-248-5680 • Fax 262-248-5685

General Manager
Richard B. Treptow

Luxury Lakeside
Inn

Experience distinctive European charm and exceptional luxury at The Geneva Inn located directly on the shores of Geneva Lake. Discover a truly relaxed style of comfort, intimate accommodations, breathtaking lake views, uncommon architectural craftsmanship and quiet seclusion in the peaceful atmosphere of this traditional English inn. Special touches include thick, fluffy bathrobes, bedtime bottled water and chocolates, oversized vintage or whirlpool baths, fully stocked private bars, free weekday newspaper delivery, early morning coffee available on each floor and exclusive use of the Inn's exercise facility. Guests are also treated to a complimentary, continental buffet breakfast served in The Grandview Restaurant. Fresh fruit and bakery items, flavored butters, delicious meats and cheeses, cereals and rich coffee and fragrant teas are offered. Hot breakfast specials also available. Enjoy a refreshing drink at the Grandview lounge or lunch outdoors on a private patio during the summer months.

Rooms/Rates
$175/$390. Special $170 packages offered Fall, Winter & Spring, Sun-Fri.
Number of Rooms: 37

Cuisine
Experience the area's best American Contemporary cuisine at The Grandview Restaurant. Featuring fresh seafood, delicious daily specials, decadent desserts. Every table offers a scenic vista of Geneva Lake through large panoramic windows.

Nearest Airport(s)
Milwaukee-Mitchell (1 hr); Chicago-O'Hare (90 min)

Directions
2 1/2 mi. S of downtown Lake Geneva, directly on Geneva Lake.

Member Since 2004

"We love the Geneva Inn and Grandview. The rooms are comfortable, the view is beautiful and the staff is friendly and courteous. Thank you so much!"

From California to Nova Scotia, SELECT REGISTRY represents the finest inns, B&Bs, and unique small hotels North America has to offer. We are proud to include among our members a number of exceptional Canadian properties. To our Canadian guests, we say, "Our innkeepers stand ready to welcome you during your travels, whether it is to the States or within Canada." To our American guests, we say, "Why not see what Canada has to offer?"

In these uncertain times, when crossing oceans is worrisome, nothing beats the exhilarating feeling of visiting an exciting new country in the security and comfort of your own car. Yes, for many millions of Americans, Canada is just a short drive away—and yet it is a whole new world!

No wonder Americans love to travel to Canada: not only do their U.S. dollars go a lot further there (which means a lot more holiday for the same amount of money), but they also get to choose between a multitude of completely different experiences.

De la Californie à la Nouvelle-Ecosse, le SELECT REGISTRY représente plusieurs auberges, cafés-couettes et petits hôtels des plus distingués en Amérique du Nord. Nous sommes fiers de pouvoir compter parmi nos membres plusieurs des plus beaux établissements canadiens. À tous les voyageurs, canadiens-français, nous vous souhaitons de merveilleux séjours dans les auberges de prestige du SELECT REGISTRY.

"We've experienced all four seasons in Canada— and we can't pick a favorite!"

There are the breathtaking vistas, mountain wildlife, Asian food and totem poles of British Columbia, the "foodie" paradise of the Niagara Peninsula (Canada's Napa Valley) and the Eastern Townships of Quebec, replete with friendly wineries and raw milk cheeses. There are festivals galore, museums, parks and world-class shopping in Toronto and Montreal as well as the fascinating culture of the Province of Quebec where French-Canadians take food and fun very, very seriously. And, never to be forgotten, the bucolic seaside charm and legendary hospitality of Canada's maritime provinces, New Brunswick, Prince Edward Island and Nova Scotia.

Many travelers have experienced all four seasons of the Northland (the winters are sunnier and less cold than you think). Traveling east to west, it would be hard to declare a regional winner. Some Canadians modestly claim to be the most hospitable of innkeepers, and a critic can't easily challenge that assertion.

Superb food, wine and service can be expected at the Canadian inns of the SELECT REGISTRY. Understated luxury, too. But above all, they offer you an exclusive glimpse of the best of Canada: its forests, crystalline lakes, affordable golf and skiing and cosmopolitan, secure and friendly cities. The Northland beckons!

"Unbelievable natural beauty, exceptional food and wine, and our friendly neighbors to the North...perfect!"

SelectRegistry.com

Alberta

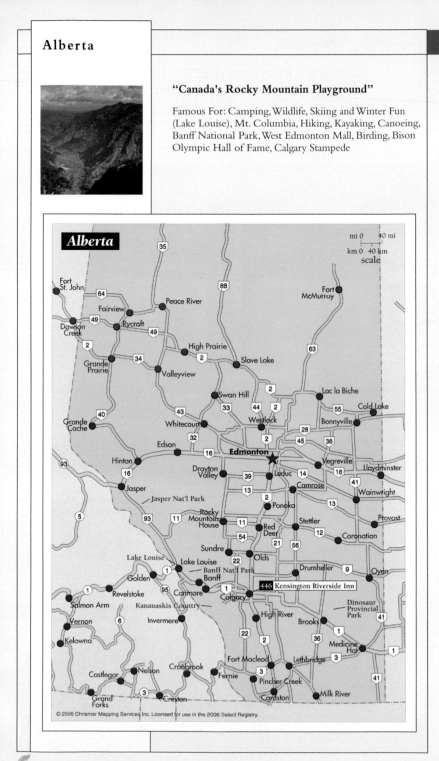

"Canada's Rocky Mountain Playground"

Famous For: Camping, Wildlife, Skiing and Winter Fun
(Lake Louise), Mt. Columbia, Hiking, Kayaking, Canoeing,
Banff National Park, West Edmonton Mall, Birding, Bison
Olympic Hall of Fame, Calgary Stampede

Alberta

Fort St. John
64
Fairview
49
Rycroft
49
49
Dawson Creek
2
Grande Prairie
34
Valleyview
Grande Cache
40
43
Whitecourt
32
Edson
16
Hinton
16
93
Jasper
Jasper Nat'l Park
93
5
11
Rocky Mountain House
11
54
Sundre
22
Lake Louise
Lake Louise
1
Golden
95
Banff Nat'l Park
Banff
Revelstoke
Canmore
Salmon Arm
1
Kananaskis Country
Vernon
6
Invermere
Kelowna
Castlegar
Nelson
Cranbrook
Fernie
Grand Forks
3
Creston

35
88
Peace River
High Prairie
2
Slave Lake
Swan Hill
33
44
2
Westlock
45
2
Edmonton
Drayton Valley
39
Leduc
13
14
2
Ponoka
Camrose
Red Deer
21
56
Stettler
12
Olds
Drumheller
9
Calgary
446 Kensington Riverside Inn
1
High River
22
2
36
Fort Macleod
3
Lethbridge
3
Pincher Creek
Cardston
Milk River

Fort McMurray
63
Lac la Biche
55
Cold Lake
28
Bonnyville
36
Vegreville
16
Lloydminster
41
Wainwright
13
Provost
Coronation
Oyen
Dinosaur Provincial Park
41
Brooks
Medicine Hat
1
41

mi 0   40 mi
km 0   40 km
scale

© 2006 Chrismar Mapping Services Inc. Licensed for use in the 2006 Select Registry.

Kensington Riverside Inn

www.srinns.com/kensingtonriverside
1126 Memorial Drive NW, Calgary, AB T2N 3E3
877-313-3733 • 403-228-4442 • Fax 403-228-9608
info@kensingtonriversideinn.com

Innkeepers/Owners
Karen & Bob Brown
General Manager
Ryan Webster
Elegant Urban Inn

paii

In the midst of Calgary's trendy Kensington district, just a short walk from the business centre of town, the Kensington Riverside Inn has made a name for itself as Alberta's only AAA Four Diamond Inn. The Inn is traditional in style and gracious in atmosphere, with 10-foot ceilings, cornices and columns throughout, and a wood-burning fireplace and bar in the living room. Guests are treated to a magnificent view of the Bow River and the downtown skyline, exceptional accommodations, first-class service and amenities galore. Shops, restaurants and a theatre are close by, as well as the Light Rail Transit System, making many of the city's attractions readily accessible. Comfort and convenience are the way in each of the 19 guest rooms, from balconies or patios to gas fireplaces and Jacuzzis, to Egyptian cotton sheets and goose-down duvets. A video and book lending library as well as voice mail and wireless Internet complete the picture. There's lots to do in and around Calgary, and the Canadian Rockies are only an hour away.

Rooms/Rates
19 Guest Rooms. $269/$404 CDN (approx. $249/$369 US). 5 room types featuring fireplaces, balconies, patios or Jacuzzis.
Number of Rooms: 19

Cuisine
A coffee tray is delivered to your room w/ the morning newspaper, followed by a gourmet breakfast in our dining room. In the evening, hors d'oeuvres are served in the living room. Chocolates by the bedside & cookies 24 hours a day. Light meals available at any time.

Nearest Airport(s)
Calgary International Airport.

Directions
From Downtown: W on 4th Avenue SW, N on 10th Street SW, W on Memorial Dr. for one block.

AAA ◆◆◆◆   *Member Since 2005*

New Brunswick: "The Picture Province"
Famous For: The Maritimes, Acadia and the Cajuns, forests, Trans-Canada Highway, Fundy National Park

Nova Scotia: "The Land of Evangeline"
Famous For: Cabot Trail, fishing, Cape Breton Highlands, harbours and coves, lobster, Christmas trees, wild blueberries

Prince Edward Island: "The Garden Province"
Famous For: Lighthouses, Confederation Centre of the Arts, Anne of Green Gables, Confederation Bridge

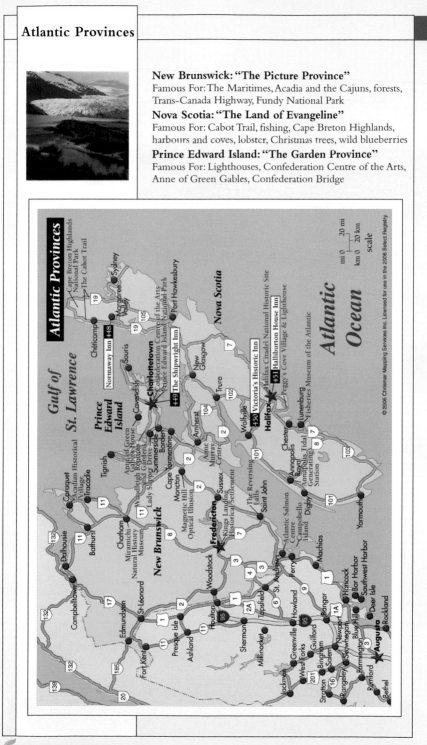

Normaway Inn

www.srinns.com/normaway
Box 138, Margaree Valley, NS, Canada B0E 2C0
800-565-9463 • 902-248-2987 • Fax 902-248-2600
normawayinn@lincsat.com

Innkeeper/Owner
David M. MacDonald

Traditional Country
Retreat/Lodge

Nestled in the hills of the Cape Breton Highlands, near the beginning of the spectacular Cabot Trail, this 250-acre property offers a 1920s inn and cabins, most with woodstove fireplaces and some with Jacuzzis. Enjoy superb food, sincere service, and choice wines. Guests often relax by the fieldstone fireplace after dinner and enjoy films or traditional entertainment nightly. Weekly fiddling concerts in music barn, tennis, hiking trails, biking, salmon and trout fishing. Arrangements for whale watching, sailing and horseback riding. 2900 foot paved air strip adjacent to property. Also, within 10 minutes of the Normaway, a large farm house on a 25 acre river property is available for weekly/daily rental. Many great hiking trails within 25 miles.

Rooms/Rates
9 Rooms, $99/$139 EP;
17 Cabins, $139/$279 EP;
3 Suites, $179/$279 EP; $45-60
per person MAP.
Number of Rooms: 29

Cuisine
June 15 - October 15. Dinner 6-9
p.m., Breakfast 7:30-10:00 a.m.
Picnic lunches.

Nearest Airport(s)
Sydney (YQY)

Directions
Trans-Canada Hwy. Jct. 7 at
Nyanza, N on Cabot Trail 17 mi.
Turn off between NE Margaree and
Lake-O-Law on Egypt Road; 2 mi.
to Inn. From Rte 19, Drive North
on Rte 19 Margaree Forks, Turn
Right, 10 miles to Egypt Road.
Turn Left on Egypt Rd, 2 mi.to Inn.

Member Since 1972

"Normaway Inn offers country fare and does so with flair."
Canadian House and Home

Shipwright Inn B & B

Innkeepers/Owners
Judy & Trevor Pye

Elegant Victorian
Breakfast Inn

www.srinns.com/shipwright
51 Fitzroy Street, Charlottetown, PEI, Canada C1A 1R4
888-306-9966 • 902-368-1905 • Fax 902-628-1905
innkeeper@shipwrightinn.com

Rooms/Rates
3 Executive suites, 1 Apartment Unit, 5 Premium suites CDN $149/$289. Open all year-round. Off-season rates apply.
Number of Rooms: 9

Cuisine
Afternoon tea/coffee and cakes. Memorable full served hot breakfast of four courses (if you have the appetite!)

Nearest Airport(s)
Charlottetown Airport - approximately a 10 minute drive.

Directions
From Confederation Bridge : TCH 1 East to the centre of Charlottetown. Turn R on Fitzroy St. go 1.5 blocks. On R before Pownal Street look for lighted red/gold sign with a gold ship model on top. From Ferry : TCH 1 West, R on Univ Av. L on Fitzroy.

Enjoy a "Unique Experience" at the award winning 5 Star Shipwright Inn. Be prepared to relax, unwind and experience our "Gentle Island" This early Victorian, Anne of Green Gables style, heritage home was built in 1865 by shipbuilder James Douse. It is located in historic Olde Charlottetown within a 3 minute walk of historic/cultural sites, waterfront, live theatre, fine dining and shopping. In keeping with the nautical theme antiques and artwork have been lovingly collected for your enjoyment. All bedrooms have polished pine floors, en-suite bathrooms, some with double Ultra Air Tubs, whirlpools and fireplaces. While savouring a memorable breakfast, beneath the dining-room chandelier, imagine how the rope insignia dinner service must have looked at the captain's table. Beautiful English garden. Safe, free parking, peaceful, comfortable and quiet. We pride ourselves on delivering warm Island hospitality, attentive service and believe in pampering our guests and exceeding their expectations.

Canada Select ★★★★★
Frommer's Best on PEI.

Member Since 1999

9+

"The outside of the Inn looks like a storybook cottage, and the inside is even better. An unforgettable experience."

Victoria's Historic Inn

www.srinns.com/victoriainn

600 Main Street, Wolfville, NS, Canada B4P 1E8

800-556-5744 • 902-542-5744 • Fax 902-542-7794

victoriasinn@eastlink.ca

Innkeepers/Owners
The Cryan Family

Elegant Victorian
Village Breakfast Inn

The Cryan family has worked tirelessly to achieve the first B&B five-star Canada Select rating in the province. Now perhaps the finest Victorian home in Nova Scotia, the Inn's professionally decorated rooms lend an intimate and first-class atmosphere, all with ensuite baths; some offer double Jacuzzis and fireplaces, with balcony or sweeping view. Travel writers say, "It is the attention to detail and the softly decorated rooms, as well as the sincere care of the innkeepers, that draw people back to Victoria's again and again for peace and relaxation in a pampered environment." Nestled in the picturesque and historic town of Wolfville, travelers are surrounded by a choice of activities. Hiking trails, scenic vistas, historic sites, award-winning dining, golf and wineries are all minutes away.

Rooms/Rates
14 Rooms, $128/$189.2 Suites, $245 CDN B&B. Open year-round.
Number of Rooms: 16

Cuisine
Hot breakfast included in room rate. Award-winning restaurants within walking distance. Selection of wines available.

Nearest Airport(s)
Halifax International Airport1 hour driving distance.

Directions
From Yarmouth: 101 E to exit #11. L off exit ramp. R onto Hwy 1. Just inside town limits on L. From Halifax Airport: Hwy. 102 S towards Halifax to exit 4B onto 101 W and Annapolis Valley (approx 15 min.) Take exit 10. Follow Hwy 1 to town. Located on R after downtown.

AAA ◆◆◆   *Member Since 1998*

"Came for one night, stayed five - perfect!"

Manager
Robert Pretty

Historic Boutique
Hotel

The Halliburton

www.thehalliburton.com
5184 Morris Street, Halifax, NS, Canada B3J 1B3
902–420–0658 • Fax 902-423-2324
information@thehalliburton.com

Rooms/Rates
29 rooms including 4 suites, rates from $140 CDN, plus tax, includes breakfast. Open year-round.
Number of Rooms: 29

Cuisine
An extensive continental breakfast is served each morning from 7-10. 'Stories' offers relaxed fine dining from 5:30 until 10:00, reservations are recommended. Fine wine, local beer and cocktails are served after 4:00 in the Library or garden courtyard.

Nearest Airport(s)
Halifax International -- CYHZ

Directions
Downtown Halifax, Barrington at Morris Street. Use Hwy #102 from Halifax International Airport or Hwy #103 from Yarmouth.

Downtown Halifax's historic boutique hotel. The Halliburton features signature dining and individually appointed guestrooms in a trio of heritage townhouses. Twenty-nine rooms and suites of various sizes, complimentary breakfast, and wireless Internet access. 'Stories' restaurant offers inventive regional cuisine in intimate dining rooms. In the summer months guests enjoy cocktails and light fare in the garden courtyard. In the autumn and winter a crackling fire invites from the cozy library. The Halliburton, was built in 1809 and was home to Sir Brenton Halliburton, the first Chief Justice of the Nova Scotia Supreme Court. More recently, the building housed Dalhousie University's prestigious law school. A short stroll from popular shops, restaurants and the Halifax waterfront.

AAA/CAA ◆◆◆ Award
Canada Select ★★★★ Award

AAA ◆◆◆   *Member Since 1998*

"The finest food we've had so far, your staff deserve much praise!"

"The Pacific Province"

Famous For: Canadian Rockies, ferries, Vancouver Island, spiral railway tunnels, Butchart Gardens

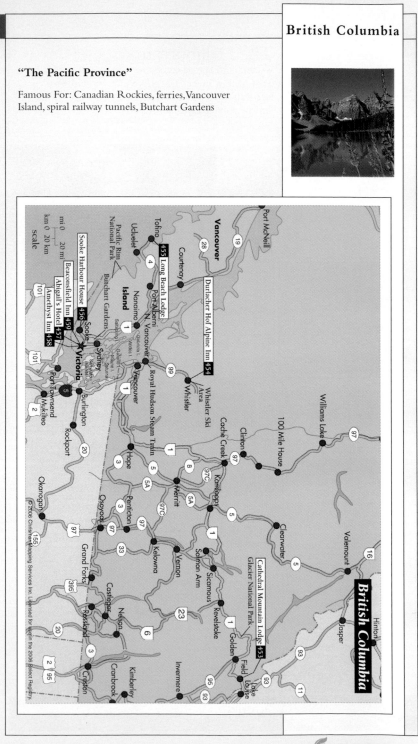

SelectRegistry.com

Innkeepers/Owners
Nancy Stibbard
General Manager
Craig Chapman

Elegant Rocky Mountain
Retreat/Lodge

 ♀

Cathedral Mountain Lodge
www.srinns.com/cathedralmountain
Yoho Valley Road, P.O. Box 40, Field, BC, Canada V0A 1G0
866-619-6442 • 250-343-6442 • Fax (250) 343-6424
info@cathedralmountain.com

Rooms/Rates
21 Cabins, $150/$350 USD.
Rates vary according to season &
cabin type.
Number of Rooms: 21

Cuisine
Complimentary continental breakfast is served from 7 - 10 a.m.
Lunch and dinner feature a range
of entree choices, emphasizing
fresh regional ingredients.

Nearest Airport(s)
Calgary International Airport

Directions
Located 200km (125 mi.) from
Calgary, Alberta. Travel W on
Trans Canada Highway 1. Go past
Canmore, Banff and Lake Louise
before crossing into B.C. 5 km
into B.C., the highway starts a
steep descent; at the bottom take
a R on Yoho Valley Rd. This will
take you directly to the lodge.

Imagine your own log cabin in the heart of the Canadian Rocky
Mountains; a stocked wood burning fireplace, down duvets, deep
soaker bathtub, tranquil sitting areas and a generous private deck
with commanding views of the magnificent Rocky Mountains
and the glacier fed Kicking Horse River. Wake up to the song of
wild birds and the call of an alpine river, to the scent of fresh pine
and the beauty of mountain wildflowers. There is no television
or telephone to disrupt your mountain escape. Your purpose is
to replenish and revive – because tomorrow you can hike, climb,
raft, canoe, bike, fish, golf and horseback ride! From leisurely strolls
to day-long expeditions, an endless array of hiking trails are just
outside your door. This is an authentic Rocky Mountain retreat
surrounded by other-worldly alpine meadows, abundant wildlife,
towering peaks and epic waterfalls. Close to the all the attractions
and activities of Yoho National Park, Lake Louise and Banff National Park, there is so much to do! Come to Cathedral Mountain
Lodge – a place where every day is like no day anywhere else.

Member Since 2003

8+

"Dining Room was exceptional. We have travelled for a month up the West coast and
this food and service is the best we have had!"

Durlacher Hof Alpine Inn

www.srinns.com/durlacherhof
7055 Nesters Rd., Whistler, BC, Canada V0N 1B7
877-932-1924 • 604-932-1924 • Fax 604-938-1980
info@durlacherhof.com

Innkeepers/Owners
Peter & Erika Durlacher
Traditional Mountain
Breakfast Inn

Nestled in the spectacular Coast Mountains of British Columbia lies Whistler Resort, home to the Durlacher Hof, an enchanting mountain retreat. Durlachers' reputation as Whistler's most welcoming and generous innkeepers is legendary. The Hof serves up the complete authentic Austrian experience from ornate exterior trimmings to the Kaiserschmarren served at breakfast. Painstaking attention to detail is evident in the cozy guest lounge and the immaculate pretty rooms all with mountain views, goose-down duvets, luxury linens and ensuite baths with jacuzzi. Durlacher Hof is part of a place that mixes old world charm with romance and a natural beauty with inviting warmth and hospitality. The natural setting of Whistler offers a bounty of outdoor activities, a quaint village, which hosts art, culture events, and intriguing shops along with a wide spectrum of international cuisine. Host location of the 2010 Winter Olympics and Paralympics.

Rooms/Rates
8 Guest Rooms. Summer $129/$239 CDN. Winter $179/$359 CDN. Ski & Golf packages. 10 days summer, 30 days winter cancellation policy, min. German spoken, Canada Select Inn ★★★★ 1/2.
Number of Rooms: 8

Cuisine
Dinners offered in Winter on selected evenings. Special culinary events in Spring and Fall. Complimentry Old Country Breakfast Buffet and afternoon refreshments. Outdoor Tea Parties in Summer. Lounge Licensed.

Nearest Airport(s)
Vancouver International 2.5 hrs.

Directions
75 miles/125 kilometres N of Vancouver on Hwy 99 (approx. 2 hours). 7 traffic lights on Hwy 99 from the 'Whistler Welcome' sign to Nesters.

AAA ◆◆◆   *Member Since 1998*

"Breakfast 'par excellence.' Upon first site, we knew Durlacher Hof would be our official return destination. We feel refreshed & refueled. Memorable."

Owner
Timothy Hackett
General Manager
Carly Hall

Luxury Beachfront Resort

🍽️ 🍽️ 🍽️ 🍷

Long Beach Lodge Resort

www.srinns.com/longbeachlodge
P.O. Box 897, 1441 Pacific Rim Highway, Tofino, BC V0R 2Z0
877-844-7873 • 250-725-2442 • Fax 250-725-2402
info@longbeachlodgeresort.com

Rooms/Rates
40 Lodge Rms $169/$529 CDN.
20 Cottages $269/$459 CDN.
Seasonal.
Number of Rooms: 60

Cuisine
The Resort's dining room is a relaxed, informal space where the emphasis is placed on fresh food, superior service & meticulous attention to detail. Our chef captures the intricate flavours of sea, field & forest with his inventive & memorable gourmet cuisine.

Nearest Airport(s)
Tofino Airport, 10km

Directions
Take Hwy 1 North from Victoria past Nanaimo. Turn west, onto Hwy 4 at the Qualicum Beach/Port Alberni exit and follow signs. Drive will take approx. 4.5 hours. Direct flights available from Vancouver and Seattle.

Experience the natural beauty, exceptional amenities and handcrafted gourmet cuisine at our luxurious beachfront resort on the West Coast of Vancouver Island. Our relaxed and inspirational coastal setting offers a perfect escape from your everyday responsibilities. Choose between accommodation in our beachfront Lodge with spectacular oceanviews or retreat to one of our tranquil, two bedroom Rainforest Cottages with full kitchens and private outdoor patios with hot tubs. You will begin to relax as soon as you enter the Lodge Great Room with its massive granite fireplace and its Douglas fir post and beam construction. Sink into an overstuffed chair, put your feet up, and gaze out at the sandy beach with the crashing surf to the lighthouse beyond. You will appreciate the attention to detail that has been lavished on each of our guest rooms, including luxurious bath amenities, bath robes, cozy duvets, decadent chocolates and waterproof rain jackets for those rainy day beach walks!

AAA ◆◆◆   *Member Since 2005*

☺ 🚭 ♿ 💳   📁 ♥ ↤   🖂 @ 🐕   🖼 ◎

"Sitting in the Great Room listening to some great music and watching the sunset was one of my top ten magical moments."

Sooke Harbour House

www.srinns.com/sookeharbour
1528 Whiffen Spit Road, Sooke, BC, Canada V0S 1N0
800-889-9688 • 250-642-3421 • Fax 250-642-6988
info@sookeharbourhouse.com

Innkeepers
Sinclair and Frederique Philip

Elegant/Romantic
Oceanfront Retreat/Inn

Cozy and enchanting, Sooke Harbour House was rated, "Second Best Country Inn in the World" by *Gourmet* Magazine and "One of the World's Top Ten Hotels" by *Travel + Leisure*. Its restaurant specializes in West Coast Canadian cuisine, especially seafood, and much of its produce comes from the Inn's organic gardens. The rooms feature stunning ocean views, wood burning fireplaces, original art, and soaker or Jacuzzi tubs. Some offer steam showers for two. Step onto your private balcony, the perfect location for watching sea lions, river otters, seals and eagles play. Activities include: kayaking, whale watching, cycling and fishing.

Member Since 2003

Rooms/Rates
28 Guest Rooms from $215/$295 U.S. (low/high) Incl. breakfast. Incl. lunch during high season. Gourmet, Spa, and Romance Getaway Packages available. Open year-round.
Number of Rooms: 28

Cuisine
Re-awaken your taste buds to the pleasures of fresh, local, seasonal culinary creations. Wine pairings from our cellar, one of the 86 best in the world, add to the adventure.

Nearest Airport(s)
Victoria, BC

Directions
23 miles W of Victoria. Take Hwy. 1 north to exit 14. Turn right onto Hwy.14 to Sooke. Turn left 2 miles past Sooke's third traffic light onto Whiffen Spit Road. We're at the end of the road, on the beach.

Canada Select 5 Star Rating "Bliss defined." - 2003 Guest

Innkeeper/Owner
Ellen Cmolik
General Manager
Marion Hansen

Elegant In Town
Breakfast Inn

Abigail's Hotel

www.srinns.com/abigails
906 McClure Street, Victoria, BC V8V 3E7
800-561-6565 • 250-388-5363 • Fax 250-388-7787
innkeeper@abigailshotel.com

Rooms/Rates
$139/$450 CDN. Honeymoon Suites, King beds, fireplaces, double Jacuzzi tubs. Charming Sunflower and Country rooms, Queen beds with soaker tubs and shower. Seasonal discounts available. Open year-round, reservations available 24 hrs.
Number of Rooms: 23

Cuisine
Our famous gourmet breakfast and complimentary evening appetizers served every evening in our fireside library. Licensed premises.

Nearest Airport(s)
Victoria International Airport

Directions
From Airport S on Hwy 17, L on Fort St., R on Vancouver St. and R on McClure St. From Downtown E on Fort St., R on Vancouver St. and R on McClure St.

Intimate, elegant and exclusive... Abigail's delivers 'Romance and the City' with its heritage ambiance and modern conveniences. Located in a peaceful cul de sac 3 blocks from downtown and the Inner Harbour. Each luxurious room has antique furnishings, cozy down duvets, air conditioning, wireless high speed internet and fresh flowers; most rooms have wood-burning fireplaces and jetted tubs. To enhance your experience, enjoy breakfast in bed or select from Celebration, Spa and Wine-Tasting Packages. Whether it's pampering yourself with a spa service in our new Spa treatment room "The Pearl", whale watching, golfing, kayaking, hiking, dining at any number of gourmet restaurants or simply relaxing in our luxurious guestrooms, it's a perfect balance of adventure and luxury you'll find only at Abigail's Hotel.

AAA ◆◆◆   *Member Since 2000*

"When I think about our stay at Abigail's Hotel, I cannot help but smile. Amenities, unparalleled service and location set Abigail's apart."

Amethyst Inn at Regents Park

www.srinns.com/amethystinn
1501 Fort Street, Victoria, BC, Canada V8S 1Z6
888-265-6499 • 250-595-2053 • Fax 250-595-2054
innkeeper@amethyst-inn.com

Innkeepers/Owners
Abel and Shelley Cheng
General Manager
John Williams

Elegant Victorian In Town
Breakfast Inn

Amethyst Inn at Regents Park is a heritage jewel and Victoria's most historically significant Inn. An award winning 1885 Victorian Mansion, which retains many original architectural features and is furnished with antiques. The preferred Inn for guests celebrating special occasions and cozy retreats. Comfortable, romantic, individually appointed accommodations offer a king or queen bed and sitting area with a fireplace. Bathrooms offer luxurious two person Jacuzzi Spa Tubs, deep soaking tubs or claw foot tubs. Mornings begin with coffee service followed by an elegant full breakfast. Enjoy visiting in the Parlor in the evening and gracious hospitality. The Inn is surrounded by heritage estates, beautiful gardens and tree lined streets. Conveniently located in the heart of Victoria and walking distance to Craigdarroch Castle, Antique Row and central to attractions. Concierge service for city and Butchart Garden tours, dining reservations, whale watching, golf and nature exploring.

Best Breakfast in Canada 2005 *Inn Traveler*.

★★★★★ Canada Select.

AAA ◆◆◆   *Member Since 2003*   Mobil ★★★

Rooms/Rates
16 romantic rooms and suites. $199/$399 CDN ($110/$330 US) Anniversary, Wedding, Elopement, Honeymoon, Spa & Sightseeing Packages. Seasonal Discounts. Open year-round. King or Queen beds, ensuite baths, two-person jacuzzi Spa tubs, fireplaces.
Number of Rooms: 16

Cuisine
Enjoy morning coffee and an elegant full breakfast. Organic, farm fresh and seasonal as available. Dining Room tables are set with linen, fine china and crystal.

Nearest Airport(s)
Victoria Int'l (YYJ) - 20 miles

Directions
HWY17 (Douglas St): L on Fort, R on St CharlesINNER HARBOUR: L on Government, R on Fort, R on St Charles. Free on-site Parking.

"We have traveled far and wide and never enjoyed an experience as delightful as Amethyst Inn. Our stay was one of those 'Beautiful Memories' that will last."

Innkeepers/Owners
Mark and Diana Havin

Elegant In Town Breakfast
Inn

Beaconsfield Inn

www.srinns.com/beaconsfield
998 Humboldt St., Victoria, BC, Canada V8V 2Z8
888-884-4044 • 250-384-4044 • Fax 250-384-4052
info@beaconsfieldinn.com

Rooms/Rates
5 Deluxe Rooms, $129/$295 CDN;
4 Suites, $229/$359 CDN.
Open year-round.
Number of Rooms: 9

Cuisine
Full breakfast, English style afternoon tea, evening sherry.

Nearest Airport(s)
Victoria International

Directions
From North: Hwy. 17 to City Centre, L on Humboldt St.; From Inner Harbor: Government St. N to Humboldt St. turn R for 4 blocks.

An Award-winning 1905 Edwardian manor located four blocks from Victoria's Inner Harbor, the Beaconsfield is the ultimate in charm, luxury and romance. Enjoy antiques, Oriental carpets, stained glass windows, fresh flowers, feather beds and down comforters, fireplaces, and Jacuzzis in most every room. The Beaconsfield Inn is situated on a quiet, tree-lined street a short 10 minute walk from shopping, restaurants and attractions. Indulge in a lovely English style afternoon tea, evening sherry hour, night time cookies and full breakfasts. *The Beaconsfield Inn has been awarded a* ★★★★★ *rating from Canada Select.*

AAA ◆◆◆   *Member Since 1994*

12+

"The Beaconsfield is...the standard by which we judge all others...," *Special Places*

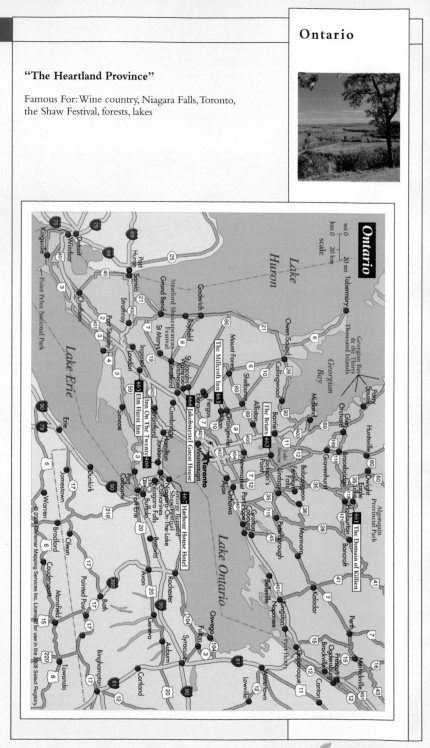

Ontario

"The Heartland Province"

Famous For: Wine country, Niagara Falls, Toronto, the Shaw Festival, forests, lakes

Innkeeper/Owner
Jean-Edouard de Marenches

Traditional Waterside Inn

Domain of Killien
www.srinns.com/domainofkillien
P.O. Box 810, 1282 Carroll Road
Haliburton, ON, Canada K0M 1S0
800-390-0769 • 705-457-1100 • Fax 705-457-3853
killien@bellnet.ca

Rooms/Rates
5 Rooms, $162/$198 CDN PP MAP; 1 Suite; 6 Chalets, $159/$224 CDN PP MAP. Open year-round.
Number of Rooms: 12

Cuisine
Breakfast and dinner. Picnic lunches available. Liquor served.

Nearest Airport(s)
Stanhope Airport

Directions
From Toronto Hwy 404 N to Davis Dr, R to 48 to 35 N, 35 N to Minden, 121 R, N to Haliburton L, W on 118, R (N) on Harburn Rd 12 km to Carroll Rd.

At the south tip of Algonquin Park, a charming inn rests on a quiet bay amidst a 5000-acre private estate of lakes, forest and rugged hills: the Domain of Killien. You can enjoy a morning game of tennis, a fly-fishing outing or later, an afternoon sail or a quiet paddle. Or you can simply Master the Art of Doing Nothing... beautifully. Summer or winter, guests have exclusive access to our hiking or nordic ski trails and to a day-cabin on a remote lake. Whatever you did today, warm and comfortable inn rooms and lakeside chalets welcome you back. Dining at the Domain is an experience to savour. Fine wines complement delicate flavours created by our team of chefs from France. The inn's full breakfast includes freshly-baked croissants and other house specialties. Year round, the Haliburton Highlands are a photographer's dream.

Member Since 1995

12+

"You come to the Domain to master the Art of doing nothing...beautifully."
Jean-Edouard

The Briars

www.srinns.com/briars
55 Hedge Rd., R.R. #1, Jackson's Point, ON, Canada L0E 1L0
800-465-2376 • 905-722-3271 • Fax 905-722-9698
info@briars.ca

Innkeepers/Owners
The Sibbald Family
Traditional Waterside
Resort

The Briars is situated on Lake Simcoe just an hour from Toronto. With its lush gardens, gracious accommodation, memorable dining and warm hospitality, The Briars is the perfect destination for any occasion. Guests enjoy rooms or suites in the inn with views of the gardens and lake, or private lakeside cottages. Three meals daily are served in the inn. Fine country dining features traditional favourites, contemporary flavours and fresh pastries prepared in The Briars kitchens. This spacious property features the warmth of an inn with the recreation of a resort. Championship golf, biking, tennis and kayaking; billiards, ping pong and exercise room; yoga and guided walks; dancing Saturday evenings. The Briars Spa provides luxurious treatments, a solarium pool, sauna and whirlpool. In winter there's also cross-country skiing and horse-drawn sleigh rides. Nearby there's antiquing, shopping, fishing and southern Ontario's many attractions. An Ontario Heritage property. Member Ontario's Finest Inns and Premier Spas of Ontario.

AAA ◆◆◆   *Member Since 1980*

Rooms/Rates
57 guest rooms, 3 private lodges, 14 private cottages/suites. $129/$249 CDN($115/$215 US approx) per person/night with all meals. Open Year Round
Number of Rooms: 90

Cuisine
Fine Country Dining: traditional and contemporary favourites; fresh herbs & fruits from the gardens. Luncheons can be packed for excursions. Light meals and entertainment in Drinkwaters Lounge and on the patio.

Nearest Airport(s)
Toronto Pearson Int'l

Directions
From Toronto: 404(N) to Davis Dr., R.(E) 6 mi. to 48; L.(N)15 mi. to Sutton; L on High St., follow signs to Jackson's Point & Briars. From W of Toronto: take ETR 407 to 404.

"The property, activities available, surroundings, comforts and amenities, happy and pleasant staff - outstanding!"

The Millcroft Inn & Spa

Innkeeper
Wolfgang Stichnothe

Traditional Country
Inn and Spa

www.srinns.com/millcroftinn
55 John Street, Village of Alton - Caledon
ON, Canada L7K 0C4
800-383-3976 • 519-941-8111 • Fax 519-941-9192
millcroft@millcroft.com

Rooms/Rates
From $265/$340 CDN per person. GUARANTEED 35% rate of exchange on US currency. B&B & Packages available. Golf nearby. 4 Diamonds from CAA/AAA.
Number of Rooms: 52

Cuisine
Continental cuisine available for breakfast, lunch & dinner. 4 Diamonds CAA/AAA. Extensive selection of wines & spirits.

Nearest Airport(s)
Pearson Int'l. (YYZ) 30 min away.

Directions
Hwy. 401W or 401E to Hwy. 410N to Mayfield Rd., W (L) to Hwy. 10 N (Hurontario) to Caledon, L on Hwy. 24 (Charleston Sideroad) 3 km to Peel Regional Rd 136 (Main St), then R (3 km), follow to stop, then L on Queen St in Alton.

Less than an hour from Toronto, the unparalleled refinement and a tranquil location amid the rolling Caledon Hills make the Millcroft Inn & Spa the Definitive Country Retreat. The inn's serene surroundings and historic charm provide a balm for the city-weary. Its riverside setting, fifty-two beautiful guestrooms (some with a fireplace, a Jacuzzi or a private outdoor hot-tub) and one hundred wooded trail-lined acres combine with the appeal of 'Four-Diamond' cuisine and vintage wines in a warmly appointed dining room for an extraordinary getaway experience. The full-service Millcroft Spa, Centre for Well-Being pampers guests with a broad range of treatments, including hydrotherapy and massage, and features fine European products. Whether you choose to read by the lounge's wood-burning fireplace, hike a sun-dappled wooded trail, or relax in the Spa, the Millcroft is ready to make your next escape the best yet. Visit the website or call for more details.

AAA ◆◆◆◆   *Member Since 1995*

"Hospitality, fine dining and its country setting make the Millcroft a perfect getaway!"

Jakobstettel Inn

www.srinns.com/jakobstettel
16 Isabella St., St. Jacobs, ON, Canada N0B 2N0
800-431-3035 • 519-664-2208 • Fax 519-664-1326
info@jakobstettel.com

Owner
Daniel P. Reeve
General Manager
Monica Frey
Victorian Luxury
Inn

This three-story Luxury Inn represents the epitome of relaxation and comfort. Built in 1898, this grand Victorian home rests on five acres, crowned by a century of towering trees and accented by groomed gardens. Enjoy a myriad of activities on the back lawn. Take a dip in our heated outdoor cabana lined heated swimming pool, invigorate tired muscles in the hot tub, serve up an ace on the tennis court, hit the walking trails along the Grand River or explore the village with it's many boutiques, craft studios, restaurants and theaters, all within walking distance of the Inn. Perhaps enjoy a massage in our outdoor gazebo. Introducing our outdoor Bar and Grill "VIXEN" Spend some time in our billiards room complete with plasma television, fireplace, and licensed bar. Make business a pleasure by meeting at the Jakobstettel Inn. We offer a luxurious setting that encourages fresh thinking outside the box. We provide an environment that sparks the brainstorming process, nurtures innovation and eases the pressures of conflict resolution.

Member Since 1995

Rooms/Rates
We have 10 disctinctly decorated rooms for your accomodations. All rooms excluding the Presidential Suite are $250 per night plus applicable taxes. The Presidential Suite is $450 per night plus applicable taxes.
Number of Rooms: 10

Cuisine
Continental breakfast is served each morning in our in-house dinning room. Lunches can be served to small groups by this area's finest chef only when pre-arranged.

Nearest Airport(s)
Kitchener-Waterloo Regional Airport

Directions
From Hwy. 401 exit Hwy. 8 W to Kitchener then Hwy. 85 N through Waterloo, choose Rd. 15 or Rd. 17 exit; in St. Jacobs turn W on Albert St.

"Thank you for a wonderful escape from reality."

Innkeepers/Owners
**Pat Frey and
Giacomo Negro**

Traditional Victorian
Country Inn

🍽 🍽 🍽 🍷

Elm Hurst Inn

www.srinns.com/elmhurstinn
415 Harris Street, P.O. Box 123, Ingersoll, ON, Canada N5C 3K1
800-561-5321 • 519-485-5321 • Fax 519-485-6579
info@elmhurstinn.com

Rooms/Rates
39 Inn Rooms (QN or 2 DB beds)
$175 CDN; 3 Fireplace Rooms
(KG bed) $199 CDN; 2 Executive
Suites (KG bed) $225 CDN;3
Jacuzzi Rooms (KG or QN bed)
$225 CDN; includes country
breakfast buffet.
Number of Rooms: 47

Cuisine
Victorian Restaurant, licensed,
private rooms, patio, award winning cuisine for breakfast, lunch
and dinner.

Nearest Airport(s)
London International Airport is
located 30 minutes away.

Directions
90 min west of Toronto, ON and
30 min east of London, ON, on
Hwy. 401 (exit 218) at Hwy. 19.

The country Inn is nestled amongst century-old maple trees
on 37 acres of land with walking trails, flowing creek and pond.
Our spacious guest rooms are uniquely decorated with picturesque views some including a fireplace or Jacuzzi tub. Rooms
include breakfast, movie channel, coffee makers & other amenities. Choose room service or dine in the Victorian Mansion. The
Elm Hurst Inn is an ideal setting for any occasion. Enjoy our
full-service Aveda spa, sauna, steam room and whirlpool. We are
perfectly situated 30 min from Stratford or 2 hrs from Detroit.
Enjoy golf, X-country skiing, great shopping, sight-seeing and
nearby tourist attractions.

AAA ◆◆◆   *Member Since 1996*

☺   🚭 ♿ 🗄 🕐 🗁 ♥ ⊷ ✂ 🖎 @   🗓 ◎

"Service was excellent and the food was great. We are already planning to come back."

Inn on the Twenty
www.srinns.com/innonthetwenty
3845 Main Street, Jordan, ON, Canada L0R 1S0
800-701-8074 • 905-562-5336 • Fax 905-562-0009
info@innonthetwenty.com

Innkeeper/Owner
Helen Young

Elegant Contemporary
Village Inn

Rooms/Rates
27 Suites, 7 two-story, 20 one-level, 5 with private garden. $194/$308 US (exchange approximate) $223/$355 CDN Open year-round.
Number of Rooms: 27

Cuisine
On the Twenty is a DiRoNA Award restaurant with regional focus. Private Dining Rooms available for up to 135. Ontario wines and beers. Full bar. Cave Spring Cellars Winery on site. Tours and tastings available daily.

Nearest Airport(s)
Buffalo, Toronto

Directions
QEW Hwy. to Victoria Ave. (Vineland Exit 57). L off the Service Road, S to Regional Rd. 81 (King St.). Turn L and go through the valley; first L at top of the hill onto Main St. 5 minutes from QEW.

This is the heart of Ontario's wine country! Renovated winery buildings boast twenty-seven suites, all with fireplaces and Jacuzzi tubs; antiques and unique art abound. The Inn is located in a charming village with artisans and antique shops. Great golf, walking and bicycling opportunities as well as the sophistication of Niagara's famous Shaw Theatre and the not-to-be-missed Falls. Our restaurant, On the Twenty, is a DiRoNA award winner and a leader in regional cuisine. Cave Spring Cellars, one of Canada's most prestigious wineries is our partner. Our full service Spa enhances any stay. The wine route beckons! A visit to Canada is a fresh experience and we are thrilled to welcome so many of our US neighbours. We are just 25 minutes from the borders at Niagara Falls and make a great on route stop to Toronto.

AAA ◆◆◆◆   *Member Since 1998*

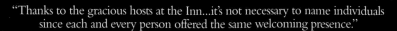

"Thanks to the gracious hosts at the Inn…it's not necessary to name individuals since each and every person offered the same welcoming presence."

Innkeepers/Owners
Susan Murray
General Manager
Ian Shulman

Elegant Waterside
Breakfast Inn

Harbour House Hotel

www.srinns.com/harbourhouse
Box 760, 85 Melville Street, Niagara-on-the-Lake, ON,
Canada L0S 1J0
866-277-6677 • 905-468-4683 • Fax 905-468-0366
inquire@harbourhousehotel.ca

Rooms/Rates
31 Deluxe Rooms & Riverview
Suites from $199 CDN. Dinner
Packages & seasonal rates.
Number of Rooms: 31

Cuisine
Harbour House features a classic
European-style buffet breakfast,
an afternoon wine and cheese
sampling and cookies at bedtime.
A shuttle service is available for
dozens of local restaurants.

Nearest Airport(s)
Buffalo, 45 min; Toronto, 60 min.

Directions
Queen Elizabeth Way (QEW) to
Exit #38 (or 38B from Toronto).
R on Glendale, follow signs for
Route #55. R on East-West Line
to Niagara Pkwy. L on Niagara
Pkwy to Wellington St. R on
Wellington to Ricardo St. R 1/2
block.

Harbour House is a wonderful blend of intimacy, quality, personality, professionalism, sensuous comfort and attention to every detail. Overlooking the Niagara River and within walking distance of the Shaw Festival, many intriguing shops and more than a dozen fine restaurants, Harbour House is just a short drive from the wonder of Niagara Falls, Niagara's world class wineries and dozens of top-flight golf courses. Perched beside Niagara-on-the-Lake's pretty yacht harbour, Harbour House has been designed in the spirit of maritime life in the 1880s—elegant simplicity, quality finishes, carefully selected antiques and unique accents. Each bedroom and suite offers whirlpool baths, fireplaces, DVD players, down duvets and featherbeds, WiFi internet access and much more. Harbour House captures the flavour of historic Niagara.

Member of Ontario's Finest Inns and CAA/AAA Four Diamond. Named best Niagara hotel by travellers on www.tripadvisor.com. Recipient of top rating of 3 Stars by Frommer's.

AAA ◆◆◆◆   *Member Since 2003*

"What sets Harbour House apart is its friendly yet impeccable service, its serene atmosphere and those heavenly beds." -Frommer's Niagara Region

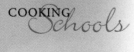

Quebec

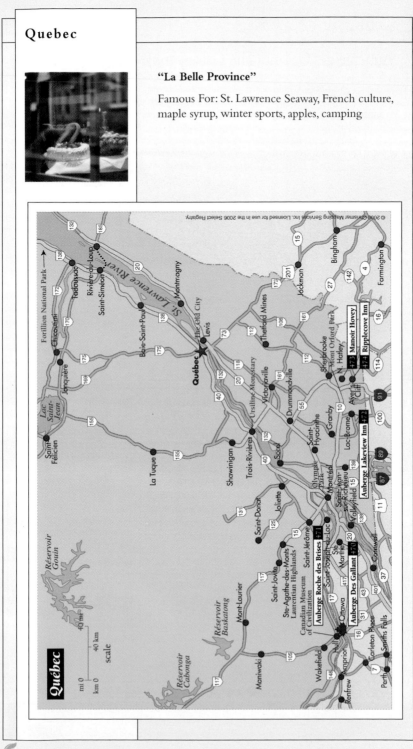

"La Belle Province"

Famous For: St. Lawrence Seaway, French culture, maple syrup, winter sports, apples, camping

Québec

Québec

scale
km 0
mi 0
40 km
40 mi

Réservoir Gouin

Réservoir Baskatong

Réservoir Cabonga

Forillon National Park →

Lac Saint-Jean

St. Lawrence River

The Old City

Chicoutimi
Jonquière
Saint-Félicien
Tadoussac
Saint-Siméon
Rivière-du-Loup
Baie-Saint-Paul
Québec
Lévis
Montmagny
Jackman
Bingham
Farmington
Sherbrooke
Mont Orford Park
N. Hatley
Ayer's Cliff
Thetford Mines
Victoriaville
Drummondville
Ursuline Monastery
Granby
Lac Brome
Saint-Hyacinthe
Sorel
Trois-Rivières
Shawinigan
La Tuque
Saint-Donat
Joliette
Montréal
Olympic Park
Saint-Jean-sur-Richelieu
Valleyfield
Cornwall
Saint-Jérôme
Saint-Joseph-du-Lac
Ste-Marthe
Ste-Agathe-des-Monts
Laurentian Highlands
Canadian Museum of Civilization
Saint-Jovite
Mont-Laurier
Maniwaki
Wakefield
Hull
Ottawa
Renfrew
Arnprior
Carleton Place
Smiths Falls
Perth

#73 Manoir Hovey
#74 Ripplecove Inn
#72 Auberge Lakeview Inn
#71 Auberge Roche des Brises
#70 Auberge Des Gallant

Auberge des Gallant (The Gallant Inn)

www.srinns.com/desgallant
1171 St - Henry Rd., Ste-Marthe, Rigaud
QUE, Canada J0P 1W0
800-641-4241 • 450-459-4241 • Fax 450-459-4667
info@gallant.qc.ca

Innkeepers/Owners
Linda and Gerry Gallant

Elegant Mountain Resort

Garden and SPA lovers will enjoy this romantic inn nestled in the heart of a bird and deer sanctuary. Enjoy award-winning French cuisine and wine list, as well as our gourmet spa! We offer wine , chocolate, and even maple sugar body wraps and facials. Elegant spacious rooms with real wood-burning fireplace and balcony overlook our five acres of beautifully appointed gardens, which in summer attract a multitude of birds and butterflies, while winter promises sleigh rides, cross country skiing and down hill skiing. Fall foliage is at its best in October, and our maple sugar shack with its 11,000 taps is open from late February to the end of April for traditional maple meals. Maple syrup is available all year round!

Rooms/Rates
24 Rooms with wood-burning fireplace & balcony, From $130 CDN/$99 US, MAP pp. for a country room and $150 CDN/$120 US, MAP pp. for a honeymoon suite. Open year-round.
Number of Rooms: 24

Cuisine
Breakfast, lunch, gourmet 5 course dinner, Sunday brunch. Extensive wine list and liquor.

Nearest Airport(s)
Montreal, Trudeau, 30 miles.

Directions
Between Montreal and Ottawa, Rte. 40 W, Exit 17, Left on Rte. 201, 3 miles & Right on St-Henri 5 miles.

Member Since 1998

"We loved the decor!!! Staff and food were excellent!" Doug & Pauline Panter
"Very friendly, warm, professional. Excellent food and service." B. Willet

Innkeeper/Owner
Gina Pratt

Elegant Country Inn

La Roche des Brises

www.srinns.com/larochedesbrises

2007, rue Principale, St-Joseph-du-Lac, QUE J0N 1M0

450-472-2722 • Fax 450-473-5878

info@rochedesbrises.com

Rooms/Rates
5 suites, $120/$180 CDN double occupancy. Open February through December 31.
Number of Rooms: 5

Cuisine
Elegant full breakfast included. Award winning fine dining with a french twist. World wines available. Roche des Brises winery on site. Tours and tasting available daily.

Nearest Airport(s)
Dorval/Pierre Eliot Trudeau Airport, 50 minutes

Directions
From South: Highway 13 North to Highway 640 West, Exit 2 Left on "Chemin Principal" for 4.7 km

The Inn is located on the outskirts of Montreal overlooking rolling hills, orchards and our vineyard with a spectacular view of Montreal. Beautifully decorated with antiques, the Inn has been awarded the Five Sun top rating by Quebec Tourism for the Laurentians. Our rooms all have King size beds and private baths and air conditioning. We also offer our guests the luxury of hot stone and grape seed massage in a relaxing ambiance. The Inn has its own pool and is close to beautiful Lake of Two Mountains. And if you take a little stroll through the vines and experience our charming fine dining restaurant or wine tasting room, revealing our renowned award winning wines, you shall feel the true nature and magic of this unique ambiance. Location: Downtown Montreal is located 30 minutes away by car or commute by train to avoid traffic. "Auberge Roche des Brises" offers a unique lodging experience in a country setting, close to the heart of Montreal.

Member Since 2005

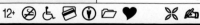

Award winning Gold Medal of the Laurentians Tourist Association.

Auberge Lakeview Inn

www.srinns.com/aubergelakeview

50, rue Victoria, Knowlton, Brome Lake, QUE, Canada
J0E 1V0

800-661-6183 • 450-243-6183 • Fax 450-243-0602
info@aubergelakeviewinn.com

Innkeeper
Chris Voutsinas

Historic Victorian
Village Inn

History... Romance... Elegance... Step thru the front door and go back 131 years in history as you enter the romantic, Victorian atmosphere of one of Quebec's most celebrated Inns. Imagine lodging and dining where Sir Wilfrid Laurier, Sir Robert Borden and the Right Hon. Arthur Meighen, former Prime Ministers of Canada, stayed. The "Lakeview Inn," built in 1874 by loyalists, is now an historic multi-award winning antique-filled Victorian Inn. Enjoy the visual splendour and ambiance of yesteryear with all of today's comforts including central air-conditioning. Beautifully decorated with antiques and hand-carved turn-of-the-century furnishings. Browse in local antique shops and boutiques. Enjoy a variety of water and summer activites. Linger over cocktails in an authentic English pub or in our garden-terrace by our heated swimming pool. Our BUSINESS CENTRE combines a relaxed atmosphere, secretarial services, audio-visual equipment, data lines and teleconferencing. For business meetings, receptions or whatever the occasion, our facilities can accomodate from five to 225 persons.

AAA ◆◆◆◆   *Member Since 2002*

Rooms/Rates
24 rooms, 4 studios, from $126CDN/$105US, MAP, pp. (gratuities included) AAA/CAA 4 diamond rating. Open year-round.
Number of Rooms:

Cuisine
Dine by candle-light in our elegant Victorian dining room where flavours of French cuisine are enhanced by an outstanding wine and Port cellar and be pampered by our "Traditional European Service."

Nearest Airport(s)
Montreal Airport

Directions
Go North on I-91 to the Canada Border. Go North on QUEBEC AUT.55 to QUEBEC AUT. 10. Take exit 90 and follow signs to Auberge Lakeview Inn.

"Lakeview Inn is the most exciting four-season destination for business, leisure, relaxation, and romance..."

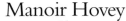

Innkeepers/Owners
Steve, Kathryn, and Jason Stafford

Elegant Waterside
Resort Inn

⭐

|O| |O| |O| ⊈

Manoir Hovey
www.manoirhovey.com
Lake Massawippi, 575 Hovey Road
North Hatley, QUE, Canada J0B 2C0
800-661-2421 • 819-842-2421 • Fax 819-842-2248
innkeeper@manoirhovey.com

Wine Spectator
AWARD OF EXCELLENCE

DiRōNA

Rooms/Rates
40 luxurious year-round rooms, mostly on the lake (US $94/$250 MAP/person/day). Many fireplaces, balconies, jacuzzis and canopy beds.
Number of Rooms: 40

Cuisine
Breakfast, lunch, dinner, cream teas. 2004 Gold Medal winner for both gastronomy and for best wine list in all of Quebec. Triple 5 Stars for cuisine, decor and service in Quebec's "Voir" Restaurant Guide. Lakeside lunches, garden cocktails, historic pub.

Nearest Airport(s)
Montreal

Directions
VT I-91 to Canadian border. Continue on Rte 55N for 29 kms to N. Hatley exit 29. Follow Rte 108 E and Manoir Hovey signs to the Inn (9 kms). Only 25 minutes from VT.

This gracious manor was built as a private estate by a wealthy Atlanta industrialist in 1900 and modeled after George Washington's Mount Vernon. The site is spectacularly nestled on 25 acres of prime lakeshore amidst celebrated English gardens and birch forest. Most of the lakeside rooms (among Quebec's most luxurious) offer combinations of fireplaces, Jacuzzis, canopy beds, and balconies. They are also equipped with Frette towels, two bathrobes, Aveda bath products, WiFi, CD player and nightly turn-down service. The Manor is also renowned for its cuisine and personalized service (2004 double gold medal winner for best restaurant and best wine list in Quebec). The addition of two small beaches, heated pool, water sports, clay tennis, massage room, X-country ski trails, skating, and many other year round recreational facilities on site (INCLUDED in the MAP rates) have made this inn an international destination in itself. We're only 25 minutes from Vermont, four hours from Boston and six and a half hours from New York City en route to Montreal and Quebec City.

AAA ◆◆◆◆   *Member Since 1973*

13+ 🚭 ♿ 🖂 ⓥ 🗁 ♥ ↔ ✕ 🖎 @ ≋ 🗔 ◎

"Wow! Most deserving of your 5 stars. Quality far surpasses other inns.
A perfect 10! Hovey certainly lived up to its reputation. The food is to die for."

Ripplecove Inn

www.srinns.com/ripplecove

700 Ripplecove Road, Lake Massawippi, Ayer's Cliff,
QUE, Canada J0B 1C0

800-668-4296 • 819-838-4296 • Fax 819-838-5541

info@ripplecove.com

Innkeepers/Owners
**Debra and Jeffrey
Stafford**

Elegant Waterside Resort
Waterside Resort

Wine Spectator

AWARD
OF
EXCELLENCE

Since 1945, Ripplecove Inn has been chosen by sophisticated travelers from around the world to get away from it all in an atmosphere of romance, privacy, refined service and luxury. The Inn resides on a beautifully landscaped 12 acre peninsula alive with English gardens, and century-old pines. A recent expansion, started in 2004, is now fully complete and has added ten additional luxurious rooms to our repertoire, as well as a full service Spa offering massage, hydro therepy, facials and a four season outdoor Jacuzzi tub. A private beach, boating, biking, tennis, heated outdoor pool and lake cruises are also all on site! Rated as one of Quebec's top 10 best places to dine, our victorian dining room and lakeside terrace offer refined cuisine and vintage wines accompanied by the strains of live piano music and sterling silver service. American visitors don't forget; Ripplecove Inn is a perfect stop over on route to Montreal or Quebec city via Interstate 91 through Vermont.

Rooms/Rates
35 Rooms, Suites and Cottages, US $114/$295MAP/person/day including dinner, breakfast and service. All rooms offer TV, TEL, A/C and designer decor Most rooms offer fireplace, private lakeview balcony and whirlpools
Number of Rooms: 35

Cuisine
Four Diamond Award cuisine in our Victorian dining room & lakeside terrace. 6000 bottle wine cellar and pub.

Nearest Airport(s)
Pierre E Trudeau Montreal

Directions
From New England take I-91 N to the Canadian border then follow Rte. 55 N to exit 21. Follow signs to Inn which is 3 miles from exit 21. Distances: Montreal 1.5 hrs, Boston 3 hrs, New York 6 hrs.

AAA ◆◆◆◆   *Member Since 1995*

"One of the most beautiful Inns we have ever stayed at! Keep up the good work!"

SelectRegistry.com

SelectRegistry.com

SelectRegistry.com

DINE WHERE THE CHEFS DINE

DiRōNA (DISTINGUISHED RESTAURANTS OF NORTH AMERICA)

THE AUTHORITY ON FINE DINING

THE
2006 DiRōNA Guide
Distinguished Restaurants of North America

• ANONYMOUS INSPECTIONS
• FINE DINING GUARANTEE

What Sets a DiRōNA Restaurant Apart?

• An independent and anonymous inspections program

• A 75-point list of inspection criteria

• North America's only fine dining guarantee

• The DiRōNA Award of Excellence cannot be purchased and is not driven by customer ratings

North America's finest restaurants are as close as your keyboard. Visit www.dirona.org to locate restaurants online or to purchase the 2006 DiRōNA Guide.

DiRōNA